ANNUAL EDITIONS

# Western Civilization

## Volume 1—The Earliest Civilizations Through the Reformation

*Fifteenth Edition*

**EDITOR**

**Robert L. Lembright**

*James Madison University*

Robert L. Lembright taught World Civilization, Ancient Near East, Byzantine, Islamic, and Greek/Roman history at James Madison University. He received his BA from Miami University and his MA and PhD from The Ohio State University. Dr. Lembright has been a participant in many National Endowments for the Humanities Summer Seminars and Institutes on Egyptology, the Ancient Near East, Byzantine History, and the Ottoman Empire. He has written several articles in the four editions of *The Global Experience*, as well as articles in the *James Madison Journal* and *Western Views of China and the Far East.* His research has concentrated on the French Renaissance of the sixteenth century, and he has published reports in the *Bulletins et memoires, Societé archaeologique et historique de la Charente.* In addition, Dr. Lembright has written many book reviews on the ancient world and Byzantine and Islamic history for *History: Reviews of New Books.*

McGraw Hill Higher Education

Boston Burr Ridge, IL Dubuque, IA New York San Francisco St. Louis
Bangkok Bogotá Caracas Kuala Lumpur Lisbon London Madrid Mexico City
Milan Montreal New Delhi Santiago Seoul Singapore Sydney Taipei Toronto

The McGraw-Hill Companies

Higher Education

ANNUAL EDITIONS: WESTERN CIVILIZATION, VOLUME 1, FIFTEENTH EDITION

Published by McGraw-Hill, a business unit of The McGraw-Hill Companies, Inc., 1221 Avenue of the Americas, New York, NY 10020.

Annual Editions is published by the **Contemporary Learning Series** group within the McGraw-Hill Higher Education division.

1 2 3 4 5 6 7 8 9 0 QPD/QPD 0 9 8

ISBN 978–0–07–351633–2
MHID 0–07–3516333
ISSN 0735–0392

Managing Editor: *Larry Loeppke*
Senior Managing Editor: *Faye Schilling*
Developmental Editor: *Debra Henricks*
Editorial Coordinator: *Mary Foust*
Editorial Assistant: *Nancy Meissner*
Production Service Assistant: *Rita Hingtgen*
Permissions Coordinator: *Lenny Behnke*
Senior Marketing Manager: *Julie Keck*
Marketing Communications Specialist: *Mary Klein*
Marketing Coordinator: *Alice Link*
Project Manager: *Sandy Wille*
Design Specialist: *Tara McDermott*
Senior Production Supervisor: *Laura Fuller*
Cover Graphics: *Kristine Jubeck*

Compositor: Laserwords Private Limited
Cover Image: © Royalty-Free/Corbis (both)

**Library in Congress Cataloging-in-Publication Data**
Main entry under title: Annual Editions: Western Civilization, Volume 1: The Earliest Civilizations Through the Reformation. 15/e.
1. Civilization—Periodicals. 2. World history—Periodicals. I. Lembright, Robert L. *comp.* II. Title: Western Civilization Volume 1.

www.mhhe.com

# Editors/Advisory Board

Members of the Advisory Board are instrumental in the final selection of articles for each edition of ANNUAL EDITIONS. Their review of articles for content, level, currentness, and appropriateness provides critical direction to the editor and staff. We think that you will find their careful consideration well reflected in this volume.

# Preface

In publishing ANNUAL EDITIONS we recognize the enormous role played by the magazines, newspapers, and journals of the public press in providing current, first-rate educational information in a broad spectrum of interest areas. Many of these articles are appropriate for students, researchers, and professionals seeking accurate, current material to help bridge the gap between principles and theories and the real world. These articles, however, become more useful for study when those of lasting value are carefully collected, organized, indexed, and reproduced in a low-cost format, which provides easy and permanent access when the material is needed. That is the role played by ANNUAL EDITIONS.

What does it mean to say that we are attempting to study the history of Western civilizations? A traditional course in Western civilization was often a chronological survey in the development of European institutions and ideas, with a slight reference to the Near East and the Americas and other places where Westernization has occurred. Typically it began with the Greeks, then the Romans, and on to the medieval period, and finally to the modern era, depicting the distinctive characteristics of each stage, as well as each period's relation to the preceding and succeeding events. Of course, in a survey so broad, from Adam to the atomic age in two semesters, a certain superficiality was inevitable. Main characters and events galloped by; often there was little opportunity to absorb and digest complex ideas that have shaped Western culture.

It is tempting to excuse these shortcomings as unavoidable. However, to present a course in Western civilization that leaves students with only a scrambled series of events, names, dates, and places, is to miss a great opportunity. For the promise of such a broad course of study is that it enables students to explore great turning points or shifts in the development of Western culture. Close analysis of these moments enables students to understand the dynamics of continuity and change over time. At best, the course can give a coherent view of the Western tradition and its interplay with non-Western cultures. It can offer opportunities for students to compare various historical forms of authority, religion, and economic organization; to assess the great struggles over the meaning of truth and reality that have sometimes divided Western culture; and even to reflect on the price of progress.

Yet, to focus exclusively on Western civilization can lead us to ignore non-Western peoples and cultures or else to perceive them in ways that some label as "Eurocentric." But contemporary courses in Western history are rarely, if ever, mere exercises in European tribalism. Indeed, they offer an opportunity to subject the Western tradition to critical scrutiny, to asses its accomplishments and its shortfalls. Few of us who teach these courses would argue that Western history is the only history that contemporary students should know. Yet it should be an essential part of what they learn, for it is impossible to understand the modern world without some specific knowledge in the basic tenets of the Western tradition.

When students learn the distinctive traits of the West, they can develop a sense of the dynamism of history. They can begin to understand how ideas relate to social structures and social forces. They will come to appreciate the nature and significance of innovation and recognize how values often influence events. More specifically, they can trace the evolution of Western ideas about such essential matters as nature, humans, authority, the gods, even history itself; that is, they learn how the West developed its distinctive character. And, as historian Reed Dasenbrock has observed, in an age that seeks multicultural understanding there is much to be learned from "the fundamental multiculturalism of Western culture, the fact that it has been constructed out of a fusion of disparate and often conflicting cultural traditions." Of course, the articles collected in this volume cannot deal with all these matters, but by providing an alternative to the summaries of most textbooks, they can help students better understand the diverse traditions and processes that we call Western civilization.

This book is like our history—unfinished, always in process. It will be revised biannually. Comments and criticisms are welcome from all who use this book. For that, an article rating form is included at the back of the book. Please feel free to recommend articles for the next edition. With your assistance, this anthology will continue to improve.

Robert L Lembright

Robert L. Lembright
*Editor*

# Contents

*Preface* iv

*Correlation Guide* xi

*Topic Guide* xii

*Internet References* xiv

## UNIT 1
## The Earliest Civilizations

**Unit Overview** xvi

These articles discuss some of the attributes of early civilizations. The topics discuss the modern methods of archaeology, an Egyptian pharaoh, the Seven Wonders, and several ancient empires.

1. **Modern Archaeology,** Brian M. Fagan, *History Today,* November 2007
Brian Fagan surveys the history of archaeology and says that a century ago, ***archaeologists*** were casually trained and worked in remote places. In the future, it will be a team effort using ***modern scientific methods*** such as DNA, tree-ring sequences, and climatic records and will come from the laboratory. 2

2. **The Queen Who Would Be King,** Elizabeth B. Wilson, *Smithsonian,* September 2006
Elizabeth B. Wilson recounts the history of ***Haptshepsut, royal wife, regent*** and finally a ***pharaoh.*** Was she a scheming stepmother to ***Pharaoh Thutmose III*** or a very effective ruler who held Egypt until her step-son came of age? 6

3. **Journey to the Seven Wonders,** Tony Perrottet, *Smithsonian,* June 2004
Though only one of the ***Seven Wonders of the Ancient World*** still stands, they still intrigue our imagination. Author Tony Perrottet details the ***Pyramids, the Lighthouse of Alexandria, the Temple of Artemis at Ephesus, the Mausoleum at Halicarnassus, the Colossus of Rhodes, the Hanging Gardens of Babylon, and the Statue of Zeus at Olympia.*** Why do these monuments still capture our thoughts after 2,000 years? 10

4. **The Coming of the Sea Peoples,** Neil Asher Silberman, *Military History,* Winter 1998
About 1200 B.C. a new military force swept southward across the Aegean Sea and into Asia Minor, Cyprus and Canaan—and even reached the borders of Egypt. Where were the ***"sea peoples,"*** and how did their weapons and tactics launch a ***military revolution*** in the ancient world? 14

5. **Before Tea Leaves Divination in Ancient Babylonia,** William W. Hallo, *Biblical Archaeology Review,* March/April 2005
William Halo discusses the use of ***hepatoscopy (a form of divination involving the inspection of animal livers)*** by the ***Assyrian kings.*** He sees parallels between ancient liver inspections and modern intelligence. 21

6. **Millennia of Murex,** Philippa Scott, *Saudi Aramco World,* July/August 2006
Although wo do not know exactly where the first use of ***Murex (a red-purple dye)*** began, it is evident, according to Philipa Scott, that the finds tell us the ***Myceneans*** had frescos decorations on it. Yet it was the ***city of Tyre in Phoenicia (Lebanon),*** which made this dye so famous that its use became associated with royal power. 24

The concepts in bold italics are developed in the article. For further expansion, please refer to the Topic Guide.

# UNIT 2
## Greece and Rome: The Classical Tradition


**Unit Overview** 28

These articles focus on Greek and Roman society. Sports, crime, politics, military conquests, women in Etruscan society, and childhood in Rome are discussed.

7. **Troy's Night of the Horse,** Barry Strauss, *Military History,* March 2007
There have been many theories as to the reality of the Trojan War, but, most historians are convinced that the ***Trojan Horse*** was a fiction. However, Barry Strauss suggests that we think of the fall of Troy as an ***example of unconventional warfare***—Bronze Age style, and that the Greeks ***must have used*** some kind of ***deceit*** to take the city. 30

8. **The First Olympics,** Betsy Carpenter, *U.S. News and World Report,* August 9, 2004
Long held beliefs about the nature of the ancient ***Olympics*** are changing, according to Betsy Carpenter. Our notions that ***only amateurs*** competed, and the reason for naked contestants is because of a ***love for the human form*** is being challenged. 34

9. **Can We Trust the Ancient Texts?,** Richard A. Gabriel, *Military History,* March/April 2008
Richard A. Gabriel says that the greatest obstacles to understanding ancient military history were the ***scarcity of reliable evidence.*** Names, dates, and details were invented or omitted, as ancient historians were more interested in writing ***moral lessons than facts.*** 37

10. **Unlocking Mysteries of the Parthenon,** Evan Hadingham, *Smithsonian,* February 2008
The ***Parthenon*** is regarded as the greatest artistic achievement of the Greek civilization, yet it has endured earthquakes, fires, looting and misguided preservation efforts. At present, a restoration effort is discovering ***new insights into the architectural plan*** of the original builders. 41

11. **Outfoxed and Outfought,** Jason K. Foster, *Military History,* January/February 2007
Jason K. Foster recounts how the superior-trained Athenian Hoplites ***(heavy armed soldiers)*** and new battle tactics overwhelmed the ancient world's greatest empire: Persia. Had Athens been defeated, ***democracy, art, culture and philosophy*** might have been lost forever. 45

12. **Mighty Macedonian,** Richard Covington, *Smithsonian,* November 2004
His victories on the battle field earned him the title ***Alexander the Great,*** but what were his motives? Was it his motivation to ***surpass his father, Philip II,*** or to ***win his mother Olympias' love,*** which enabled him to conquer the ***Persian Empire?*** 48

13. **Etruscan Women,** Ingrid D. Rowland, *Archaeology Odyssey,* May/June 2004
The author tells us that the Etruscan Women's ***freedom of action, appetite for wine, and their loose morals*** were scandalous to the Greeks and later, to the Romans. They were powerful, dignified, elegant, and aristocratic, and seemed to be equal to men. 53

14. **Rome's Craftiest General,** James Lacey, *Military History,* July/August 2007
***Publius Cornelius Scipio "Africanus"*** learned the art of war at a very young age against Rome's greatest enemy, ***Hannibal Barca.*** Although Scipio and the Romans were first defeated, he eventually gained a command to take Spain from Carthage and then met Hannibal at Zama in 202 B.C. The latter was the crowning achievement of his career and gave him the title, ***"Africanus" or "victor of Africa",*** but it was to be his last important command. 56


The concepts in bold italics are developed in the article. For further expansion, please refer to the Topic Guide.

**15. The End of the Roman Empire,** Bryan Ward-Perkins, *History Today,* June 2005
Did the invasions from the fifth century to the seventh century destroy Roman Civilization, or were the barbarians peacefully incorporated? Bryan Ward-Perkins says that his archaeological investigations suggest that sophisticated Roman life disappeared and that war was the reason for this. 59

# UNIT 3
## The Judeo-Christian Heritage

**Unit Overview** 62

The articles in this section examine the Hebrew religion, Jesus, and Mary Magdalene.

**16. The Volcano Explains Everything—Or Does It?,** Manfred Bietak, *Biblical Archaeology Review,* November/December 2006
According to a TV film, "The Exodus Decoded," the volcanic explosion on Thera (Santorini) is the basis for the Hebrew Exodus. Manfred Bietak lists a number of problems associated with this explanation. 64

**17. Holy Family Values,** Lisa Miller, *Newsweek,* December 18, 2006
Lisa Miller details how the world into which Jesus was born and reared shaped morals for 2,000 years. She further explains how Jewish traditions became Christianity's customs. 67

# UNIT 4
## Muslims and Byzantines

**Unit Overview** 70

Three selections discuss the Late Roman or Byzantine civilization as well as important political and philosophical figures in the Muslim world.

**18. Adrianople,** Joe Zentner, *Military History,* October 2005
Joe Zentner describes how ***Emperor Valens'*** bad tactics resulted in his death and the triumph of cavalry over infantry at the ***Battle of Adrianople*** in 378 AD. This permitted an influx of Germanic people to the West, while the East survived. 72

**19. The Survival of the Eastern Roman Empire,** Stephen Williams and Gerard Friell, *History Today,* November 1998
The ***Eastern Roman Empire*** had long-term advantages over the West: a strategically located capital, shorter frontiers, and a wealthier economic base. The first-century emperors evolved rules of imperial succession, control of top army commands, opposition to federated settlements, and a centralized pool of administrative, fiscal, and diplomatic experience. This enabled the East to avoid the destruction, which happened in ***the Western Roman Empire.*** 76

**20. Islam's First Terrorists,** Clive Foss, *History Today,* December 2007
The ***Kharijites*** emerged in the late seventh century and caused chaos during the Arab civil wars. Although they flourished in chaotic times and were able to set up a few states, none of these states lasted. Their insistence on ***democracy*** undermined a strong leadership, while their ***fanaticism*** led to internal splits. 81

The concepts in bold italics are developed in the article. For further expansion, please refer to the Topic Guide.

21. **Rediscovering Arabic Science,** Richard Covington, *Saudi Aramco World,* May/June 2007
Richard Covington recounts the fascinating history of Islamic science from the 8th to the 15th centuries and says that Islam produced a tremendous abundance of scientific knowledge. The study of ***mathematics, chemistry, physics, medicine, geometry, and cartography*** were far advanced than in the Western societies. It was not until 1258, with the Mongol destruction of Baghdad, and the later emergence of the Ottoman Empire, that Islamic science fell into decline. **85**

# UNIT 5
# The Medieval Period

**Unit Overview** **96**

These selections examine the medieval world. Topics include empire building, military conquests, and culture.

22. **A Turbulent Reputation,** Michael Staunton, *History Today,* April 2007
Michael Staunton recounts the various opinions of ***Thomas Becket*** through the centuries. Becket, even in his own time, was seen either as a ***great saint*** who was murdered in defiance of his king, ***or as an arrogant troublemaker.*** **98**

23. **What Did Medieval Schools Do For Us?,** Nicholas Orme, *History Today,* June 2006
When the Roman Civilization evaporated in England during the 5th century, learning inclined more into/toward the monasteries, where Latin Grammars were developed to teach those who knew no Latin. By the 12th century, school became what we would call ***modern:*** they ***moved away from the monasteries, had full-time teachers, and they were more in number.*** Many more children—boys and girls—were literate. **102**

24. **Lackland,** Nick Barratt, *History Today,* March 2004
Although King Henry II of England and his son Richard I the Lionhearted are considered good rulers, Henry's second son, ***John,*** truly does merit his bad reputation in history. Nick Baratt says it was John's loss of Normandy in 1204 and his defeat at the Battle of Bovines in 1214, which brought about the creation of the ***Magna Carta.*** **106**

25. **The Fourth Crusade and the Sack of Constantinople,** Jonathan Phillips, *History today,* May 2004
What caused the knights of the ***Fourth Crusade*** to sack Constantinople and establish a Latin Empire, which lasted from 1204 to 1261? Jonathan Phillips says that it was a ***clash of cultures***—the Byzantines saw themselves as superior to the West and the Westerners saw the Byzantines as effeminate and duplicitous. **110**

26. **East Meets West in Venice,** Richard Covington, *Saudi Aramco World,* March/April 2008
Richard Covington says that without Muslim trade, Venice would not have existed. It became the trade center of Europe; importing silk, spices, carpets, ceramics, and manuscripts, while carrying on diplomacy from the 8th to the 16th centuries. **114**

27. **Genghis Khan,** Timothy May, *Military History,* July/August 2007
Timothy May discusses why the ***Mongols*** were so successful in conquering an empire. They had a ***complex military system,*** which involved the ***molding of steppe tactics with the new weapons or strategies*** they encountered. They ensured the ***army was properly trained*** to execute these new tactics. And they were better informed about their opponents than those in other medieval lands, so for 150 years they suffered no serious defeats. **122**

The concepts in bold italics are developed in the article. For further expansion, please refer to the Topic Guide.

**28. How a Mysterious Disease Laid Low Europe's Masses,**
Charles L. Mee Jr., *Smithsonian,* February 1990
The great ***Bubonic plague*** of the fourteenth century destroyed a third of Europe's population and had profound psychological, social, religious, economic, and even artistic consequences. Charles Mee spells out the causes, symptoms, and effects of the epidemic that altered ***medieval life.*** **127**

# UNIT 6
## Renaissance and Reformation

**Unit Overview** **132**

The following articles discuss Byzantium, the Renaissance, politics, culture, and the importance of religion in Western Europe.

**29. The Guns of Constantinople,** Roger Crowley, *Military History,* September 2007
For lack of funds, the last ***Byzantine Emperor Constantine XI*** could not hire a Hungarian cannon-maker, and so it was ***Sultan Mehmed II*** who was offered this new weapon. Richard Crowley says that this ***new military invention meant the end of medieval castle construction and siege warfare.*** **134**

**30. Joan of Arc,** Kelly DeVries, *Military History,* January/February 2008
Kelly DeVries says that ***Joan of Arc's*** fame comes from ***her skill at leading men into battle against great odds.*** She inspired later generals to adopt her tactics, such as ***direct engagements and frontal assaults.*** These things later made her celebrated and a saint. **138**

**31. The Luther Legacy,** Derek Wilson, *History Today,* May 2007
***Martin Luther*** has been seen as an advocate of ***individual freedom, intellectual repression, nationalism, spirituality and secularism.*** But as Derek Wilson says this did not make Luther a dry philosopher but a flesh-and-blood fallible human being. He was a ***theologian who lived his theology.*** **142**

**32. Explaining John Calvin,** William J. Bouwsma, *The Wilson Quarterly,* New Year's Edition 1989
John Calvin's image in history is well established. The religious reformer has been credited with—or blamed for—promoting the ***capitalist work ethic, individualism,*** and ***Puritanism.*** His biographer, William Bouwsma, says our image of Calvin as a cold, inflexible moralist is mistaken. According to the author, Calvin's life and work were full of "the ambiguities, contradictions, and agonies" of a troubled time. **145**

**33. The Third Way,** Phillip E. L. Greene, *History Magazine,* October/November 2004
Phillip Greene recounts the history of the ***Anabaptist*** movement in Europe. It began with the ideas of the Swiss theologian, ***Ulrich Zwingli,*** who rejected infant baptism in favor of adult baptism. However, Zwingli broke with his own followers and they went on to form the ***Moravian Brethern, Hutterites, Mennonites, and Amish.*** **150**

**34. Vlad Dracula's War on the Turks,** Will Romano, *Military History,* October 2003
Will Romano recounts the military exploits of one of the most famous anti-Turkish crusaders in history, ***Vlad Tsepes.*** Ruling the area of ***Wallachia (Romania),*** Vlad tried to secure his land from the Turks as well as the Holy Roman Empire. In doing so, he gained one of the most famous reputations of vicious ***cruelty, unparalleled until modern times.*** **154**

The concepts in bold italics are developed in the article. For further expansion, please refer to the Topic Guide.

**35. Women in War,** John A. Lynn, *Military History,* October 2007
In the armies of 16th century Europe, there was a women for every man. The tasks performed by camp women were ***prostitution, laundry, meal preparation, commerce, and heavy camp labor.*** The import of women in the field is recounted by John A. Lynn. **159**

**36. Will the Real Henry VIII Please Stand up?,** Eric Ives, *History Today,* February 2006
***Henry VIII*** might be one of the most famous of all English monarchs, but how well do most understand him? Eric Ives says that there were three important ideas guiding Henry—***egoism***—the conviction that he had superior wisdom; an ***ability to deny reality or facts when as he wanted to;*** and ***insecurity*** in comprehending sex and the king. **163**

***Test-Your-Knowledge Form*** **168**
***Article Rating Form*** **169**

The concepts in bold italics are developed in the article. For further expansion, please refer to the Topic Guide.

# Correlation Guide

The *Annual Editions* series provides students with convenient, inexpensive access to current, carefully selected articles from the public press. **Annual Editions: Western Civilization, Volume 1: The Earliest Civilization through Reformation, 15/e** is an easy-to-use reader that presents articles on important topics such as *ancient Greece, Islam, medieval society,* and many more. For more information on *Annual Editions* and other *McGraw-Hill Contemporary Learning Series* titles, visit www.mhcls.com.

This convenient guide matches the units in **Western Civilization, Volume 1, 15/e** with the corresponding chapters in one of our best-selling McGraw-Hill History textbooks by Sherman/Salisbury.

| Annual Editions: Western Civilization, Volume 1, 15/e by Lembright | The West in the World, Volume 1: To 1715, 3/e by Sherman/Salisbury |
|---|---|
| **Unit 1:** The Earliest Civilizations | **Chapter 1:** The Roots of Western Civilization: The Ancient Middle East to the Sixth Century B.C.E. |
| **Unit 2:** Greece and Rome: The Classical Tradition | **Chapter 2:** The Contest for Excellence: Greece, 2000–338 B.C.E. Timeline: The Big Picture<br>**Chapter 3:** The Poleis Become Cosmopolitan: The Hellenistic World, 336–150 B.C.E.<br>**Chapter 4:** Pride in Family and City: Rome from Its Origins Through the Republic, 753–44 B.C.E. |
| **Unit 3:** The Judeo-Christian Heritage | **Chapter 5:** Territorial and Christian Empires: The Roman Empire, 31 B.C.E. to 410 C.E. |
| **Unit 4:** Muslims and Byzantines | **Chapter 6:** A World Divided: Western Kingdoms, Byzantium, and the Islamic World, ca. 376–1000 |
| **Unit 5:** The Medieval Period | **Chapter 7:** The Struggle to Bring Order: The Early Middle Ages, ca. 750–1000<br>**Chapter 8:** Order Restored: The High Middle Ages, 1000–1300<br>**Chapter 9:** The West Struggles and Eastern Empires Flourish: The Late Middle Ages, ca. 1300–1500 |
| **Unit 6:** Renaissance and Reformation | **Chapter 10:** A New Spirit in the West: The Renaissance, ca. 1300–1640<br>**Chapter 11:** "Alone Before God": Religious Reform and Warfare 1500–1648 |

# Topic Guide

This topic guide suggests how the selections in this book relate to the subjects covered in your course. You may want to use the topics listed on these pages to search the Web more easily.

On the following pages a number of Web sites have been gathered specifically for this book. They are arranged to reflect the units of this Annual Editions reader. You can link to these sites by going to *http://www.mhcls.com.*

**All the articles that relate to each topic are listed below the bold-faced term.**


**Archaeology**

1. Modern Archaeology
2. The Queen Who Would Be King
3. Journey to the Seven Wonders
7. Troy's Night of the Horse
10. Unlocking Mysteries of the Parthenon
13. Etruscan Women
15. The End of the Roman Empire
16. The Volcano Explains Everything—Or Does It?

**Art**

10. Unlocking Mysteries of the Parthenon

**Babylonia**

5. Before Tea Leaves Divination in Ancient Babylonia

**Bible**

16. The Volcano Explains Everything—Or Does It?
17. Holy Family Values

**Byzantium**

18. Adrianople
19. The Survival of the Eastern Roman Empire
25. The Fourth Crusade and the Sack of Constantinople
29. The Guns of Constantinople

**Christianity**

17. Holy Family Values
22. A Turbulent Reputation
31. The Luther Legacy
32. Explaining John Calvin
33. The Third Way

**Culture**

3. Journey to the Seven Wonders
5. Before Tea Leaves Divination in Ancient Babylonia
6. Millennia of Murex
8. The First Olympics
10. Unlocking Mysteries of the Parthenon
13. Etruscan Women
21. Rediscovering Arabic Science
23. What Did Medieval Schools Do For Us?
35. Women in War

**Disease**

28. How a Mysterious Disease Laid Low Europe's Masses

**Education**

23. What Did Medieval Schools Do For Us?

**Egypt**

2. The Queen Who Would Be King

**England**

22. A Turbulent Reputation
24. Lackland
36. Will the Real Henry VIII Please Stand up?

**Europe**

15. The End of the Roman Empire
23. What Did Medieval Schools Do For Us?
25. The Fourth Crusade and the Sack of Constantinople
26. East Meets West in Venice
28. How a Mysterious Disease Laid Low Europe's Masses
30. Joan of Arc
31. The Luther Legacy
32. Explaining John Calvin
33. The Third Way
34. Vlad Dracula's War on the Turks
35. Women in War

**Greece, ancient**

3. Journey to the Seven Wonders
7. Troy's Night of the Horse
8. The First Olympics
9. Can We Trust the Ancient Texts?
10. Unlocking Mysteries of the Parthenon
11. Outfoxed and Outfought
12. Mighty Macedonian

**France**

30. Joan of Arc

**Islam**

20. Islam's First Terrorists
21. Rediscovering Arabic Science
26. East Meets West in Venice
29. The Guns of Constantinople
34. Vlad Dracula's War on the Turks

**Italy**

26. East Meets West in Venice

**Jews and Judaism**

16. The Volcano Explains Everything—Or Does It?

**Medieval society**

22. A Turbulent Reputation
23. What Did Medieval Schools Do For Us?
24. Lackland
25. The Fourth Crusade and the Sack of Constantinople
26. East Meets West in Venice
28. How a Mysterious Disease Laid Low Europe's Masses

**Middle East**

20. Islam's First Terrorists
21. Rediscovering Arabic Science
25. The Fourth Crusade and the Sack of Constantinople
26. East Meets West in Venice
27. Genghis Khan
29. The Guns of Constantinople

**Military**

4. The Coming of the Sea Peoples
7. Troy's Night of the Horse
11. Outfoxed and Outfought

12. Mighty Macedonian
14. Rome's Craftiest General
15. The End of the Roman Empire
18. Adrianople
25. The Fourth Crusade and the Sack of Constantinople
27. Genghis Khan
29. The Guns of Constantinople
30. Joan of Arc
34. Vlad Dracula's War on the Turks

## Olympics

8. The First Olympics

## Persia, ancient

11. Outfoxed and Outfought

## Reformation

31. The Luther Legacy
32. Explaining John Calvin
33. The Third Way

## Religion

16. The Volcano Explains Everything—Or Does It?
17. Holy Family Values
31. The Luther Legacy
32. Explaining John Calvin
33. The Third Way

## Roman civilization

14. Rome's Craftiest General
15. The End of the Roman Empire
18. Adrianople
19. The Survival of the Eastern Roman Empire

## Science

1. Modern Archaeology
21. Rediscovering Arabic Science

## War

4. The Coming of the Sea Peoples
7. Troy's Night of the Horse
11. Outfoxed and Outfought
12. Mighty Macedonian
14. Rome's Craftiest General
15. The End of the Roman Empire
18. Adrianople
25. The Fourth Crusade and the Sack of Constantinople
27. Genghis Khan
29. The Guns of Constantinople
34. Vlad Dracula's War on the Turks
35. Women in War

## Women

2. The Queen Who Would Be King
13. Etruscan Women
20. Islam's First Terrorists
30. Joan of Arc

# Internet References

The following Internet sites have been selected to support the articles found in this reader. These sites were available at the time of publication. However, because Web sites often change their structure and content, the information listed may no longer be available. We invite you to visit *http://www.mhcls.com* for easy access to these sites.

# Annual Editions: Western Civilization, Volume 1

## General Sources

**Archaeological Institute of America (AIA)**
*http://www.archaeological.org*

Review this site of the AIA for information about various eras in human history. It presents news about the activities and research of the AIA, AIA/IAA-Canada, and other archaeological research institutions and organizations around the world.

**The History of Costumes**
*http://www.siue.edu/COSTUMES/history.html*

This distinctive site illustrates garments worn by people in various historical eras. Clothing of common people is presented along with that worn by nobility. Provided by C. Otis Sweezey, the site is based on a history of costumes through the ages that was originally printed between 1861 and 1880.

**Library of Congress**
*http://www.loc.gov*

Examine this Web site to learn about the extensive resource tools, library services/resources, exhibitions, and databases available through the Library of Congress in many different subfields of historical studies.

**Smithsonian Institution**
*http://www.si.edu/*

Access to the enormous resources of the Smithsonian, which holds some 140 million artifacts and specimens in its trust for "the increase and diffusion of knowledge," is provided at this site.

## UNIT 1: The Earliest Civilizations

**Hypertext and Ethnography**
*http://www.umanitoba.ca/faculties/arts/anthropology/tutor/aaa_presentation.html*

This site will be of great value to people who are interested in culture and communication. Brian Schwimmer addresses such topics as multivocality and complex symbolization.

**NOVA Online/Pyramids—The Inside Story**
*http://www.pbs.org/wgbh/nova/pyramid/*

Take a virtual tour of the pyramids at Giza through this interesting site. It provides information on the pharaohs for whom the tombs were built.

**The Oriental Institute/University of Chicago**
*http://www.oi.uchicago.edu/OI/default.html*

Open this site to find information on ancient Persia, Mesopotamia, Egypt, and other topics in ancient history.

## UNIT 2: Greece and Rome: The Classical Tradition

**Diotima/Women and Gender in the Ancient World**
*http://www.stoa.org/diotima/*

This site features a wide range of resources on women and gender in the ancient and classical world.

**Exploring Ancient World Cultures**
*http://eawc.evansville.edu*

This electronic, college-level textbook has been designed by a worldwide team of scholars. Especially useful are the links to related Web sites. Learn about Greece and Rome, the pyramids of Egypt, and many more eras and topics.

**WWW: Classical Archaeology**
*http://www.archaeology.org/wwwarky/classical.html*

Useful information and links regarding ancient Greek and Roman archaeology are provided at this site.

## UNIT 3: The Judeo-Christian Heritage

**Institute for Christian Leadership/ICLnet**
*http://www.iclnet.org*

This site of the Institute for Christian Leadership, a Christian organization, presents documents and other resources of use in the study of early Christianity. Internet links are provided.

**Selected Women's Studies Resources/Columbia University**
*http://www.columbia.edu/cu/libraries/subjects/womenstudies/*

Click on extensive links to information about women in religion and philosophy and a wealth of other topics.

## UNIT 4: Muslims and Byzantines

**ByzNet: Byzantine Studies on the Net**
*http://www.thoughtline.com/byznet/*

This Web site offers a brief historical overview of the Byzantine Empire, a collection of maps, and a comprehensive list of emperors.

**Islam: A Global Civilization**
*http://www.templemount.org/islamiad.html*

This site presents information on Islamic history. It chronicles the basic tenets of the religion and charts its spread, including the period of the Umayyad Dynasty in Spain.

## UNIT 5: The Medieval Period

**EuroDocs: Primary Historical Documents from Western Europe**
*http://eudocs.lib.byu.edu*

This collection is a high-quality set of historical documents. Facsimiles, translations, and transcriptions are included as well as links to information on Medieval & Renaissance Europe, Europe as a Supernational Region, and individual countries.

**Feudalism**
*http://www.fidnet.com/~weid/feudalism.htm*

Feudalism is covered in great detail at this site, which offers subjects such as feudal law, agriculture, development in Europe during the feudal period, and feudal terms of England, as well as primary source material.

# Internet References

**The Labyrinth: Resources for Medieval Studies**

*http://www.georgetown.edu/labyrinth/*

Labyrinth provides easy-to-search files in medieval studies. As a major site for topics in medieval history and lore, make it a primary stop for research.

**The World of the Vikings**

*http://www.worldofthevikings.com*

For information on Viking ships and travel—and other aspects of Viking life—visit this site from Past Forward Ltd.

## UNIT 6: Renaissance and Reformation

**Burckhardt: Civilization of the Renaissance in Italy**

*http://www.idbsu.edu/courses/hy309/docs/burckhardt/burckhardt.html*

Jacob Burckhardt's famous book on the Renaissance is available chapter by chapter on the Net at this site.

**Elizabethan England**

*http://www.springfield.k12.il.us/schools/springfield/eliz/elizabethanengland.html*

Prepared by senior literature and composition students in Springfield High School (Illinois), this unusual site covers Elizabethan England resources in some detail: Historical Figures and Events, Everyday Life, Arts and Architecture, Shakespeare and His Theatre, and Links to Other Sources.

**1492: An Ongoing Voyage/Library of Congress**

*http://lcweb.loc.gov/exhibits/1492/*

This site provides displays examining the causes and effects of Columbus's voyages to the Americas and explores the mixture of societies coexisting in five areas of the Western Hemisphere before the arrival of the Europeans. It then surveys the Mediterranean world at a turning point in its development.

**History Net**

*http://www.historynet.com/*

The National Historical Society site provides articles on a wide range of topics, with emphasis on American history, book reviews, and special interviews.

**The Mayflower Web Pages**

*http://www.mayflowerhistory.com/*

These Web pages represent thousands of hours of research, organization, and typing. The site is a merger of two fields: genealogy and history.

**Sir Francis Drake**

*http://www.mcn.org/2/oseeler/drake.htm*

Sir Francis Drake and, in particular, his "famous voyage"—the circumnavigation of the world during the reign of Queen Elizabeth I—are the focus of this site. It is provided by Oliver Seeler's site, The History Ring.

**Society for Economic Anthropology Homepage**

*http://sea.org.ohio-state.edu/*

This is the home page of the Society for Economic Anthropology, an association that strives to understand diversity and change in the economic systems of the world. The site presents data on the organization of society and culture, a topic of interest to students of the Renaissance and Reformation.

# UNIT 1

# The Earliest Civilizations

## Unit Selections

1. **Modern Archaeology,** Brian M. Fagan
2. **The Queen Who Would Be King,** Elizabeth B. Wilson
3. **Journey to the Seven Wonders,** Tony Perrottet
4. **The Coming of the Sea Peoples,** Neil Asher Silberman
5. **Before Tea Leaves Divination in Ancient Babylonia,** William W. Hallo
6. **Millennia of Murex,** Philippa Scott

## Key points to Consider

- How do modern archaeological methods differ from those of the past?
- Was Hatshepsut a wicked step-mother or an effective ruler?
- What were the Seven Wonders of the ancient world and why do they capture our thoughts even after 2,000 years?
- Who were the "Sea Peoples" and how did their weapons and tactics launch a military revolution in the ancient world?
- By what methods did kings in Mesopotamia learn about the future? Are there parallels in today's world?
- What is the connection between the city of Tyre and dyes? Why was this dye famous all over the ancient world?

## Student Web Site

www.mhcls.com/online

## Internet References

**Hypertext and Ethnography**

*http://www.umanitoba.ca/faculties/arts/anthropology/tutor/aaa_presentation.html*

**NOVA Online/Pyramids—The Inside Story**

*http://www.pbs.org/wgbh/nova/pyramid/*

**The Oriental Institute/University of Chicago**

*http://www.oi.uchicago.edu/OI/default.html*

Civilization is a relatively recent phenomenon in human experience. What exactly is civilization? How do civilized people differ from those who are not civilized? How is civilization transmitted?

Civilization, in its contemporary meaning describes a condition of human society marked by an advanced stage of artistic and technological development and by corresponding social and political complexities. Thus, civilized societies have developed formal institutions for commerce, government, education, and religion—activities that are carried out informally by pre-civilized societies. In addition, civilized people make much more extensive use of symbols. The greater the complexity of civilized life, the greater the requirement of a much wider range of specialized activities.

Symbolizations, specialization, and organization enable civilized societies to extend greater control over their environments. Because they are less dependent than pre-civilized societies upon a simple adaptation to a particular habitat, civilized societies are more dynamic. Indeed, civilization institutionalizes change. In sum, civilization provides us with a wider range of concepts, techniques, and options to shape our destinies.

In the West, the necessary preconditions for civilization first emerged in the great river valleys of Mesopotamia and Egypt. There we find the development of irrigation, new staple crops, the introduction of the plow, the invention of the wheel, mathematics, science, improved sailing vessels, and metallurgy (see "Before Tea Leaves Divination in Ancient Babylonia" and "Millennia of Murex"). These developments revolutionized society. Population increased, became more concentrated and complex. The emergence of cities or "urban revolution" marked the beginning of civilization.

Civilization combines complex social, economic, religious, and political structures with a corresponding network of ideas and values. The Sumerians organized themselves in city-states that were headed by kings who acted in the name of the local patron deity. The Egyptians developed the first centralized and authoritarian system based on loyalty to divine pharaohs (see "The Queen Who Would Be King"). The Assyrians used force and intimidation to shape an international empire.

These early civilizations allowed for little individualism or freedom of expression. As historian Nels M. Bailkey notes in *Readings in Ancient History: Thought and Experience from Gilgamesh to St. Augustine* (2002), "their thought remained closely tied to religion and found expression predominantly in religious forms." Elaborate myths recounted the deeds of heroes, defined relations between humans and the gods, and generally justified the prevailing order of things. Thus, myths reveal something of the relationship between values and the social order in ancient civilizations.

We are inclined to make much of the limitations of ancient systems of thought and authority. Yet, the record of the Mesopotamians and Egyptians demonstrates, the civilizations potential for innovation and collective accomplishment from the beginning. They developed mathematics, monumental architecture, law, astronomy, art, timekeeping and monetary systems, and literature rich in diversity and imagination. The records of ancient civilization note not just the cruelty and destruction of the age but also the awakening concern for justice and moral righteousness. These early civilizations are also notable for their heroic efforts to bring nature under human control.

Philip Coblentz/Brand X Pictures/PictureQuest

For a time, the great river valleys remained islands of civilization in a sea of barbarism. The spread of civilization to rain-watered lands required the outlying areas to find the means to produce a food surplus and to develop the social mechanisms for transferring the surplus from farmers to specialists. The first condition was met by the diffusion of plow agriculture; the second by cultural contacts that came through conquest, trade, and migration.

Several satellite civilizations evolved into great empire. Such enterprises grew out of conquest; their initial success and later survival typically depended upon their relative capacity to wage war. "The Coming of the Sea Peoples" describes how an ancient military revolution affected the balance of power in the Near East and furthered cultural exchange between diverse and dispersed societies. The problem of governing scattered and often hostile subjects required that the conquerors create new patterns of authority. The growth of the Assyrian and Persian empires was not mere acts of conquest; it was innovations in government and administration. The earliest efforts to impose and maintain imperial hegemony must have been both crude and cruel.

# Modern Archaeology

**Archaeology continues to be an irresistible lure to publishers, broadcasters and the general public. And the last fifteen years have seen an extraordinary number of spectacular finds across the globe and equally spectacular revelations from ever more sophisticated lab techniques.**

BRIAN M. FAGAN

The Terracotta Army, the royal tombs of Ur, and Olduvai Gorge's Zinjanthropus boisei: some archaeological discoveries of the twentieth century are household names. However, for the most part, we excavators work in quiet anonymity, far from the blaring headlines, despite the efforts of university public relations officers to promote even a minor find as being of international significance. In the popular eye we're still romantic figures, perhaps a trifle eccentric, who poke into royal tombs and dig in the shadow of pyramids. The epic work of Austen Henry Layard at Nineveh and of John Lloyd Stephens in the Maya rainforest in the 1840s, and of Heinrich Schliemann at Troy and Mycenae a generation later, set the tone. Lost civilizations emerging from clinging vines, and, above all, pharaohs' gold, are irresistible lures for the romantically inclined. That redoubtable traveller Rose Macaulay was seduced by her rambles through long-deserted cities, and wrote in her classic travelogue *The Pleasure of Ruins* (1953) of 'the marble and gold of palaces, the laurel and jasmine of gardens, [that] are now brambles and lagoons; the house built for Caesar is now dwelt in by lizards.' The study of the past, though now a highly specialized science, will never escape the lure of ruins.

Part of the romance of discovery comes from the personalities of the major archaeologists of a century ago. Hollywood's Indiana Jones is said to be a composite of at least three genuine excavators of yesteryear. Many of the great discoverers were compelling figures, such as Leonard Woolley of Ur (1880–1960) or Harriet Hawes (1871–1945) who excavated the Minoan village at Gournia on Crete almost alone in the first years of the twentieth century, when the site was inaccessible except by mule; or palaeoanthropologists Louis (1880–1960) and Mary Leakey (1913–96) of Olduvai Gorge fame.

The world of archaeology was an intellectual village in their day, where everyone knew everyone else and the gossip was ferocious. Just a handful worked outside the narrow confines of Europe, the Mediterranean, and North America. In 1959, the year Mary Leakey found Zinjanthropus, there were under a dozen archaeologists in sub-Saharan Africa and less than a handful in Australia and New Zealand. Considering the small numbers and the shoestring budgets, the quantity of important discoveries was astonishing.

Today, the number of archaeologists working around the world has mushroomed to perhaps 10,000. Many of them are engaged in heritage and monuments administration, but a large number are actively involved in excavation and discovery. The great expansion of archaeology coincided with the explosion of higher education during the 1960s, at the same time as radiocarbon dating burst on the study of the remote past like a thunderclap. I vividly remember the nervous frisson that swept through our comfortable world when radiocarbon samples suddenly dated the beginnings of agriculture in southwestern Asia previously thought to have occurred in the fifth millennium BC—to 6,000 BC and then even earlier. Soon afterward another new method, potassium argon dating, pushed human origins back to at least 2 million years ago. More recently, even earlier human ancestors date to at least 4 million.

Today's archaeology bears less and less resemblance to that of a half century ago. The best excavators of the 1950s were maestros of their craft. Their successors have refined digging and archaeological survey into a fine-grained science, by the use of subsurface radar and other technologies to probe the earth, and by close collaboration with scientists from many disciplines—everyone from botanists to ice-core climatologists, even beetle and earthworm specialists. Many recent discoveries have come from the laboratory rather than the trench, through work on hominin fossils, artefacts, on human bone and occasionally surviving tissue, and from cutting-edge research on ancient DNA. We can 'excavate' a person's ancestry through their genes, trace their lives through bone strontium, and analyze the traces of their last meals from pottery buried with them in their tombs. We know more about the medical history of pharaoh Rameses II than he did himself. We've become experts on ancient feasts and emperors' wines, on sources of stone axes and the conservation of ancient mummies.

Yet, we too are enjoying a triumphal era of archaeological exploration. More important discoveries have been made in the past fifteen years than since Victorian times. We may not discover a forgotten civilization in a week or excavate entire cities with huge armies of local workers as our forebears could do, but today's discoveries are equally dazzling in their range and complexity. Archaeological finds still encompass the golden and the spectacular, witness the flamboyant tombs of the Moche Lords of Sipan, dating to about AD 400, found on Peru's north coast in 1989. But most major discoveries reveal the lives of ordinary people, the folk who laboured far from the limelight. The great strengths of archaeology lie in its ability to study human societies as they change over enormous periods of time, and to look at them as functioning entities, not just at royal courts or richly adorned cemeteries. And at places like medieval Winchester or Colonial Jamestown in Virginia, the spade still does much to flesh out historical records and to reveal the bustling diversity of medieval and early modern communities.

Many of the revelations of recent years have transformed our knowledge of early human evolution from a ladder-like progression to an intricate tree of evolving hominins. We are now certain that tropical Africa was the cradle of humankind over 4 million years ago. We also know that an astounding diversity of potential human ancestors roamed the East African savanna between 2 and 3 million years ago, among them the genus Homo, known from East Turkana in northern Kenya and from Ethiopia's Afar. New fossil discoveries tell us that Don Johanson's famous Lucy, the diminutive 4-million-year-old Ethiopian hominin known as Australopithecus afarensis which he found in 1974, had gorilla-like characteristics, but walked upright and was at home in the trees. We also now know that by 2 million years ago more advanced humans, generically known as Homo erectus, had appeared in Africa and that some of their descendants were living in what is now Georgia in Central Asia 1.8 million years ago. And a remarkable find of about eighty human fossil fragments, many of them children, in deep caves in the Sierra de Atapuerca in northern Spain, dates to about 780,000 years ago—remote ancestors of the Neanderthals.

One of the great controversies of archaeology revolves around the origins of Homo sapiens, but the discoveries of recent years leave us in little doubt that our ancestry lies in sub-Saharan Africa. The 1980s brought mitochondrial DNA (mtDNA) into the headlines, DNA that is inherited through the female line, with the then-controversial theory of an African Eve, of genetically ancestral populations south of the Sahara about 180,000 years ago. Then came the discovery by Tim White of Homo sapiens skulls at Herto in eastern Ethiopia which date to about 160,000 years ago, and a raft of less well-known discoveries that revealed traces of more modern human behaviour in many places throughout Africa in later millennia.

Another scientific advance, Accelerator Mass Spectrometry (AMS) radiocarbon dating, now allows us to date tiny specks of charcoal, even individual seeds, and this has enabled us to trace the great diaspora that carried modern humans through the late Ice Age world in the last 100,000 years. Thanks to AMS, we now know that modern humans had replaced Neanderthals in Europe after 45,000 years ago. (DNA from Neanderthal bones shows that the two populations could not interbreed.) Homo sapiens was well established in East Asia before 60,000 years ago, in Australia and New Guinea by 45,000, and on the Solomon Islands by 30,000. There were Ice Age wallaby hunters in Tasmania by 35,000 years ago. But many enigmas remain, notable among them the diminutive humans excavated on the island of Flores, Indonesia, dating to about 18,000 years ago. Do these people, nicknamed the Hobbits, and known scientifically as Homo floresiensis, represent an entirely new species of dwarf human, or are they medically abnormal? The injury is still out.

Three quarters of a century ago, the prehistorian Vere Gordon Childe (1892–1957), a genius at popularizing archaeology, wrote of a 'Neolithic Revolution' in southwestern Asia, which saw people domesticate crops and animals and settle down in permanent villages, a development that he claimed to have taken place in southwestern Asia around 4,000 BC. Today, new excavations and sophisticated flotation methods that recover large samples of wild and domesticated seeds by passing them through fine sieves and water, show that the origins of farming and animal domestication go back to at least 9,000 BC. The German archaeologist Klaus Schmidt has shown that human society had changed dramatically even before agriculture began. At Gobelki Tepe in southeastern Turkey, he has uncovered a series of subterranean shrines with carved monoliths, which appear to be places that commemorated the dead, the ancestors. Such a concern may have developed as growing populations of hunter-gatherers exploited ever-smaller territories and developed much closer ties to ancestral lands.

Hawaii, New Zealand, and Rapa Nui, some of the most remote landmasses on Earth, had been settled by Polynesians by about AD 800. Meticulous excavations and AMS radiocarbon dates are now pinpointing the dates of first settlement with much greater precision, but mysteries remain. Did Polynesians sail even further eastward and land on the coast of South America? The answer may come from the DNA extracted from bones of chickens. A handful of bones from a site in Peru share identical DNA with Polynesian birds, hinting at human contact between native Americans and Polynesians at least a century before the Spaniards arrived in the Americas.

The Sutton Hoo ship, the Maya lord at Tikal in Guatemala—some of archaeology's most dramatic finds are tombs, graves, and mummies. The past two decades have produced more sensational burials from southwestern Asia. Iraqi archaeologists have unearthed the sepulchres of three Assyrian queens of the eighth century BC, buried under the floor of a palace at Nimrud. An international team of excavators has uncovered the undisturbed tombs of at least three generations of kings at Qatna, Syria, from the sixteenth century BC. Qatna itself was a powerful state between 1900 and 1350 BC, a dominant but now little-known partner in eastern Mediterranean trade for many centuries. Other burial discoveries, like those of the Golden Mummies at Bahariyah, Egypt, made international headlines. But perhaps the most remarkable discoveries involve less exalted individuals, like the Amesbury Archer, buried near Stonehenge in about 2470 BC. Strontium analysis of his teeth reveals that he was brought up in Central Europe, startling testimony to the distances that people travelled during the Early Bronze Age. The archer was a metalsmith, perhaps one of the first in Britain, which may account for his high prestige.

Royal tombs and art have always gone hand-in-hand. Even before the days of states and monarchs, the artistic traditions of the past are closely tied to belief and ritual which is why the sensational discovery in 1994 of Chauvet cave in France's Ardeche is of such importance. It is a magnificent gallery of Cro-Magnon art that has been sealed since at least 24,000 years ago. The earliest paintings date to at least 31,000 years ago and are of a level of sophistication that rivals the famous friezes at Altamira and Lascaux, which are half their age. (So is an ivory mammoth figurine of 35,000 years ago found in Vogelherd cave in southern Germany in 2005.) Even more importantly, Chauvet will give us unparalleled insights into some of the rituals that unfolded in the dark cave. And thanks to AMS radiocarbon dating, it will be possible to decipher the multiple layers of animal drawings on the walls.

In 2001, the Mayan archaeologist William Saturno made a stunning find of early Maya art in a buried room at San Bartolo, Guatemala, a frieze of the creation featuring the Maize God of primordial tradition and some of the earliest known Maya glyphs, dating to between 400 and 200 BC. In Maya society, and many others of the past, there was no boundary between the world of the living and the supernatural realm—which is why it is important that we attempt to comprehend the intangible. Much cutting-edge research in archaeology now focuses on religion and ideology, topics considered inaccessible a generation ago. For instance, the lords of Moche, a coastal Peruvian state of the early first millennium AD, were aware that coastal fisheries would occasionally be interrupted by what we now call El Nino episodes, when the ocean currents temporarily reverse. The anchovy fisheries would vanish as cold water ceased to flow to the sea surface. Exotic tropical fish brought by a south-flowing current appeared off the Moche homeland; at the same time, savage rainstorms would descend on the coastal desert and generations of irrigation works would be swept away within hours. In 1995 Steve Bourget of the University of Texas and a team of Peruvian colleagues uncovered the remains of sacrificial victims in a small plaza at the great Moche shrine of Huaca del Luna, where they also found murals of tropical fish such as eagle rays and swimming crabs. This suggests that the Moche lords incorporated the hazards of El Ninos into the complex ideology that propagated their special relationship to the supernatural world. Such ideology gave these lords with the authority to rule during periods of chaos, when the people might question their infallibility as divine rulers.

The broad sweep of archaeological discovery covers all time periods, and includes sites above and below water and long forgotten cities. It has also moved into much more recent times. William Kelso has uncovered the foundations of the first English houses in North America at the 1607 settlement of Jamestown, Virginia—despite the almost universal historical and scientific opinion that the entire settlement had been washed away by the waters of the James River. Kelso eventually located the remains of an entire lost settlement, and thousands of artefacts from it. The Peruvian archaeologist Ruth Shady Solis did the same when she investigated the extensive plazas and pyramids of the 4,600 year-old city of Caral on the Peruvian coast north of Lima in the late 1990s. This remarkable settlement extends the date of cities in the Andes back in time by more than 2,000 years.

Archaeology particularly excels when it uncovers people with no trace in the historical record, the anonymous artisans and labourers who laboured in the shadows, building pyramids, temples, and fortifications. Mark Lehner has spent several field seasons exploring the long-vanished workers' community close to the pyramids of Giza. He uncovered dwellings, the town cemetery, which tells us much about the skilled artisans of Giza, and the facilities where teams of labourers baked bread and prepared the dried fish that were the staple rations of the entire pyramid workforce. Lehner's finds and recent survey work on the Giza Plateau is transforming our understanding of the pyramids and those who built them.

Perhaps the greatest contribution of archaeology in the past two decades is the way in which excavation after excavation has been able to document the great, often unsuspected, diversity of ancient societies, not only in the teeming streets of growing cities, but in ethnic enclaves, slave plantations, and military barracks. Time and again, as was the case in Annapolis, Maryland, where finds of African ritual artefacts show how anonymous groups like slaves tried to maintain their cultural identities in the face of oppression and powerful doctrines of social inequality.

Archaeologists have long sought the past under the surface of the oceans, since scuba-diving technology has provided a means of investigating ancient shipwrecks. Among them is the Uluburun ship, which foundered off southern Turkey in 1310 BC, laden with a rich cargo from at least ten regions of the eastern Mediterranean world, and which was excavated over eleven years up to 1994. Underwater archaeology is not a treasure hunt, as many people still believe, but it has the same goals as excavation on land—to understand human behaviour. The underwater discoveries of recent years result from investigations that have this firmly in mind. Some boats may even be excavated on land: David O'Connor and Matthew Douglas Adams have studied some of the world's earliest boats far up the Nile at Abydos, and have shown how boats played a fundamental role in ensuring the immortality of the earliest pharaohs. At the mouth of the Nile, the French scholar Franck Goddio is mapping Alexandria's imposing Classical harbour and also investigating warships sunk during the epochal Battle of Aboukir Bay in 1798, where Nelson destroyed an anchored French fleet.

Underwater investigations involve complex detective work, which continues long after excavation is complete. Thirty years of investigation has produced a remarkably complete portrait of the warship HMS Pandora, wrecked on Australia's Great Barrier Reef, while transporting Bounty mutineers in 1791. The wreck of the American Civil War submarine Hunley was discovered in 2000, and research on its crew members is still in its early stages as technicians probe delicately through the compacted sludge of the interior.

A century ago, the archaeologist was usually an amateur, casually trained and often working in a remote land with few assistants. Excavators like Howard Carter in the Valley of the Kings, Alfred Kidder in the southwestern United States, and Leonard Woolley in Mesopotamia had a genius for improvisation on minimal budgets. Carter moved Tutankhamun's treasures in mining cars along track relaid every few hundred metres, in 100[degrees]F (37[degrees]C) heat. Woolley recovered the wooden frame of a Sumerian lyre by the simple expedient of pouring plaster of Paris into small holes in the ground. Such achievements pale alongside the miracles of modern science, which allows a researcher to reconstruct the countenances of our forebears, to trace ancestry with DNA, and to work with European climatic records deduced from tree-ring sequences that extend back over 10,000 years. From solitary adventurers, we have turned into team workers, with much of our work conducted far from the heat of a trench. Many of the most sensational discoveries of the twenty-first century will come in the laboratory. Today we can locate new sites from space, tell the direction of the wind on the day of an ancient hunt, and say whether a stoneworker of 10,000 years ago was left-handed. We may have accounted for the world's 'lost' civilizations, but the work of understanding those who created them and our humbler forebears has hardly begun.

The soil still holds many secrets, but it doesn't take a genius to predict the most spectacular find of the coming century. The great burial mound of China's First Emperor Shi Huangdi, who died in 210 BC, remains unexplored. The sheer scale of his mausoleum beggars the imagination. The terracotta regiment and other offerings unearthed around the sepulchre hint at the extraordinary riches inside the burial mound. Shi Huangdi's tomb is said to contain a map of China with the rivers delineated in mercury. Remote sensing has detected traces of a large wooden structure inside the mound. So far Chinese authorities have postponed any excavations, on the grounds that they lack the resources and skills needed to investigate this ultimate in royal sepulchres. But when they do, the finds will surely dwarf those of other ancient rulers.

---

**BRIAN M. FAGAN** is a emeritus professor of Archaelogy at the University of California and the Editor of *Discovery! Unearthing the New Treasures of Archaelogy* (Thames & Hudson, 2007).

# The Queen Who Would Be King

## Was she a scheming stepmother or a strong and effective ruler? History's view of the pharaoh Hatshepsut has been revised.

Elizabeth B. Wilson

It was a hot, dusty day in early 1927, and Herbert Winlock was staring at a scene of brutal destruction that had all the hallmarks of a vicious personal attack. Signs of desecration were everywhere; eyes had been gouged out, heads lopped off, the cobra-like symbol of royalty hacked from foreheads. Winlock, head of the Metropolitan Museum of Art's archaeological team in Egypt, had unearthed a pit in the great temple complex at Deir el-Bahri, across the Nile from the ancient sites of Thebes and Karnak. In the pit were smashed statues of a pharaoh—pieces "from the size of a fingertip," Winlock noted, "to others weighing a ton or more." The images had suffered "almost every conceivable indignity," he wrote, as the violators vented "their spite on the [pharaoh's] brilliantly chiseled, smiling features." To the ancient Egyptians, pharaohs were gods. What could this one have done to warrant such blasphemy? In the opinion of Winlock, and other Egyptologists of his generation, plenty.

The statues were those of Hatshepsut, the sixth pharaoh of the 18th dynasty, one of the few—and by far the most successful—females to rule Egypt as pharaoh. Evidence of her remarkable reign (c. 1479–1458 B.C.) did not begin to emerge until the 19th century. But by Winlock's day, historians had crafted the few known facts of her life into a soap opera of deceit, lust and revenge.

Although her long rule had been a time of peace and prosperity, filled with magnificent art and a number of ambitious building projects (the greatest of which was her mortuary or memorial, temple at Deir el-Bahri), Hatshepsut's methods of acquiring and holding onto power suggested a darker side to her reign and character. The widowed queen of the pharaoh Thutmose II, she had, according to custom, been made regent after his death in c. 1479 B.C. to rule for her young stepson, Thutmose III, until he came of age. Within a few years, however, she proclaimed herself pharaoh, thereby becoming, in the words of Winlock's colleague at the Metropolitan, William C. Hayes, the "vilest type of usurper." Disconcerting to some scholars, too, was her insistence on being portrayed as male, with bulging muscles and the traditional pharaonic false beard—variously interpreted by those historians as an act of outrageous deception, deviant behavior or both. Many early Egyptologists also concluded that Hatshepsut's chief minister, Senenmut, must have been her lover as well as a coconspirator in her climb to power—the so-called evil genius behind what they viewed as her devious politics.

Upon Hatshepsut's death in c. 1458 B.C., her stepson, then likely still in his early 20s, finally ascended to the throne. By that time, according to Hayes, Thutmose III had developed "a loathing for Hatshepsut . . . her name and her very memory which practically beggars description." The destruction of her monuments, carried out with such apparent fury, was almost universally interpreted as an act of long-awaited and bitter revenge on the part of Thutmose III, who, Winlock wrote, "could scarcely wait to take the vengeance on her dead that he had not dared in life."

"Of course, it made a wonderful story," says Renée Dreyfus, curator of ancient art and interpretation at the Fine Arts Museums of San Francisco. "And this is what we all read when we were growing up. But so much of what was written about Hatshepsut, I think, had to do with who the archaeologists were . . . gentlemen scholars of a certain generation."

A new exhibition, "Hatshepsut: From Queen to Pharaoh"—co-curated by Dreyfus and fellow scholars Cathleen Keller, professor of Near Eastern Studies at the University of California at Berkeley, and Catharine Roehrig, curator of Egyptian art at the Metropolitan—aims to set the record straight. The show, which began a national tour at the Fine Arts Museums of San Francisco's de Young Museum last fall and continued on to the Metropolitan Museum in New York City, is currently on view through December 31 at the Kimbell Art Museum in Fort Worth, Texas.

The first major exhibition devoted to Hatshepsut, the show brings together some 300 objects from the tombs, temples, palaces and private lives of the ruler and her contemporaries. Ranging from colossal sphinxes and stone stelae to cosmetic containers and elaborate gold jewelry, these objects dazzlingly confirm something not even Hatshepsut's detractors have denied—that her reign set new standards of craftsmanship, taste and luxurious living, in both life and death.

Perhaps more important, the exhibition and its accompanying 340-page catalog also bring together a wealth of recent archaeological scholarship that contradicts many long-held beliefs about this much-maligned pharaoh and affirms her place in history as a strong, capable and largely beneficent ruler, whose path to power may have had more to do with political necessity than personal ambition.

Hatshepsut was born at the dawn of a glorious age of Egyptian imperial power and prosperity, rightly called the New Kingdom. Her father, King Thutmose I, was a charismatic leader of legendary military exploits. Hatshepsut, scholars surmise, may have been born about the time of his coronation, c. 1504 B.C., and so would still have been a toddler when he famously sailed home to Thebes with the naked body of a Nubian chieftain dangling from the prow of his ship—a warning to all who would threaten his empire.

Hatshepsut seems to have idolized her father (she would eventually have him rebuffed in the tomb she was having built for herself) and would claim that soon after her birth he had named her successor to his throne, an act that scholars feel would have been highly unlikely: There had been only two—possibly three—female pharaohs in the previous 1,500 years, and each had ascended to the throne only when there was no suitable male successor available. (Cleopatra would rule some 14 centuries later.)

Normally, the pharaonic line passed from father to son—preferably the son of the queen, but if there were no such offspring, to the son of one of the pharaoh's "secondary," or "harem," wives. In addition to Hatshepsut—and another younger daughter who apparently died in childhood—it's believed that Thutmose I fathered two sons with Queen Ahmes, both of whom predeceased him. Thus the son of a secondary wife, Mutnofret, was crowned Thutmose II. In short order (and probably to bolster the royal bloodlines of this "harem child"), young Thutmose II was married to his half sister Hatshepsut, making her Queen of Egypt at about age 12.

Historians have generally described Thutmose II as frail and ineffectual—just the sort of person a supposedly shrewish Hatshepsut could push around. Public monuments, however, depict a dutiful Hatshepsut standing appropriately behind her husband. But while she bore her husband a daughter, Neferure (her only known child), Hatshepsut failed in the more important duty of producing a son. So when Thutmose II died young (c. 1479)—possibly still in his 20s—the throne went, yet again, to a "harem child." Duly named Thutmose III, this child was destined to become one of the great warrior kings of Egypt. But at the time of his father's death, he was likely an infant—a "hawk . . . still in the nest"—and deemed too young to rule.

In such cases, it was the accepted New Kingdom practice for widowed queens to act as regents, handling the affairs of government until their sons—in this case, stepson/nephew—came of age, and Hatshepsut (more or less automatically, it seems) got the assignment. "I think it would have been pretty much the norm for Hatshepsut to step in," says Peter Dorman, an Egyptologist at the University of Chicago and a contributor to the exhibition catalog. "But it's also quite clear that Thutmose III was recognized as king from the very start."

Monuments of the time show Thutmose III—still a child, but portrayed in the conventional manner as an adult king—performing his pharaonic duties, while Hatshepsut, dressed as queen, stands demurely off to one side. By the seventh year of her regency, however (and it may have been much earlier), the formerly slim, graceful queen appears as a full-blown, flail-and-crook-wielding king, with the broad, bare chest of a man and the pharaonic false beard.

But why? To Egyptologists of an earlier generation, Hatshepsut's elevation to godlike status was an act of naked ambition. ("It was not long," Hayes wrote, "before this vain, ambitious, and unscrupulous woman showed . . . her true colors.") But more recent scholarship suggests that a political crisis, such as a threat from a competing branch of the royal family, obliged Hatshepsut to become pharaoh. Far from stealing the throne, says the Metropolitan's Roehrig, "Hatshepsut may have had to declare herself king to protect the kingship for her stepson."

It's an interpretation that seems to be supported by Hatshepsut's treatment of Thutmose III during her reign. "He wasn't under house arrest for those 20-odd years," says Roehrig. "He was learning how to be a very good soldier." And it's not as if Hatshepsut could have stepped down when her stepson came of age. "Once you took on the attributes of kingship," explains Dreyfus, "that was it. You were a god. It's not queen for a day, it's king for all time."

Hatshepsut probably knew her position was tenuous-both by virtue of her sex and the unconventional way she had gained the throne—and therefore appears to have done what canny leaders have often done in times of crisis: she reinvented herself. The most obvious form this took was having herself portrayed as a male pharaoh. As to why, "No one really knows," says Dorman. But he believes it may have been motivated by the presence of a male co-ruler—a circumstance with which no previous female ruler had ever contended.

"She was not pretending to be a man! She was not cross-dressing!" says exhibition co-curator Cathleen Keller, pointing out that inscriptions on Hatshepsut's statues almost always contain some indication of her true gender—a title, such as "Daughter of Re," or feminine word endings, resulting in such grammatical conundrums as "His Majesty, Herself."

Hatshepsut also took a new name, Maatkare, sometimes translated as Truth (maat) is the Soul (ka) of the Sun God (Re). The key word here is maat—the ancient Egyptian expression for order and justice as established by the gods. Maintaining and perpetuating maat to ensure the prosperity and stability of the country required a legitimate pharaoh who could speak—as only pharaohs could—directly with the gods. By calling herself Maatkare, Hatshepsut was likely reassuring her people that they had a legitimate ruler on the throne.

One important way pharaohs affirmed maat was by creating monuments, and Hatshepsut's building projects were among the most ambitious of any pharaoh's. She began with the erection of two 100-foot-tall obelisks at the great temple complex at Karnak. Reliefs commemorating the event show the pair, each weighing about 450 tons, being towed along the Nile by 27 ships manned by 850 oarsmen. Dedicated to the sun god Re, they were sheathed in shimmering electrum, a combination of gold and silver.

Hatshepsut carried out her public works program across the empire, but it was concentrated in the area around Thebes, the dynastic and theological center of the Thutmoside dynasty, where she built a network of imposing processional roadways and sanctuaries. At Deir el-Bahri, just across the Nile from Thebes, she erected her magnum opus—an immense memorial temple, used for special religious rites connected to the cult that would guarantee Hatshepsut perpetual life after death.

Dramatically sited at the base of towering limestone cliffs, the temple, which is regarded as one of the architectural wonders of the ancient world, is approached through a series of terraced colonnades and courtyards that appear to ascend up the very side of the mountain. Despite the enormous scale of the complex—roughly the length of two and a half football fields—its overall impression is one of lightness and grace, unlike the fortress-like temples of her predecessors.

The temple's lower levels featured pools and gardens planted with fragrant trees. Supersized images of Hatshepsut were everywhere. Some 100 colossal statues of the female pharaoh as a sphinx guarded the processional way. Lining the terraces were more images of the ruler (some more than ten feet tall) in various devotional attitudes—kneeling with offerings to the gods, striding into eternity, or in the guise of Osiris, the mummiform god of death and resurrection.

Miraculously, a number of these statues—some reassembled, others still in a fragmentary state—survive and are included in the current exhibition. Most are massive, masculine and meant to be seen from a distance. But not all. For example, an exquisitely carved granite statue reunited for the show—the head and lower parts are owned by the Metropolitan; the torso comes from Leiden's Rijksmuseum—is a rare example of Hatshepsut depicted as both female and pharaoh. Only slightly larger than life-size, it shows her, slender, with small, rounded breasts, seated on her throne and wearing the pharaonic nemes, or head cloth. Some scholars believe the statue is from an early phase of Hatshepsut's rule, before she fully adopted a masculine persona; others believe there were certain contexts in which she felt comfortable being portrayed as the woman she was. This image may have been used for cult offerings at her memorial temple and seen only by a privileged few. As depicted in this statue, she has large almond eyes, a slightly aquiline nose, narrow chin and confident, quiet smile. Does it reflect Hatshepsut's actual appearance? Or, like so much pharaonic portraiture, does it simply conform to the artistic conventions of the time? Hatshepsut's mummy has never been identified, so we cannot know for sure.

Hatshepsut's temple also featured a series of reliefs marking the achievements of her reign, including a storied trading expedition to the mysterious and distant land called Punt, believed to be somewhere on the coast of the Red Sea, perhaps in current-day Eritrea. The reliefs show the Egyptians loading their boats in Punt with an array of highly prized luxury goods—ebony, ivory, gold, exotic animals and incense trees. "Never," reads an inscription, "were such things brought to any king since the world was."

As a work of art, of architecture and of self-glorification, Hatshepsut's memorial temple was an enormous enterprise that must have involved an army of workers. It's almost certain, scholars agree, that Senenmut, the official overseer of works at Deir el-Bahri, was the mastermind, if not the actual architect, of the temple. He had most likely begun his climb to power during the reign of Thutmose II, when he was appointed tutor to Hatshepsut's daughter, Neferure. But his influence soared with Hatshepsut's accession to the throne. In time he acquired some 93 titles, the most prestigious of which was Great Steward of Amun (the god of Thebes), which put him in charge of all of Karnak's building and business activities.

Many of Senenmut's monuments to himself (some 25—a staggering number for a nonroyal) mention his exceptional access to the throne; he was a "true confidant" of the pharaoh and the "one upon whose utterances his Lord relied." But earlier scholars' belief that Senenmut was the real force behind Hatshepsut's rule—not "even a woman of the most virile character could have attained such a pinnacle of success without masculine support," wrote historian Alan Gardiner in 1961—has now been largely discounted by experts as a woeful underestimation of Hatshepsut.

Did she and Senenmut share more than power? Probably not, most scholars have concluded. "I think Hatshepsut was too conscious of her position to have gotten involved with him physically," says Keller. Dorman agrees but allows that the pharaoh and her favorite minister may well have been victims of speculation and gossip. He cites a crude drawing scrawled on a Deir el-Bahri wall that shows a man thought to be Senenmut having sex with a woman in pharaonic headdress. "It could be them," says Dorman. "Whether it reflects reality or not, we don't know."

Senenmut's fate is a mystery. His privileged position allowed him to build a splendid tomb for himself near Hatshepsut's—which is in the Valley of the Kings, just west of Deir el-Bahri —but he apparently never occupied it. The tomb suffered major damage, including the smashing of his impressive, if unused, stone sarcophagus. It was long thought that either Hatshepsut or Thutmose III were the culprits, but recent scholarship suggests some combination of religious upheaval, tomb robbers and natural collapse.

Hatshepsut's own tomb was cut into the base of the cliffs on the east side of the Valley of the Kings, and was large enough to accommodate both her sarcophagus and that of her father—reburying him in her tomb was yet another attempt to legitimize her rule. It's believed that Hatshepsut died (possibly in her late 40s) around 1458 B.C., the year that Thutmose III first used the title "Ruler of Maat."

Thutmose III's destruction of Hatshepsut's monuments has long been recognized as a conscientious—and very nearly successful—attempt to obliterate her name and memory from history. But was it, as many early Egyptologists had assumed, an act of revenge and hatred? In recent decades, scholars have reexamined the archaeological evidence and come to the startling conclusion that the destruction, presumed to have been initiated soon after Hatshepsut's death, was actually not begun until some 20 years later, toward the end of Thutmose III's own long reign (c. 1458–1425 B.C.). "I think that people recognize now, because it happened so late in Thutmose III's reign, that it wasn't personal animosity," says Dorman of the rampage. "For some reason, Thutmose III must have decided it was necessary to essentially rewrite the official record of Hatshepsut's kingship"—which meant eradicating all traces of it to suggest that the throne had gone directly from his father to him.

While numerous theories abound, most contemporary Egyptologists agree that the effort to delete any evidence of Hatshepsut's rule had something to do with Thutmose III's concerns about the succession of power after his death. Was there some threat to the legitimacy of his own son, Amenhotep II, who in fact did succeed him? Possibly but Dorman suggests that Hatshepsut's unconventional reign may have been too successful, a dangerous precedent "best erased," he writes in the catalog, "to prevent the possibility of another powerful female ever inserting herself into the long line of Egyptian male kings."

The story of Hatshepsut's reign will probably never be complete. "She's like an iceberg," says Joyce Tyldesley, scholar and author of the 1996 biography Hatchepsut: The Female Pharaoh. "On the surface we know quite a lot about her. But there's so much we don't know."

"I see her as I do Elizabeth I," says Roehrig. "Someone who was probably trained from childhood to be a representative of the royal family. And you are put in extraordinary circumstances and you rise to the occasion. You do what's necessary to get the job done." Tyldesley agrees, but she also feels that Hatshepsut may have been keenly conscious of her exceptional place in history. "This is just speculation," she says, "but I think she was almost aware that she might be forgotten or that her actions would be misunderstood." Toward the end of her reign, Hatshepsut erected a second pair of obelisks at Karnak. On one the inscription reads: "Now my heart turns this way and that, as I think what the people will say—those who shall see my monuments in years to come, and who shall speak of what I have done."

---

New Yorker **ELIZABETH B. WILSON** has written about culture and the arts for such publications as *ARTnews and Art & Antiques*.

# Journey to the Seven Wonders

## Though only one of the ancient marvels still stands, they still engage our imagination—and launch a thousand tours—more than two millennia later.

Tony Perrottet

Visitors to the Lobby of the Empire State Building in Midtown Manhattan are often surprised to find a series of pictorial stained-glass panels. Added in the 1960s, they were meant to link the great skyscraper to other engineering triumphs. These triumphs, however, are not the great symbols of American modernity you might expect—other massive steel-and-concrete structures like the Hoover Dam or the Panama Canal—but the Seven Wonders of the Ancient World.

The colorful lobby paintings make no attempt at accuracy. Rather, they echo fantasies of the ancient monuments that have been current since the Renaissance—but they are mysteriously inspiring all the same: the Pyramids of Giza, the Pharos of Alexandria, the Temple of Artemis in Ephesus, the Mausoleum at Halicarnassus, the Colossus of Rhodes, the Hanging Gardens of Babylon, the Statue of Zeus at Olympia.

Why should a collection of monuments more than two millennia old still capture the imagination—especially when six of the seven are no longer standing?

"It's that word 'wonder,' " says David Gilman Romano, professor of classics at the University of Pennsylvania. "If you just called them the Seven Architectural Marvels, it wouldn't have the same impact." Then, too, the one that does survive—the Pyramids of Giza—is sufficiently stunning to convince us that the ancients weren't exaggerating the splendor of the other six.

It's also our passion for ordering the world. "We are living in a time very much like that of the Hellenic period," says Larissa Bonfante, professor of classics at New York University. "The Greeks loved to have things categorized—they loved anything out of the ordinary—and so do we." In our chaotic age, bombarded as we are with new technologies and rapid cultural change, we still seem to yearn for the security of mutually acknowledged "greats"—whether it be Impressionist painters, *Citizen Kane,* the Washington Monument, Cartier-Bresson photographs or the Hanging Gardens of Babylon.

One of the first-known lists of wonders was drawn up in the third century B.C., when a Greek scholar at the Library of Alexandria, Callimachus of Cyrene (305–240 B.C.), wrote a treatise called "A collection of wonders in lands throughout the world." The essay has been lost, but his choices may have become the basis for later selections, such as the famous list attributed to the engineer Philo of Byzantium around 250 B.C. Of course, the whole idea of Seven Wonders started with antiquity's fondness for the number seven: being indivisible, it gave each of its elements equal status and so enjoyed a privileged position in numerology.

The list also reflected a shift in Western attitudes toward the world, as thinkers began to celebrate man-made creations along with those of the gods. In the wake of Alexander the Great's conquests of the Persian Empire and parts of India (334–325 B.C.), Greeks marveled at their own achievements. "Like the sun," raves Philo of the Hanging Gardens, "beauty dazzling in its brilliance."

From their inception, the ancient Wonders were also rooted in human curiosity. In fact, the sites originally were not called "Wonders" at all, but *theamata,* "things to be seen," preferably in person. In the Hellenic era, wealthy and erudite Greeks traveled by land and sea around the cultural centers of the eastern Mediterranean, broadening their education firsthand. Although the lands conquered by Alexander the Great had dissolved into separate kingdoms by the time Philo compiled his list, they were still ruled by Greek-speaking dynasties, and while travel was not yet as safe as it would become under the Roman Empire, the network of Greek culture extended far and wide, offering an open invitation to explore.

Today one can follow the itinerary of an ancient traveler as he—a peripatetic Greek scholar of that time was almost always male—sought out the magnificent Seven. Along the route, he would find passable highway inns and cheap roadside restaurants. At the sites themselves, professional tour guides called *exegetai,* or "explainers," jostled for commissions ("Zeus protect me from your guides at Olympia!" prayed one first-century B.C. antiquarian worn down by their harangues). There were papyrus guidebooks to consult before departing and vendors with whom to haggle over souvenirs: a cheap glass vial engraved with an image of the Pharos of Alexandria has been found by archaeologists as far away as Afghanistan.

## The Statue of Zeus at Olympia

Departing in the Shadow of the Acropolis from Athens, the traditional center of ancient learning, a scholar-tourist of 250 B.C. would likely have set off on his grand tour with a couple of servants and a pair of pack mules to carry the luggage. The first and easiest Wonder to visit was the great sculptor Phidias' (c. 485–425 B.C.) Statue of Zeus (completed around 435 B.C. at Olympia, a religious sanctuary in southern Greece and the site of the Olympic Games. An energetic walker could cover the 210 miles in ten days. Arriving at Olympia, visitors beheld a walled enclave where a trio of Doric temples, 70 altars and hundreds of statues of past Olympic victors created a dazzling sculpture garden. The most impressive of the structures was the Temple of Zeus, built between 466 and 456 B.C. and resembling the Parthenon in Athens. Through its grand bronze doors, a constant stream of travelers passed into the flickering torchlight, there to behold a glowering, 40-foot-high, gold-and-ivory figure of the King of the Gods seated on a throne, his features framed by a leonine mane of hair.

"It seems that if Zeus were to stand up," wrote the Greek geographer Strabo, who visited the statue early in the first century B.C., "he would unroof the temple." Beyond its stunning size, viewers were struck by the majesty of the image's expression—even stray dogs were said to be cowed. The sculptor had captured both Zeus' invincible divinity and his humanity. Roman general Aemilius Paullus (c. 229–160 B.C.), an earlier visitor, "was moved to his soul, as if he had beheld the god in person," while the Greek orator Dio Chrysostom wrote that a single glimpse of the statue would make a man forget his earthly troubles.

## The Colossus of Rhodes

From Olympia, our intrepid traveler would have caught a merchant ship from the isthmus of Corinth, sailing eastward some 300 miles across the pellucid waters of the Aegean. Since there was no exclusive passenger service, one simply negotiated a price with the ship's captain and took a place on deck. One's servants would arrange the creature comforts, leaving the traveler to enjoy the view and make small talk with fellow passengers.

Arriving a few days later at their destination, the bustling island of Rhodes, the travelers would have been greeted with a breathtaking sight. There, towering majestically above the island's port, so crowded with ships' masts that it was said to resemble a field of wheat, stood a 110-foot-high Colossus—a gleaming bronze statue of the Greek sun god Helios. It was long believed that the statue straddled the harbor entrance, but modern archaeologists say this would not have been possible with the bronze-casting techniques available to the sculptor, Chares of Lindos, when he erected it between 294 and 282 B.C. While not even a drawing of the statue survives, scholars theorize the Colossus was an upright figure holding a torch aloft in one hand not unlike the Statue of Liberty; Helios' face was quite possibly modeled after Alexander the Great's. Yet, for all its majesty, the Colossus turned out to be the most fragile Wonder of them all—standing for only 56 years before collapsing in an earthquake in 226 B.C. "Even lying on the ground, it is a marvel," wrote Roman scholar Pliny the Elder in the first century A.D. "Few people can even put their arms around the figure's thumb, and each of its fingers is larger than most statues."

## The Temple of Artemis in Ephesus

The Colossus would have made an appropriate introduction to the opulence of Asia Minor (modern Turkey), where the temple of Artemis mixed Oriental splendor and Hellenic artistry. Size mattered in the ancient world, and in the ostentatious port of Ephesus, citizens built their greatest temple to tower above the city skyline. Though the Parthenon of Athens was regarded as the most perfectly proportioned of all buildings, the Temple of Artemis overwhelmed it in scale. Estimates suggest the interior was about 425 feet long and 255 feet wide, making it nearly as cavernous as New York City's Grand Central Terminal. One hundred twenty-seven columns, painted in gaudy colors, supported its huge ceiling; some visitors felt lost in the dizzying forest of pillars, as imposing as sequoia trunks. Guides warned tourists not to stare at the temple's polished white-marble walls lest they be struck blind by their brilliance. Swathed in clouds of incense, a statue of the mother goddess beckoned with open arms. This was not the svelte, athletic huntress Artemis of Greek lore but a majestic, maternal creation from the East, whose multiple breasts hung like papayas from her torso. Among eunuch priests offering sacrifice at the statue's feet, silversmiths peddled souvenir miniatures of the temple and goddess for the pagan faithful. "Only in Heaven has the Sun ever looked upon its equal," gushed Greek author Antipater around 100 B.C.

## The Mausoleum at Halicarnassus

No less splendor graced the Mausoleum, rising 140 feet into the air like a gigantic wedding cake above the turquoise harbor of Halicarnassus, now the modern port of Bodrum on the so-called Turkish Riviera, about 60 miles from the Colossus. Built, legend has it, around 350 B.C. for King Mausolos, the ruler of Caria, by his grief-stricken sister-wife, Artemisia, the Mausoleum was an art lover's fantasy whose tiers teemed with more than a hundred statues of heroes, kings and Amazon warriors, carved by the five greatest Greek sculptors of the day. "Even today," noted Pliny the Elder in 75 A.D., "the hands of the sculptors seem to vie with one another in artistry" The glittering confection was topped with a statue believed to be of the dead king and his wife riding a golden chariot.

## The Lighthouse of Alexandria

Sailing south to Egypt, a journey of several days, travelers up to 50 miles out to sea could spot the fifth—and the only practical—ancient Wonder: the Pharos, or lighthouse, of Alexandria, whose orange flame guided ship pilots along the Nile

Delta's treacherous coastline. Looming above Alexandria's busy Eastern Harbor and surrounded by palm trees and statues of the Pharaohs, the 445-foot, three-tiered limestone tower was taller than the Statue of Liberty. At its pinnacle, a giant burning brazier topped by a statue of Zeus provided a suitably theatrical arrival to the city where Europe, Africa and Asia met. Once ashore, visitors hastened to Alexandria's Great Library to observe the scientists, astronomers and geographers who labored in what amounted to the first government-funded think tank, the Mouseion. It was these learned men who had produced the lighthouse.

## The Pyramids of Giza

Eventually, our Seven Wonders tourist would likely have torn himself away from Alexandria's pleasures to sail up the Nile and gaze upon the oldest and most impressive wonder of them all—the Pyramids of Giza, three pyramids that rise, even to this day, from the undulating sands of the Giza Plateau. (For thousands of years, the Great Pyramid of Giza was the tallest and most precise stone building in the world.) The pyramids were especially dazzling in the Greek era when they were still sheathed in white limestone and covered by hieroglyphics and graffiti, glistening brilliantly in the desert sun. Surrounding the pyramids, the remains of ancient temples dating back to the Old Kingdom—the apogee of Egyptian military power and artistic skill circa 2500 B.C.—dotted the landscape. Shaven-headed priests, acting as tour guides, pretended to translate the pyramids' hieroglyphics, which they said described the construction of the monuments, including even what the Egyptian workmen who built them, between around 2580 and 2510 B.C., ate on the job.

## The Hanging Gardens of Babylon

The final site on our traveler's itinerary would have been the most difficult to visit. He would have had to sail to Antioch, in Syria, then follow 500 miles of desert tracks, either on horseback or by carriage, to gaze upon the gardens' splendor. Babylon, lying some 45 miles south of modern Baghdad, was once widely regarded as the most intoxicating urban center in the world. Travelers entered the city through the Ishtar Gates, inlaid with blue glazed bricks bearing images of lions, bulls and dragons, only to behold a forest of towering ziggurats, obelisks and smoking altars by the Euphrates River.

The Hanging Gardens—a rooftop paradise of sculpted terraces, shade, and perfumed flowers—rose majestically above the human sprawl, watered by a hydraulic irrigation system. ("A work of art of royal luxury . . . suspended above the heads of spectators," noted Greek engineer Philo around 250 B.C.) The gardens had been built by King Nebuchadnezzar II (604–562 B.C.) for his wife, a princess from Media, a fertile kingdom by the southern Caspian Sea, who was homesick for greenery; it was said Alexander the Great gazed upon them from his deathbed in the royal palace in 323 B.C.

But much about the gardens is unknown, including their exact location. "The Hanging Gardens, by their very nature, cannot be definitively found," says Richard A. Billows, professor of history at Columbia University "They would not leave a very clear footprint that says 'this must have been the spot.' This isn't helped by the fact that there is no clear idea of what the gardens looked like."

Though only one of the Seven Wonders survives, it and the sites of the six others still launch a thousand package tours each year. Fascination with the Pyramids of Giza is certainly understandable; even stripped of their gleaming limestone—Arab conquerors used it as building material in the Middle Ages—the pyramids' majesty, antiquity and bulk continue to astonish visitors, even if their first glimpse is from a crowded Cairo suburban highway.

But our fascination with the "missing" Wonders is harder to explain. Two of them exist only as fragments on display in museums; others have been scorched entirely from the earth. And yet, they remain curiously compelling. Phidias' Statue of Zeus at Olympia was taken to Constantinople in the fourth century A.D. and was later destroyed in a palace fire, but the sanctuary itself—near the first Olympic Stadium through overgrown ruins buzzing with bees—remains one of the most visited attractions in Greece. All that is left of the Temple of Zeus is its foundation, but the spot where the statue stood has been identified. In 1958, archaeologists found, some 50 yards from the temple ruins, the workshop in which the artist Phidias sculpted the statue in the fifth century B.C.—including pieces of ivory and the base of a bronze drinking cup engraved with the words "I belong to Phidias" in classical Greek.

In Rhodes, hordes of tourists cluster each summer at Mandraki Harbor, where the Colossus is thought to have stood. Around A.D. 650, more than eight centuries after its collapse, it was broken up by Arab plunderers and sold as scrap metal. Today, not a toenail remains, though local entrepreneurs peddle souvenir T-shirts, spoons and cups emblazoned with the statue's image. (In 1999, the citizens of Rhodes announced a memorial to be built on the site, though work has yet to begin.)

As for the two Wonders of Asia Minor—the Temple of Artemis and the Mausoleum—they were devastated by earthquakes, barbarians and vengeful Christians. Scraps of both lie in the British Museum in London, but their sites are hauntingly bare. In an ironic genuflection to the cycles of history, chunks of the Mausoleum's original masonry were used to refortify the Castle of St. Peter at Bodrum, which was restored in the 1970s as a museum dedicated to underwater archaeology.

And, as the city of Alexandria reminds us, there is always hope for finding "lost" Wonders. In 1994, Asra el Bakri, an Egyptian filmmaker creating a documentary about Alexandria's Eastern Harbor, noticed some huge stone blocks just below the water's surface off Fort Qait-Bey; on a promontory at the heart of the old city. Within a year, French marine archaeologists had catalogued just under 3,000 chunks of masonry, some of which is thought to be the lighthouse, scattered about the ocean floor. Soon they were raising the magnificent statues that once stood by its side. The sculptures are believed to have fallen there during earthquakes that struck the region from late antiquity to the 14th century A.D.

"As a news story, it was definitely very sexy" says Colin Clement, spokesman for the Centre d'Etudes Alexandrines (CEA), the French organization leading the work. "It seemed like everyone wanted to film or photograph what we were doing." More recently, marine archaeologists discovered the frame of a nearly 40-foot-high double door that was once part of the lighthouse. Using computer graphics, CEA archaeologists are now piecing together how the edifice would have looked and functioned. "Little by little, from campaign to campaign, we have more results," says Jean-Yves Empereur, director of the CEA, emphasizing that he is attempting to reconstruct all of ancient Alexandria graphically, not just a single monument.

One tour company, ignoring warnings that the harbor's untreated sewage may cause typhoid, offers recreational diving to the lighthouse stones as well as to two dozen fragmented sphinxes on the sea bottom. For its part, the Egyptian government has floated plans for an underwater marine park, which tourists would visit in glass-bottomed boats. "Why not?" says Clement. "What's the point of doing the work if it's just for a few academics reading fusty obscure journals?"

Of course, one Wonder has dropped off today's grand tour entirely—the Hanging Gardens. "Things have been going very badly for Babylon over the last 20 years," says Harriet Crawford, chairman of the British School of Archaeology in Iraq. Saddam Hussein's "reconstruction" program, begun in 1987, devastated the Mesopotamian city's venerable ruins. As a self-styled new Nebuchadnezzar, Hussein built a luxurious palace on a hill above the excavations of the original royal palace, then ordered the ancient edifice rebuilt using bricks stamped with his name. The Hanging Gardens—Babylon's trademark feature—played a key role in this farce: courtyards and passageways were built to integrate the supposed site of the gardens into the reconstruction. Ironically new research carried out by Stephanie Dalley and others of the Oriental Institute at Oxford University suggests the gardens may not have been in Babylon at all, but in Nineveh, the ancient capital of Assyria in what is now northern Iraq. Nor are they thought to have been built by Nebuchadnezzar, but an Assyrian king, Sennacherib.

Misguided though it was, the work in Babylon shows the power of the past to shape the present. In seeking to connect himself to Iraq's most glorious era, "Hussein saw the significance of Babylon," says Crawford. "He used it as a symbol of national identity and triumph, to unite all the factions in Iraq."

The fate of the original Seven Wonders has long provoked a wide spectrum of reactions, from melancholy meditations on human vanity to the transience of man's achievements. But if their most obvious lesson is that our finest creations will one day turn to rubble, it is a lesson that we resolutely refuse to learn. Which is only as it should be, as the ancient Wonders' durability if only in our imagination—so eloquently testifies.

---

Travel writer **Tony Perrottet** is the author of *Pagan Holiday: On the Trail of Ancient Roman Tourists* (Random House, 2002).

# The Coming of the Sea Peoples

## A low-tech revolution in Bronze Age battlefield tactics changed the history of the Western world.

NEIL ASHER SILBERMAN

In the long annals of Western military history, one important group of battlefield innovators—whose archaeological traces have been uncovered from mainland Greece to the coasts of Lebanon and Israel—has often been overlooked. Around 1200 B.C., a wave of sword-wielding warriors streamed southward across the Aegean and eastward toward Asia Minor, Cyprus, and Canaan. By around 1175, some of them had reached the borders of Egypt, where they were finally repulsed by the land and sea forces of Pharaoh Ramesses III. Yet in their stunning military successes throughout the region, these warriors exerted an enormous impact on the development of ancient warfare and proved instrumental in the transformation of Mediterranean society. In subsequent centuries, the rising kingdoms of Israel and Phoenicia and the city-states of Classical Greece all adopted their tactics, arms, and strategic mentality.

Who were these invading forces and where did they come from? What was it about their weapons and tactics that proved to be so deadly to the great Late Bronze Age empires—and so influential in shaping the societies that succeeded them? For the past 150 years, historians have recognized that the twelfth century B.C. was a time of great upheaval, in which ancient empires were toppled and new societies were born. They have ascribed this dramatic transformation not to innovations in warfare but to vast population movements, spearheaded by a coalition of northern tribes and ethnic groups who are mentioned repeatedly in ancient Egyptian inscriptions—and whom nineteenth-century scholars dubbed the "Sea Peoples" or the "Peoples of the Sea." These Sea Peoples were not simply Bronze Age Vikings but were a haphazard collection of farmers, warriors, and craftspeople, as well as sailors who originated in the highlands of the Balkans and the coastlands of Asia Minor. Their only common trait seems to have been their movement across the Mediterranean toward the centers of trade and agriculture of the Near East.

Their impact on the Near Eastern empires was dramatic, though scholars are deeply divided on the reasons. Some maintain that the Sea Peoples were displaced from their homelands by famine, natural disasters, or political breakdown and were able to overcome the sophisticated, cosmopolitan empires of the Mediterranean by their sheer barbarian savagery. Others suggest that a closer analysis of the historical records and archaeological remains from this period can pinpoint a more specific agent of change connected to the era's vast population movements. There is reason to believe that only a small, specialized class of professional warriors, in the midst of the much more massive migratory waves, was responsible for the military attacks of the Sea Peoples. As a skilled caste of mercenary foot soldiers who drifted southward to find employment in kingdoms throughout the region, this group of Sea Peoples had both the tactical know-how and the weaponry to recognize—and demonstrate—just how pitifully vulnerable the great Late Bronze Age powers had become. The civilization of the Late Bronze Age (c. 1550 to c. 1200 B.C.), to which these northern mercenary contingents gravitated, was typified by grand monuments, opulent palace cultures, and some of the most complex administrative and accounting systems the Mediterranean world had ever seen. In Egypt, the powerful pharaohs of the New Kingdom resided amid the splendor of Thebes in Upper Egypt. There they prospered from the rich agricultural produce of the Nile valley and enjoyed the luxury goods acquired from a far-flung trade network reaching from Africa and the southern coast of Arabia to the islands of the Aegean Sea. To the north of Egypt, in the city-states of Canaan, on the island of Cyprus, and at the cosmopolitan port of Ugarit, local dynasties ruled over docile peasant populations and vied with one another for diplomatic or commercial advantage. In the vast continental expanse of Asia Minor, the Hittite empire maintained its feudal rule from the stronghold of Hattusas. And across the Aegean Sea, on mainland Greece, Crete, and the islands, a unique palace-based civilization of regional rulers, with their coteries of servants, craftsmen, priests, and mercenary forces, comprised the chivalric society that was at least partially reflected in the physical details of Homer's *Iliad.*

Despite these differences in styles and traditions, all the empires of the Late Bronze Age were united in their dependence on a single military technology. No self-respecting kingdom could exist for long without attack forces based on the light battle chariot, which was then the most sophisticated and reliable vehicle of war. The chariots of this period were constructed with

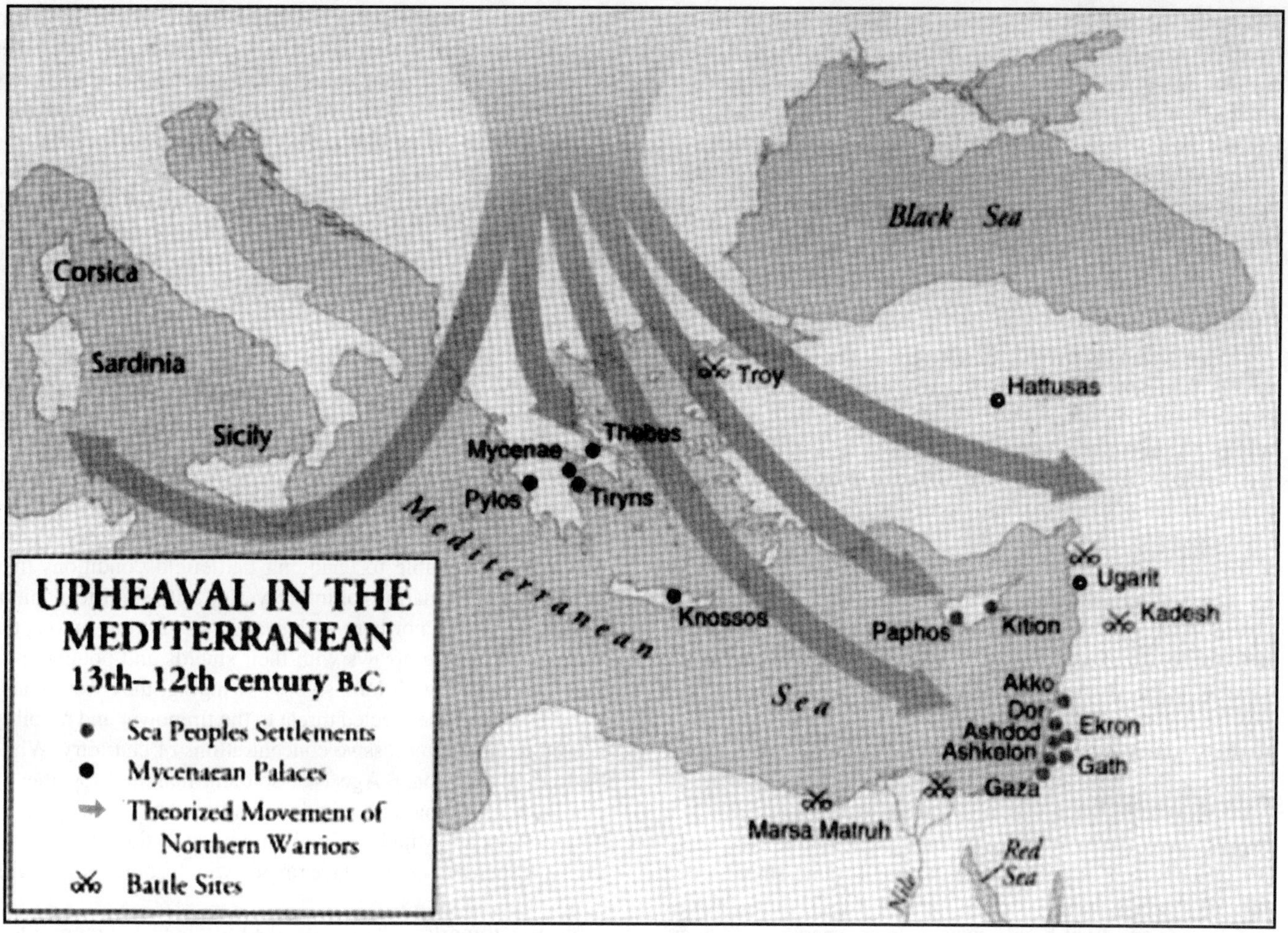


Geosystems, Columbia, MD

Not long after appearing in Egypt, Sea People warriors fought for the Egyptians at Kadesh (c. 1275 B.C.). They would become agents of radical change, likely bringing down Mycenaean civilization and enfeebling the great empires of the ancient world.

considerable skill—and at considerable cost—from sturdy yet highly flexible laminates of wood and bone that enabled them to travel at high speed and with great maneuverability. Propelled by a specially bred and trained two-horse team, the chariot was manned by a professional driver and a combat archer, whose composite bow, also constructed of laminated materials, could launch arrows with extraordinary accuracy and force. These factors all added up to make the light chariot a high-powered, highly mobile weapons delivery system that could swoop down on static infantry forces with frightening speed and velocity.

The figure of the charioteer—as an embodiment of individual skill and courage—became, in many respects, a symbol for the age. The firepower of the new-style chariots was so overwhelming on the battlefield that no ruler who hoped to maintain his throne against his local or regional rivals could afford to be without them—any more than any truly modern nation can afford to be without an effective air force. As a result, Bronze Age kings, pharaohs, and princes scrambled to assemble chariot forces. And just as the kings and potentates of other eras strutted in the guise of knights-errant, cavalry officers, or naval commanders, Late Bronze Age Egyptian pharaohs and Mycenaean, Hittite, and Canaanite kings were all grandly depicted on their monuments in the pose of triumphant charioteers. Yet as the chariot buildup continued through the fourteenth and thirteenth centuries B.C., and as chariot formations gradually rendered infantry battles obsolete in conflicts between rival city-states or empires, a costly arms race began to get out of control.

By the time of the Hittite-Egyptian confrontation at the battle of Kadesh in Syria in 1275 B.C., relatively modest chariot corps of a few dozen vehicles had expanded to enormous contingents. At Kadesh, the Hittite chariot corps alone numbered at least 3,500 vehicles. This placed a strain on even the wealthiest kingdoms. The cost of chariots and horses was substantial. And the skilled craftsmen, chariot drivers, archers, and horse trainers required to maintain the battle-readiness of a kingdom's chariot force could—and did—demand lavish personal support, generous land grants, and conspicuously privileged status at each court they served. Thus, at times of shortage brought about by drought, flood, disease, or poor crop yields, the demands of the charioteers and their staffs could force individual kingdoms toward the breaking point. And yet the Late Bronze Age powers had all become dangerously dependent on this method of warfare. Little wonder, then, that when its tactical vulnerability was discovered, the whole edifice came tumbling down.

The result was one of the great turning points in history dubbed by some the Great Catastrophe. Within the span of just a few decades before and after 1200 B.C., the Bronze Age civilizations of Greece and Asia Minor were shattered, and Egypt gradually lost its role as a regional superpower. At the same time, the sudden arrival and settlement of new peoples on Cyprus and along the coast of Canaan ushered in a new era of small kingdoms and city-states.

Just beyond the confines of the civilized regions of the Mediterranean world, in the mountainous areas of the Balkan peninsula and in the rugged hinterlands of western and southern Asia Minor, the chariot had no power. It was suited only to action on the relatively level battlefields of the lowlands and the plains. On the occasions when the great empires felt the need to mount punitive expeditions against the inhabitants of the highlands, they dispatched infantry forces for brief, brutal demonstrations of force. For the most part, however, the highlanders were left alone as long as they handed over the demanded tribute and did nothing to interfere with the main routes of trade. Among the tribal societies of these regions, internal disputes were settled in contests of single combat between experienced professional warriors. Archaeological finds from warriors' tombs across western and central Europe, from Scandinavia to the Black Sea, have provided evidence of this mobile, deadly kind of hand-to-hand warfare, waged with long, two-edged swords that could be swung with enough momentum to decapitate an opponent or cut off a limb. Small round shields seem also to have been used to deflect rapid parries. Helmets of various designs and light body armor of many shapes and materials were also common in this individualistic style of war. In terms of weaponry and personal aggressiveness, the warriors of the frontier areas were much more formidable than the typical infantries of the Mediterranean empires, whose members were usually conscripted from the local peasantry, poorly trained, and armed only with short daggers, spears, or clubs.

The reason for the neglect of the infantry by the Mediterranean empires was the overwhelming importance accorded to chariot forces, which comprised the main tactical elements. Lines of chariots would charge against each other like modern tank forces, and, having penetrated or outflanked the opposing formation, would wheel around quickly and charge against the opposing chariots again. Foot soldiers were used in the decidedly secondary capacities of guard duty, road escort, frontier patrols, and routine police work. The only battlefield function reserved for foot soldiers was as "runners" who raced behind and among the chariots, snatching up fallen enemy booty and finishing off wounded enemy chariot crews. This mopping-up function was of little tactical significance. But by the time of the battle of Kadesh, the appearance of a new kind of runner proved to be an omen of the way that subsequent wars in the Mediterranean region would be waged—and won.

In a provocative new book entitled *The End of the Bronze Age: Changes in Warfare and the Catastrophe, ca. 1200 B.C.*, Robert Drews, a professor of ancient history at Vanderbilt University, argues that the arrival of northern-style warriors in the Mediterranean upset the unquestioned domination of the chariot. By so doing, it undermined the foundations of the regimes the chariots were meant to defend. Drews notes that barely ten years before the battle of Kadesh, Egyptian hieroglyphic reliefs recorded the ominous movements of a people named the "Sherden," who had arrived "in their warships from the midst of the sea." Wearing trademark horned helmets and armed with long swords and small round shields, they obviously made a profound impression on the Egyptians. By the time the Egyptian chariot forces moved north to confront the Hittites, contingents of Sherden had been recruited by the Egyptians to serve as bodyguards and particularly deadly "runners" among the chariots.

In contrast to the usual runners, who merely mopped up after the chariot charges, the Sherden apparently became an independent offensive force. They are shown in the reliefs of the battle of Kadesh using their weapons to slash, hack, and dismember enemy charioteers. Their weapons, which were originally designed for individual combat, made Sherden warriors far more mobile and adaptable to changing battlefield conditions than the traditional formations of infantry. And with significant numbers of aggressive, northern-style warriors swarming among the chariots, deflecting arrows with their shields and pouncing on disabled vehicles with long swords swinging, they would have posed a sudden, unexpected threat to the firepower and mobility of even the most impressive concentrations of chariotry. While the traditional Bronze Age foot soldiers marched together in relatively slow-moving formations and used weapons such as clubs and spears, which had only a limited radius of effectiveness, the Sherden seem to have ranged widely, pouncing on vulnerable chariot crews.

No less important, they possessed weapons far more effective in combat than those of standard Bronze Age foot soldiers. Ancient pictorial representations of Sherden runners suggest that they were also skilled in the use of the hunting javelin, commonly used in this period for felling wild game. In combination with the long sword, the hunting javelin would have been especially deadly. Drews makes a persuasive—if admittedly speculative—case for suggesting that these new weapons could transform units of runners into an effective battlefield strike force. "For the 'hunting' of chariot horses the javelin must have been ideal," Drews writes, "although it seldom would have killed the horse that it hit, the javelin would have surely brought it to a stop, thus immobilizing the other horse, the vehicle and the crew."

The battle of Kadesh ended in a stalemate between the Egyptians and the Hittites, ushering in a brief period of military balance between the two powers. But by the middle of the thirteenth century B.C., new groups of northern warriors armed with long swords and javelins were drawn in increasing numbers toward the centers of the Late Bronze Age empires, where they were destined to upset the delicate geopolitical balance. Initially, they found employment as mercenaries just as the Sherden had done. Among the names mentioned in Egyptian records and in the archives of Ugarit and the Hittite empire were—in addition to the Sherden—groups known as the Shekelesh, Tursha, Lukka, Shardana, and Ekwesh. Linguistic analysis of these names has enabled scholars to identify them with peoples mentioned in classical and biblical literature: Sicilians, Tyrrhenians, Lycians, and Achaean Greeks. The Sherden have been identified as a group originating on the island of Sardinia, or, according to some scholars, as its eventual conquerors.

It is important to recognize, however, that these Sea Peoples mentioned in the ancient records were not entire nations displaced from their homelands, but a particular military caste represented by warriors from many ethnic groups. Like the pirates and freebooters of the seventeenth-century Caribbean, their many separate nationalities were as conspicuous as the threatening uniformity of their weapons and hand-to-hand fighting techniques.

Archaeologists are generally agreed that the relative tranquility of the Late Bronze Age world following the battle of Kadesh was rocked sometime after 1250 B.C. by a great wave of destructions and upheavals that seems to have begun in the Aegean basin. The Mycenaean palace of Thebes in Boeotia was destroyed and abandoned. The flourishing city of Troy, guarding the trade routes to the Black Sea, was likewise destroyed in a great conflagration, to be succeeded by a much more modest settlement. There is suggestive evidence that these destructions may not have resulted from normal clashes between chariot forces. The hasty construction of a great fortification wall across the Isthmus of Corinth and the strengthening of the defenses around other Mycenaean palace complexes may reflect apprehensions about a far more pervasive danger, perhaps a threat by potential attackers that Bronze Age chariotry would have been unable to withstand. And those apparent fears of attack and conquest seem to have been justified, for by the middle of the next century, the destruction of all the Mycenaean palace complexes was virtually complete.

There may, of course, have been many specific, local reasons for this wave of upheaval. In some places, rivalries between regional centers could have led to the violence. In others, widespread social unrest caused by growing inequalities in late Bronze Age society may have led to local uprisings and the overthrow of the palace elite. Yet in a thought-provoking hypothesis that has already aroused considerable scholarly discussion, Drews pulls together tactical analysis, archaeological evidence, and the colorful testimony of heroic Greek myth to offer a novel reconstruction of the events. He suggests that the legendary accounts of the attacks against Thebes by a coalition of champions (immortalized by Aeschylus in his play *Seven Against Thebes*) and Homer's epic poem about the sack of Troy by Agamemnon's forces preserve memories of the first dramatic triumphs of free-lance northern infantry concentrations, fighting in the new style.

The gradually increasing scope of such encounters may suggest that news of the vulnerability of chariot forces spread among northern mercenary contingents. And in this very period, a wave of northern warriors now made their way southward in search of plunder, not employment. In looking anew at Homer's poetic metaphors about the epic battle between Achaeans and Trojans, it may well be—as Drews suggested—that the repeated description of the Achaean hero Achilles as "fleet-footed," and the characteristic description of the Trojans as "horse-taming," preserve memories of an epic clash between foot soldiers and horse-powered troops. Even though the *Iliad* was set down in writing several centuries later, at a time when chariot warfare had long been abandoned, the vivid image of Achaean soldiers streaming from the Trojan Horse may eloquently express, at least in mythic language, the sudden emergence of a new style of infantrymen—whose hidden power was revealed in an age of horse-based warfare. In their conquest of Troy, the Achaean foot soldiers departed from the empty wooden horse, thereby symbolically leaving behind the horse (and chariot) as the preferred weapons platforms of the age.

The violent events in the Aegean do not seem to have affected the great capitals and emporia of the Near East—at least not immediately. International commerce continued throughout the thirteenth century B.C., and a certain measure of prosperity was enjoyed in the royal courts of the Near East. New Kingdom Egypt (where at least some Sea People had gone to find work as mercenary runners) therefore beckoned as a tempting target for plundering attacks. The aging pharaoh Ramesses II (c. 1279–c. 1212 B.C.), after having emerged from the battle of Kadesh in a military stalemate with the Hittites, still presided over a vast territory and trade network extending from Canaan, south to Nubia, and as far west as Libya. Excavations at Late Bronze Age port cities and recovered cargoes from sunken merchant ships of this period throughout the eastern Mediterranean have emphasized the volume of international trade—and the extent of interaction between nations, cultures, and ethnic groups during this cosmopolitan age. Only recently have excavations uncovered the ruins of a once busy Late Bronze Age trade depot—littered with sherds of pottery from Mycenaean Greece, Egypt, Cyprus, and Canaan—on a sandy island known as Bates's Island off the coast of Egypt's western desert, about 120 miles east of the modern border with Libya.

It was surely no coincidence or accident that the first major attack by northern warriors on Egypt was launched from this direction. Far from being an isolated wilderness, Libya was connected to Egypt by land and sea trade routes. At a time of reported famine, it was a Libyan leader named "Meryre, Son of Did," who instigated the first major operation in which a coalition of northern warriors played a prominent role. Scholars have always puzzled over how and why Libyans forged a coalition with the various Sea Peoples. Yet the archaeological evidence of an offshore trade depot so close to Libya indicates that it was not a cultural backwater but on one of the main routes in the movement of people and goods. It is entirely conceivable that Meryre was aware of events going on elsewhere in the eastern Mediterranean, possibly through the contact his subjects had with the polyglot gangs of sailors, stevedores, and workers who were drawn into the networks of long-distance trade. More important, he seems to have been keenly aware of the recent—one might even say revolutionary—developments in the art of warfare. Indeed if Meryre had heard about recent successes achieved by northern warriors in direct assaults on chariot forces in Greece and Asia Minor, his subsequent actions in recruiting Sea People warriors for his own campaign would suddenly be understandable.

Why else would he contemplate an invasion of Egypt with only foot soldiers? If he were planning a less organized infiltration of the border lands, he would not have needed to form the grand coalition he did. Yet soon after the death of Ramesses II around 1212 B.C., Meryre began to organize a campaign against the western Nile Delta, for which he gained the cooperation of a number of warrior bands. Later Egyptian records note that they came from "the northern lands"—which could indicate an origin in any of the territories along the northern shores of the Mediterranean. The specific mention of Ekwesh, Lukka, Sherden, Shekelesh, and Tursha (identified as Achaeans, Lycians, Sardinians, Sicilians, and Tyrrhenians) suggests that Meryre's appeal attracted recruits from many lands. He promised them a share of the fertile territory and booty to be gained in attacking the forces of the new pharaoh, Merneptah, the long-lived Ramesses' already elderly son. Seen in the context of the times, Meryre thus made an audacious tactical gamble: in recruiting tens of thousands of northern-style foot soldiers along with his own sizable infantry contingents, he was confident that he could overcome the Egyptian chariotry.

As things turned out, Meryre lost his gamble but proved to be a strategist ahead of his time. Merneptah's chariots met the advancing Libyan-Sea People coalition in midsummer 1208 B.C. in the western desert, at a site probably not far from the later and also fateful battlefield of El Alamein. The Egyptian forces reportedly slew 6,000 Libyans and more than 2,200 of the invading Ekwesh, with significant casualties suffered by the other Sea Peoples as well. Yet the list of spoils taken in the battle by the Egyptians gives a clear indication of the novel nature of the encounter: more than 9,000 long swords were captured from the invaders—with only an utterly insignificant twelve Libyan chariots being seized. For the time being, the pharaoh's chariots had prevailed over massed formations of swordsmen and javelineers. But new troubles were not long in coming for the pharaoh. Frontier populations in other regions were growing restless, and Merneptah soon had to undertake a punitive campaign into Canaan, where he was forced to reassert his control over some important cities and pacify the highlands. In typically bombastic prose he reported one of the most gratifying outcomes of the encounter: "Israel is laid waste; his seed is not!" The clear, if mistaken, implication was that this people had been so thoroughly defeated that they or their descendants would never appear on the stage of history again.

The quotation, which comes from Merneptah's so-called Victory Stele at the Temple of Karnak, contains this earliest mention of the people of Israel outside the Bible, and it may also indicate the extent of the tactical revolution spreading throughout the Mediterranean world. For in the hill country of Canaan at precisely this period, c. 1250–c. 1200 B.C., archaeologists have discovered the sudden establishment of scores of hilltop villages throughout the modern area of the West Bank. Being far from the lowland Canaanite urban centers and outposts of Egyptian presence in fortresses along the coast and major trade routes, they represent the earliest settlements of the Israelites. Their defense against outside powers was not based on chariot warfare but most likely on coordinated militia campaigns. Certainly the biblical books of Joshua and Judges are filled with references to the defeat of the Canaanite kings and the destruction of their chariot forces. Although many historians have come to question the historical reliability of the story of the Israelite Exodus from Egypt, the vivid scriptural account of the drowning in the Red Sea of the pharaoh's pursuing army—and its great chariot corps—might preserve in dreamlike narrative an indelible historical memory of an era of great victories over chariotry.

The threats by northern-style raiders against Egypt and the other great centers of the Bronze Age civilization continued to intensify in this period, with port cities, fortresses, temples, and trade depots throughout the region put to the torch, and in some cases never fully reoccupied again. It is likely that in the spreading chaos, movements of people grew more frequent. Warriors and mercenaries were on the move, of course, but so were other groups formerly serving as craftsmen, servants, or functionaries in the palace centers that had been destroyed by hostile attacks. All of these groups were the "Sea Peoples," both the victims and the perpetrators of the spreading wave of violence. In certain places on Cyprus and along the coast of Canaan, settlers from the Aegean world arrived to establish new communities in the ruins of destroyed Late Bronze Age cities. And the characteristic Mycenaean-style pottery they produced at sites such as Ashkelon, Ekron, and Ashdod in Canaan clearly indicates that whether they themselves were marauders or refugee craftsmen and officials from the destroyed palace-centers of the Aegean, the course of their lives and communities had been disrupted by upheavals throughout the Mediterranean world.

Although it is impossible to follow precisely the sequence of raids, conquests, and refugee colonizations in Greece, Cyprus Egypt, and Canaan, there is suggestive evidence that the use of new weapons and tactics by the invaders continued to play a crucial role. In the rubble of the great trading emporium of Ugarit on the coast of modern Syria, for example, excavators have found a number of hunting javelins scattered in the destruction ruins. And the discovery of several newly cast long swords (one even bearing the royal cartouche of Merneptah!) hidden away in hoards at the time of the city's destruction may reflect a desperate, last-ditch effort by some local commanders to equip their forces with the same deadly weapons borne by the marauding Peoples of the Sea.

The last and greatest of attacks by contingents of northern warriors against the centers of Bronze Age civilization is memorialized in exacting detail on the outer walls of the Egyptian temple of Medinet Habu in Upper Egypt, built by Pharaoh Ramesses III, who ruled from c. 1186 to c. 1155 B.C. The Medinet reliefs depict what was one of the most notable events of Ramesses' reign: thousands of Egyptian foot soldiers, sailors, and archers are shown engaged in battles on land and sea against a bizarrely costumed coalition of invaders, who include—in addition to the Sherden and the Shekelesh of the earlier invasions—people known as the Tjekker, Denyen, Weshesh, and Peleset (whom scholars have identified as the biblical Philistines).

This invasion was apparently different and far more threatening than earlier actions. The tone of Ramesses III's official inscription accompanying the pictorial representations conveys an atmosphere of deep crisis that gripped Egypt when word arrived that seaborne and overland coalitions of northern warriors "who had made a conspiracy in their islands" were approaching. Although the precise origin of these warrior bands has never been pinpointed, the mention of "islands" suggests that the threat came from the direction of the Aegean Sea. Ramesses' chronicle goes on to trace the progress of the invaders across the region, in which many separate actions seem to have been combined for rhetorical purposes to heighten the drama of the events.

"All at once the lands were removed and scattered in the fray," reported the inscription in tracing the path of the invaders southward from the Hittite empire, through the cities of Cilicia, Cyprus, and Syria, toward Canaan, which was also known as Amor. "No land could stand before their arms from Hatti, Kode, Carchemish, Arzawa, Alayshia on, being cut off at one time. A camp was set up in one place in Amor. They desolated its people, and its land was like that which has never come into being. They were coming forward to Egypt, while the flame was being prepared before them," the inscription continued. "They laid their hands upon lands as far as the circuit of the earth, their hearts confident and trusting, 'Our plans will succeed!' "

In retrospect, we can see that Pharaoh Ramesses III was placed in an impossible situation in the Great Land and Sea Battles of 1175 B.C. When this last and greatest wave of Sea Peoples' invasions burst upon Egypt, Ramesses was forced to confront forces that had proved they could successfully overcome chariots—which remained the backbone of the Egyptian defense. In response, he apparently tried to change radically the fighting capabilities of his forces—as many desperate, doomed warlords have attempted to do throughout history. Indeed, as analysis of the Medinet Habu reliefs suggests, the vaunted Egyptian chariotry played almost no role in the fighting. Ramesses III's inscriptions can be seen as a commemoration of the heroism of his own infantry. He boasted that the Egyptian foot soldiers—once scorned as insignificant tactical factors—had fought "like bulls ready on the field of battle" and that the militiamen who engaged the enemy in hand-to-hand fighting aboard their ships "were like lions roaring on the mountaintops." No less significant is the fact that in one scene Ramesses himself is depicted as an unmounted archer—not a charioteer—with his two royal feet firmly planted on the bodies of fallen Sea People enemies.

Yet in discarding the ethos and discipline of chariot warfare on which his empire had become so dependent—and in mobilizing his foot soldiers to fight on the same terms and with the same weapons as the invaders—Ramesses sealed the fate of New Kingdom Egypt as surely as a defeat at the hands of the Sea Peoples would have done. For even though the Sea Peoples' invasion was repulsed, and some of the Sea Peoples, like the Philistines, were permitted to settle peacefully in colonies along the nearby coast of Canaan, Egypt would never regain its former strength. The Egyptian Empire—like all other Late Bronze Age kingdoms—had been built and maintained over hundreds of years as a towering social pyramid in which the king, his court, officers, and chariot forces reserved the pinnacle for themselves. The new method of marshaling units of highly mobile, highly motivated infantry against chariot forces required unprecedentedly large numbers of trained fighters. Egypt was never a society that viewed its general population as much more than beasts of burden; to accord peasant recruits respect and intensive training within the armed forces was something that the highly stratified society of New Kingdom Egypt found extremely difficult to do. The strict hierarchy began to crumble, and the growing power of mercenary units and local infantry bands caused widespread social unrest. By the end of the twelfth century, the power of New Kingdom Egypt was ended, and the country entered a new dark age. In contrast, the new world that unfolded in the centuries after the appearance of the Sea Peoples in Greece, Cyprus, Asia Minor, and Canaan drew its strength from the new cultural pattern, which was based on the solidarity and military might of local levies of foot soldiers, not elite units of courtly charioteers.

Chariot forces would again be used on the field of battle—as in the later campaigns of the Assyrian empire in the ninth and eighth centuries B.C.—but only in a supporting role to the infantry. And with the development of effective tack and stirrups during the subsequent centuries, the chariot could be dispensed with altogether, except perhaps as a battlefield conveyance for generals and kings. The Sea People warriors themselves were eventually assimilated into the general populations of the refugees from the great upheavals. Along the coast of Canaan and on Cyprus, new societies derived from Mycenaean models and led by descendants of refugees were born. Even in the rising kingdoms of Israel, Phoenicia, Aramea, Cilicia, Phrygia, and the city-states of Greece, where new forms of military and social organization emerged after the end of the Bronze Age, the legacy of the Sea Peoples—though dramatically transformed—could still be perceived. Just as the fleet-footed Achaean warrior Achilles became the role model for the citizen soldier of the archaic Greek polis, the image of the young David, surrounded by his band of mighty men of war, remained a cherished biblical symbol of national solidarity. And there were to be even more far-reaching developments in the use of large infantry formations as the kingdoms of Assyria and Babylonia swelled into great empires with enormous populations. Eventually, the massive formations of infantry units evolved into the Macedonian phalanx and the Roman legion.

The sweeping scenario of scattered contingents of Sea People warriors streaming together from their distant islands and hill country homes to overcome the elite chariot forces of the Bronze Age Mediterranean has not been without its critics. Scholars who still favor explanations such as natural disasters, generalized social breakdown, or the gradual cultural shift from Bronze Age chariot empires to Iron Age infantry kingdoms are skeptical of a single military cause. But without minimizing the possibility that natural or economic crises may indeed have undermined the political order and intensified social tensions, there is much to be said for the contention that only something as dramatic as the introduction of new weapons and tactics could have triggered violent upheavals on such a massive scale.

And there is, even beyond the specific questions of this remote period, a far more basic historical point. We must not merely see the episode of the "Sea Peoples" as a bizarre and bloody episode that took place in a far-off region more than

3,000 years ago. The long swords, javelins, and body armor of the invading Sea Peoples may seem quaintly rustic to us in a day of Stealth fighter-bombers and Tomahawk missiles. Yet they offer an important object lesson in the way that complacent dependency by great powers on expensive and complex military technology can suddenly be undermined. The grand catastrophe of the end of the Bronze Age and the role of the Sea Peoples in it should show us how unexpectedly simple weapons in the hands of committed warriors can topple great empires. Societies in any age can become dangerously presumptuous about the invulnerability of their advanced military technologies. Over centuries or even decades the society molds itself, in its religion, political order, and social hierarchy, to conform to the dominant technology. If that technology is undermined by groups with little stake in preserving the existing system, the results can be catastrophic. Today we speak of terrorists with homemade bombs and shoulder-fired missiles, but at the end of the Late Bronze Age in the eastern Mediterranean, it was northern warriors with long swords and hunting javelins who laid the groundwork for a dramatic transformation of society.

---

**NEIL ASHER SILBERMAN** is an author and historian specializing in the ancient history of the Near East. He is a contributing editor to *Archaeology* magazine.

# Article 5

# Before Tea Leaves Divination in Ancient Babylonia

**The administration was determined to go to war, but it lacked the necessary public support. Fortunately there was timely intelligence, especially from southern Iraq, that victory was assured. Am I referring to the CIA and Washington in 2003 C.E.?**

WILLIAM W. HALLO

No, this is Nineveh in 652–648 B.C.E., the administration was headed by King Ashurbanipal, and the intelligence came from a diviner who had studied the liver of an animal slaughtered for that purpose. This common practice is the subject of Danish Assyriologist Ulla Koch-Western-holz's *Babylonian Liver Omens,* which is primarily a scholarly translation and presentation of cuneiform texts devoted to hepatoscopy, or divination by means of the liver, the favored organ for extispicy (divination from sheep entrails).

Here's the diviner's report: "[If the omen for] the decimation of the army is situated on the right side of the 'head lift' of the liver: It is an omen of Shamash-shum-ukkin who waged war against Aššurbanipal the beloved of the great gods and defeat seized him in the midst of battle and before Aššurbanipal the king of the world he [. . .]: It is not favorable for Shamash-shumukkin" (CT 35:38:14–17) [a collection of cuneiform tablets in the British Museum]. According to Koch-Westenholz, the "if-clause" (known in Assyriology as the protasis) was realistic (based on the actual shape of the liver), but the prediction was fabricated to please the king of Assyria in his great war against his rebellious brother, who ruled Babylonia.

There are other parallels between ancient liver divination and modern intelligence. For one thing, it was expensive, involving not only the fee to the diviner but the sacrificial slaughter of possibly of two or even three animals so that the total number of omens obtained from their entrails would result in a decisive majority of answers on one side of the question or the other. As a result, the use of liver divinations was largely confined to the royal administration, which had at its disposal the necessary resources, while private persons mostly resorted to less expensive and less sophisticated methods. A second reason for the limited use of liver divination was that its predictions were never wrong: If events turned out other than foretold, the fault lay not with the prediction but with the protasis—that is, inadequate account had been taken of ancillary phenomena surrounding the actual taking of the omens and this would be duly considered in the future. As a result, increasingly elaborate handbooks of omens were produced to cover all possible (and many impossible) contingencies. Third, even if the king could at times encourage the production of omens favorable to his plans, more often he stood in awe of the learned specialists on whom he depended for the interpretation of their secret lore. So, for example, Esarhaddon, who extended the Assyrian Empire in the seventh century B.C.E. to its farthest limits, was nevertheless so much under the spell of his diviners (and physicians) that he left a whole dossier of inquiries to the Sun god Shamash and lived his whole life in fear of an early demise, which indeed came to pass. His son Ashurbanipal also followed his example.[1]

In ancient Israel, the Mesopotamian king was an object of ridicule for his dependence on divination. In Ezekiel 21:21–23, Jerusalem's fate hangs in the balance as the king of Babylon halts his army on its westward march through Syria to await divination not only by the liver (hepatoscopy) but also by arrows (belomancy) and *teraphim* (perhaps, small household idols) before deciding which road to take for his next conquest. As it was expressed by Balaam, that quintessential Mesopotamian diviner from Petor on the Euphrates, "Lo, there is no augury in Jacob, no divining in Israel: Jacob is told at once, yea Israel, what God has wrought" (Numbers 23:23). For Israel, the place of the diviner was taken by the seer and then the prophet—though less to predict the future than, in Martin Buber's terms, "to confront man with the alternatives of decision." As the first of the literary prophets declared, "Indeed, my Lord God does nothing without having revealed His purpose to His servants the prophets" (Amos 3:7).

Not that all forms of divination were forbidden to Israel. The *Urim* and *Thummim* widely resorted to by both Saul and David represented a binary sort of psephomancy (from the Greek words meaning divining from pebbles) that essentially provided only yes-or-no answers, with *Thummim* probably standing for yes and *Urim* for no. (When Saul prays *hava thammim* [1 Samuel 14:41], the text should probably be emended to *hava thummim*—give a yes!)[2] The cup that Joseph employed for divining (Genesis 44:5) constituted a form of lecanomancy—that is, interpretation by the shape of oil in water. The words that Jonathan used to determine whether God would deliver the Philistine garrison into his hands (1 Samuel 14:10), or earlier the words by which Abraham's servant decided he would know the right bride for his master's son (Genesis 24:12–14), represent legitimate forms of cledonomancy or divination by a (chance) word.

All these simple and inexpensive methods were also known in Mesopotamia, but they were not deemed worthy of ancient scholarly attention, and no handbooks were created to catalogue their interpretations. Handbooks were reserved for divination by such phenomena as the heavenly bodies (astrology), freak births among humans and animals (teratoscopy) and dreams (oneiromancy). Particular attention was paid to the ingredients in a food offering to a deity: incense (libanomancy), flour (aleuromancy), oil (lecanomancy) and especially the entrails of sacrificial sheep (extispicy).[3]

It is to this last technique that Koch-Westenholz has dedicated her book, but so vast is the cuneiform literature devoted to this particular technique of divination that in nearly 600 pages and plates (the latter are expertly drawn hand copies of the cuneiform texts), she was able to cover only three of the ten "chapters," comprising 27 of the estimated 100 tablets that once made up the canonical series, together with their commentaries, extract texts and other ancient scholarly apparatus. Between these chapters, more than 3,000 individual omens are presented, painstakingly reconstructed from more than 200 discrete cuneiform tablets and fragments of tablets (many of them published here for the first time).

All these omens are of the form: "if (the configuration of a given part of the liver is such and such), then this presages (such and such an outcome)." The "then-clause" is known in Assyriology as the apodosis. Since **BAR** readers are not exclusively veterinarians, they may be spared the protases, with their detailed descriptions of a dozen parts of sheep livers and gall bladders. Instead a brief overview of the predictions in the apodoses will suffice.

The great majority of the predictions deal with the royal house, the kingdom or the commonweal. There are references to the outcome of campaigns, battles or sieges, the health and welfare of the king (often referred to as "the prince") and other members of the royal family and its entourage, to the weather, the success or otherwise of the harvest or the flocks, and the interactions between the monarchy and its subjects. Some omens refer specifically to great kings of the past. For example, "Omen of Sargon whose troops were shut in by rainstorm and exchanged weapons among themselves." Or "Destruction: omen of Ibbi-Sin, king of Ur." Private concerns are far rarer in the apodoses; examples include the prediction that "a snake will bite a man" and that "the patient will continue to waste away but will live." There are also omens that have a double signification, one for the king and another for the "commoner" (Akkadian *muškenu*; compare Hebrew *misken,* Arabic *miskin,* French *mesquin*), as for example "If (the extispicy) concerns the campaign, the enemy will defeat me. If it is a commoner's sacrifice: Attack."[4]

Only a relatively few omens concern women, and then mainly in their relationships to children or husbands. For example: "The man's wife will bear a son;" "A woman who does not [has not] give[n] birth easily will give birth easily;" or "A man's wife will write again and again about killing her husband: 'Kill my husband and marry me!' "

How can we explain the ancient Mesopotamian fascination with extispicy? I have long ago suggested an economic motive: It was inspired, at least in part, by an aversion to wastefulness. For the individual, offering up a sheep or ram from his own flock meant true sacrifice, not only in the literal sense of "making holy" that which was to be offered to or at least shared with the deity, but also in the modern sense of giving up something dear and precious to oneself. The edible parts of the animal could be consumed by the deity in the form of its statue, and what the deity deigned to leave uneaten (in effect, everything) was available for the priest and ultimately for the worshiper. But the entrails and certain organs were considered inedible. So what better use to make of organs such as the lung and liver than for divination? The king was constrained by no such economies, but he took over the practice and extended it to decision-making in all realms of public policy, which explains the public character of the great majority of the liver omens. And if enough of them predicted a favorable outcome, for an impending battle, for instance, they tended to become a self-fulfilling prophecy: Armies became fired up with the enthusiasm imparted by the favorable prognosis.

And how to explain the Israelite disdain for extispicy? Sacrifice took an entirely different form in ancient Israel. The deity was not worshiped in the form of a statue, but was unseen. The meat sacrifice was divided among worshiper, priest and deity,

## Glossary

**astrology:** study of heavenly bodies
**teratoscopy:** study of freak births among humans and animals
**oneiromancy:** divination based on dreams
**libanomancy:** study of incense offered to deities
**aleuromancy:** study of flour offered to deities
**lecanomancy:** study of oil offered to deities
**extispicy:** study of entrails of sacrificial sheep
**psephomancy:** divination based on pebbles
**belomancy:** study of arrows
**hepatoscopy:** study of animal livers
**cledomancy:** divination by a chance word

## Cuneiform Tablets: Who's Got What?

There is no official tally of the number of ancient Mesopotamian cuneiform tablets held by the world's museums, but experts agree that there are roughly half a million. The largest collection by far is in the possession of the British Museum, in London, which has approximately 130,000 of them. Next, in roughly descending order, are Berlin's Vorderasiatisches Museum, the Louvre in Paris, the Museum of Ancient Orient in Istanbul, the Baghdad Museum and Yale University's Babylonian Collection, which, with 40,000 tablets, has the largest holding in the United States. A close second is the University of Pennsylvania's Museum of Archaeology and Anthropology. Many tablets have lain in these collections for a century without being translated, studied or published.

with the deity's portion "wholly burnt" so that it went up (hence Hebrew *'olah,* literally "that which goes up"; translated in the Greek Septuagint as *holokaustos,* literally "burnt whole") in smoke whose odor was pleasant or soothing (*rei'ach nichoach*) to God. In Israel, there was no squeamishness about, nor prohibition against, eating the liver, hence no reason for with-holding it from the sacrifice and no economic motive to use it instead for divination.

*Babylonian Liver Omens* provides a fascinating, panoramic look at a world and a worldview that shares the Biblical stage with Israel yet differs from it so fundamentally that it silhouettes the latter by contrast as vividly as other aspects of that world highlight it by positive comparison.

## Notes

1. Compare Ivan Starr, *Queries to the Sungod: Divination and Politic in Sargonid Assyria* (State Archives of Assyria 4, 1990), especially pp. 187–199, 255–257; and Simo Parpola, *Letters from Assyrian and Babylonian Scholars* (State Archives of Assyria 10, 1993), pp. 253–270.
2. On the frequent references to receiving a "firm yes" (*annu kinu*) in extispicy, see Starr, *Queries,* p. xvi; for a different view, see Cornelis van Dam, *Then Urim and Thummim: a Means of Revelation in Ancient Israel* (Winona Lake; In: Eisenbrauns, 1997), especially pp. 197–214.
3. Ulla Jeyes, "Divination as a Science in Ancient Mesopotamia," *Jaar-bericht Ex Oriente Lux* 32 (1991–1992), pp. 23–41, especially p. 23.
4. Found on p. 283, line 17 of the book under review; see also note 702 for a list of these from other divination series.

# Millennia of Murex

**Among the more unlikely "marriages" arranged by human ingenuity is the one between the Chinese domesticated silk moth, *Bombyx mori,* and the Mediterranean sea snails of the Muricidae, or murex, family. The sea snails produce a pigment that, when brought together with silk, led to the world's longest-lasting fashion statement.**

PHILIPPA SCOTT

Murex is the dye first famous as "Tyrian purple," named for the city of Tyre, today in Lebanon but 3000 years ago the center from which that energetic trading nation, the Phoenicians, controlled a far-flung luxury trade in murex-dyed silks. Later, the dye was known as "royal purple" or "imperial purple," from the Roman and Byzantine emperors who reserved the color for members of the imperial family.

The search for stable, brilliant textile dyes is an ancient one. Early dyers experimented with plants, lichens, colored earths, stones containing metallic oxides, insects, blood, seaweeds—and shellfish. Shell mounds, pits full of shells and stretches of seashore made up of millions of crushed shells are continually being discovered, forcing archeologists and historians to reassess dates and boundaries. Archeologists working in Qatar, along the Gulf coast of the Arabian Peninsula, have recently uncovered shell middens—discard heaps—that date to the 18th century BC and are composed mostly of the *Thais savigni* species of murex. Nearby were pits with hearths and dye pots more than a meter (39") in diameter. Until this discovery, historians believed the story of murex purple dyes began around 3000 BC with the Minoan civilization of Crete, and was then advanced by the enterprising Phoenicians. Now it seems probable that the use of shellfish dyes developed as independently in what is today Qatar as it did in the Mediterranean and the Americas.

In the Mediterranean there are 16 species of Muricidae. Three that are common to the eastern Mediterranean were specifically fished for dye: *Murex trunculus, Murex brandaris* and *Thais haemastoma* (also called *Purpura haemastoma*). The earliest, most complete written account of early dyeing techniques comes from Pliny the Elder in the first century of our era, but researchers have recently found that Pliny either misunderstood certain processes or was misinformed—or perhaps intentionally misled by craftsmen reluctant to fully reveal their techniques. For example, it might be true, as Pliny claimed, that honey was a traditional ingredient in the murex formula, or there may be a lost legend about it, or a belief in some symbolic potency of which today we know nothing. However, modern methods of chemical analysis have found honey to be of no practical use in murex dyeing.

**The name "Phoenician" is adapted from the Greek *phoinix,* meaning "purple-red."**

The Minoan civilization of Crete endured some two millennia, from roughly 3000 BC to 1000 BC. Excavations there have revealed houses decorated with frescoes that used murex purple as a paint. Some earthen floors have been found to contain crushed murex shells as aggregate—an example of recycling from about 1500 BC. Murex shells appeared as a design motif on pottery and on carved gemstones. From frescoes, painted figures and pottery, we know that the Minoans wove fine wool cloth that was profusely patterned and colored; however, we do not know whether the designs were woven, embroidered, appliquéed or printed, for archeologists have not yet found any of the textiles themselves.

The extensive Minoan trading network operated by barter, coinage not having yet been invented, and cloth was among the most important trading elements. To the south, Egypt was a significant trading partner, and the Papyrus Anastasy, a New Kingdom document written about 1400 BC (now in the Victoria Museum in Upsala, Sweden), includes 70 formulae for dyeing wool, most of which deal with purple. There is a vivid description of a purple dyer: "His hands stink, they have the smell of decaying fish. His eyes are overcome with exhaustion."

From the 15th century BC or earlier, murex dyeing was also carried on along the north coast of Syria at the port of Ugarit, at Mina al-Bayda. Here, archeologists' finds include lots of crushed shells and part of a pot still stained with purple. Surviving Ugaritic texts describe a thriving commerce in purple wool and purple cloth. They mention wool being dyed in the yarn, an indication that craftsmen may have practiced pattern weaving. An Assyrian chemist's text gives a formula for murex purple dye. Eastward in Mesopotamia, Babylonians dressed sacred idols in purple cloth.

## It's a Purple World

Beyond the Mediterranean, there are a number of other sea snails useful for dyeing. Some 140 species flourish off the shores of North and South America. Of these, *Purpura patula, Purpura persica* and *Purpura aperta* inhabit the Gulf of Mexico, and these are still valued today in Central America, where women use them to color skeins of yarn. Sun and saltwater cause the pigment to oxidize on the fibers into an attractive but uneven purple. Unlike the Mediterranean types of murex, which must be crushed in order to obtain the tiny sac of pigment, the gland on the American shellfish is closer to the surface, and the creature can be persuaded to squirt its secretion onto the yarn. Afterward, the shellfish can be put back into the sea, given time to recover, and used again. Threads colored in this way tend to retain a fishy smell, however. The dyes in many pre-Columbian textiles and the purple paint in the Nahuatl codices have been analyzed and found to be shellfish purple.

In ancient Japan yet another type of shellfish was used. In the waters around Scandinavia and the British Isles, the Anglo-Saxons called purple dye fiscdeag ("fish dye"), and in the seventh century the Venerable Bede wrote about red and purple dyes obtained from sea snails. In Australia, although there are equivalent shellfish, no evidence has yet been found that these were ever used for textile dyeing.

But it was another seafaring nation of traders, the Phoenicians, who were destined to become irrevocably linked with murex purple dye. The name "Phoenician"—and "phoenix," the legendary bird reborn in the flames—is derived from the Greek *phoinix,* meaning "purple-red." (*Murex* comes to us from Latin, derived from the Greek *muax,* or "purple fish.") It was the Phoenicians who developed and promoted the Mediterranean murex market. Herodotus tells us that Tyre, built on an island and the neighboring mainland, was founded in 2759 BC. Archeology supports this as a roughly probable date for the arrival and settlement of this Semitic people from somewhere further south. The geography of their long, narrow country, with its high mountains sloping toward the coastal plain, made the Phoenicians look naturally outward to the sea.

The sea meant trade, and by the eighth century BC, the Phoenicians were established as traders, craftsmen and daring seafarers, and Phoenician sarcophagi depict wealthy businessmen. Perhaps because good business required efficient accounting, the Phoenicians invented an alphabet which was passed on to and adapted by the Greeks—and which became the origin of our own today. Phoenician vessels traveled as far as the British Isles, where they traded for tin in Cornwall and tin, gold, silver and copper in Spain.

All around the Mediterranean there are wide stretches of beaches composed of crushed murex shells, silent witnesses to the geographical scope and longevity of the Phoenician dyeing industry. One famous Phoenician dye-works was near Cadiz, in the south of Spain; others were in present-day Tunisia, where Carthage was a Phoenician colony. At all these sites, the shellfish were crushed, and the pigment extracted, processed, mixed and used. Gravestones of "purple merchants" (*purpurarii or negotiatores artis purpurariae*) often show a set of scales or hanks of yarn, indicating that here too yarn was dyed before weaving, enabling it to be used for woven patterns and embroidery.

On the supply end, the "marriage" of silk and murex may have occurred relatively early. Strands of Chinese silk—the remains of a decorative net, perhaps—have been identified in the hair of an Egyptian mummy dating from 1000 BC, long before an established trade network is thought to have existed—a reminder of the importance of keeping an open mind to the reassessment of historical knowledge. The East–West land and maritime routes that became known as the Silk Roads are generally considered to have been "opened up" during the time of the Han and the Roman Empires, but already during the sixth century BC, Greek vessels carried silk to the Mediterranean via trading settlements around the Black Sea. The Chinese, who kept close account of all silk production outside their borders, recorded that Syria was a silk producer by the fifth century of our era.

The commercial success and enduring appeal of murex was based on solid science. Silk and wool are both protein fibers obtained from living creatures and, as such, they both have carboxyl and amino groups available to which dyestuffs can bond, unlike such plant fibers as cotton, linen, hemp, nettle and jute. Silk, as strong as steel, weight for weight, is also highly absorbent, which makes it easier to dye than any other fiber. This meant it required less dye to achieve more effect. Results ranged the palette from heavy ultramarine blues and purples to gentle lilacs, mauves and pinks, all depending on dye mixture and timing. Silk, it turned out, was more than a chemically compatible partner for murex: Both were labor-intensive in use, extremely expensive and long-lasting, and the Phoenicians justified the high prices they demanded for murex because so little pigment was obtained from the glandular secretions of each shellfish. (See "How Murex Works")

When Alexander the Great's troops, marching east in 324 BC, took the Achaemenid winter capital Susa (in today's Iran), they found a vast store of purple robes and cloth in the royal treasury. Afterward, Alexander's generals criticized their leader for swanning around in the all-purple robes "like a Persian." To the austerity-loving Greek mind of the time, only a show-off would don such ostentatious luxury. Not long afterward, however, possibly thanks to captive Phoenician dyers, the Greeks learned purple technology themselves. Purple dye works have been excavated in Corinth, and murex shells were depicted on certain Greek coins. Archeologists excavating the royal Macedonian graves at Vergina found the bones of Cleopatra, Philip II's youngest wife and Alexander the Great's stepmother, wrapped in a breathtaking fabric of the finest purple wool, delicately woven with gold thread. A fragment of that royal shroud has recently been analyzed and proved, not surprisingly, to have been dyed with murex.

The Phoenicians continued trading until the late fourth century BC, when the gradual incorporation of their cities into the

Greek empire effectively put an end to a separate Phoenician identity. However, their dyeing and textile skills continued to flourish in the Levant and Syria.

By the time Julius Caesar returned to Rome from Egypt in 47 BC, his mind awash with thoughts of Cleopatra's perfumed purple sails, the number of purple stripes or emblems on any Roman male's outer garment was an indication of his rank, authority and prestige. This prompted imitations and became a fashion. Artists and orators donned purple. Nero, who had a habit of taking things to extremes, wore all-purple robes, and it was he who issued a decree that anyone else who did so would be executed.

In the breakaway Syrian state of Palmyra, grown rich from the Silk Roads trade, statues show its citizens elaborately coiffed and bejeweled, and the folds of their carved robes drape in silk's inimitable manner. Murex purple has been identified in some of the Palmyran silks discovered in graves and funeral towers. When Palmyra fell to Rome in the year 273, its queen, Zenobia, was paraded through the streets of Rome in golden chains—and we may be reasonably certain that she also wore murex-dyed silks from Palmyran looms.

## How Murex Works

At first, the mucus-like glandular secretions of all types of murex are colorless or faintly yellow. The glands of the American species are close to the surface, which means the animals can be squeezed lightly, then replaced in the water alive, but in the Mediterranean, the species must be crushed. Exposure to sunlight and air causes rapid oxidization, turning the secretions into a purple pigment. If this is immediately rubbed onto fabric (or, as in a Phoenician legend, a dog's muzzle), it will stain. Each shellfish, however, produces very little pigment, and although this method of rubbing the pigment onto thread or fabric is used in the Americas, it was not practical for Phoenician commercial purposes. Murex produce most of their secretions in early spring, the season when Sirius, "the Dog Star," is high in the northern hemisphere's sky, and thus the legend of Melcarth (Hercules) and his dog may in fact be a folktale reminding people of this seasonal advantage.

A pigment is a coloring agent, but to become a dye that will attach itself permanently to fibers, it needs to be processed. Murex is chemically related to the indigo dye family (which includes woad), and all these need to be processed in dyeing vats in an alkaline solution. Usually this meant a mixture of saltwater, wood ash, fermented urine or lime-water. (The salt stops the shellfish's flesh from rotting, just as salt-curing preserves meat). No doubt dyers had their own formulae, each with varying quantities, reduction times and so on.

Once the dye had been made, it could be used to color cloth or unwoven yarn, or it could be dried and made into a powder, which could then be stored or transported and later reconstituted. After the cloth or yarn had been dyed, its color could be brightened by rinsing in an acetic-acid bath, such as diluted vinegar.

The trickiest question is, how many sea snails were required for dyeing? Enormous numbers have always been quoted, and indeed the dyeing vats used in ancient Qatar had a capacity of more than 600 liters (160 gal).

One experiment in 2001 with woollen fleece found that good color could be obtained on one gram of wool ($1\frac{1}{30}$ oz) with just three snails, though darker hues and a more uniform color could be obtained by using a more concentrated dye solution and less wool. Excellent uniformity of dyeing was obtained using three successive one-gram samples of wool, 20 medium-sized snails (total weight, with shells, about 360 grams [13 oz]) and about 200 milliliters (6¾ oz) of sodium carbonate, or washing soda, as the alkaline solution—just enough to cover all the snails. The minimum recipe to produce uniform purple color was seven snails and 70 milliliters ($2\frac{1}{3}$ oz) alkaline solution.

Based on these findings, the researchers calculated that dyeing a robe, cloak, mantle, toga or other garment that weighed only a kilogram (2.2 lb) to a deep shade would require not fewer than 10,000 snails.

But it was in the eastern Roman Empire of Byzantium that the murex purple fashion reached its all-time apogee. When Emperor Constantine established his new city, Constantinople, in 330, the Byzantines embraced the symbolism of purple. Ancient Phoenicia and Syria became Byzantine territories. Syrian merchants were accorded special privileges in the imperial city, for they brought the most desirable dyestuffs and the most desirable purple-dyed silk, some already woven and some as thread, to supply the imperial weaving ateliers. The Byzantine silk industry was strictly regulated by guilds, and silks of both purple and purple-and-gold were imperial monopolies. Many Byzantine laws regulated the sale, production and wearing of purple, and punishment for their breach was severe.

If in Rome a single stripe of murex purple had signified wealth, prestige and, at times, even aristocracy, how much more magnificent was a Byzantine subject dressed in a purple garment or—better yet—in a purple silk garment? More prestigious still were purple silk garments woven with gold thread, in patterns of varying degrees of intricacy. And what of the Byzantine imperial children, literally and in every symbolic sense "born to the purple," raised in the *porphyra,* a room with pillars and a floor of polished purple porphyry, hung all around with perfumed purple drapes? As a finishing touch, there was also imperial footwear, crimson or scarlet, sandals or boots, for men and women alike.

**For the Turks, and the Arabs as well, purple did not hold the same symbolic meanings that it held for Phoenicians, Romans and Byzantines.**

Of all the shades obtained from murex, the Byzantine favorite was a dark violet color sometimes described as "cockroach." Exerting a strict monopoly on murex, the Byzantines colluded with the Syrian merchants to maintain and protect this market. Foreign rulers begged for trading privileges that would include Byzantine silks, and a gift of Byzantine silk was a treasure indeed. It may be difficult for us to imagine today, accustomed as we are to the easy worldwide availability of silk, but it is no exaggeration to say that in the Byzantine economy and in Byzantine diplomacy, the central position of their fabulous silks is loosely comparable to the role of crude oil in today's world.

All around the Mediterranean, throughout the Roman Empire, from Phoenician times until the collapse of the Byzantine Empire and the fall of Constantinople in 1453, purple meant glamour, royalty, aristocracy, wealth and power. Authors have often borrowed this symbolism: In 1400, Geoffrey Chaucer wrote of "the venom of Tyre" and "the bright fleeces of the land of Syria" and, quoting St. Jerome, warned, "wives that are apparelled in silk and in precious purple are not able to clothe themselves in Jesus Christ." Shakespeare's image of Cleopatra's royal barge conjures romance: "Purple the sails, and so perfumed that the winds were lovesick with them." And Byron: "The Assyrian came down like a wolf on the fold / And his cohorts were gleaming in purple and gold."

Our ancestors thus understood "purple" in a broader, more symbolic sense than we do today. Many a student in recent times has puzzled over Homer's "wine-dark sea," in *The Iliad:* The sea can be dark blue, they wonder, but surely not wine-colored. As a color, however, "purple" encompassed all the shades that could be obtained from the murex family of shellfish, from ultramarine to pink. Which color resulted depended on what species' pigment went into the dye pot, what it was or wasn't mixed with, for how long and how many times the yarn or cloth was dyed and even the season in which the shellfish had been harvested. Faced with such a rainbow, "purple" was not so much a color as a notion, a status.

The demise of murex purple has been variously attributed to the seventh-century Arab conquest of the Levant and to overfishing, but most writers and textile historians blame the Turks. Historian Stephen Runciman, in his *Fall of Constantinople,* wrote that two great secrets were lost when Constantinople fell to the Ottoman Turks in 1453: the military formula for making "Greek fire," and the dyeing techniques of Tyrian purple.

But there were other factors. In 1202, the Fourth Crusade sacked and looted Constantinople, and the Byzantines and their great city never fully recovered. As always throughout history, skilled craftsmen were part of the booty taken back to Italy, and among them were textile workers whose skills and knowledge boosted the fledgling Italian silk industry, which suddenly, around this time, began to flourish.

It is also true that for the Turks, and the Arabs as well, purple did not carry the same symbolic freight as for the Byzantines. To Muslims, green and red were the colors of life and royalty. Ottoman superstitions held black and purple to be unlucky colors. Although purple at times conferred distinction, during times of war it was an omen of death. But still, the Ottoman Turks were always canny about their textile trade, and they had no compunction about continuing to manufacture Byzantine-style silks, complete with figures of Jesus, for the Orthodox Church in Russia. Despite some claims that Byzantine dye works and weaving factories were destroyed by the Turks, we know that murex dyeing continued under the Ottomans, for the dye has been identified recently in at least one silk examined by Turkish textile historians, and the Topkap holdings contain other silks that, when analyzed, may well prove to be murex.

There is also the element of alum. With the collapse of the Byzantine Empire, the Ottomans began to control the lucrative trade in this vital ingredient used for mordanting textile dyes (and also for preparing leather). Alum had always been a major Byzantine export to Europe, and to the Ottomans it promised a no less vital revenue for the sultans' coffers. But in 1460, Italians discovered a plentiful source of alum on their mainland. The Pope immediately claimed the deposits as church property, simultaneously enriching the Church and dealing a blow to Ottoman commerce.

Then, a 1467 papal decree stated that the murex purple, previously used on cardinals' robes, should be replaced by scarlet, a color intended to bring the cardinals onto a level equal with kings. The new "cardinal purple" was dyed with a mixture of indigo and kermes, the "beetle dye" from which English takes its word *crimson*—via the Arabic *qirmizi.* By this color shift, said the Pope, the Ottomans would lose valuable revenue and the Church would gain it, the better to wage war against them.

Yet a further blow to the murex industry lay ahead. The European discovery of the Americas brought cochineal, a crimson dye obtained from the insect of the same name (*Dactylopius coccus*). It proved less expensive than either murex or kermes. From the 16th century, with no more need to go through the laborious processes of obtaining pigment from sea snails, Turkish dyers, as others, began mixing cochineal with indigo to obtain shades formerly obtained from shellfish. (Logwood imported from Sri Lanka also gave a deep, purplish-red color, but in 1630 a complaint is recorded from the velvet-makers of Bursa, who considered this to be an inferior dye.)

Things changed further in the 19th century when chemists discovered how to make synthetic colors. When William Henry Perkin, an 18-year-old English student and lab assistant of the German chemist Wilhelm von Hofmann, accidentally discovered the dye mauveine in 1856, he initially called it "Tyrian purple," thinking, mistakenly, that he had rediscovered the dye of the ancients. When Queen Victoria chose mauve for her Jubilee dress in 1887, she was perhaps the first monarch ever to wear silk that had been dyed to that shade without the aid of either the venerable murex or the upstart cochineal.

Fashion being a fickle jade, the murex market, so stable and central for millennia, had finally faded. The marriage was over. The silkworm had spurned the shellfish, first for a beetle, and finally for a chemist.

---

London-based free-lance writer **Philippa Scott** is a textile historian and author of several books, including *The Book of Silk* (2001, Thames & Hudson).

# UNIT 2

# Greece and Rome: The Classical Tradition

## Unit Selections


7. **Troy's Night of the Horse,** Barry Strauss
8. **The First Olympics,** Betsy Carpenter
9. **Can We Trust the Ancient Texts?,** Richard A. Gabriel
10. **Unlocking Mysteries of the Parthenon,** Evan Hadingham
11. **Outfoxed and Outfought,** Jason K. Foster
12. **Mighty Macedonian,** Richard Covington
13. **Etruscan Women**, Ingrid D. Rowland
14. **Rome's Craftiest General,** James Lacey
15. **The End of the Roman Empire,** Bryan Ward-Perkins


## Key points to Consider

- Why did the Greeks invent the story of the Horse in the Trojan War?
- What are some of the new ideas concerning the Ancient Olympics?
- What is the problem with many ancient texts?
- What is the new perspectives concerning the Parthenon?
- How did the Athenians win over the Persians at Marathon?
- What were the motives behind Alexander the Great's victories, that enabled him to conquer the Persian Empire?
- Why were the Etruscan Women scandalous to the Greeks and Romans?
- Why is Publius Cornelius Scipio famous in Roman history?
- What might have brought about the end of the Roman Empire?

## Student Web Site

www.mhcls.com/online

## Internet References

**Diotima/Women and Gender in the Ancient World**
*http://www.stoa.org/diotima/*

**Exploring Ancient World Cultures**
*http://eawc.evansville.edu*

**WWW: Classical Archaeology**
*http://www.archaeology.org/wwwarky/classical.html*

It has been conventional to say that, for the West, civilization began in Mesopotamia and Egypt, but that civilization became distinctly Western in Greece. These matters no longer go undisputed; witness recent academic debates of Martin Bernal's thesis that Greek civilization derived its culture from the older cultures of Egypt and the Eastern Mediterranean.

Those disputes aside, the Greek ideals of order, proportion, harmony, balance, and structure (see "Unlocking Mysteries of the Parthenon")—so pervasive in classical thought and art—inspired Western culture for centuries, even into the modern era. Their humanism, which made humans "the measure of all things," not only liberated Greek citizens from the despotism of the Near East, but also encouraged them, and us, to attain higher levels of creativity and excellence.

Though the Greeks did not entirely escape from the ancient traditions of miracle, mystery, and authority (see "Can We Trust the Ancient Texts?"), they nevertheless elevated reason and science to new levels of importance in human affairs, and they invented history, as we know it. It was their unique socio-political system—the polis—that provided scope and incentives for Greek culture. Each polis was an experiment in local self-government. But to many modernists, the Greek order was tainted because it rested on slavery and excluded women from the political process.

For all its greatness and originality, classical Greek civilization flowered only briefly. After the great Athenian victory over the Persians at Marathon (see "Outfoxed and Outfought"), the weaknesses of the polis system surfaced during the Peloponnesian Wars. After the long conflict between Athens and Sparta, the polis ceased to fulfill the lives of its citizens as it had in the past. The Greeks' confidence was shaken by the war and subsequent events.

But it was not the war alone that undermined the civic order. The Greek way of life depended upon unique and transitory circumstances—trust, smallness, simplicity, and a willingness to subordinate private interests to public concerns. The postwar period saw the spread of disruptive forms of individualism and the privatization of life.

Eventually, Alexander the Great's conquests and the geographical unity of the Mediterranean, enabled the non-Greek world to share Greek civilization (see "Mighty Macedonian"). Indeed, a distinctive stage of Western civilization, the Hellenistic age, emerged form the fusion of Greek and Oriental elements. At best, the Hellenistic period was a time when new cities were built on the Greek model, a time of intellectual ferment and cultural exchange, travel and exploration, scholarship and research. At worst, it was an era of amoral opportunism in politics and derivative art styles.

Later, the Greek idea survived Rome's domination of the Mediterranean. The Romans themselves acknowledged their debt to "conquered Greece." Modern scholars continue that theme, often depicting Roman culture as nothing more than the practical application of Greek ideals to Roman life. In addition, the Roman Republic invented an effective system of imperial government and a unique concept of law, which was carried on during the reign of the Empire.

Royalty-Free/Corbis

The Romans bequeathed their language and law to Europe and preserved and spread Greek thought and values. The Greeks provided the basis for cultural unity of the Mediterranean; and the Romans provided the political unity. Between themselves, they forged and preserved many of the standards and assumptions, upon which our traditions of civilization are built—the classical ideal.

# Troy's Night of the Horse

## The Trojans got tricked, but did the Greeks need a wooden horse?

Barry Strauss

He is the last Greek at Troy. Pale in the morning light, he looks like a weak, ragged runaway. But looks can deceive. Sinon, as he is called, claims to be a deserter—the only Greek remaining when the entire enemy and its cursed fleet had suddenly departed. But can he be trusted? His name, Sinon, means "pest," "bane" or "misfortune" in Greek, leading some historians to consider it a nickname, like "the Desert Fox" for German General Erwin Rommel, or a generic name, like "Bones" for a military doctor. Sinon played a key role in the plot to take Troy, although he is often forgotten, overshadowed by the most famous trick in Western civilization.

The famous horse may be imagined as a tall and well-crafted wooden structure, towering over the wildflowers of the Scamander River plain. Its body is made of the pine of Mount Ida, a tree known today as Pinus equi troiani, "Trojan Horse Pine and renowned since antiquity as a material for shipbuilding. The horse's eyes are obsidian and amber, its teeth ivory. Its crest, made of real horsehair, streams in the breeze. Its hooves shine like polished marble. And hidden inside are nine Greek warriors.

Everyone knows the story. The Greeks are said to have packed up their men, horses, weapons and booty, set fire to their huts, and departed at night for the nearby island of Tenedos, where they hid their ships. All that they left behind was the Trojan Horse and a spy, Sinon, pretending to be a deserter.

The Trojans were amazed to discover that after all those years, the enemy had slunk home. But what were they to do with the Horse? After a fierce debate, they brought it into the city as an offering to Athena. There were wild celebrations. The Trojans underestimated the cunning of their adversaries. That night, the men inside the horse sneaked out and opened the city's gates to the men of the Greek fleet, who had taken advantage of Troy's drunken distraction to sat back from Tenedos. They proceeded to sack the city and win the war.

Everyone knows the story, but nobody loves the Trojan Horse. Although scholars disagree about much of the Trojan War, they nearly all share the conviction that the Trojan Horse is a fiction. From Roman times on, there have been theories that the Trojan Horse was really a siege tower, or an image of a horse on a city gate left unlocked by pro-Greek Antenor, or a metaphor for a new Greek fleet because Homer calls ships "horses of the sea," or a symbol of the god Poseidon, who destroyed Troy in an earthquake, or a folk tale similar to those found in Egyptian literature and the Hebrew Bible. There has been every sort of theory about the Trojan Horse except that it really existed.

Many of these theories sound convincing, particularly the horse-as-siege engine, since Bronze Age Assyrians named their siege towers alter horses, among other animals. But sometimes a horse is just a horse. Although epic tradition might exaggerate the details of the Trojan Horse and misunderstand its purpose, that the object existed and that it played a role in tricking the Trojans into leaving their city without defenses might just be true.

More about the Horse presently: In the meantime, back to the spy whom the Greeks had left behind. Although Sinon is less dramatic than the famous Horse, he was no less effective as an agent of subversion, and he inspires far more confidence as a genuine historical figure. The Trojan Horse is unique and improbable, although not impossible. But Sinon plays a well-attested role in unconventional warfare as it was waged in the Bronze Age.

In Virgil's retelling in the Aeneid, Sinon pretends to be a deserter in order to work his way into Troy. He testifies that the Greeks have left for good and argues that the Trojan Horse is a genuine gift and not some trick. Eventually, after a stormy debate, the Trojans decide to bring the Horse into the city.

Deceit is not unique to the Trojan saga; it was a fundamental ingredient in Hittite military doctrine. Consider some examples: A king broke off the siege of a fortress at the approach of winter, only to send his general back to storm the unsuspecting city after it had gone off alert. A general sent agents into the opposing camp before battle, where they pretended to be deserters and tricked the enemy into letting down his guard. Another king attacked a neighbor via a roundabout route to avoid enemy scouts. Nor were the Hittites alone in their use of trickery. For example, the siege of one Mesopotamian city by another involved sneak attacks at night and the impersonation of an allied unit of soldiers in an attempt to lull the besieged into opening their gates. (It failed.)

Think of the fall of Troy not as a myth about a Horse but as an example of unconventional warfare, Bronze Age style. The Trojan Horse might be better known as the Trojan Red Herring. Everyone focuses on the Horse, but the real story lies elsewhere. In fact, it would be possible to leave out the Trojan Horse and yet tell a credible and coherent narrative of the capture of Troy much as the ancients told it.

Without the Trojan Horse, the story might go like this: The Greeks decided to trick the Trojans into thinking they had gone

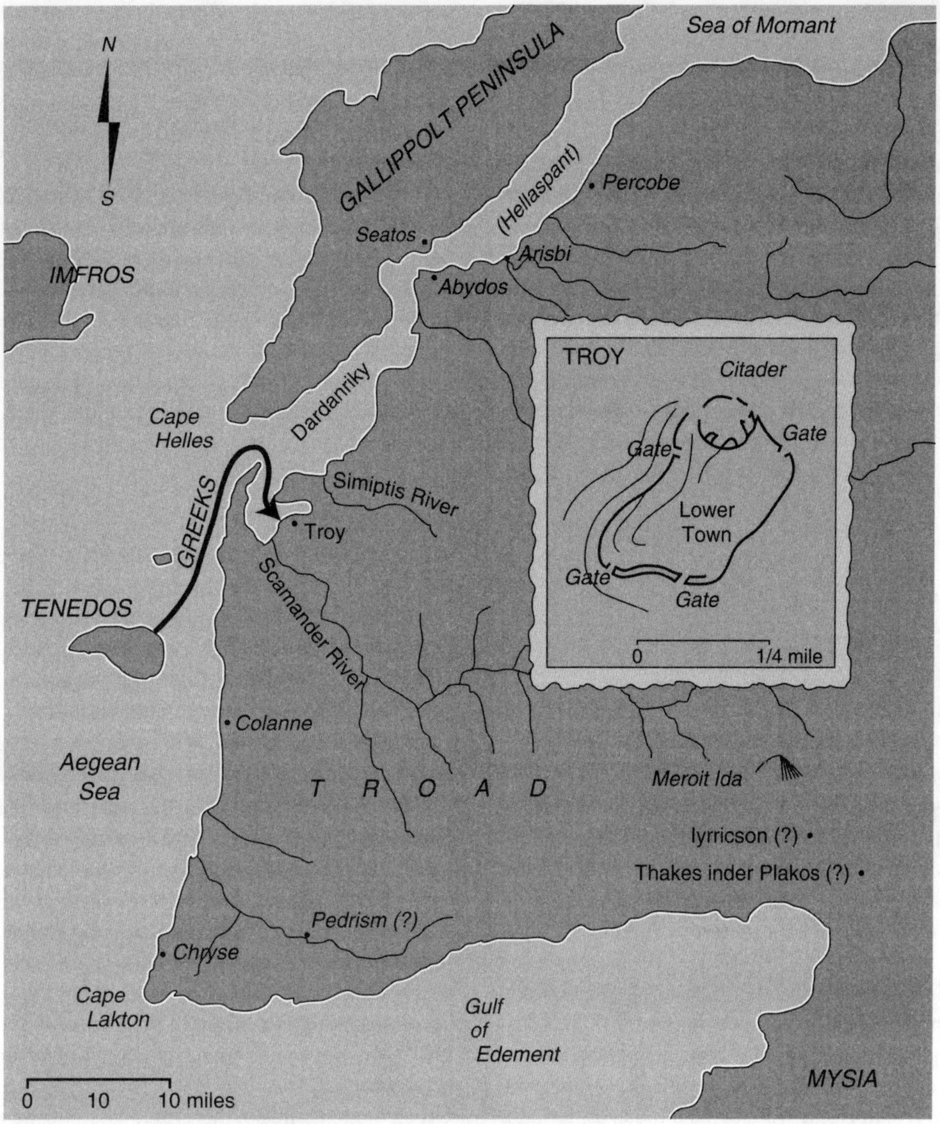

Tricking the Trojan defenders, the Greeks likely withdrew to the island of Tenedos, some seven miles away, before springing their surprise attack.

home when, in fact, they had merely retreated to Tenedos. Once they had lulled the enemy into dropping his guard, they planned to return in a surprise attack—at night. To know when to move, the Greeks would look for a lighted-torch signal, to be given by a Greek in Troy who had pretended to turn traitor and desert. Signals were used often in ancient battles, most famously at Marathon (490 BC), when a Greek traitor in the hills flashed a shield in the sunlight to communicate with the Persians. In the clear skies of the Mediterranean, fire signals could be seen from far off. They were visible as smoke signals during the day and as beacons at night. Tests show that the signals were visible between mountaintops up to a distance of 200 miles.

At the sign, the Greeks would row back rapidly to Troy. The final part of the plan required a few men inside Troy to open the city gate. These men might either have been Trojan traitors or Greeks who had sneaked into the city. With the emergency supposedly over, Troy's gatekeepers would not have proved difficult to overcome.

Compare the set of tricks by which the south Italian port city of Tarentum was betrayed in turn to Hannibal and then to the Romans. In 213 BC a pro-Carthaginian citizen of Tarentum arranged for Carthaginian soldiers to come back with him from a nighttime hunting expedition. The soldiers wore breastplates and held swords under their buckskins; they even carried a wild boar in front, to appear authentic. Once the city gate was opened to them, they slaughtered the guards, and Hannibal's army rushed in. Four years later, the Romans under Fabius Maximus recaptured the city by having a local girl seduce the commander of Hannibal's garrison. He agreed to guide Roman troops over the walls at night while Fabius' ships created a distraction at the harbor wall on the other side of town. Although these events took place 1,000 years after the Trojan War, they could easily have been carried out with Bronze Age technology.

The Greek plan at Troy was to trick the enemy into dropping his guard. It worked: the Trojans relaxed. At that point, one Greek inside the city lit a signal fire to bring the Greek fleet back and then others opened a gate.

The island of Tenedos (now Bozcaada) lies about seven miles (six nautical miles) from the Trojan harbor. The Greeks might have moored their ships in one of the sheltered coves on the island's east coast, near Troy but out of sight. At a rate of about five knots (about that of a 32-oared Scandinavian longship traveling 100 miles), they could have covered the distance in little more than an hour. That is, in daylight; the trip would no doubt have taken longer at night. But the Sack of Ilium claims it was a moonlit night, and, anyhow Bronze Age armies knew how to march by night. So the trip from Tenedos took perhaps no more than two hours. From the Trojan harbor it was another five miles by land to Troy. It was nighttime, and the road was primitive, but the Greeks knew it well. They could have covered the distance in three hours. Athenian sources claim the month was Thargelion, roughly modern May. At that time of year, sunrise at Troy is 5:30–6 A.M., sunset 8–8:30 P.M. If the Greeks left Tenedos at, say, 9 P.M., and if everything went without a hitch, they would have arrived at Troy between 2 and 3 A.M., that is, about three hours before sunrise. A forced march may have gotten the Greeks to Troy an hour or so earlier.

To carry out their plan, the Greeks had had to infiltrate a small group of soldiers into the city. But they did not need the Trojan Horse to do so. Odysseus had already sneaked in and out of the city on two separate occasions shortly before. People came and went through the gates of Troy throughout the period of the war, making it all the easier now to trick the gatekeepers into letting in a handful of disguised Greek warriors.

Once inside the city, all the Greeks needed was arms, which a determined man would not have found difficult to get. Hardened commandos could easily have overpowered a few Trojan soldiers and seized their shields and spears. Ancient cities under attack were also often betrayed from within. Not even weapons could stand up to "dissatisfaction and treachery," says an Akkadian poem. Troy no doubt had its share of Trojans who preferred dealing with the Greeks to prolonging the misery of war.

But if the Trojan Horse was not strictly necessary to the Greeks' plan, it might well nonetheless have been part of it. The Trojan Horse would certainly be more believable if ancient history recorded another occasion on which a similar ruse was employed. But how could it? The Trojan Horse was such a famous trick that it could have been used only once.

According to Homer, it was Odysseus who conceived of the idea and Epeius, known otherwise as the champion boxer at the funeral games of Patroclus, who built the Horse. Certainly the Greeks had the technology to build it. Ancient fleets usually sailed with shipwrights because wooden ships constantly need repairs, and Linear B texts (ancient inscribed clay tablets) refer both to shipwrights and carpenters as professions. There would have been no shortage of men in the Greek camp to do the job.

And there would have been no question about whether or not a statue of an animal would catch the Trojan king's fancy. Bronze Age monarchs liked animal imagery. A Babylonian king of the 1300s BC, for example, had specifically asked the pharaoh for a gift of realistic figures of wild animals, with lifelike hides, made by Egyptian carpenters. But which animal should the Greeks build at Troy? A Trojan Dog would have been insulting; a Trojan Lion frightening; a Trojan Bull or Cow would have thrown Greek cattle raids in the enemy's teeth. But a horse symbolized war, privilege, piety, popularity and Troy itself.

Horses are expensive, and in the' Bronze Age they were usually used in military context, rarely as farm animals. Rulers of the era often sent horses as a gift between kings, while ordinary Trojans might cherish a figure of a horse. In the Late Bronze Age, horse figurines, made of baked clay, were collected throughout the Near East. Excavators recently found a clay model of a horse in Troy of the 1200s BC. Finally, there was the religious connotation: As a votive offering, the horse was all but an admission of Greek war guilt, a symbolic submission to the gods of the horse-taming Trojans.

The Horse could have been used to smuggle a small number of Greek soldiers into the city, but the chances of detection were very high. Although the traditional story of the Trojan Horse cannot be ruled out, it seems more probable that, if the Horse did exist, it was empty. There were simpler and less dangerous ways of smuggling soldiers into the city. The Horse's main value to the Greeks was not as a transport but as a decoy, a low-tech ancestor of the phantom army under General George Patton that the Allies used in 1944 to trick the Germans into expecting the D-Day invasion in the area of Pas de Calais instead of Normandy.

Epic tradition has some Trojans accepting the Horse as a genuine sign that the Greeks had given up while others remain skeptical. The debate lasted all day, according to Virgil, or three days, according to Homer. The Sack of Ilium identifies three camps: those who wanted to burn the Horse, those who wanted to throw it down from the walls and those who wanted to consecrate it to Athena. The length of the debate was in direct proportion to the stakes. The safety of the city as well as individual careers were hanging on the decision.

Virgil makes much of Priam's daughter Cassandra, an opponent of the Horse who enjoyed the gift of prophecy but suffered the curse of being ignored. This story does not appear in Homer, or what we have of the Epic Cycle. One person who does feature in the tradition is the Trojan priest Laocöon, a staunch opponent of the Greeks, who wanted to destroy the Horse. In Virgil, the debate over the Horse comes to an end when Laocöon and his sons are strangled by two snakes from the sea. The Sack of Ilium apparently places this event after the Horse had already been brought into town. Surely the snakes are symbolic; surely Laocöon and his boys were killed not by a sea snake but by a member of the pro-Greek faction, and so, therefore, by someone perceived as a tool of a signifier of evil like a snake.

Laocöon's snakes may well be rooted in Anatolian Bronze Age religion, local lore of the Troad, or both. Hittite literature made the snake a symbol of chaos and the archenemy of the Storm God. It makes sense for a snake to foil the Storm God's servant, the Trojan priest who was trying to save his city. The Troad, meanwhile, is rich in fossil remains of Miocene animals such as mastodons and pygmy giraffes, and these objects might have made their way into myth. For example, an Iron Age Greek painter probably used a fossilized animal skull as a model for a monster that Heracles is supposed to have defeated on the shore of Troy. So the story of Laocöon's murder by monsters from the sea may well have Trojan roots.

Laocöon's fate convinced Aeneas and his followers to leave town; they withdrew to Mount Ida in time to escape the Greek onslaught. Virgil famously tells a different story, in which Aeneas stays in Troy, fights the Greeks and then at last escapes the burning city while carrying his elderly father, Anchises, on his back. But the account in the Sack of Ilium, which records Aeneas' departure, strikes a more credible note. Aeneas would not have been eager to die for Priam, a king who had never given Aeneas the honor that he felt he was due. His homeland was south of the city, in the valley of Dardania beside the northern slopes of Mount Ida. What better place to regroup if Aeneas believed that Troy was doomed?

Helen played a double game. She had helped Odysseus on his mission to Troy and learned of his plan of the Horse. Now she tried to coax the Greeks out of the Horse, but Odysseus kept them silent—or perhaps the Horse was empty. Helen is supposed to have gone back home that night and prepared herself for the inevitable. She had her maids arrange her clothes and cosmetics for her reunion with Menelaus.

Whether or not there was a Trojan Horse, and whether or not the Trojans brought it into town and dedicated it to Athena, it is easy to imagine them celebrating the end of the war. They treated themselves to a night of partying, according to the Sack of Ilium. It was now, when the Trojans were occupied, that Sinon supposedly gave the prearranged torch signal. Once watchers on Tenedos saw it, the expedition to take Troy rowed rapidly back to the mainland.

Surprise, night and Trojan drunkenness would have given the Greeks substantial advantages, but taking Troy would require hard fighting nonetheless. Experienced warriors, the Trojans would have recovered quickly after their initial shock. If the battle began in darkness it no doubt would have continued into the daylight hours. The epic tradition offers a few details of Trojan resistance. The Greek Meges, leader of the Epeans of Elis, was wounded in the arm by Admetus, son of Augeias. Another Greek, Lycomedes, took a wound in the wrist from the Trojan Agenor, son of Antenor.

But what the tradition highlights, of course, is Greek victory. Admetus and Agenor, for instance, did not savor their successes, because that same night one was killed by Philoctetes and the other by Neoptolemus. A Greek named Eurypylus, son of Euaemon, killed Priam's son Axion. Menelaus began his revenge by killing Helen's new husband, Deïphobus, brother of Paris and son of Priam. But the Greek with the reputation for scoring the most kills during the sack of Troy is Achilles' son, Neoptolemus. Among his victims, besides Agenor, were Astynous, Eion and Priam himself, either at the altar of Zeus—no doubt the Storm God, where the Trojan king had sought shelter—or, as some say, at the doors of the palace because, not wanting to violate a god's altar, Neoptolemus was careful to drag his victim away first.

As for the Trojan women, tradition assigns Andromache to Neoptolemus and Cassandra to Agamemnon. Locrian Ajax had attempted to seize Cassandra but violated the altar of Athena or a Trojan goddess, which made the Greeks loath to reward him and thereby earn divine enmity.

Prudent Bronze Age warriors knew better than to insult an enemy's god. For example, when Hittite King Shuppiluliuma I conquered the city of Carchemish around 1325 BE, he sacked the town but kept all his troops away from the temples of Kubaba and Lamma. He bowed to the goddesses instead.

Priam's daughter Polyxena was, according to the Sack of Ilium, slaughtered at the tomb of Achilles as an offering to the hero's ghost. Little Astyanax, Hector's son, was murdered by Odysseus—thrown from the walls, in one version—lest he grow up and seek vengeance.

And then there was Helen. The Little Iliad states that Menelaus found her at home, in the house of Deïphobus. Menelaus' sword was drawn to seek vengeance on the agent of his humiliation and suffering, but Helen had merely to undrape her breasts to change his mind. It is the sort of story that we can only wish is true.

So much for the epic tradition. What do other Bronze Age texts and the archaeological excavations tell us about the sack of Troy?

Bronze Age documents show that however brutal the sack of Troy may have been, it would have conformed to the laws of war. Cities that did not surrender would, if they were captured, be destroyed. This role goes as far back as the first well-documented interstate conflict, the border wars between the two Sumerian city-states of Lagash and Umma between 2500 and 2350 BC.

When the Greeks sacked the city, they put Troy to the torch. Archaeology discloses that a savage fire destroyed the settlement level known as Troy VIi (formerly referred to as Troy VIIa). Blackened wood, white calcined stone and heaps of fallen building material were found in a thick destruction layer of ash and dirt that varied from about 20 inches to 6 feet deep. That inferno can be dated, according to the best estimate, sometime between 1230 and 1180 BC, more likely between 1210 and 1180.

The flames must have spread fast. One house in the lower city tells the story: A bronze figurine, as well as some gold and silver jewelry, was left abandoned on the floor of a room. The inhabitants had clearly fled in panic.

Imagine Troy's narrow streets clogged, and imagine the cries of disoriented refugees, the wailing of children; the growls and snorts, bleating, high-pitched squeals and relentless howls and barks of terrified barnyard animals (in the Bronze Age, typically kept within the town walls at night). Imagine too the clatter of arms, the clang and whistle of cold bronze, the cheers of the avengers, the whiz of javelins in flight, the reverberation of a spear that has found its mark, the holler and thud of street fighting, the surge of wails and curses, the gush and choking of pain, and much of it muffled by a fire burning fast and furious enough to sound like a downpour.

Archaeology draws a picture that is consistent with a sack of Troy. Outside the doorway of a house on the citadel, for example, a partial human male skeleton was discovered. Was he a householder, killed while he was defending his property? Other human bones have been found in the citadel, scattered and unburied. There is also a 15-year-old girl buried in the lower town; the ancients rarely buried people within the city limits unless an attack prevented them going to a cemetery outside town. It was even rarer to leave human skeletons unburied—another sign of the disaster that had struck Troy.

Two bronze spear points, three bronze arrowheads, and two partially preserved bronze knives have been found in the citadel and lower town. One of the arrowheads is of a type known only in the Greek mainland in the Late Bronze Age. The lower town has also yielded a cache of 157 sling stones in three piles. Another supply of a dozen smooth stones, possibly sling stones, was found on the citadel, in a building beside the south gate that looked to the excavators like a possible arsenal or guardhouse.

None of this evidence proves beyond doubt that Troy was destroyed in a sack. The fire that ravaged the city could have been caused by accident and then been stoked by high winds. If Troy was destroyed by armed violence, were the Greeks responsible? The archaeological evidence is consistent with that explanation but does not prove it.

---

This article is excerpted from Barry Strauss' book *The Trojan War,* published by Simon & Schuster in 2006.

# The First Olympics

## The early Greek games were not as pristine as we like to imagine.

BETSY CARPENTER

Amid fears that terrorists will mount an attack at this summer's Athens Olympics, it's tempting to take solace in visions of the earliest games as a more innocent and civilized gathering. After all, isn't Greece, the cradle of western civilization, promoting a worldwide cease-fire during the 2004 games, just like the Olympic Truce of ancient times?

Not quite, says a group of scholars and authors who are taking a closer look at ancient texts and art and other archaeological artifacts, and puncturing cherished myths about the original games. To be sure, Greek cities generally granted travelers safe passage to and from the competitions. But many continued warring even as their athletes competed in the hallowed stadium at Olympia. Once, an army even invaded Olympia's Sacred Grove in the middle of a wrestling match, while spectators critiqued soldiers' martial skills from the sidelines.

Indeed, almost every dewy-eyed notion about the ancient games is shriveling in the light of the revisionist scholarship. The Greeks' high-minded athletics were all about agility, speed, and coordination—right? Hardly. Two of the most popular events at the ancient games were the four-horse chariot race—which often ended in gory pileups—and a ferocious, no-holds-barred brawl known as the pankration. The ancient Olympians were highborn amateurs who competed for the pure love of sport, their sole prize a crown of olive leaves? Not at all. Indeed, Greek athletes trained hard under highly paid coaches and reaped rewards ranging from tax breaks to huge cash prizes. "All the vices of our modern games," writes Tony Perrottet in his new book The Naked Olympics, "were present at their birth."

**Spectators.** In this post-9/11 world, attending the Olympics is not for the risk-averse. But that's not new, scholars say. In ancient times, spectators had to be not just adventurous but in robust health. While some fortunate sports fans took boats to the games, most walked to Olympia in the blistering late summer heat, over steep trails and roads snaking through the mountains of Arkadia.

Arriving travelers found few amenities. According to Perrottet, Olympia had only one inn, which was reserved for dignitaries, so spectators slept under the stars or in makeshift tents. Sports fans had to use nearby pine forests and dry riverbeds as latrines because there were no toilets until A.D. 150. The air was hazy with the smoke from thousands of cooking fires lit morning and night. And water was in short supply. Archaeologists have excavated nine wells. Still, water had to be hauled in by mules throughout the five-day extravaganza, and physicians were kept busy caring for those who had collapsed from heatstroke.

Despite the creature discomforts, the games were wildly popular, with between 40,000 and 70,000 celebrants arriving from all over the Mediterranean world. Most were men, although some had young, unmarried daughters in tow, perhaps to broaden their marriage prospects. Married women were strictly forbidden; host city Elis even had a law stating that any matron who dared attend would be thrown off a nearby cliff. Why the ban? It was surely easier for the men to carouse with their women out of the way. And carouse they did, with prostitutes of both sexes at lavish, nightly feasts. But perhaps they also weren't pleased at the prospect of their wives' drooling over the athletes who, unlike today's Olympians, competed entirely in the nude.

Some modern scholars have argued that the Greek custom of disrobing before engaging in athletics hearkened back to hunters' rituals. Others believe that it was symbolic of the democratic nature of Greek sports. "But only recently have we begun to admit that ancient athletics had an erotic dimension," comments Donald Kyle, professor of history at the University of Texas-Arlington. The Greeks not only competed in the buff; they oiled themselves beforehand until they glistened. Not surprisingly, gymnasiums, to which most freeborn Greek men belonged, were prime pickup spots, where older men chased buff, beautiful youths.

Few athletes stayed gorgeous for long, however. Boxing and the pankration were particularly brutal events. Ancient bronzes and reliefs of competitors depict facial gashes, cauliflower ears, and bloodied, broken noses. In Olympic boxing, most blows were directed to the head, and contestants wore a tough, laminated "glove" designed to protect the hand rather than face, reports Stephen Miller in his recent book Ancient Greek Athletics. Matches had no rounds or time limits—contests ended when one man couldn't continue or signaled defeat by raising a finger on one hand.

During one infamous match that had dragged on into early evening, the contestants, Damoxenos of Syracuse and Kreugas of Epidamnos, agreed that each would accept an undefended blow. Kreugas went first, delivering a punch to his opponent's head. Still standing, Damoxenos jabbed Kreugas with his fingers straight out, piercing his rib cage. Damoxenos yanked out his intestines, killing him on the spot. Damoxenos was expelled, although seemingly on a technicality: The judges deemed the disemboweling to be several blows (one for each finger) instead of the single agreed-upon blow.

The pankration, the most popular of the contact sports at Olympia, was a vicious mix of wrestling, boxing, and street fighting in which punches, kicks to the groin, shoulder and ankle dislocations, and chokeholds all were allowed. Only biting and eye gouging were forbidden. One famed pankratiast at the 364 B.C. Olympics, who specialized in breaking his opponents' fingers, earned the nickname "Mr. Digits."

The dramatic and often-lethal four-horse chariot race must have had much the same lure for the ancients as stock car racing has for spectators today. Forty teams with brightly painted chariots crowded the track, known as the hippodrome. The race consisted of 12 laps around the course—and two turning posts, the loci of innumerable spills and collisions. A passage by Sophocles paints a lurid picture of one crash: "As the crowd saw the driver somersault, there rose a wail of pity for the youth, as he was bounced onto the ground, then flung head over heels into the sky. When his companions caught the runaway team and freed the blood-stained corpse from his rig, he was disfigured and marred past the recognition of his best friend."

**Paid amateurs.** The idea that the ancient Olympics took place under amateur rules is "nonsense," according to David Young, a professor of classics at the University of Florida and author of *A Brief History of the Olympic Games*. First of all, victors profited royally from their wins. Many cities gave them free meals and front-row seats at local sporting events for the rest of their lives. They were also presented with oxen, generous pensions, huge cash prizes, and even slaves. By the early sixth century B.C., Athens awarded victors 500 drachmas—the equivalent of $700,000 today. The money was a form of insurance as well as a reward for a job well done: Athletes usually competed for their native cities, but some accepted money to switch allegiances—not unlike free agency today. Astylos of Kroton, for instance, won in 480 for Syracuse after winning in 488 and 484 for Kroton.

The original Olympians also were professionals in the sense that they trained and competed virtually full time. Entrants in the very earliest games may well have honed their abilities in the margins of their regular working lives. One early winner was said to be a cook, another a goatherd. But by the classical period, roughly 470 to 350 B.C., top athletes were shuttling among major, pan-Hellenic games at Delphi, Isthmia, and Nemea, in addition to Olympia, as well as myriad less-prestigious sporting events, known as "money games."

Moreover, the ancients were just as serious about training regimes as professional athletes are today. In the late fifth century B.C., for instance, meat diets were thought to enhance performance. Celebrated wrestler Milo of Kroton reputedly once ate 40 pounds of meat and bread at a sitting. And like modern Olympians, the ancients pushed themselves to the point of injury. Decrying this "extreme" conditioning, the physician Galen wrote: "Perhaps someone will say that they have a blessing in the pleasure of their bodies. But how can [that be] if during their athletic years they are in constant pain and suffering not only because of their exercises but also because of their forced feedings? And when they reach the age of retirement, their bodies are essentially if not completely crippled."

Also like today, cities competed for the winningest coaches. The Greek historian Herodotus describes the peripatetic career of Demokedes, a trainer from Kroton, who was lured away to Aigina for a salary equivalent to 12 times that of a skilled worker. A year later, he took a job in Athens for almost double that, and the following year a position on the island of Samos, off the coast of Asia Minor, for more still. (There, his luck ran out, at least temporarily. Samos was conquered by the Persian King Darius, who was so pleased to learn that the famed trainer was in residence that he wouldn't let him leave. Eventually, Demokedes escaped, however, and made his way to Kroton, which took him back in.)

**Hostilities.** There is no ancient equivalent of the horror of 1972 Olympics in Munich, where 11 Israeli athletes were killed after being taken hostage by Palestinian terrorists. The Greeks certainly were brutal enough in their ways of vengeance and war to undertake such an act. But they admired athletes as paragons of human physical excellence, so they didn't target them in their endless feuds.

Still, much like today, cities fought over control of the games—and the money, prestige, and political power that went along with hosting them, according to David Romano, an adjunct professor of classical studies at the University of Pennsylvania. Around 365 B.C., for instance, the Arkadians took Olympia by force, and in 364, they hosted the games. The wrestling portion of pentathlon was in progress when the Elean Army marched in to take back Olympia. A pitched battle ensued in the Sacred Grove, where, according to ancient author Diodorus, spectators cheered on soldiers fighting hand to hand. The Arkadians won, but before the next Olympiad, they gave in to pressure from their allies to return Olympia to Elis, which forever after refused to recognize wins from the 364 games.

Much of our mythology about the original Olympics is rooted in Victorian England in the late 1800s, when formal athletic competitions were starting to spring up. According to Young, the aristocracy wanted to compete but not against working class stiffs, so with the aid of a few "obliging classical scholars," he says, they dreamed up the idea that Greek athletes were aristocrats who practiced only an hour or two a day and didn't profit from their wins. A few years later, when Baron

Pierre de Coubertin and other gentlemen advocates of an Olympic revival sought to ensure that modern Olympians would be drawn from the upper classes, the fiction was again trotted out. Avery Brundage, who presided over the International Olympic Committee from 1952 to 1972, put the finishing touches on the story, arguing that the ancient games degenerated and were finally abolished when they "lost their purity and high idealism" and became a business.

Our modern notion that the original Olympics were a force for peace is not entirely myth. In 476 B.C., Greek cities put aside their feuds long enough to repel the Persian Army, and in the wake of that victory, they agreed to allow an Olympic appeals board to settle future differences. For a brief, shining decade the agreement actually was upheld. Archaeologists have unearthed at Olympia a sheet of bronze detailing the board's verdict in two cases. But within a few years some cities had rejected the board's authority, and by 431, most Greek cities were embroiled in the Peloponnesian War.

Still, the ancients upheld the Olympic truce for more than a millennium. Moreover, the games were never canceled, points out Miller—not in 480, with the Persians on the doorstep, not during the Peloponnesian War, not even in the first century A.D. when the Roman Emperor Nero fiddled with the program to suit his fancy. By contrast, in a little over a century the modern Olympics have been canceled three times because of wars and disrupted by three major boycotts. Perhaps, writes Miller, "we need to study ancient practices more closely, after all."

## Highlights of Ancient Times

Sometime during the 10th century B.C., a cult of Zeus was formed at Olympia, in the valley of the river Alpheus, where locals sacrificed animals to the god and hosted an agrarian festival.

At the first Olympics in 776 B.C., the sole event was a footrace of about 200 meters.

Milo of Kroton was the only wrestler to show up at the 520 B.C., games. Apparently, no one dared compete against the famed strongman, who ultimately won in at least six Olympiads.

In 420 B.C., the Olympic host city Elis forbade Spartan athletes from competing on a technicality. At the time, Sparta was at war with Athens, with which Elis had concluded a treaty.

In A.D. 67, after accepting hefty bribes, the Olympic judges awarded Roman Emperor Nero the wreath in the chariot race, even though he'd been thrown from his vehicle and did not complete the course.

Around A.D. 150, Olympia finally got running water—from an enormous marble drinking fountain shaped like an open oyster shell and fed by water from an aqueduct.

After a slow decline, the ancient games ended in A.D. 393, when Christian Roman Emperor Theodosios I forbade the use of pagan religious sites, including Olympia's Temple of Zeus.

*Article 9*

# Can We Trust the Ancient Texts?

## Sources for all Greek and Roman military history amount to a handful of translated ancient texts. How accurate are they?

RICHARD A. GABRIEL

Some were found lying alive with their thighs and hams cut, laying bare their necks and throats, bid them drain the blood that remained in them. Some were found with their heads plunged into the earth . . . having suffocated themselves by overwhelming their faces with the earth which they threw over them. A living Numidian, with lacerated nose and ears, stretched beneath a lifeless Roman who lay upon him . . . for when the Roman's hands were powerless to grasp his weapon, turning from rage to madness, he had died in the act of tearing his antagonist with his teeth.

Pretty vivid stuff but there is no way to tell if it is true. This description of the 216 BC Battle of Cannae was written 200 years after the actual events for which no eyewitness accounts exist, and the historian, Titus Livius, or Livy, had no military experience.

What often passes as ancient history turns out to be dramatic representations of what the writers thought may have occurred. And yet one cannot examine the wars and battles of antiquity without reference to these accounts. The modern historian studying Greek and Roman military history is a prisoner of the ancient texts.

The single biggest obstacle to our understanding of ancient military history is the scarcity of reliable evidence. The Greeks' invention of history as a search for a rational explanation and understanding of events, expressed in written prose or oral recitation, created a means by which ancient historians could record events in a manner still comprehensible in the modern age. Three centuries later the Greeks passed on their invention to the Romans. The consequence was an archive of written texts on which the modern study of Greek and Roman military history is based. Unfortunately, some of the information contained in those texts is unreliable, biased, incomplete or even false.

The modern reader is right to suspect that there is something different about history as written by ancient historians: Greek and Roman historians were often less concerned with a factual accounting of events than with writing something that taught moral lessons or guided the behavior of powerful political classes or individuals. This didactic approach to history often focused on the deeds of great men.

Moreover, ancient historians expected their work to be recited more than read, and their concern for rhetoric led to the incorporation of great, but fictitious, speeches attributed to famous generals and kings. If the bare facts were insufficient for an effective presentation, then the known facts could be adorned, modified or variously combined in the interest of heightened drama. Names, numbers, exact dates, chronology and geographic details of battles were frequently inaccurate, invented or sometimes omitted.

These military "histories" were often written long after the events they describe; only a few address events contemporary with their authors. Ancient writers usually did not check the validity of their sources—a mostly impossible task in any case, as few usable archives existed and would probably have required lengthy and dangerous journeys to get to them. Some ancient historians simply repeated accounts from earlier sources, telling them in a different, often more dramatic fashion. Thus, Livy (59 BC–AD 17) relies primarily on Polybius' (c. 200-118 BC) account of the Second Punic War for his military narrative, while Dio Cassius (c. AD 150-235), writing more than a century later, relies on Livy's account for the same war. Often, sources available to the writer in his time cannot be referenced because they have since been lost. For example, the works of two of Polybius' most valuable sources, Sosylus and Silenus, Greek "war correspondents" who traveled with Hannibal, are lost to us. The sources Herodotus (c. 484–425 BC) used for the Greco-Persian Wars are little more than monument inscriptions and a collection of oral tales. There are exceptions: Campaigns of Alexander, by Arrian (c. AD 87–145), is a trustworthy account of Alexander the Great's life based on earlier eyewitness accounts by Nearchus, Ptolemy and Aristobulus, all soldiers who participated in Alexander's campaigns.

Today, military historians are also the prisoners of the surviving translations, most of which contain errors introduced when they were translated from Greek to Latin or simply copied by medieval monks, who often lacked language skills and knowledge of the military subjects. The most common errors involved numbers. The monks had limited knowledge of ancient numerical systems and regularly mistranslated or transposed numerical values, sometimes substituting completely new numbers of their own. Ancient historians had a tendency to exaggerate the number of enemy combatants and casualties in the first place, and that was compounded by the monks' errors, further distorting the facts. Rates of march, distances, weights, numbers of animals, the widths of rivers and streams, and terrain heights are usually expressed numerically, so such distortions affect the information most important to today's military historian.

Writers of ancient texts dealing with military history can be divided into three categories: (1) those with no military experience who wrote years after the events; (2) those with some military experience who wrote years after the events; and (3) those with military experience who participated in the events about which they wrote.

Herodotus, Appian (c. AD 95–165), Livy and Dio Cassius all fall into the first category. Appian's Roman History covered all the wars fought by the Romans from their early history through Trajan's campaigns. Polybius' works and Livy's War With Hannibal are the basic source materials for the Punic Wars. Dio Cassius' work is extensive but flawed in its reliance on uncriticized sources and its dependence on Livy as a major source. Herodotus' account of the Greco-Persian Wars is more dramatic novel than military history, its technical details of things military often suspect. These sources are more valuable for general themes than for exact details and must be treated with caution.

Polybius, Tacitus (c. AD 56–117) and Arrian fall into the second category. Polybius' Histories is the best account of military events, details and tactics pertaining to the Second Punic War and Scipio Africanus' role. Cavalry commander of the Achaean League, Polybius fought in the Achaean War and commanded Greek troops before being taken as a hostage to Rome, where Scipio's family befriended him. He had access to all of Scipio's papers, interviewed major commanders of the Second Punic War and visited some of the battlefields about which he wrote. Thus, his account of Roman warfare is written with an accomplished military eye and is generally accurate.

Arrian also served as a cavalry officer, seeing action in Dacia. Later, as governor of Cappadocia, he commanded two legions and may have participated in Trajan's campaign against the Parthians. His treatment of Alexander's campaigns is based on eyewitness accounts and is the most reliable source for Macedonian tactics and military organization.

Tacitus was a legion commander but apparently did not see combat. His greatest work is the Annals, which provides the only extant descriptions of Roman legionary warfare and equipment of the 1st century.

Firsthand military experience, alas, is no guarantee of historical accuracy, and even experienced soldier-historians cannot always be trusted to put aside their own biases. Sallust (c. 86–35 BC), for example, was an experienced soldier who saw combat in the civil war in Illyricum and Campania and later in North Africa. Yet Jugurthine War, his account of the Roman conflict against Jugurtha the Numidian, is generally untrustworthy as to numbers, dates, distances and size of forces. Josephus (c. AD 37–100), another combat veteran who commanded troops both for and against Rome, is a good source for the details of Roman equipment and arms hut is otherwise untrustworthy. His primary work, *The Jewish War,* an account of the great uprising against Rome, may have been commissioned by the Romans.

Among those soldier-historians who wrote contemporary accounts of battles in which they fought, Thucydides (c. 460–395 BC), Caesar (100–44 BC), Xenophon (c. 431–352 BC) and Aeneas Tacticus (4th century BC) are especially valuable.

Thucydides wrote the definitive account of the Peloponnesian Wars. He fought on land and at sea in that war, witnessing 5th century Greek phalanx warfare and trireme naval tactics. He probably participated in or saw every major engagement of the war. Thucydides' command of tactical and strategic realities of that period is unrivaled.

In his Commentaries, Caesar offers firsthand narratives of dozens of legion battles and sieges, including the siege of Alesia in Gaul and the battle at Georgovia, making him the best source for Roman military capabilities in the 1st century BC.

Xenophon was an Athenian mercenary captain who spent most of his life in military service. He served all over the eastern Mediterranean in the pay of several Greek states and even fought in the Persian army. Xenophon participated in or witnessed dozens of Greek vs. Greek and Greek vs. Persian battles and is the best source for 4th century BC Greek land warfare. His best work is Anabasis, an account of his service to Persian King Cyrus, the defeat at Cunaxa and his command of the Greek troops in retreat for more than a thousand miles across Asia Minor. A cavalryman, he wrote a short work on cavalry command appended to a treatise on horsemanship, the earliest extant work of its kind.

Aeneas Tacticus was one of the earliest Greek writers on military matters. He wrote several didactic works on warfare, but the only one known to exist is How to Survive Under Siege, a detailed manual on defending a fortified city. A Greek mercenary captain of the Peloponnese, Aeneas served in the Aegean and Asia Minor and participated in several battles, including the 362 BC Battle of Mantinea. His work is especially valuable for its plethora of historical illustrations of Greek warfare.

Although the shortcomings of these ancient texts were well known, for many years there was little else on which historians could draw. The study of ancient military history was left largely to classicists, who could read the texts in the original Latin and Greek. But while classicists' forte is language, few are trained military historians. They have long perceived military history as a minor field, thus paying it scant attention.

A European university education of the 19th century consisted largely of a classical education in which the original texts were read. Many university graduates of the aristocratic classes became high-ranking military officers, who did pore over the accounts of ancient warfare for modern lessons. Soldier-historians such as Basil Liddell-Hart, J.F.C. Fuller, Hans Delbrück and Georg Veith revised accounts of the ancient battles based on their own experiences with military training and war.

Two developments in the late 19th century led to a more empirical study of ancient military history. First, the 19th century was an age of invention and discovery in which the scientific impulse required carefully measured confirmation of all propositions before they could be accepted as fact. For the first time, military historians were able to apply new findings from psychiatry, medicine, nutrition, human endurance studies, cartography, metallurgy, engineering and other fields to the study of ancient warfare.

Second, the 19th century saw the emergence of modern war on an unprecedented scale. Large standing and reserve armies required the precise management of men and materiel. This gave rise to tabular organization and implementation, including calculations of how much food and water each soldier required; how quickly a brigade could march under different conditions; how many mules and wagons were needed to transport men and supplies over a given distance and how long they could be sustained in the field; as well as what kinds of wounds could result from different types of attacks and how many of the wounded would die from hostile fire, accidents or disease. Military science replaced what had once been the "art of war."

The new approach was further spurred by the reserve mobilization system used by European armies of the day. While standing armies were relatively small, reserve units were enormous, comprising almost every male adult between the ages of 18 and 45. Between the Crimean War and World War I, many of these reservists saw combat or at least underwent military training. The reservists included professors and university students who learned the new science of war and its attendant tables, schedules and measurements, then returned to the universities, creating an impetus for more empirical analysis of the ancient warfare texts.

By the beginning of the 20th century the new approach was gaining credibility, and professors who were not classicists but ancient military historians began securing positions at European universities, only to have the disruption and carnage of World War I decimate the ranks of the new scholarship and bring it to a halt. After the war, surviving professors who still had posts to fill and classes to teach tried to reestablish the new discipline. They produced a number of groundbreaking empirical works, like Johannes Kromayer and Georg Veith's Battle Atlas of Ancient Military History and Hans Delbrück's four-volume History of the Art of War. The postwar political turmoil and the catastrophe of World War II in Europe again eclipsed the study of ancient military history. The subject had never been popular in the United States, and the study of ancient military history remains today a comparatively minor discipline.

The last two decades have seen the emergence of an empirical approach to ancient military history in the United States and Europe, prompted by an electronic revolution that has brought the contents of the world's libraries and the work of distant scholars to the historian's desktop. This same revolution has increased communication among scholars. There are also the beginnings of financial support for such research: Oxford University, for example, sponsored the re-creation of a 4th century trireme to test its operational characteristics.

New research has added to the tools the ancient historian can now apply to the texts. J.F. Lazenby's and J.K. Anderson's work on Greek warfare, Victor Davis Hansong study of the Battle of Cannae, and Philip Sabin's research on the battles of the Punic Wars have added to our understanding of the mechanics of close combat and the respective roles played by fear, exhaustion and "battle pulses." Markus Junkelmann's real-life experiments measuring the carrying loads, speed and endurance of actual soldiers have raised new questions about these factors in ancient warfare. Donald Engels' excellent study on the logistics of Macedonian armies has been supplemented by Jonathan Roth's analysis of the logistics of Roman armies from 264 BC to AD 235. (Karen Metz's and my efforts at "experimental archaeology" have provided insights into the killing and wounding power of ancient weapons.) In short, today's ancient historians now have at their disposal a new set of tools with which to analyze the ancient battle accounts, thus revising and enriching our understanding of what war was like in those times.

One of the most important factors in our understanding of ancient warfare, the terrain on which the battles were fought, has remained mostly beyond our ken. Urbanization, industrialization and two world wars have altered the landscape of the ancient battlefields beyond recognition. (At this writing, the battlefield of Chaeronea in Greece is under development as a shopping mall.)

This was not the case before and just after World War I. Then, Johannes Kromayer, chair of the Department of Ancient Military History at Leipzig University, and Georg Veith, director of the War Office archives in Vienna, located and mapped the major battlefields of antiquity. Employing military cartographic teams, they spent a decade visiting these battlefields and overseeing the production of color topographic maps for each site. After consulting the most famous European military historians of the day, Kromayer and Veith superimposed illustrations of troop dispositions and maneuvers on each map. Their Battle Atlas of Ancient Military History comprised 168 color contour maps of all major Greek and Roman battlefields from the Greco-Persian Wars (499–448 BC) through Octavian's campaign in Illyria (35–34 BC).

The atlas was published between 1922 and 1928 as several individual folios. Due to the expense and time required to publish the work, only a small number of complete sets found their way into the hands of scholars or libraries. The devastation of World War II destroyed many of these copies, and in 2008 only 28 complete copies remained, most secured in rare book rooms and not permitted to circulate. This year the Canadian Defence Academy in Kingston, Ontario, will republish one of the last complete atlases remaining in private hands and make it available to scholarly and military libraries in Canada and Europe. With the republication of Kromayer and Veith's work, military historians will be able to travel back in time and examine the blood-soaked ground of antiquity.

For further reading, Richard Gabriel recommends: The Ancient Historians, by Michael Grant, and The Roman Historians, by Ronald Mellor.

Writers of ancient texts dealing with military history fall into three categories:

1. Those with no military experience who wrote years after the events.
2. Those with some military experience who wrote years after the events.
3. Those with military experience who participated in the events about which they wrote.

## Ancient Historians & the Wars They Covered

Xenophon c. 431–352 BC Greco-Persian Wars
Thucydides c. 460–395 BC Peloponnesian Wars
Herodotus c. 484–425 BC Greco-Persian Wars
Polybius c. 200–118 BC Punic Wars
Aeneas Tacticus 4th century BC Peloponnesian Wars
Sallust c. 86–35 BC Jugurthine War
Julius Caesar 100–44 BC Roman Wars
Livy 59 BC–AD 17 Punic Wars
Appian c. AD 95–165 Roman Wars
Arrian c. AD 87–145 Alexander's campaigns
Tacitus c. AD 56–117 Roman Wars
Josephus c. AD 37–100 Jewish War
Dio Cassius c. AD 150–235 Punic Wars

Greco-Persian Wars 499–448 BC
Peloponnesian Wars 460–404 BC
Punic Wars 264–146 BC
Macedonian Wars 215–148 BC
Campaigns of Alexander the Great 338–323 BC
Jugurthine War 112–105 BC
Gallic Wars 58–51 BC
Roman Civil Wars 49–30 BC
Jewish War AD 66–73

# Unlocking Mysteries of the Parthenon

## Efforts to restore the ancient temple of Athena are yielding new insights.

EVAN HADINGHAM

During the past 2,500 years, the Parthenon—the apotheosis of ancient Greek architecture—has been rocked by earthquakes, set on fire, shattered by exploding gunpowder, looted for its stunning sculptures and defaced by misguided preservation efforts. Amazingly, the ancient Athenians built the Parthenon in just eight or nine years. Repairing it is taking a bit longer.

A restoration project funded by the Greek government and the European Union is now entering its 33rd year, as archaeologists, architects, civil engineers and craftsmen strive not simply to imitate the workmanship of the ancient Greeks but to re-create it. They have had to become forensic architects, reconstructing long-lost techniques to answer questions that archaeologists and classical scholars have debated for centuries. How did the Athenians construct their mighty temple, an icon of Western civilization, in less than a decade—apparently without an overall building plan? How did they manage to incorporate subtle visual elements into the Parthenon's layout and achieve such faultless proportions and balance? And how were the Parthenon's builders able to work at a level of precision (in some cases accurate to within a fraction of a millimeter) without the benefit of modern tools? "We're not as good as they were," Lena Lambrinou, an architect on the restoration project, observes with a sigh.

If the Parthenon represents "the supreme effort of genius in pursuit of beauty," as the 19th-century French engineer and architectural historian Auguste Choisy declared, at the moment it looks more like a construction site. Ancient masonry hides behind thickets of scaffolding, planks and steel poles. Miniature rail tracks connect sheds that house lathes, marble cutters and other power equipment. In the Parthenon's innermost sanctuary, once the home of a massive ivory-and-gold statue of Athena, a gigantic collapsible crane turns on a concrete platform.

Though heavy equipment dominated the hilltop, I also found restorers working with the delicacy of diamond cutters. In one shed, I watched a mason toiling on a fresh block of marble. He was one of some 70 craftsmen recruited for the project from Greece's sole remaining traditional marble school, located on the island of Tinos. His technique was exacting. To make the new block exactly match an old, broken one, the mason used a simple pointing device—the three-dimensional equivalent of a pantograph, which is a drafting instrument for precisely copying a sketch or blueprint—to mark and transfer every bump and hollow from the ancient stone to its counterpart surface on the fresh block. On some of the largest Parthenon blocks, which exceed ten tons, the masons use a mechanized version of the pointing device, but repairing a single block can still take more than three months. The ancient workers were no less painstaking; in many cases, the joints between the blocks are all but invisible, even under a magnifying glass.

The Parthenon was part of an ambitious building campaign on the Acropolis that began around 450 B.C. A generation before, the Athenians, as part of an alliance of Greek city-states, had led heroic victories against Persian invaders. This alliance would evolve into a de facto empire under Athenian rule, and some 150 to 200 cities across the Aegean began paying Athens huge sums of what amounted to protection money. Basking in glory, the Athenians planned their new temple complex on a lavish, unprecedented scale—with the Parthenon as the centerpiece. Surviving fragments of the financial accounts, which were inscribed in stone for public scrutiny, have prompted estimates of the construction budget that range from around 340 to 800 silver talents—a considerable sum in an age when a single talent could pay a month's wages for 170 oarsmen on a Greek warship. The Parthenon's base was 23,028 square feet (about half the size of a football field) and its 46 outer columns were some 34 feet high. A 525-foot frieze wrapped around the top of the exterior wall of the building's inner chamber. Several scholars have argued that the frieze shows a procession related to the quadrennial Great Panathenaia, or the festival "of all the Athenians." By incorporating this scene of civic celebration, the scholars suggest, the Parthenon served not merely as an imperial propaganda statement but also as an expression of Athens' burgeoning democracy—the will of the citizens who had voted to fund this exceptional monument.

When the current restoration effort began in 1975, backed by $23 million from the Greek government, the project's directors believed they could finish in ten years. But unforeseen problems arose as soon as workers started disassembling the temples. For example, the ancient Greek builders had secured the marble blocks together with iron clamps fitted in carefully carved grooves. They then poured molten lead over the joints to cushion them from seismic shocks and protect the clamps from corrosion. But when a Greek architect, Nikolas Balanos, launched an enthusiastic campaign of restorations in 1898, he installed crude iron clamps, indiscriminately fastening one block to another and neglecting to add the lead coating. Rain soon began to play havoc with the new clamps, swelling the iron and cracking the marble. Less than a century later, it was clear that parts of the Parthenon were in imminent danger of collapse.

Until September 2005, the restoration's coordinator was Manolis Korres, associate professor of architecture at the National Technical University of Athens and a leading Parthenon scholar. He has spent decades poring over every detail of the temple's construction. In a set of vivid drawings, he depicted how the ancient builders extracted some 100,000 tons of marble from a quarry 11 miles northeast of central Athens, roughly shaped the blocks, then transported them on wagons and finally hauled them up the steep slopes of the Acropolis. Yet all that grueling labor, Korres contends, was dwarfed by the time and energy lavished on fine-tuning the temple's finished appearance. Carving the long vertical grooves, or flutes, that run down each of the Parthenon's main columns was probably as costly as all the quarrying, hauling and assembly combined.

Today's restorers have been replacing damaged column segments with fresh marble. To speed up the job, engineers built a flute-carving machine. The device, however, is not precise enough for the final detailing, which must be done by hand. This smoothing of the flutes calls for an expert eye and a sensitive touch. To get the elliptical profile of the flute just right, a mason looks at the shadow cast inside the groove, then chips and rubs the stone until the outline of the shadow is a perfectly even and regular curve.

The ancients spent a lot of time on another finishing touch. After the Parthenon's exposed marble surfaces had been smoothed and polished, they added a final, subtle texture—a stippling pattern—that Korres says dulled the shine on the marble and masked its flaws. With hundreds of thousands of chisel blows, they executed this pattern in precisely ordered rows covering the base, floors, columns and most other surfaces. "This was surely one of the most demanding tasks," Korres says. "It may have taken as much as a quarter of the total construction time expended on the monument."

With such fanatical attention to detail, how could the Parthenon's architects have finished the job in a mere eight or nine years, ending somewhere between 438 and 437 B.C.? (The dates come from the inscribed financial accounts.) One key factor may have been naval technology. Since the Athenians were the greatest naval power in the Aegean, they likely had unrivaled mastery of ropes, pulleys and wooden cranes. Such equipment would have been essential for hauling and lifting marble blocks.

Another, counterintuitive possibility is that ancient hand tools were superior to their modern counterparts. After analyzing marks left on the marble surfaces, Korres is convinced that centuries of metallurgical experimentation enabled the ancient Athenians to create chisels and axes that were sharper and more durable than those available today. (The idea is not unprecedented. Modern metallurgists have only recently figured out the secrets of the traditional samurai sword, which Japanese swordsmiths endowed with unrivaled sharpness and strength by regulating the amount of carbon in the steel and the temperature during forging and cooling.) Korres concludes that the ancient masons, with their superior tools, could carve marble at more than double the rate of speed of today's craftsmen. And the Parthenon's original laborers had the benefit of experience, drawing on a century and a half of temple-building know-how.

Moreover, the restoration team has confronted problems that their ancient Greek counterparts could never have contemplated. During the Great Turkish War in the late 17th century—when the Ottoman Empire was battling several European countries—Greece was an occupied nation. The Turks turned the Parthenon into an ammunition dump. During a Venetian attack on Athens in 1687, a cannonball set off the Turkish munitions, blowing apart the long walls of the Parthenon's inner chamber. More than 700 blocks from those walls—eroded over time—now lay strewn around the Acropolis. For five years, beginning in 1997, Cathy Paraschi, a Greek-American architect on the restoration project, struggled to fit the pieces together, hunting for clues such as the shape and depth of the cuttings in the blocks that once held the ancient clamps. Eventually, she abandoned her computer database, which proved inadequate for capturing the full complexity of the puzzle. "Some days were exhilarating," she told me, "when we finally got one piece to fit another. Other days I felt like jumping off the Acropolis." In the end, she and her co-workers managed to identify the original positions of some 500 of the blocks.

Looming over each restoration challenge is the delicate question of how far to go. Every time the workers dismantle one of Balanos' crude fixes, it is a reminder of how destructive an overzealous restorer can be. As the director of the Acropolis Restoration Project, Maria Ioannidou, explains, "we've adopted an approach of trying to restore the maximum amount of ancient masonry while applying the minimum amount of new material." That means using clamps and rods made of titanium—which won't corrode and crack the marble—and soluble white cement, so that repairs can be easily undone should future generations of restorers discover a better way.

There have been some bravura feats of engineering. The 1687 explosion had knocked one of the massive columns out of position and badly damaged its bottom segment. A serious earthquake in 1981 damaged it further, and the entire column appeared at risk of toppling. The obvious procedure was to dismantle the column, one segment after another, and replace the crumbling section. Korres, hoping to avoid "even the smallest departure from the column's perfection and authenticity of construction," designed a metal collar that exerts precisely controlled forces to grasp a column securely without harming the stone. In the early 1990s, after the careful removal of the overhead blocks and lintels, the collar was suspended by turnbuckles (adjustable connectors) inside a mounted, rectangular steel frame. By tightening the turnbuckles, the team raised the 55-ton column less than an inch. They then removed the bottom segment—which they repaired with fresh marble to an accuracy of one-twentieth of a millimeter—and slid it back into position. Finally, they lowered the rest of the column into place on top of the repaired segment. "It was a bold decision to do it this way," Korres says. "But we were young and daring then."

Perhaps none of the Parthenon's mysteries stirs more debate than the gentle curves and inclinations engineered throughout much of its design. There is hardly a straight line to be found in the temple. Experts argue over whether these refinements were added to counter optical illusions. The eye can be tricked, for instance, into seeing an unsightly sag in flat floors built under a perched roof like the Parthenon's. Possibly to correct this effect, the Athenians laid out the Parthenon's base so that the 228-by-101-foot floor bulges slightly toward the middle, curving gradually upward between 4 and 4 1/2 inches on its left and right sides, and 2 1/2 inches on its front and back. One theory holds that this slight upward bulge was built simply to drain rainwater away from the temple's interior. But that fails to explain why the same curving profile is repeated not only in the floor but in the entablature above the columns and in the (invisible) buried foundations. This graceful curve was clearly fundamental to the overall appearance and planning of the Parthenon.

And then there are the columns, which the Athenians built so that they bulged slightly outward at the center. This swelling was termed entasis, or tension, by Greek writers, perhaps because it makes the columns seem as if they are clenching, like a human muscle, under the weight of their load. Again, some scholars have long speculated that this design might compensate for another trick of the eye, since a row of tall, perfectly straight-sided pillars can appear thinner at the middle than at the ends.

No matter the motivation for these refinements, many early scholars assumed that crafting such visual elements imposed tremendous extra demands on the Parthenon's architects and masons. (One wrote of the "terrifying complications" involved.) No architectural manuals survive from the Classical Greek era, but today's experts suspect the temple builders could add curves and inclined angles with a few relatively simple surveying tricks. "If you're building without mortar, every block . . . must be trimmed by hand," notes Oxford University archaeologist Jim Coulton. "Although tilts and curvatures would require careful supervision by the architect, they don't add a lot to the workload."

Still, how could each column segment be measured so that all would fit together in a single, smoothly curving profile? The likely answer was found not in Athens but nearly 200 miles away in southwestern Turkey. In the town of Didyma rises one of the most impressive relics of the ancient world, the Temple of Apollo. Three of its 120 colossal columns still stand, each nearly twice the height of the Parthenon's. The wealthy trading city of Miletus commissioned the temple in the age of Alexander the Great, around 150 years after the Parthenon's completion. The gigantic ruins testify to a project of grandiose ambition: it was never finished despite 600 years of construction efforts. But thanks to its unfinished state, crucial evidence was preserved on temple walls that had not yet undergone their final polishing.

A few years after the Parthenon restoration began, University of Pennsylvania scholar Lothar Haselberger was on a field trip exploring the Temple of Apollo's innermost sanctuary. He noticed what seemed to be patterns of faint scratches on the marble walls. In the blinding morning sunlight the scratches are all but invisible, as I discovered to my initial frustration when I searched for them. After the sun had swung around and began grazing the surface, however, a delicate web of finely engraved lines started to emerge. Haselberger recalls, "All of a sudden I spotted a series of circles that corresponded precisely to the shape of a column base, the very one at the front of the temple." He realized he had discovered the ancient equivalent of an architect's blueprint.

Then, just above the outline of the column base, Haselberger noticed a pattern of horizontal lines with a sweeping curve inscribed along one side. Could this be related to entasis, also evident in the towering Didyma columns? After carefully plotting the pattern, the answer became clear: it was a profile view of a column with the vertical dimension—the height of the column—reduced by a factor of 16. This scale drawing must have been a key reference for the masons as they carved out one column segment after another. By measuring along the horizontal lines to the edge of the curve, they would know exactly how wide each segment would have to be to create the smooth, bulging profile. Manolis Korres believes that the ancient Athenians probably relied on a carved scale drawing similar to the one at Didyma in building the columns of the Parthenon.

Haselberger also traced a labyrinth of faint scratches covering most of the temple's unfinished surfaces. The lines proved to be reference drawings for everything from the very slight inward lean of the walls to details of the lintel structure supported by the columns. There were even floor plans, drafted conveniently right on the floor. As the temple's stepped platform rose, each floor plan was copied from one layer to the next. On the topmost floor, the builders marked out the positions of columns, walls and doorways.

The discoveries at Didyma suggest that the temple builders operated on a "plan-as-you-go" basis. "Clearly, a lot of advance planning went into a building like the Parthenon," Coulton says. "But it wasn't planning in the sense that we'd recognize today. There's no evidence they relied on a single set of plans and elevations drawn to scale as a modern architect would."

Still, the Parthenon remains something of a miracle. The builders were steered by tradition, yet free to experiment. They worked to extreme precision, yet the final result was anything but rigid. A commanding building, with supple and fluid lines, emerged from a blend of improvised solutions.

But the miracle was short-lived. Only seven years after the construction of the Parthenon was completed, war broke out with Sparta. Within a generation, Athens suffered a humiliating defeat and a devastating plague. The story of the Parthenon resembles an ancient Greek tragedy, in which an exceptional figure suffers a devastating reversal of fortune. And from Korres' perspective, that calamity is all the more reason to restore the greatest remnant of Athens' golden age. "We wanted to preserve the beauty of what has survived these past 2,500 years," he says. "A reminder of man's power to create, as well as to destroy."

---

**Evan Hadingham** is senior science editor of PBS's *NOVA* series. The *NOVA* program "Secrets of the Parthenon" airs January 29, 2008.

## *Article 11*

# Outfoxed and Outfought

### Why Darius' superior Persian army and navy lost to the Athenians at Marathon.

Jason K. Foster

On the morning of September 17, 490 BC, some 10,000 Greeks stood assembled on the plain of Marathon, preparing to fight to the last man. Behind them lay everything they held dear: their city, their homes, their families. In front of the outnumbered Greeks stood the assembled forces of the Persian empire, a seemingly invincible army with revenge, pillage and plunder on its mind.

The Athenians' feelings are best expressed by Aeschylus, who fought in the Persian wars, in his tragic play The Persians: "On, sons of the Hellenes! Fight for the freedom of your country! Fight for the freedom of your children and of your wives, for the gods of your fathers and for the sepulchers of your ancestors! All are now staked upon the strife!"

The two sides faced each another directly, waiting for the fight to start. The Athenians stalled for days, anticipating reinforcements promised by Sparta. But they knew they could not wait for long. The Persians, expecting as easy a victory as they had won against enemies so many times before, were in no hurry.

The Greeks, knowing the time for battle had come, began to move forward. Ostensibly, they advanced with focus and purpose, but beneath this firm veneer, as they looked on a vastly larger enemy—at least twice their number—many must have been fearful of what was to come. The Persian archers sat with their bows drawn, ready to loose a barrage of arrows that would send fear and confusion through the Greek ranks.

"The Athenians advanced at a run towards the enemy, not less than a mile away," recounted the historian Herodotus. "The Persians, seeing the attack developed at the double, prepared to meet it, thinking it suicidal madness for the Athenians to risk an assault with so small a force—rushing in with no support from either cavalry or archers."

Had the Persian archers been allowed to loose their bows, the battle might have ended before it had truly begun. Fighting their doubts and fears, the Athenians seized the initiative and rushed the Persians. Confronted by such a bold move and realizing their infantry would be pressed into action sooner than expected must have shaken Persian confidence.

The two Athenian commanders, Callimachus and Miltiades (the latter having fought in the Persian army himself), used their knowledge of Persian battle tactics to turn the tide further in their favor. As the clatter of spears, swords and shields echoed through the valley, the Greeks had ensured that their best hoplites (heavily armed infantry) were on the flanks and that their ranks were thinned in the center. Persian battle doctrine dictated that their best troops, true Persians, fought in the center, while conscripts, pressed into service from tribute states, fought on the flanks. The Persian elite forces surged into the center of the fray, easily gaining the ascendancy. But this time it was a fatal mistake. The Persian conscripts whom the Hellenic hoplites faced on the flanks quickly broke into flight. The Greeks then made another crucial decision: Instead of pursuing their fleeing foes, they turned inward to aid their countrymen fighting in the center of the battle.

By then, the Persians were in a state of utter confusion. Their tactics had failed, their cavalry was absent and their archers were useless. Their more heavily armed and armored opponents, who could sense that victory was close, were attacking them from three sides and pushing them into the sea. The Persians fled back to their ships. Many of the Athenians, buoyed by their success, dragged several of the Persian vessels to shore, slaughtering those on board.

When the day was over, the Greeks had won one of history's most famous victories, claiming to have killed about 6,400 Persians for the loss of only 192 Athenians. The Spartans eventually arrived, but only after the battle was long over. To assuage their disbelief in the Athenians' victory, they toured the battlefield. To their amazement, they found the claim of victory was indeed true. The Athenians had defeated the most powerful empire in the Western world.

Around the 5th century BC, the Persians under Cyrus the Great had rapidly expanded their domain. By the time of Darius I, the Persian empire covered most of southwest Asia and Asia Minor, reaching as far as the easternmost boundaries of Europe. The Persians demanded tribute and respect from all they dominated. The Greek cities in Asia Minor eventually decided to throw off the Persian yoke. Through those revolts, the assistance of the Athenians and the ensuing Battle of Marathon, the wheels had been set in motion to end Persian domination.

How did this sequence of events come to pass? From the time he ascended the throne, Darius, like all the kings before him, needed to conquer and add to the empire that his forebears had passed to him, to establish his worth as a ruler and maintain control. Establishing and retaining authority over such a vast dominion required thousands upon thousands of troops. To pay for the soldiery and to maintain the grandeur of the Persian capital, Persepolis (which Darius built to demonstrate his greatness), he needed more than the tribute from subjugated states. He needed to conquer more cities and territory to expand his treasury.

To the east of ancient Persia (modern-day Iran and Iraq) lay India and the Orient; expansion there held unknown dangers. To take this route, Darius would risk overextending his empire. To the west lay the inhospitable Libyan desert. To the north were the barbarian lands of the Scythians. Expansion into Europe seemed the most promising option, but the scattered city-states of Greece constituted a major roadblock to Darius' ambitions.

Before he could move on Greece, Darius had to achieve complete submission within his existing territories, and an empire of Persia's size was impossible to control centrally. Therefore, the Persians had established local governors or satraps, whose main role was to oversee the day-to-day functioning of their provinces and to ensure that all tribute was collected and sent to the capital. Many of these satraps ruled as tyrants. Understandably, the Greek cities east of the Aegean Sea would become restless and desire change when they cast a glance westward at the seeds of democratic society planted in Athens.

Dissent first began to appear on the island of Naxos, which revolted in 502 BC. The Naxians appealed to the despot of the Ionian city of Miletos, Aristagoras, for assistance. He agreed, meaning to take control of the island once the revolt had been crushed. For his plan to succeed, he enlisted the aid of Artaphernes, Darius' brother and the satrap of Lydia (modern-day Turkey). Aristagoras' tangled web fell apart when the plot against the Naxians failed. Owing the Persian emperor and his brother money and promised conquests, Aristagoras had no option but to incite his own people to revolt.

The revolt of Miletos led other cities to follow suit. The Ionian Greeks had also maintained strong trade and cultural ties with their kin on mainland Greece. Forced to pay tribute to a distant king, feeling the tyrannical push of the Persian governors and encouraged by the Athenians, many of these city-states decided to revolt. Athens sent 20 triremes (oar-propelled warships) to Ephesus. Their hoplites and the citizens of Miletos marched on the Lydian capital of Sardis and sacked it. On hearing of this in Persepolis, Darius was infuriated; according to legend, he instructed one of his servants to remind him three times daily of this Athenian outrage so he would never forget it.

The revolts in Ionia and an excuse to wreak vengeance on Athens gave Darius the perfect pretext to implement his plans of expansion in Europe. When he looked toward mainland Greece, he must have seen a disjointed conglomeration of city-states that bickered and fought among themselves. It must have seemed unlikely that such cities would form any lasting alliances and be capable of repelling a powerful foe. As the ruler with the largest army in the world, and with the success of his predecessors on which to build, Darius must have thought that one way or another victory would be assured.

In 492 BC, Darius gave Mardonius, his satrap in Thrace (northern Greece), command of 600 ships that sailed across the Hellespont (the Dardanelles) and along the coast. As it rounded Mount Athos, however, the fleet was destroyed by a freak storm, an event that would prove to have great significance. The Greeks took it as an encouraging omen that the gods must surely be on their side. Herodotus claims—with questionable accuracy—that the storm destroyed 300 ships and killed 20,000 men.

Two years later, Darius sent another 600 ships in a second attempt. Expecting little resistance, he sent emissaries to the cities of Greece asking for their submission and demanding offerings of earth and water. Most cities in the north and in Macedonia submitted to his demands. But war became inevitable when the Athenians refused, and the Spartans went even further and killed the Persian envoy.

A second Persian expedition was launched under the command of Datis and Darius' nephew, Artaphernes. As they moved across the Aegean, they subdued many of the island cities such as Naxos and Delos. Eventually they reached Eritrea, a large island off the Attic coast, and made their way to Marathon. Herodotus explains why the Persians chose to land at Marathon: "The part of Attic territory nearest Eritria—and also the best ground for cavalry to maneuver in—was at Marathon. To Marathon, therefore, Hippias directed the invading army, and the Athenians, as soon as the news arrived, hurried to meet it."

Marathon was also chosen to draw the Athenians away from Athens. While the hoplites were engaged on the field, the Persians planned to send their ships around the coast and easily capture the undefended city. The Persian plan was twofold: They knew that if the Athenian army was defeated outside of Athens, the city's civilian inhabitants would have no choice but to submit.

Almost immediately after hearing the news of the Persian landing, the Athenians sent a runner named Pheidippides to Sparta to ask for their assistance. The Spartans promised to send aid, but with a major qualification: No help would be forthcoming until the Carneia (a religious festival) was over. The Spartan refusal to commit troops before then left the Athenians with three choices: march out and meet the Persians at Marathon; defend the pass at Pallini; or stay in the city and defend its walls.

The Athenians chose Marathon. There were several reasons for this. The food supplies they would need to survive a protracted siege came from the surrounding countryside of Attica, which could easily be cut off by the encamped Persian army. The soon-to-be-vaunted Athenian navy was at that time little more than a flotilla and had no chance of defeating the Persian fleet. If the Persians were able to blockade both the land and sea, Athens could not withstand a sustained siege. The pass at Pallini was high in the mountains, but the Persians had sufficient forces to continue to attack pass defenders until Pallini fell.

Confronting the Persians at Marathon offered the Greeks several tactical possibilities. As stated by Herodotus, the geography of the plain of Marathon was significant in the Persian decision-making. Measuring approximately 10 miles long and three miles wide, it was flanked by boggy marshlands. A large, flat plain, it was perfect for the use of the Persians' main strike weapon: cavalry.

When the Athenians reached Marathon, they found the Persians camped along the coast. Obviously, the Greeks needed to take the high ground. Both sides sat encamped for nine days, each waiting for the other to make the first move. The Persians believed that the longer they stayed, the greater the fear that would rattle their opponents.

The outnumbered Athenians and their Plataean allies played for time in hopes that the Spartan hoplites would join them—not only to strengthen their numbers but because Spartan military renown stretched all the way to Persepolis, and a Spartan presence would surely dent Persian confidence. On the other hand, the longer the Persians stayed, the more cities would submit to them, lowering the confidence of the Athenian troops.

A meeting was held in the Greek camp to resolve the issue. The 10 Athenian generals (each of the original tribes that had first formed Athens had an elected general) voted, with five in favor of immediate battle and five voting to wait for the Spartans' arrival. According to Herodotus, it was the influence of Miltiades that swayed the decision. "With you it rests, Callimachus," he allegedly said, "either to lead Athens to slavery or, by securing her freedom, to leave behind to all future generations a memory far beyond even those who made Athens a democracy. For never since the time the Athenians became a people were they in so great a danger than now." Whether Miltiades was as influential as Herodotus made him out to be is uncertain; however, Callimachus voted in favor of starting the battle. Herodotus also stated that while each general normally took a daily turn in overall command, many of the lesser generals handed their turn over to Miltiades.

With approximately 1,000 Plataeans bolstering the Athenian ranks, the Hellenic forces mustered some 10,000 hoplites. The Persians may have numbered as high as 48,000. Familiar with the tactics and strengths of their enemy, the Greeks knew the Persian cavalry had to be taken out of the calculations. The Persians could not use the cavalry on one side because of the marshland. Nor could they use it on the opposite flank, as the Athenians had buried large stakes in the ground. It seems likely that the Persians, even without the use of either flank, would have used their premier weapon, but for whatever reason, the Persian cavalry was away from the battlefield. Miltiades may well have learned of the Persian cavalry's absence and then decided it was time to attack.

The absence of Persian cavalry is one of the reasons for the Greek victory. The second is that the Persians were completely unprepared for and unable to adapt to the Greeks' tactics. Persian battle tactics that previously had served them well entailed stationing their archers at the front to fire volley after volley of arrows into the enemy ranks, wreaking havoc and instilling fear. Once that objective was achieved, Persian infantry would move in to slaughter the confused opposition, with cavalry used only to complete the task when the enemy was routed.

The Greeks held an advantage at Marathon in the equipment of their infantry. An Athenian hoplite carried a heavy, 9-foot spear, wore a solid breastplate and carried an almost body-length shield. The Persian infantryman, in contrast, wore little more than robes and carried a shorter sword and a wicker or cane shield. Therefore, close-quarter combat favored the Athenians. The Persian disadvantage was exacerbated by the Greek use of the phalanx formation—an eight-hoplite by eight-hoplite square. The hoplites at the from would interlock their shields, as would the men to the side, forming an almost impenetrable barrier. Because of their lesser numbers, the Greeks had to thin their formation out, but even that would eventually further serve their purpose.

Although they had won a great victory, the Athenians knew the Persian threat had not passed, and they quickly marched back to prepare the defense of Athens from the attack they were certain would come. In an amazing feat of strength and endurance, they marched at double time directly from the battlefield and managed to reach the city before the Persian ships arrived.

With time of the essence, the Athenians dispatched Pheidippides to inform Athens' populace of their victory before the troops arrived. The tale goes that after running the 26 miles from Marathon to Athens, Pheidippides exclaimed: "Rejoice! We conquer!" then died from exhaustion. Whether true or not, that is the source of the modern-day marathon race; the distance of the modern race reflects the distance Pheidippides ran.

Even though the future battles of Salamis and Plataea were fought against a greater Persian threat, had Marathon ended in defeat, those later battles would never have occurred. Themistocles, who fought at Marathon, saw that Athens had been lucky the first time, and had the Persians conducted their campaign differently, the outcome might well have been different. Hence, soon after Marathon he successfully petitioned to have Athens build a stronger navy, which led to its success at Salamis.

Marathon smashed the myth of Persian invincibility, an achievement that lent a critical measure of confidence to the Greeks who fought the Persians again at Salamis and Plataea. It meant that many of the same commanders who served at Marathon were at the later battles and had knowledge of the Persian mind, and in the longer term, it would lead Alexander the Great on his conquest of Asia and the eventual decline and downfall of the Persian empire.

While most credit the second installment of the Persian wars with the birth of the Athenian renaissance, one could argue that Marathon was the catalyst for, and much of the reason behind, the Athenians' belief that they were on par with the Spartans—which allowed them to flourish. Had Marathon been a defeat and Athens annihilated, the Western democracy, culture, art and philosophy that developed from this period in history might have been lost, and the Western world today could be very different.

**Jason K. Foster** is a London-based teacher and historian specializing in ancient Rome, Greece and Egypt.

For further reading, he recommends: *The Histories,* by Herodotus; and *Plutarch's Rise and Fall of Athens.*

# Mighty Macedonian

## *Alexander the Great*

RICHARD COVINGTON

Taking measured steps around a lush garden terrace in ancient Egypt, Anthony Hopkins as the Macedonian general Ptolemy dictates his memoirs of helping Alexander the Great conquer the world. While he strolls beneath the palm trees of the ancient library in Alexandria—in reality, a sprawling movie set at Shepperton Studios outside London—the aged ruler of Egypt delivers a bombshell. "We killed him," Ptolemy says.

Literally? Or metaphorically? With Oliver Stone writing and directing, you never know for sure, even though the notion that Alexander was poisoned by his generals is "as dead as doornails," says Robin Lane Fox, a British biographer of Alexander who worked as a consultant on the movie. Stone, after all, defended the multiple-gunmen conspiracy theory of the Kennedy assassination in his 1991 movie, *JFK.*

In the library scene, Ptolemy, portrayed by Hopkins as a world-weary old soldier, says that if Alexander's men didn't literally poison his body, their refusal to follow him deeper into India surely poisoned his spirit. "I never believed in his dream," he says. "The dreamers exhaust us."

True enough, no conqueror ever dreamed so exhaustively as Alexander the Great. In the fourth century B.C., the Macedonian warrior-king attacked the Persian Empire, the most powerful realm in the world, with almost 50,000 soldiers—then ranged across three continents for more than a decade, subduing tens of millions of people. By the time Alexander died in June 323 B.C., six weeks shy of his 33rd birthday, his empire stretched from the Balkans to the Himalayas—an unprecedented kingdom that spanned what is now Greece, Turkey, Lebanon, Syria, Jordan, Israel, Egypt, Iraq, Kuwait, Iran, Afghanistan, Pakistan and parts of India, Turkmenistan, Uzbekistan and Tajikistan.

Despite his imperialist accomplishments, Alexander has always seemed a melancholy figure, possessed by what the ancient Greeks called *pothos,* a passionate yearning. Once, when court philosopher Anaxarchus described the infinite number of worlds in the universe to him, Alexander broke down crying. "There are so many worlds," he lamented, "and I have not yet conquered even one."

It was this pothos, as much as his military genius, that would make him a romantic hero—to the 17th-century English poet John Dryden, to Sigmund Freud, to world leaders from Julius Caesar and Napoleon to Dwight David Eisenhower. Others, such as St. Augustine and Dante, reviled him as a murdering, plundering bandit. Frank Holt, an Alexander authority at the University of Houston, estimates that more than 2,000 books and articles have been written about him in the past 40 years.

Yet the truth about Alexander remains elusive. For one thing, as Cambridge University's Paul Cartledge (author of *Alexander the Great: The Hunt for a New Past*) points out, none of his actual words was recorded verbatim. Although there were several written eyewitness accounts of Alexander's campaigns, they survive only as fragments written down centuries later by sympathetic interpreters. Other writers suppressed or distorted events to make him look heroic or demonic, depending on their agendas.

Historians' verdicts vary. Some view Alexander as a charismatic, visionary leader intent on constructing a fusion of East and West, while others condemn him as a cruel and unstable megalomaniac, an ancient Stalin or Hitler who cared less about unifying mankind than consolidating control over as much territory as he could grab. A third camp credits Alexander with bringing Western notions of civilization to the East, using methods that seem brutal by today's standards but were acceptable in their time. Perhaps historians are divided because the man himself was divided—swinging wildly from blind wrath to acts of selfless generosity.

Historical novelists like Mary Renault and Valerio Manfredi have eagerly mined the Alexander legend, but few filmmakers have tackled the subject. Director Robert Rossen's 1956 *Alexander the Great,* with Richard Burton, was a heavy-handed dud. Since the success of *Gladiator* in 2000, however, "swords-and-sandals" epics—last in vogue with *Ben-Hur* in 1959 and *Spartacus* in 1960—are back, and at least three Alexander films are in the works—by Baz Luhrmann (director of *Strictly Ballroom* and *Moulin Rouge*), due out next year; by Ilya Salkind (producer of *Superman*); and by Stone, whose $150 million juggernaut with Colin Farrell in the title role is due to open across the country this month.

"Basically, I wanted to do the film as an experiment," says Stone, "to see if Alexander's motivations hold up today." Taking a break from editing the movie at a studio west of Paris in June, the director sounded more like a star-struck fan than notorious

Hollywood maverick. "He was the Sun God, the star of all time, Joe DiMaggio, Mickey Mantle rolled into one," Stone says. "Some historians put him down . . . in a class with Genghis Khan and Attila the Hun, but they miss the point. No tyrant ever gave back so much. His life was not about money for himself, but about his growing curiosity, engaging and fulfilling his intellect, his consciousness."

There's substantial agreement on one issue: Alexander's military prowess. "He would've made mincemeat of any Roman who came over the hill," says biographer Lane Fox.

"Julius Caesar would've gone straight back home as fast as his horse could carry him." And Napoleon? "Alexander would've wiped him out too. Napoleon only fought dodos."

Alexander personally spearheaded his attacks, suffering severe arrow, lance, sword and knife wounds. As Roman historian Arrian said of Alexander around A.D. 150, "The sheer pleasure of battle, as other pleasures are to other men, was irresistible." Once, when he found himself stranded without a ladder atop a fortress surrounding Multan in present-day Pakistan, he jumped straight down alone into the midst of the enemy, instead of leaping outside the walls to safety. Managing to fend off his attackers until help arrived, he received a nearly fatal arrow wound that may have punctured his lung. When his doctor insisted that officers hold him down to keep him from squirming, Alexander waved them away, sitting stoically as the surgeon sliced the deeply embedded barb out of his chest. "As a warrior and strategist," Lane Fox says, "no one compares to Alexander."

Born in July 356 B.C. in Pella, near the Aegean coast in then Macedonia (now Greece), Alexander was the only son of the ruthless King Philip II and the hot-tempered Olympias. (After Philip died, she killed Philip's last wife, Eurydice, and Eurydice's baby daughter, Europa.) At the time of Alexander's birth and right up until Philip's assassination 20 years later, Alexander's father was preoccupied with consolidating the Macedonian Empire through diplomacy, political marriage, intrigue and war—particularly against the rebellious Greeks to the south. Although Macedonians spoke Greek and regarded themselves as Greek, the Athenians, Thebans and citizens of other Greek city-states dismissed them as culturally inferior hicks.

According to Peter Green, professor emeritus of classics at the University of Texas at Austin, Olympias spoiled her son outrageously; he idolized her in return. The love-hate relationship that Alexander had with his father, says Green, was "an ambivalent blend of genuine admiration and underlying competitiveness." From his father, Alexander is believed to have inherited courage, quickness of decision and intellectual perceptiveness. His mother, who may have tried to turn their son against his father, gave him a will stronger than Philip's, as well as fervent religiosity.

When the prince was a young boy, he eyed a black stallion, Bucephalas, that neither the king nor anyone else could control. As the horse stymied rider after rider, Alexander noticed that he reared at the sight of his own shadow. When Alexander's turn came, he calmly stroked the animal, turned his head into the sun so that he could not see his shadow and galloped off in triumph. "My boy, you must find a kingdom big enough for your ambitions," Philip declared. "Macedonia is too small for you." Alexander rode Bucephalas until the war horse died in 326 B.C. fighting elephant-mounted brigades in present-day Pakistan.

During his early teens, Alexander was taught by Aristotle, who inspired the prince's lifelong interest in biology, medicine and zoology. Ultimately, Alexander broke ranks with his tutor on an issue that was to become critical for the future empire. Unlike Aristotle, who viewed non-Greeks as barbarians, the Macedonian Alexander was less prejudiced, and would come to rely on conquered Persians and other foreigners to play prominent roles governing his far-flung territory.

Alexander was a handsome youth with shoulder-length blond hair, prominent forehead, ruddy complexion and "a certain melting look in his eyes." Historical sources suggest Alexander was bisexual, an orientation that bore no stigma in his day. He had at least two male lovers—his childhood friend and fellow soldier Hephaestion, and the Persian eunuch Bagoas—and fathered a child with his Sogdian wife, Roxane, and perhaps one with his Persian mistress. Even so, he had an ambivalent attitude toward sex. "Sex and sleep alone make me conscious that I am mortal," he supposedly once remarked.

Raised to believe that he was descended from both the Greek heroes Achilles and Herakles, the young Alexander acquired a zealous reverence for the ancient Greek myths. He loved to recite passages from the plays of Euripides, and he slept with a dagger and a well-thumbed copy of the *Iliad* beneath his pillow during his campaigns.

In the year 336 B.C., as Philip entered an outdoor theater to preside over a wedding, he was fatally stabbed by a bodyguard named Pausanias. Although it was widely rumored that Olympias, recently rejected by the king in favor of a younger wife, colluded in the murder, Lane Fox says the idea that her son had a hand in the assassination is "a bit wild."

Nevertheless, Stone's film, playing with the son's possible Oedipal feelings for Olympias, keeps both of them on the hook. "Anybody who's a dramatist has to ask if Alexander and his mother had a role in Philip's death," the director counters with a conspiratorial grin. Unlike Oedipus, who did not know the man he killed was his father at the time of the murder, Alexander would have been fully aware of his crime's enormity.

Just 20 years old, Alexander seized the throne, summarily murdering or exiling a number of rivals. Within a year, he reasserted control over the recalcitrant cities and tribes that had frustrated Philip, expanding the boundaries of the Macedonian kingdom north to the Danube and west toward the Adriatic. When Thebes revolted, he slaughtered or sold into slavery some 30,000 citizens, then razed the city, except for temples and the house of the revered poet Pindar. After this example, Athens and the other Greek cities—with the stubborn exception of Sparta—pledged allegiance to the young king. Perhaps more important, they also promised him soldiers and financial support for an invasion of Persia.

In May 334 B.C., Alexander sailed his army three miles across the Hellespont (Dardanelles strait) in present-day Turkey, casting his spear into the sandy shore to dramatically claim all of Asia as his "spear-won prize," in the Roman historian Curtius' vivid first-century imagery.

After defeating an advance Persian force at the Granicus River 60 miles northeast of Troy and fighting all across Asia Minor, Alexander faced off against the Persian king Darius III at Issus in southern Turkey. Though sources disagree on the exact numbers, Alexander probably faced a larger force of Persians, across a narrow plain. Alexander's cavalry, backed by archers and by infantry wielding 16-foot-long pikes, smashed through the enemy in well-orchestrated charges. Alexander spurred Bucephalas headlong toward Darius, who spun his chariot around in retreat and ultimately made a successful getaway.

The conquest continued. Following a grinding, seven-month siege, Alexander captured the island fortress of Tyre, in present-day Lebanon; Egyptians, oppressed by the Persians, welcomed him as a liberator. Sailing down the Nile to the Mediterranean, the 24-year-old sovereign came across a former Persian fortress with a superb natural harbor that he chose as the site of his future Egyptian capital, the first of several Alexandrias he would establish as he swept east.

The young ruler still craved a clear-cut victory to lay claim to all of Persia. Darius, meanwhile, was conscripting a stupendous new army from the farthest reaches of his empire, gathering his forces in the Persian winter capital of Babylon. The Persian ruler (who hadn't taken Alexander seriously enough the first time they faced off) finally marched more than 200,000 men 275 miles north to the open plain at Gaugamela, where he deployed cavalry clad in chain mail, chariots equipped with scythe blades on their wheels, and mounted elephants.

With 47,000 men, Alexander was spectacularly outnumbered. When his senior generals advised him to attack at night to even the odds, he indignantly retorted, "I will not demean myself by stealing victory like a thief." The king slept late on the day of battle, coolly emerging with an all-or-nothing plan. He ordered one wing of his cavalry to charge Darius' far left flank, another to aim for the far right, leaving his own infantry vulnerable in the center. As Darius' mounted corps tore away in opposite directions to meet the Macedonian squadrons, Alexander spurred a wedge of riders straight into the heart of the Persian ranks, splitting them in two. The gamble worked. Within minutes, the battle turned into a debacle. The Persians sounded a retreat, and Darius again slipped away on horseback.

After Alexander occupied Babylon, he continued his triumphant march east to Persepolis, the ceremonial center of Persia. He marveled at the dazzling gilt, bronze and marble palace and the hundred-columned hall where kings reigned from a golden throne. Inside the treasury he seized 3,000 tons of gold and silver, among the richest hoards in history.

Alexander and his officers celebrated with a feast. The inebriated king grabbed a torch and set fire to the tapestries and beams of the massive palace. Other drunken revelers joined him, stoking the inferno to the accompaniment of flutes and singing. Within hours, Persia's hallowed shrine was a smoking ruin.

Darius ranged across the countryside in what is now northern Iran, trying to rebuild his devastated army. Alexander, in pursuit, caught up with him too late. Bessus, one of the monarch's own generals, had murdered Darius and proclaimed himself king. At about this time, Alexander was making a critical transformation, one that would later alienate his troops but lead to a dramatic cultural shift. Hoping to solidify control over his new territories, he adopted Persian dress and customs and invited former adversaries into his inner circle. To win the support of his new subjects, Alexander even ordered a royal burial in Persepolis for Darius. But "the sight of their young king parading in outlandish robes, and on intimate terms with the quacking, effeminate barbarian nobles he had so lately defeated, filled [his troops] with genuine disgust," Green writes in his biography *Alexander of Macedon, 356–323 B.C.*

When Alexander was informed that disgruntled soldiers were plotting to kill him, he arrested seven of the alleged conspirators, including Philotas, the son of Parmenio, a venerated general who had fought under both Philip and Alexander. Although the evidence against Philotas was weak, he and the others were stoned to death. Then, anticipating that Parmenio would seek revenge for his son's execution, Alexander had the 70-year-old commandant stabbed to death. The killings had a chilling effect on Alexander's men. "From now on, Alexander never trusted his troops," Green says. "The feeling was mutual."

But Alexander still thirsted for conquest. He led his unhappy men over the Hindu Kush, to capture Bessus and take control of his home province of Bactria in what is now northern Afghanistan. Crossing the 11,600-foot snow-bound passes in April, many of the soldiers suffered severe frostbite and snow blindness. Bessus and his Persian troops, caught off-guard by Alexander's risky offensive, retreated into Sogdiana (present-day Uzbekistan, Turkmenistan and Tajikistan). But Bessus' Sogdian allies, fearing Alexander's attack, handed him over. Alexander ordered Bessus' ears and nose cut off, then likely had him crucified.

In just five years, Alexander had toppled the mighty Persian Empire and expanded his empire eastward 2,500 miles. Yet he was far from content, and his control over his men was slipping. In the summer of 328 B.C., Alexander set up headquarters in Maracanda (now Samarkand in modern-day Uzbekistan). When he started boasting about his victories at yet another drunken banquet, Cleitus, a grizzled cavalry officer who had saved Alexander's life at the Granicus River, bluntly reminded him how much he owed his father and the Macedonian veterans. Incensed, Alexander accused Cleitus and other senior officers of cowardice. "Those who died defending you are the lucky ones," Cleitus roared back at him. "At least they never lived to see Macedonians thrashed with Median rods or kow-towing to Persians before they can have an audience with their own king!" Screaming that this was yet another plot against him, Alexander grabbed a spear and ran his beloved comrade through the chest, killing him instantly. Immediately, the king was possessed by remorse. Yanking the spear out of Cleitus' body, he tried to impale himself on it. After a few officers jerked it away from him, he shut himself up in his tent for days, grieving.

Eventually, Alexander rallied, prodding his multinational crew of Macedonian, Persian and Bactrian soldiers toward the next goal: India. En route, the 28-year-old became smitten with

Roxane, a princess captured in the siege of a Sogdian fortress and "the loveliest woman in Asia, after Darius's wife," according to Arrian, a second-century Greek biographer rarely given to exaggeration. Marrying for love in 327 B.C., the pragmatic Alexander also calculated that an alliance with a noble family from outer Persia would help legitimize his power.

Pushing farther east to the Hydaspes River (now the Jhelum River in Pakistan), the Macedonians faced off against the Indian king Porus at a crossing some 70 miles southeast of present-day Islamabad. Alexander's 50,000 troops vanquished a force of 35,000 soldiers and 200 mounted elephants, but his men proved no match for monsoon season. "It was pelting with rain, the men were terrified, there were snakes everywhere," says Lane Fox. "They were lost and did not feel they could go on any more."

Standing in front of the assembled ranks near the Hyphasis River, Coenus, a senior commander, did the unthinkable: he pleaded with Alexander to go home. Furious, the young king said that anyone who left would be considered a deserter, then stormed off to sulk in his tent for two days. But when Alexander's personal seer reported that the signs to continue east into India were unfavorable, the king used this excuse to save face and turn back to Macedonia. On hearing of Alexander's change of heart, the exhausted veterans erupted in cheers. Even in retreat, the contrarian Alexander scorned the known route home—back over the Hindu Kush to Babylon—in favor of leading his flotilla of 1,800 ships down the unfamiliar Jhelum, Chenab and Indus rivers to the Indian Ocean and hence west to the Persian Gulf.

It was far from smooth sailing. En route, hostile tribes put up fierce resistance—and were pitilessly exterminated. Cartledge views this trail of blood as one prolonged "fit of frustration at having been forced by his own troops to turn back." In July 325, nine months after setting sail, the Macedonians finally reached the Indian Ocean.

Still focused on building his empire, Alexander concocted an audacious scheme to revive ancient sea routes for transporting gold, spices, ivory and precious stones from India to the Middle East. The idea was that ships carrying food and supplies would sail up the coast of the Arabian Sea while Alexander led soldiers over a parallel inland route. The ships would drop off food for the army at prearranged intervals, while the soldiers in turn would supply the fleet with fresh water. If this land-sea relay made it to the Persian Gulf on a dry run, merchants could follow the same itinerary.

The scheme would prove to be one of Alexander's gravest mistakes, subjecting his men to what Lane Fox calls "the most hellish match that [he] could possibly have chosen." In the oppressive night—the only time the sprawling caravan could move—the temperature seldom dipped below 95 degrees. Worst of all, monsoon winds delayed the fleet after Alexander's departure; the navy and army never met up, forcing both to subsist on the limited food and water they had brought with them. Reportedly, by the end of the two-month march, 15,000 of Alexander's men, or nearly half of the corps accompanying him, had perished—more than all the men killed in battle. The fleet, in contrast, reached the Iranian coast almost intact.

Back in Kirman, Persia, Alexander did little to mend relations with his men. He executed 6 of 20 provincial governors, and deposed two more. Then, in what Cartledge describes as a "reign of terror," he executed 600 men from his own garrisons for rape and pillaging in his absence. At Susa, he commanded 90 of his officers to marry aristocratic Persian women to strengthen the political bonds between Macedonians and Persians.

Despite the growing tensions—and crises like the sudden death of his lover, the soldier Hephaestion—Alexander still "hunted, diced, played ball, joked and banqueted" with his men. At one of these banquets, Alexander downed his usual enormous quantity of wine, then collapsed with a fever. Twelve days later, on June 10, 323 B.C., he died, probably of malaria. Just before he expired, he was asked to name a successor. Alexander weakly answered that the empire should go "to the strongest," Arrian wrote. "I foresee a great funeral contest over me."

With Alexander gone, the empire was riven by dissent, with his commanders fighting over territory. Roxane and her son, Alexander IV, born six weeks after the king's death, were murdered by a distant relative when the boy was 12 or 13; so was the king's mother, Olympias. As Alexander's embalmed body was being transported to Macedonia in a magnificent chariot, Ptolemy hijacked it to Alexandria, where it would stay for six centuries. Lane Fox speculates that the coffin later disappeared, probably destroyed in riots in the third century A.D.

Although Alexander's empire splintered shortly after his death, Greek arts, science and culture continued to pervade Middle Eastern and Asian societies for centuries. In Egypt, Greek physicians taught the study of human anatomy. In Babylon, Greek physicists devised a technique to electroplate silver to copper. Greek city planning prevailed in the many towns the king had established and was widely adopted elsewhere. Greek myths and philosophy spread well beyond the former empire's borders.

Alexander's legacy has long been a matter of debate. Cleitarchus, a fourth-century B.C. historian from Alexandria, portrays the king as a cruel, paranoid alcoholic. Eratosthenes of Cyrene, a third-century B.C. scholar at the Alexandria library, suggests that Alexander's conquests opened the eyes of the Greeks to other civilizations. Plutarch ventures the opposite—that Alexander civilized Persians, Sogdians and others. Johannes Gustav Droysen, a 19th-century German historian, proposes that the Macedonian king wanted above all to unify the entire world. Yet the modern historian Brian Bosworth dismisses such idealism, comparing Alexander's Indian campaign to Cortez's genocidal war against the Aztecs and condemning the king as a cold-blooded imperialist.

Lane Fox says that "the fashion of the moment is to take a sour view of Alexander." But he adds: "You've still got to explain why so many people followed him with such devotion for so long."

"These days," says director Stone, a Vietnam veteran, "we have a strong antipathy for conquerors, but in Alexander's time, war was a way of life and soldiering a much more honorable profession."

As many historians conclude, it was his achievements as a commander on the field of battle that justify the name Alexander the Great. He was a military genius, and a hero to his men. He never asked them to do something he would not do himself, and he bore the wounds to prove it. He also shared his vast riches with his men. When he challenged his army to take the most difficult route, to do the impossible, they amazed themselves when they succeeded. At the Hyphasis River near Amritsar, when his soldiers pressured him to turn back, they may well have been too hasty. Alexander's promised land of India was nearly in their grasp.

Nowhere did Alexander articulate what was behind his all-consuming desire to master the world. To speculate that he was trying to surpass his father and win his mother's love, as some psychohistorians have done, is to take the easy way out. It may be, as Ptolemy wistfully concludes in the Stone film, that Alexander was blessed and cursed with an eternally unsatisfied longing, a pothos even he could not fathom. Perpetually racing the gods, his destiny remained exactly where it served him best—just out of reach.

---

Paris-based author **Richard Covington** last wrote for *Smithsonian* about Cambodia's Angkor temples in February 2004.

# Etruscan Women

## *Dignified, Charming, Literate and Free*

INGRID D. ROWLAND

Most travelers' tales from the ancient world have been told by men, so its not surprising that their yarns devote special attention to the local women they encounter. The most famous of all those ancient travelers, Homer's Odysseus, trooped off to Troy in pursuit of Helen of Sparta, lingering nine years on the Maltese island of Gozo with Calypso, touched down on the North African coast with the Lotus-Eaters, sailed past the Sirens of Sorrento en route to Circe's lair, popped out naked from behind a bush to approach Nausicaa of Corfu, and finally settled on the little island of Ithaca with his wife, Penelope—who still bests them all through her irresistible combination of integrity and intelligence.

Later sailors would have said, however, that Odysseus's 10-year itinerary left one huge gap: Homer makes only one reference to the Etruscans—the literate and sophisticated people who by the eighth century B.C.E. were inhabiting the region of central Italy bounded by the Arno and Tiber rivers and the Tyrrhenian Sea, a region corresponding to modern-day Tuscany. Moreover, in that one reference, Homer transforms the Etruscans into the seven-headed monster Scylla (her name means "the Bitch"), who snatches seven men from Odysseus's ship as it passes through the Straits of Messina.

The Athenian playwright Euripides, in his tragedy *Medea* (431 B.C.E.), was already claiming that Scylla stood in Homer's epic for the Etruscan pirates who jealously guarded access to the sea that still bears their name—the Greek word for "Etruscan" was "Tyrrhenian."

Perhaps only those monstrously fierce Etruscan pirates could have kept such an inveterate swain as Odysseus from working his charms on Etruscan women, those ravishing creatures who had already begun to captivate the Greeks of Homer's time. Perhaps we see something of their legendary allure in Circe, the witch of Monte Circeo (south of Rome), who serves Odysseus's men a potion that turns them into pigs before she hops happily into bed with the hero. Etruscan women's freedom of action, their appetite for wine and their loose morals were the talk of their Greek and, later, their Roman neighbors. In his *Histories,* the fourth-century B.C.E. Greek historian Theopompus of Chios could hardly contain his leering fascination:

> Sharing wives is an established Etruscan custom. Etruscan women take particular care of their bodies and exercise often, sometimes along with the men, and sometimes by themselves. It is not a disgrace for them to be seen naked. They do not share their couches with their husbands but with the other men who happen to be present, and they propose toasts to anyone they choose. They are expert drinkers and very attractive.

Theopompus's account, which goes on to discuss public displays of affection, spouse-swapping and boy toys, is almost certainly exaggerated. The men and women who recline together in the painted banquet scenes from Tarquinian tombs, in a set of famous sarcophagi from Cerveteri (one in the Louvre and two in Rome's Villa Giulia Museum), and on sculpted relief decorations from buildings at Murlo and Acquarossa seem overwhelmingly to be married couples, whether they are divine or mortal. Their conviviality comes nowhere near Roman standards of probity—a Roman general was never supposed to laugh. But look at the banquet scenes from the tombs at Tarquinia, for example, and you will see nothing like the ribald parties held by the Greeks, with courtesans and Ganymedes; if anything, they resemble lively family outings in modem Tuscany.

The images of banquets begin as early as the sixth century B.C.E., the probable date of the Cerveteri sarcophagi and the architectural ornaments from Murlo and Acquarossa. Wealthy women, their pale skin set off by flushed cheeks and deep red lips, flaunt big earrings and close-fitting rounded caps much like those favored by their contemporaries along the Ionian coast of Asia Minor. Their finely woven dresses crinkle like Venetian silk scarves, and their soft red shoes, with flashy pointed toes, seem only natural on the ancestors of a Tuscan shoemaker named Cuccio Cucci. Their names, when we have them, are as sonorous as they are peculiar: Tanchvil, Larthia, Thania. Tanchvil—with its root *evil,* or "gift" must mean something like "Dorothy" (Greek for "God's gift").

One sixth-century B.C.E. Tanchvil entered Roman legend as Tanaquil, the resourceful wife of Lucumo, the fifth king of

Rome. As the Roman historian Livy tells the story, Lucumo, despite his thoroughly Etruscan name (*lauchme* means "chief"), was in fact the son of a Demaratus of Corinth, one of many Greek men who seem to have settled down along the shores of the Tynhenian Sea with an Etruscan wife. (The epitaph of another Etruscanized Greek, Larth Hipucrate, is still preserved in Lucumo's home town of Tarquinia.)

Tanaquil shares some characteristics with Homer's Circe: She has the gift of oracular vision, and she is a charmer of magical appeal. Her sage advice is what transforms Livy's Lucumo into a king. Upon ascending to the throne, Lucumo takes a new name, Tarquinius, and is later described as Priscus, meaning "The Early." Livy credits Tarquinius Priscus with most of the innovations that made Rome a real city—proper drainage, city planning, lavish temples, legal institutions—but he implicitly ascribes the king's authority to Tanaquil. Livy lived from 59 B.C.E. until 17 C.E., and his account of Tanaquil shows how consistently, half a millennium after Tanaquil and Tarquinius Priscus lived, the Romans continued to view Etruscan women as strong, influential participants in public as well as private life.

Not all the charms of Etruscan women were natural: A fifth-century B.C.E. tomb from Tarquinia shows dark-haired men reclining alongside wives as strikingly blonde as the angels in some 15th-century C.E. Tuscan paintings. Tuscan women of the Renaissance bleached their hair with a combination of sunlight and lemon juice. Etruscan women must have used much the same recipe. They perfumed themselves with scented oils, sold in tiny, exquisite Corinthian vases or glass vessels. They applied their cosmetics with ivory sticks and combed their hair with ivory combs, checking the results in the burnished golden glow of their bronze mirrors. The backs of many of these mirrors are incised with mythological scenes, often with written labels suggesting that Etruscan women were readers. These mirrors now provide important clues to Etruscan myth, Etruscan religion and some times even to the Etruscan language: One image of Leda and the swan is labeled "Lata" and "Tusna"—allowing the linguist Jaan Puhvel to add another word to an Etruscan vocabulary that still remains frustratingly small. Other mirrors simply show naked ladies with wings; thus the owners' charms are given mythological form.

The way the Etruscans—male and female—chose to memorialize themselves tells us much about the way they lived. The repertory of decorations on Etruscan ash urns from Chiusi and Volterra favors active scenes: battles, chariot races, hunting, whether the deceased is a man or a woman. Perhaps Etruscan men had the final say in the kinds of images they wanted associated with themselves and their wives. Or perhaps the unusual freedom Etruscan women enjoyed gave them a taste for action, in this way distinguishing them from their Greek and Roman counterparts.

The second-century B.C.E. sarcophagus of Larthia Seianti, from the Seianti family of Chiusi, was discovered in 1877 and now resides in the Florence Archaeological Museum. That of her relative Seianti Hanunia Tlesnasa, likewise discovered in the 19th century, traveled as far as the British Museum. (At the time, the city of Chiusi sold Etruscan antiquities without much concern for provenance, or even authenticity; in newspaper advertisements, the city encouraged buyers to order the kinds of artifacts they wanted!) Seianti Hanunia Tlesnasa's sarcophagus, however, was so authentic that it still contained the lady's mortal remains, which were recently analyzed by a team of curators and a forensic physician. Wealthy and well-connected as Seianti Hanunia Tlesnasa must have been, her life could not have been easy, it turns out. At the age of about 18, she was injured in what may have been a riding accident. The mishap crushed her pelvis and left her limping, and probably in constant pain. None the less, she lived into her 50s. (Medicine in Etruria was subject to all the drawbacks of an era before anesthesia and antibiotics, but the Etruscans did develop a sophisticated dentistry, which included bridges with prosthetic teeth.)

Both Larthia Seianti and Seianti Hanunia Tlesnasa recline on what could either be a banqueting couch or a bed; a sarcophagus of comparable size in the Chiusi museum shows another wealthy woman lying in bed with the covers up to her chin. More modest urns show the deceased wrapped in a blanket and curled up in a deep, comforting sleep. Quite a different picture of death, and of bereaved parenthood, is provided by an urn at Volterra, which has an extraordinary image of a skinny baby staring with huge eyes into the unknown, heart-breakingly lonely on its narrow blanket.

Two fourth-century B.C.E. Etruscan sarcophagi from Vulci, now side-by-side in the Museum of Fine Arts in Boston, show two couples from two generations of the same family reclining on their marriage-beds. The older pair, Larth Tetnies and Tanchvil Tarnai, wear the elaborate clothes in which most Etruscans dress up to face the afterlife, but Arnth and his wife, Visnai, despite their stylish Greek-inspired coiffures, lie daringly naked, looking deeply into each other's eyes for all eternity, as devoted, and with the same kind of attractive maturity, as Odysseus and Penelope.

Attractive maturity is less evident in an elderly, homely Etruscan couple from Volterra, stretched out on a banqueting couch, their wrinkled skin and piercingly shrewd expressions shown without compromise—though so, too, is the solidity of their bond to each other. In order to look into her husband's face while reclining beside him, the wife must twist her body around with all the agility of a contortionist. It is typical of Etruscan artistry to emphasize a powerful emotional tie at the expense of a strictly accurate depiction of physical reality. The director of Volterra's Guarnacci Museum, Gabriele Cateni, suggests that the couple may have commissioned this traditional Etruscan sarcophagus as late as the first century B.C.E., making it a touching document not only of two individuals but also of their entire culture, gradually disappearing under the steady pressure of Roman domination.

Conquest by the Romans eventually destroyed whatever was left of Etruscan literature, except for the ritual books whose use continued, remarkably, into the sixth century of the Common Era. It is doubly frustrating, therefore, to see how many of the little alabaster sarcophagi in which the Etruscans of Volterra buried their dead show women with wax writing tablets or folded linen books. What were they reading and writing? Pliny the Elder (23–79 C.E.) mentions an Etruscan writer of tragedies,

Volnius (whom the Etruscans themselves would have called Velnie), and we see ample evidence of the singers and dancers who must have helped to transmit the Greek and local myths we see depicted on temples, tombs, furniture, clothing, utensils and dishes. But most of what we know about Etruscan life is strictly material, as concrete as the spindles and loom weights from which Etruscan women produced their luxurious robes, the luxuries great and small for which Etruria was famous throughout the Mediterranean world.

How could the women of Etruria not have been the envy of their Greek and Roman counterparts? Look at Greek painted vases from the sixth century B.C.E., those colorful depictions of banquets and symposia, and the only women you will find are the prostitutes called *hetairai,* dancing and playing their pipes, posing no threat at all to the men gathered for an evening of heady intellectual debate. The banquet hall was certainly no place for a proper Athenian lady. Roman women led similarly restricted lives, sober and silent in the presence of men.

What a contrast, then, were the freedoms enjoyed by Etruscan women, who dined alongside Etruscan men, partaking of their wine without reservation. And in death, too, Etruscan women were not shortchanged, their burials rivaling those of their husbands, brothers and uncles, filled with great quantities of luxurious goods. The Larthias and Tanchvils and Thanias we encounter on sarcophagi and wall paintings were unusual in the ancient world. Powerful, dignified, elegant and aristocratic, they not only inhabited the world of men, they seem to have been every bit their equals.

# Rome's Craftiest General

## *Scipio Africanus*

JAMES LACEY

Publius Cornelius Scipio Africanus learned the art of war in the hardest and bloodiest of all forums—on the battlefield against Hannibal. As a 17-year-old, he followed his father, Roman consul Publius Cornelius Scipio, into Northern Italy on Rome's first engagement against the Carthaginian military genius at the Ticinus River. Though it would be the first of Rome's many defeats at Hannibal's hands, Scipio personally distinguished himself by charging a superior force of the Carthaginian cavalry to save his father's life. Over the next three years Scipio probably fought at both the Battles of Trebia and lake Trasimene, where Hannibal annihilated two more Roman armies, and was certainly present to witness Rome's greatest defeat at Cannae, where some 60,000 Romans perished in a single day's fighting.

At the end of that horrific day Scipio found himself amid a body of survivors who had cut their way through the Carthaginian center and regrouped a few miles away at Canusium. Hearing that a group of young Roman patricians was planning to desert, 20-year-old Scipio burst into their meeting place. One by one, he forced the waverers, at sword-point, to swear an oath never to desert Rome. After that he exacted a second oath that they would kill anyone else attempting to forsake the empire.

Scipio had performed exactly as expected of him. Facing defeat, a Roman leader was expected neither to die gloriously with his troops nor to consider surrender. Instead, he was to reconstitute whatever forces could be salvaged from the fiasco and ready them for the next effort. There was no shame in defeat, only in giving up.

On the other side, Hannibal was being handed a lesson in Roman perseverance—one that should have been absorbed by his father during the First Punic War. Despite suffering three successive routs at Hannibal's hands, Rome never considered surrender or a negotiated end to the Second Punic War. What's more amazing, though Hannibal's army continued to rampage through Italy for a dozen years and was to win several more major battles, Rome had the strategic wisdom to send many of its best legions to fight in other theaters. Roman legions' presence in Macedonia and Sicily, for instance, ensured that Hannibal was unable to draw upon those regions for supplies or reinforcements. It was from Spain that Hannibal drew the core of his strength, so Rome concentrated its major foreign push there. If the legions could strip Spain away from Carthage, Hannibal would be cut off from the mines that financed his army and from his most reliable source of fresh troops.

Though Roman armies made steady progress in Spain for a half-dozen years after Cannae, the strategy ended abruptly in 211 BC when, on the eve of the Battle of the Upper Baetis, Rome's Spanish allies deserted and went over to the enemy. The now overwhelming Carthaginian force nearly wiped out the Roman army, commanded by Scipio's father. Both his father and uncle were killed. A remnant Roman force managed to hold out on a small patch of land in northeast Spain.

At this low ebb, the Roman senate called for a replacement to command the demoralized Roman force in Spain. As it was apart from the main theater facing Hannibal, and because Rome could not afford to send the Spanish legions much in the way of reinforcements, no senior Roman generals stepped forward. Finally, the senate called an assembly of the people to elect a proconsul for the "honor." As Livy relates, "They [the Roman voters] looked round at the countenances of their most eminent men . . . and muttered bitterly that their affairs were in so ruinous a state that no one dared take command in Spain." Spotting a unique opportunity, Scipio declared himself a candidate, though at 24 he was not officially old enough for the post. Age notwithstanding, he was unanimously elected.

Arriving in northern Spain the following year, Scipio learned of three Carthaginian armies operating in various regions, each of them larger than his own. Roman discipline and tactical ability still made it probable Scipio would defeat any single opposing force. But that could involve weeks of careful maneuvering, during which time his opponents would surely put aside their personal differences and join forces. So Scipio seized on the idea of striking at New Carthage, the main Punic base in Spain.

Defenses at New Carthage (modern-day Cartagena) were considered so strong that only a thousand Punic mercenaries had been left to guard the city The closest reinforcements were two weeks away It was a plum for the picking, but only if Scipio could keep his intentions secret. As he spent the winter preparing his army, Scipio shared his plans with only one trusted subordinate, Laelius. When he launched his campaign in early spring, neither the army nor its senior commanders had any idea of his plans. By force-marching south 40 miles a day,

Scipio's 25,000 infantry and 2,500 cavalry arrived in less than a week to confront the city's stunned defenders. Simultaneously, Laelius arrived by sea with 35 Roman war galleys to blockade the port.

Just shy of the city walls, Scipio's army stopped and began digging a fortified camp. While the Romans dug, the Carthaginians manned the walls and hastily armed 2,000 citizens as reinforcements. New Carthage was a natural strongpoint, surrounded on three sides by water, but the defenders knew they needed time to prepare. To stall, they sallied out with 2,000 men to disrupt Roman preparations. Refusing to meet the Carthaginian onrush, Scipio instead withdrew his pickets to lure the defenders closer to his camp. His intention was to isolate the Carthaginians' best fighters far from the refuge of the city gates.

Scipio met the initial charge with his less experienced soldiers, but steadily fed in reserves to ensure there were fresh troops on the front line. Eventually, the consul sent the *Triarii* (battle-hardened men of the third line) into action. This proved too much for the Carthaginians, who broke in a rout. The Romans pursued and nearly forced the gates before they could be closed. Pressing the attack, the legionnaires began to scale the walls, but the defenders thwarted each attack. By midafternoon, Scipio ordered his exhausted troops back to camp to recoup.

The Carthaginians were at first elated, but as dusk arrived their joy turned to dismay when the legions advanced once again. It was time for Scipio's master-stroke: He had learned that the ebb tide reduced water levels in the lagoon north of the city, making it fordable. As his main force began its assault, the consul sent 500 chosen men to march across the lagoon and attack an undefended section of the wall. By then, the defenders were hard-pressed to hold off the frontal assault. The chosen 500 scaled the wall unnoticed and quickly made their way to the main gate just as the legionnaires outside began smashing away at it with heavy axes. Attacked from both front and rear, the defenders panicked, and New Carthage fell.

Just one week after launching his first military campaign, Scipio had upset the balance of power in Spain. He had deprived the Carthaginians of their main supply base, captured almost 20 war galleys and now held a large part of the Carthaginian treasury. Just as important, he recovered more than 300 noble hostages the Carthaginians had taken from Spain's most powerful tribes as a guarantee of good behavior. Despite the fact that many of these hostages had come from tribes that had betrayed his father, Scipio treated them honorably and allowed them to return home. That bit of wisdom, coupled with Scipio's proven ability to win, brought more Spanish allies into the Roman camp. Scipio used them, but was never so foolish as to trust them.

After consolidating his position at New Carthage, Scipio led his legions against the Carthaginian army under Hannibal's brother, Hasdrubal, winning a marginal victory at the Battle of Baecula in 208 BC. Either as a result of this battle or according to an earlier plan, Hasdrubal soon left Spain and marched his army into Italy to reinforce his brother. The Carthaginians arrived in Italy only to be destroyed by a Roman force led by the consul Nero. Hannibal learned his reinforcements had been wiped out when his brother's head was thrown over the wall of his camp.

Back in Spain, Scipio had only two armies to contend with, though by now they had combined forces. In 206 BC, with about 45,000 men—less than half of them well-disciplined legionnaires—Scipio marched against a Punic army nearly double that size, led by a different Hasdrubal and another of Hannibal's brothers, Mago. The armies met near Ilipa, north of Seville. For the next few days the opponents sized each other up. For each of these demonstrations, Scipio put his best troops, his two legions and Latin allies, in the center, while his Spanish allies held the flanks. To match the Romans, the Carthaginian commanders put their best African troops in the center and their own Spanish allies on the flank.

After several days of such preliminary moves, Scipio suddenly reversed his formation, putting a legion on each flank and the Spaniards in the center. Before Hasdrubal and Mago could adjust their own lines, the legions began to advance, while Scipio held his Spanish allies back. Instead of moving in the more typical line formation, Scipio advanced in columns, which allowed him to close the distance with the Carthaginians at an unheard-of speed. Then, at the last moment, the legions wheeled into line and smashed the Carthaginian flank. The Spaniards soon broke and ran for safety.

Throughout this decisive stage of the battle, Hasdrubal was unable to maneuver his center to help his flanks because Scipio's Spanish allies still menaced his front. Their flanks ultimately routed, the usually reliable African mercenaries in the center also ran for camp. That night, Hasdrubal's Spanish allies deserted. What was left of the Carthaginian army tried to escape in darkness during a storm, but was pummeled by Roman pursuers.

With Spain secured, Scipio returned to Rome. After a bitter political battle with jealous rivals, he secured permission to lead a Roman army into Africa and attack the base of Carthaginian power. Permission was only grudgingly granted, however, and the senate refused to allow him to recruit for the expedition, limiting his force to the two legions already in Sicily. But they couldn't prevent Scipio from enrolling eager volunteers. According to ancient historians, they came because "to fight under so brave and gallant a captain as Scipio was an adventure all good soldiers welcomed." That said, one suspects the promise of rich plunder was at least as much of a draw.

By allowing him to take Legions V and VI, the senate didn't think it was doing Scipio a service. These legions comprised survivors of Cannae. Following that rout, the defeated soldiers were sent to serve in exile—a degradation in direct contrast to the praise the senate bestowed on Cannae survivors of noble birth. These men keenly felt the stain of dishonor, and each year they petitioned the senate to allow them to return to Rome and prove their valor in battle against Hannibal. They were ignored.

Scipio understood such men and their desire for redemption. To him they were not simply the losers from Cannae. They were the men who by dim of sheer hard fighting had cut their way through an encircling army and re-formed to protect the Republic. He praised them and honored their service, and they in turn gave him utter devotion. Around this core of combat-hardened veterans Scipio spent a year training his volunteers and preparing the logistics required to support an invasion of Carthage's home territories.

In 204BC Scipio's force sailed for North Africa and laid siege to the Carthaginian stronghold of Utica. The defenders held strong, their resistance buoyed by the promise of a large Carthaginian relief army. In time, Carthage did manage to assemble a large force, under the joint command of Hasdrubal and a local king, Syphax, who had previously pledged his support to Scipio. Despite overwhelming military superiority, however, Hasdrubal was reluctant to attack, perhaps recalling the drubbing he'd received at Ilipa.

Scipio took full advantage of the Carthaginian general's indecision to suggest peace talks, an offer that was eagerly accepted. Over the next several days, Roman emissaries, accompanied by their slaves, made their way to the two enemy camps. As the emissaries negotiated, the slaves—actually Roman centurions—roved around the camp, noting its layout and defensive works. To maintain the illusion these spies were actually slaves, several of them submitted to public whippings for having wandered off without permission.

Their familiarity with the enemy camp emboldened Scipio to conduct the most dangerous of operations—a nighttime assault on a fortified enemy position. The consul was about to find out whether his faith in the disgraced legions was misplaced. They didn't disappoint.

In a single night of brutality, Scipio's army massacred upwards of 40,000 of the enemy (twice their own number) and sent the rest into flight. Incredibly, Hasdrubal managed to raise another army in only a month and marched once again to engage Scipio. But no army so hastily raised and organized was a match for battle-disciplined legions, which made short work of this new army. Faced with these twin disasters and no army left in North Africa that could oppose Scipio, Carthage was forced to recall Hannibal from Italy. For all practical purposes, Rome had won the Second Punic War. But there was still one great battle left to be fought.

At Zama, in 202 BC, Scipio and Hannibal finally met on the field of battle. Each had about 40,000 men at his disposal, but—unlike at Cannae—this time the Romans had the better mounted force, thanks to King Masinissa, who swung his superb Numidian cavalry out of the Carthaginian orbit over to the Roman side. Scipio, like Hannibal, placed this cavalry on the flanks, and each organized his infantry in three lines. But Scipio also made a major tactical change to the standard Roman formation by separating his maniples, opening wide lanes through his lines.

After some initial skirmishing, Hannibal sent his 80 war elephants forward. But this was a different Roman army than the one he had faced at Cannae—tougher and more disciplined, led by men accustomed to Hannibal's tactics. Faced with the choice of smashing into the heavily armed legionnaires or running unimpeded through the gaps in their formations, most of the elephants took the path of least resistance and passed harmlessly through the Roman army. Others, frightened by the blasts of massed Roman trumpeters, ran down their own cavalry.

Noting the chaos, Laelius and Masinissa took the cavalry on each flank and charged the Carthaginian horsemen. These horsemen quickly retreated, with Roman and Numidian cavalry in close pursuit. As the cavalry departed, the legions crashed into the lead Carthaginian line, pressing the mercenaries hard until they turned to escape. But the second line refused to break formation, and as the Romans continued their advance, the Carthaginians began fighting each other. Ultimately, men in the second line also broke and ran for the rear, where they met a similar reception from the third line.

As the defeated first two lines skirted around the ends of Hannibal's final line, Scipio recalled his troops to within bow shot of the Carthaginians. Before them stood Hannibal's seasoned veterans, rested, unbowed and in numbers almost equal to his own. Scipio, rather than replace the exhausted legionnaires in his leading ranks, re-formed them into a tightly packed formation and moved the Triarii to each flank, intending to overlap the enemy line. In a testament to Roman discipline, the legions quickly negotiated these complex maneuvers in the face of an unbeaten enemy.

Given a short breather, the Romans came forward at a quickened pace, until at about 20 paces they let fly their throwing spears and drew their short swords. The advance became a rush as thousands of screaming Romans hurled themselves upon the Carthaginian line. For long minutes the issue remained in doubt, until at the peak of battle the Roman and Numidian cavalry returned to the battlefield and charged into the Carthaginian rear. With cavalry at the rear and the Triarii collapsing their flanks, Hannibal's veterans finally did the unthinkable—they broke.

Though Hannibal himself escaped, his army was lost and Carthaginian military power broken. Rome was now the uncontested master of the Western Mediterranean. Scipio's victories earned him tremendous popular support but also numerous enemies, envious of his popularity. Though he later accompanied his brother on a war of conquest in Asia Minor, he was never again to hold real power in Rome. Under constant legal attack, he ultimately went into a bitter retirement, dying at an early age.

How Rome treated its most victorious general was not lost on such future successful commanders as Marius, Sulla and Caesar. For them the overriding lesson of Scipio's fall from grace was that if you wanted to rule, you needed to return home with your legions.

---

For further reading, **JAMES LACEY** recommends: *Scipio Africanus: Greater Than Napoleon*, by B. H. Liddell Hart.

# The End of the Roman Empire

## *Did It Collapse or Was It Transformed?*

BRYAN WARD-PERKINS

It used to be unquestioned that the Roman empire in the West fell to violent and bloody invasion that resulted in the death of a civilization, and the start of a 'dark age', from which it would take Europe centuries to recover. Recent scholarship, however, has tended to downplay the violence, and to challenge a concept of post-Roman cultural decline. New orthodoxies are emerging: that the barbarians were peacefully 'accommodated' into the empire to serve as its defenders; and that Roman culture was quietly 'transformed' into a new guise.

In the late 1970s I worked with a team of archaeologists on the site of Luna, a Roman city in northern Italy, on the coast about halfway between Pisa and Genoa. Ancient Luna, like hundreds of other towns across the empire, enjoyed the full range of Roman urban amenities: bath-buildings with piped water; paved roads with a drainage and sewerage system beneath them; a theatre and amphitheatre; a number of imposing temples; a full complement of civic buildings including a marble-paved forum square and a basilica for commercial and political transactions; and some splendid private houses, decorated in fresco, mosaic and marble. In the searing heat of July, one of the Roman houses was particularly attractive—its main reception rooms had floors of cool marble, and opened out onto a shaded courtyard, with raised flower beds and a fountain playing at its centre. The prosperity of the city was also attested by a remarkable range of high-quality and eminently functional domestic articles. For instance, third- and fourth-century citizens were eating off glossy plates and bowls from North Africa, and even cooking in casseroles from the same region. These vessels are found in large quantities, and were clearly very widely available. Like other Roman towns, Luna's prosperity depended partly on a flourishing local agriculture, and partly on more specialized production and trade, in its case the extraction and export of the white marble now known as Carrara marble—much of imperial Rome was built in this stone.

My own interest, however, was in the history of the city in the period when the empire in the West disintegrated and disappeared. During the fifth century, Italy, after centuries of peace, faced invasion and devastation, first by armies of Goths (who sacked Rome itself in 410), and then by Vandals, raiding by sea from their north African base at the port of Carthage. The Mediterranean, which had been a peaceful commercial lake for five centuries, was contested between rival Germanic kingdoms, and became a place where raiders, as well as traders, operated. In the sixth century, Italy's troubles continued, with a long war for mastery between the Goths and the forces of the surviving east-Roman (or 'Byzantine') empire, with its capital in Constantinople. This war ended in Byzantine victory, but was followed, almost immediately, by the invasion of another Germanic people, the Lombards. The Lombards, however, failed to capture the whole of Italy, which became a divided and contested peninsula. Luna suffered directly from some of these upheavals—a large Gothic army passed through its territory in 412, and during the long Lombard-Byzantine wars it became an isolated outpost of Byzantine power, surrounded by Lombard territory. As a coastal city, it must have suffered badly from the slow decline of Mediterranean trade that has been charted by recent archaeology.

What we found had happened to the city in the fifth to seventh centuries was both striking and depressing. Sometime in the fourth or fifth centuries, the marble quarries, which were the source of much of Luna's wealth, were abandoned—and they remained closed for some 700 years thereafter. At roughly the same date, the monumental buildings of the city were progressively allowed to fall down, or were demolished, their decorative marble elements broken into pieces and used as building materials. The great basalt slabs of the Roman roadways were gradually covered over and lost under patchy gravel surfaces. The aqueduct was interrupted, piped water no longer reached the city, and its fountains fell silent, compelling the inhabitants to dig wells through the ancient monuments to the water-table beneath. The houses of the aristocracy decayed, and were buried under rubble—one of them became the site of a graveyard. Eventually, the town of Luna disappeared altogether.

The specific remains that we were excavating consisted of the scant traces of two simple wooden houses built in the sixth century A.D.—with post-holes, dry-stone footings for timber walls, and beaten earth floors. Each house was made up of two small rooms, one probably for humans, and the other for animals. These unprepossessing dwellings were built over the square of the Roman forum, the monumental heart of the ancient city. By the time they were built, all the Roman monumental buildings and shops of the forum had been abandoned and despoiled of their marble fittings, and the square itself was already covered in a deep layer of silt. These simple post-Roman houses, and the startling contrast that they presented with the imposing underlying Roman structures, seemed to point to a remarkable drop in economic and technological complexity, and in levels of material comfort. A city of mortared stone and marble, was replaced by a settlement of wood, thatch and beaten earth. Furthermore, good quality domestic goods and other indicators of sophistication and prosperity also totally disappeared: the sixth-century inhabitants of Luna, unlike their ancestors, hardly used coins at all, and almost the only pottery available to them were simple cooking-pots.

From working at Luna, and from visiting many other Roman cities with a similar history, I formed an unshakeable impression that the disappearance of the Roman world was a shattering, and negative, event in human history. But, in the very years that I was documenting this post-Roman collapse, scholars elsewhere were engineering the downfall of such conventional views. The seeds of this change had been planted in 1971, when Peter Brown published his World of Late Antiquity, a book which was to have a remarkable effect on how the end of the ancient world was viewed by historians. Brown defined and described a period, which he termed 'Late Antiquity', stretching from the third century to the eighth century A.D.; but he saw it as characterized not by the disappearance of Roman sophistication and civilization, but by lively and positive developments. Brown invited his readers to reject the old language of 'decline and fall' and to embrace instead a vision of this as a period when Roman culture was transformed and revitalized.

The spread and impact of Brown's new interpretation was slow but inexorable. He is a brilliant historian who writes beautiful prose, and he is a bewitching performer in a lecture or seminar. In the early 1970s, as an undergraduate in Oxford, I attended a course of his lectures in All Souls on early Egyptian monasticism, not because I understood much of what he was saying (I was studying later periods and his detailed arguments went way over my head), but because the way he talked, and his empathy with those tough old men of the Egyptian desert, were truly enthralling. Under his influence, the way that historians, and some archaeologists, describe the last centuries of the Western Empire and their immediate aftermath changed markedly. For instance, a massive recent research project into the fourth to eighth centuries, sponsored by the European Union, was entitled the 'Transformation of the Roman World'. The very title of this project rejects the notion of any abrupt break at the end of the Roman empire; the underlying vision is instead of a Roman World seamlessly 'transformed' into the Europe of Charlemagne. The many Germanic peoples who entered the empire in the fifth and sixth centuries (Goths, Vandals, Franks, Burgundians, Sueves, Thuringians, Alamans, Lombards and others) are no longer seen as invaders who, wittingly or unwittingly, severely damaged the well-being of the Roman world, but as peaceful settlers in a world that continued much as before.

As a reinterpretation of the political and military history of the disintegration of the western empire, this is radical enough. But can the new upbeat thinking about the end of the Roman world be reconciled with the gloomy evidence of material collapse from Luna, and from hundreds of other similar sites across the ancient world? I think not, though efforts have been made by others to square this circle. For instance, some archaeologists have argued that one of the most striking changes at the end of the Roman period—the almost universal switch from solid stone and brick buildings, to much less permanent structures in perishable materials—was caused by cultural choice rather than economic necessity. They argue that it is possible to construct complex, sophisticated and highly decorated structures over the simple post-holes which are the only evidence we have for the buildings of post-Roman times; and that building in stone was merely a fashion—a way of expressing political and ideological allegiance to Rome—which was dropped when the empire disappeared. According to this way of thinking, the descendants and successors of the Roman aristocracy abandoned their villas, with their solid walls and floors, tiled roofs, bath-buildings, and under-floor heating, not because they were forced to, by a collapse in economic and technological sophistication, but because they actually preferred to live in wooden halls.

I find this deeply implausible: tiled roofs are, quite simply, much more durable, brick and stone floors far easier to keep clean, and stone walls more weatherproof, than their equivalents in perishable materials; and heating systems and hot baths are both effective and very pleasant indeed—much more so than a smoking open fire in the middle of a hall, and a bowl of lukewarm water. The evidence of buildings will, however, always remain controversial, because it is impossible in most cases to reconstruct with confidence, from the scant remains we find in the soil, what a post-Roman building was really like to live in. But if we look at domestic pottery, an inescapable picture emerges of technological and economic collapse at the end of the Roman period, leading to a dramatic regression in living standards. And there is little prospect of arguing it away in terms of ideological and cultural choice.

The Romans produced pottery vessels to high standards, in enormous quantities, and shipped them widely. As we have already seen, in third- and fourth-century Italy even a cooking-pot might often be imported from North Africa. Furthermore—and this is very important—good quality pottery, whether made in the region, or imported, was available at all levels of society. Fine tablewares, and imported amphorae for the storage and transport of liquids are discovered not just on the coast and in towns and rich villas, but also on inland sites and humble farmsteads.

Because pottery survives so well in the soil and because individual potsherds can be both dated and provenanced (reliably attributed to particular production sites), we know a remarkable amount about the trade in ancient pottery. We also know, from the objects themselves, that the vast majority of Roman pottery is of a quality not exceeded, in Europe, in terms of consistency and quality, before factory-made products became widely available in the eighteenth century. This judgement is based not on aesthetic considerations but on practical values. Roman pots are tough and hold liquids well; they are light and pleasant to handle; and they have smooth surfaces that are easy to clean. Furthermore, from the excavation of production sites we know a lot about the scale and levels of complexity involved in making some of the best-quality Roman wares. Excavators at a south Gaulish pottery, la Graufesenque near modern Millau, have found graffiti that record the stacking of great communal kilns, firing up to 30,000 vessels at a time. At the same site, a pit was discovered full of near-perfect vessels, discarded because they were not quite of a high enough quality; some of these pots had a hole punched through their base, in order to prevent them slipping into circulation—a remarkable testimony to Roman quality control.

Almost none of this sophistication survived into post-Roman times. In some provinces—particularly Britain—the regression was startling: even the potter's wheel, widespread in Roman times, wholly disappeared for over two hundred years. Pottery of the early Anglo-Saxon period, and also pottery of the same date from unconquered western Britain, is rare and poor in quality—of badly selected clay, hand-shaped, and fired on an open fire. The resulting vessels are porous and very friable—many would score low marks as first efforts in pottery at an infants' school. Elsewhere, the changes were slightly less dramatic and less sudden, but they were still very remarkable. On Mediterranean sites like Luna, the extraordinary and abundant range of tablewares available in Roman times became very rare in the fifth and sixth centuries, and eventually disappeared altogether; and kitchenwares, which were pretty much all that remained, became more or less restricted to a single bulbous design of pot. To explain these developments in terms of cultural change rather than of economic and technological regression, one has to work very hard indeed, perhaps imagining a culture with access to large numbers of metal vessels which replaced pottery but were all eventually recycled so they left no trace in the archaeological record!

If the archaeological evidence that points to a severe post-Roman regression cannot be squared with the historians' cheerful view of 'Late Antiquity', how has the latter come about? Partly, it is through the optimism of some archaeologists themselves, who explain all change in terms of altered cultural values. But largely it is because historians like Peter Brown examine entirely different aspects of the human condition, and therefore come to radically divergent impressions about the same periods of the past. The 'World of Late Antiquity' tends to be defined in spiritual and religious terms, as the period when Christianity became established and defined, and, slightly later, Islam emerged as the dominant religion of the southern Mediterranean. If we take these as the key things that happened in our period, then there is no problem in depicting the third to eighth centuries as a 'Golden Age' of continuous and positive development. It is certainly true that with the conversion of the Germanic kingdoms, and the eventual spread of Christianity into areas like Ireland and Scotland, far more souls were saved in these centuries than under the Roman empire.

I may be wrong to believe that the disintegration of a complex economy, and a consequent collapse of living standards mattered even more than momentous religious developments, and that they mark a decisive break in Western history—but I don't think I am. The changes that archaeologists have documented affected kings and peasants alike: palaces, as much as rural farmsteads, were far less impressive and comfortable in post-Roman times than they had been under the empire. These changes even affected God and his saints, currently the focus of much of the writing by historians on Late Antiquity. The cult of saints grew steadily through late Roman and post-Roman times, and was not slowed by the disintegration of the Roman world. But if we look at the size of the churches built for these saints, there is a dramatic shrinkage between late Roman and post-Roman times. In the fourth century, huge churches were built over the graves of the martyrs—Old St Peter's, for instance, erected by Constantine to honour Rome's premier bishop, was a massive five-aisled basilica about 100 metres long, with an atrium almost the same size again. However, by the seventh century, new churches in the West seldom exceeded 20 metres in length. Fortunately for the saints, many great churches of earlier times were still maintained—if they had had to rely on post-Roman builders, their living-conditions would have become very cramped indeed.

All the evidence suggests that most of the sophisticated features and creature-comforts that characterized Roman life, disappeared in the West in the fifth to seventh centuries, to such an extent that the change can accurately be seen as the 'end of a civilization'. Furthermore, the close coincidence of date between this collapse and the Germanic invasions of the fifth and sixth centuries suggests, beyond all reasonable doubt, that the change was caused by the disruption of war and the disintegration of the peaceful trading-world that was the Roman empire. Western Europe did eventually emerge out of the resulting slump, but it took perhaps a thousand years to regain the levels of economic activity and the high standards of living that had so impressed me in Roman Luna.

## For Further Reading

Peter Brown, *The World of Late Antiquity: From Marcus Aurelius to Muhammad* (Thames and Hudson, 1971); Averil Cameron, *The Later Roman Empire,* A.D. 284–430 (Fontana, 1993) and *The Mediterranean World in Late Antiquity,* A.D. 395–600 (Routledge, 1993),Walter Goffart, Barbarians and Romans A.D. 418–584. *The Techniques of Accommodation* (Princeton University Press, 1980); J. H. W. G. Liebeschuetz, *The Decline and Fall of the Roman City* (Oxford University Press, 2001); Peter Heather, *The Fall of the Roman Empire* (Macmillan, 2005).

**Bryan Ward-Perkins** is Lecturer in Modern History and Fellow of Trinity College, Oxford. His book *The Fall of Rome and the End of Civilization* is published by Oxford University Press in June, 14.99 [pounds sterling].

# UNIT 3

# The Judeo-Christian Heritage

## Unit Selections

16. **The Volcano Explains Everything—Or Does It?,** Manfred Bietak
17. **Holy Family Values,** Lisa Miller

## Key points to Consider

- What does the Island of Thera (Santorini) have to do with the Hebrew Exodus?
- What traditions shaped the Christian religion?
- Why is there a controversy surrounding Mary Magdalene?

## Student Web Site

www.mhcls.com/online

## Internet References

**Institute for Christian Leadership/ICLnet**

*http://www.iclnet.org*

**Selected Women's Studies Resources/Columbia University**

*http://www.columbia.edu/cu/libraries/subjects/womenstudies/*

Western civilization developed out of the Greco-Roman world, but it is also indebted to the Judeo-Christian traditions. If Western civilization derives the concept of humanism and materialism, and philosophy, politics, art, literature, and science from the former, it derives its God and forms of worship from the latter. It is difficult to separate these traditions, for Judeo-Christian heritage comes to us through a Hellenistic filter.

On one hand, the history of the Jews seems similar to those of other small kingdoms of the Near East that were closely situated to powerful empires such as the Babylonians, Assyrians, and Persians. Yet of all the ancient peoples, only the Jews had had a lasting influence. What appears to differentiate the Jews from all the rest, writes historian Crane Brinton, is "The will to persist, to be themselves, to be a people." The reappearance of Israel in the modern world, some 2,000 years after the Romans destroyed the Jewish client-state is remarkable.

The legacy of the Jews is a great one. It includes a rich literary tradition found in their sacred texts. They have also bequeathed to Western civilization their unique view of history; a linear and miraculous God, who intervenes in history to guide, reward, or punish his Chosen People (see "The Volcano Explains Everything—Or Does it?"). The Jewish religion also gave birth to the concept of morality found within the Ten Commandments, the moral wisdom of the prophets and a messianic expectation, which inspired Christianity and other religions. Their monotheism and their god, Yahweh, formed the model for the Christian and Muslim ideas of God.

A brief comparison of Yahweh and the Greek god Zeus illustrates the originality of the Jewish conception. Both gods began as warrior deities of tribal cultures. But Zeus was chiefly concerned with Olympian affairs rather than human ones. Yahweh, on the other hand, was more purposeful and had few interests except for his people. And unlike Zeus, who was not the creator of the universe, Yahweh had created the Universe and ordered the humans to rule over nature.

Certainly Christianity bears the stamp of Judaism. Jesus himself was a Jew. To his early followers, all of them Jews, he satisfied the prophetic messianic messages inherent in Judaism. The New Testament recounts the growth and spread of Christianity from an obscure Jewish sect in Palestine to a new religion with great appeal in the Roman world. Yet Jesus remains shrouded in mystery, for there is a lack of firsthand evidence. The Gospels, the greatest and most familiar sources, contain wide gaps in their accounts of his life. Nonetheless, they remain a profound record of early Christian faith. The essay "Holy Family Values" recounts the world of Jesus and how Jewish mores became Christian customs.

As it separated from Judaism, Christianity took on a new dimension, including the promise of private salvation through participation in the sacraments. From the beginning, its theology reflected the teachings of St. Paul, who changed the focus from converting the Jews to spreading the faith among the Gentiles. Then, as it took hold in the Near East, Christianity absorbed some Hellenistic elements, Stoicism, Platonism, and the Roman pantheon. This prepared the way for a fusion of classical philosophy and Christianity. The personal God of the Jews and Christians became the abstract God of the Greek philosophers. Biblical texts were given symbolic meanings that might have confounded an earlier, simpler generation of Christians. The Christian view of sexuality, for instance, became fraught with multiple meanings and complexities. In effect, Christianity was no longer a Jewish sect; it had become Westernized. It would become a principal agent for Westernization of the much of the world.

The Palma Collection/Getty Images

# The Volcano Explains Everything—Or Does It?

## Does this crater from an ancient volcanic eruption hold the answer to the mysteries of the exodus?

Manfred Bietak

Canadian Documentarian Simcha Jacobovici, in cooperation with James Cameron, director of *Titanic,* has masterminded a two-hour TV special dealing with the oft-treated—and oft-mistreated—Exodus narrative. The Biblical account provides the principal pillar of the script. Every sentence of the Biblical text is taken literally in quite a fundamentalist fashion.

Until now, Biblical scholars have not found specific archaeological evidence for the Exodus. This perspective—the archaeological evidence—is purportedly now supplied by Jacobovici and backed up, we are led to believe, with opinions of scholars working in the field. Technically the film is brilliantly produced—flashy and full of unusual special effects. The digital age has clearly arrived in this film, and no effort has been spared to find scholarly support from a whole series of experts (including the author of this review) whose research involves them in one way or another in the Exodus story.

The chronology proposed in the film is based on the volcanic eruption at the Mediterranean island of Thera (modern Santorini), more than 500 miles from Egypt, and the phenomena that followed. In the film, the Biblical narrative is explained in terms of this eruption and its aftereffects. According to the conventional chronology, this volcanic eruption is dated around 1500 B.C.E. The aftereffects of the eruption seem, at first glance, to be described in an Egyptian inscription known as the "Tempest Stela," which dates to the reign of Pharaoh Ahmose (c. 1540–1515 B.C.E.), the founder of the Egyptian New Kingdom who transformed his domain into a kingdom encompassing not only the whole of Egypt but also starting to acquire areas of the Near East. In order to do this, Ahmose had to defeat and probably expel a part of the population living under the Hyksos, Asiatics then ruling Egypt. He did this in about 1525 B.C.E., thus liberating northern Egypt from a foreign dynasty and their people. The scenario of Near Easterners (Asiatics) living for a long time in Egypt and finally being driven out provides the alleged historical background through which Jacobovici explains the Israelite presence in Egypt, followed by their exodus. The ten plagues are explained as the natural aftereffects of the volcanic eruption.

Nearly two millennia ago, the Jewish historian Josephus suggested a connection between the Hyksos expulsion from Egypt and the Proto-Israelites of the Biblical Exodus story. Few Egyptologists today would support that idea, however, although it is still alive among some Old Testament scholars such as John Bimson of the University of Liverpool, who was given the opportunity to comment on this scenario in Jacobovici's film. Most Biblical scholars, however, would date the Exodus, if they do not consider it largely legendary, to the Ramesside Period (c. 1295–1070 B.C.E.), that is, if we exclude the end of this era, about 250 to 350 years after the Hyksos expulsion from Egypt.

The idea of associating the Thera eruption with the unusual tempest in the Tempest Stela of Ahmose has also been suggested a number of times,[1] although the idea has also been refuted.[2] And the association of the Exodus with the Thera eruption is also not new. Already in 1981, Hans Goedicke, then professor at The Johns Hopkins University, compared the features in the Exodus narrative with a volcanic eruption and its aftereffects.* However, according to Goedicke, Thera erupted not in the reign of Ahmose but (according to his interpretation of the Speos Artemidos inscription) half a century later, during the reign of Queen Hatshepsut (c. 1477–1457 B.C.E.).

In Jacobovici's film a number of leading scholars in the field are interviewed. One is left to wonder why only snippets of their interviews are included. From the snippet of the interview with Professor Donald Redford of Pennsylvania State University, for example, we are given the impression that he is a super-fundamentalist. I know him to be in fact quite the opposite. [A reporter for the Canadian newspaper *The Globe and Mail* interviewed Redford about the film and reports that Redford "dismisses most of the film's points as fantasy."—**Ed.**] I am confident that the most important parts of Redford's interview were left on the cutting room floor because they collided with the theories advanced in the film.

The same thing happened to me Short statements from my interview, cut out of context, come across as seeming to support the film's argument. In fact, I objected to dating the Exodus story

* Hershel Shanks, "The Exodus and the Crossing of the Red Sea, According to Hans Goedicke," *BAR*, September/October 1981.

## Water into Blood?

In 1986 an eruption of gases beneath Lake Nyos, Cameroon, caused dissolved iron particles in the lake to mix with oxygen and form iron hydroxide (rust), which turned the water a reddish color. Producer Jacobovici uses this phenomenon and its after-effects to explain how several of the Biblical plagues—the Nile turning into "blood" (Exodus 7:14–24), the infestation of frogs (Exodus 8:1–15) and the outbreak of boils (Exodus 9:8–12), among others—occurred as a result of earthquakes that also caused the eruption at Thera. However, our author argues that gases could not have seeped into the Nile Delta as they did at Lake Nyos. He explains that the delta is composed of layers of sand and compact silt over a kilometer thick that would have prevented subterranean gases from leaking into the sediments and the water in any significant quantity. Moreover, the Bible says the water turned into blood, not just into reddish water.

to the Hyksos period and the reign of Ahmose. And I objected, not because I wanted to steer clear of Biblical chronology and history (the film claims that I was afraid of the Egyptian authorities—nonsense), but because archaeology does not provide any trace of Israelites before the Iron Age (shortly before 1200 B.C.E.). Written evidence is provided for the first time on the so-called Israel Stela from the fifth year of Pharaoh Merneptah's reign (c. 1209 B.C.E.). It is probably no coincidence that likely evidence of Proto-Israelites appears in the archaeological record in Egypt in the latter half of the 12th century B.C.E.in the remains of a typical structure known as a Four-Room House, considered the customary housetype of Israelites throughout the Iron Age until the Babylonian Exile.*

The disadvantage of placing the Exodus at the end of the Hyksos period, as Jacobovici chooses to do, is that one has to cope with some odd anachronisms in the Biblical text, but he does not deal with these. The Bible says, for example, that Hebrew slaves built the store-city of Ramesses (Exodus 1:11), but the Ramesside period was hundreds of years after the Hyksos period. Similarly with the Biblical reference to the "Way of the Philistines," which the fleeing Israelites avoided on their way out of Egypt (Exodus 13:17)—but there were no Philistines in the Hyksos period. By using the lower chronology for the Exodus—to the Ramesside period—as is generally accepted by scholars, at least such grave anachronisms could be avoided. Placing the Exodus even later, into the time of Ramesses III or Ramesses IV (12th century B.C.E.) would make the expression "Way of the Philistines" meaningful.

Pharaoh Seqenenre of the 17th Dynasty (16th century B.C.E.) was killed by the Israelites, according to this film. This is presented as a fact. This so-called fact is based on an actual fact; Seqenenre was killed with Near-Eastern battle-axes (as we learn from a forensic examination). This is typical of the film's logic: Because Seqenenre was killed with Near-Eastern battle-axes, it must have been the Israelites who were responsible for this happening.

The film identifies Ahmose as the pharaoh of the Oppression and of the Exodus because the Tempest Stela is dated to Ahmose's time. The stela's description of a tempest, perhaps an extremely violent rainstorm, that caused darkness in Egypt seems to fit with the volcanic eruption of Thera. According to the film, the Exodus can be "securely" associated with the Thera eruption.

The film should have made clear to the audience that, in fact, this argument skates on thin ice. First of all, the date of the Thera eruption is not settled. Radiocarbon dates place it at about 1720 B.C.E.; however, on historical grounds, it can be argued that it occurred in 1500 B.C.E. or even slightly later. Jacobovici's contention holds water, so to speak, only if 1500 B.C.E. proves correct.

What is, however, highly unlikely is that Egypt was shrouded in a cloud of volcanic ash. Vulcanologists and oceanographers have clearly shown (based on sediment accumulation) that the ash from the eruption was transported northeastward, across Asia Minor. The dark clouds never reached Syria, Palestine or Egypt.

The Theran pumice that does appear at Egyptian sites[3] most likely arrived by sea or by trade. Jacobovici shows some of this pumice from my site of Tell el-Dab'a as proof of his position. However, the Theran pumice that massively appears at Tell el-Dab'a and at some other Egyptian and southern Palestinian sites is from the Tuthmoside period and later (several generations after Pharaoh Ahmose). The tephra-particles found in the Nile Delta by Daniel Stanley of the Smithsonian Institution were not found in a datable context and, according to our petro-graphic scientist, Max Bichler, were too large to be windborne.[4] All this means that it is highly unlikely that volcanic signals from Thera affected Egypt, except that tsunamis may have inundated the northern parts of the delta.

Also, the numerous sequelae of the Thera eruption that the film uses to explain the plagues are not always reasonable. For example, the evaporation of gases from the ground, killing only the oldest son (the tenth plague), sleeping as a kind of privilege in a bed while the other children would be sleeping on the roof, is hardly convincing. What about the elderly parents and the social dignataries who slept in beds? Why did they survive the creeping gas? It is also difficult to explain volcanic gases creeping or seeping through sediments in the Nile Delta. These sediments are more than a kilometer thick and consist of layers of both sand and compact silts.

To prove that Israelite slaves worked for the pharaohs, the film takes us to the turquoise mines at Serabit el-Khadem in the Sinai with its well-known Proto-Sinaitic inscriptions (the first alphabetic script, written in a Semitic idiom). Here Jacobovici uses a highly conjectural decipherment ("God save us") proposed long ago for the still-not-fully deciphered script. But, in any event, these inscriptions can now be dated to the 12th Dynasty (19th century B.C.E.),[5] more than 300 years before Ahmose.

Biblical figures such as Joseph, Jacob and Moses are presented in the film as if they were fully substantiated historical figures, firmly set into Egyptian history. Proof of Jacob and Joseph in the Hyksos period consists of nine bullae (seal impressions) with the so-called throne name of the Hyksos Yaqub-her (Yaqub = Jacob) that were found at Tell el-Dab'a/Avaris, exactly "in the layer, where one would expect them to be." This, according to the film, came after a painstaking search for evidence of Joseph. Jacobovici interviewed me as director of the excavations at Tell el-Dab'a/Avaris. I spoke of a puzzle in connection with these bullae, but

* Manfred Bietak, "Israelites Found in Egypt," *BAR*, September/October 2003.

Jacobovici made a cut at this point and declared that the puzzle is solved if we apply his Biblical chronology and identify the seals with Biblical Jacob. My puzzle, however, was an entirely different one. All of these bullae of Yaqub-her dating to the Hyksos era were not found in the level where one would have expected to find them, but in a layer of the late Tuthmoside period (second half of the 15th century B.C.E.). This obviously did not interest the film producer. Nor was he concerned with the fact that Biblical names have a wide distribution in the Near East, and the people with these names were not necessarily Israelites. Besides that, the identification with the Biblical Jacob is naïve. The Bible does not tell us of a royal status for Jacob, and the name Joseph does not appear on these bullae.

Perhaps the most serious blunder of the film involves a hieroglyphic inscription on a granite Egyptian templenaos from El-Arish, now in the Ismailia Regional Museum, dating to the 30th Dynasty (fourth century B.C.E.). Jacobovici, who is no Egyptologist, proceeds to interpret a few hieroglyphs in this inscription completely out of context, based on the pictorial appearance of the signs: three waterlines and two knives. According to him, these signs should be read as signifying a parting of the water. In reality the inscription involves a mythic lake known as the "Lake of the Two Knives" or phonetically as *Yam Desdes.* The name Desdes is also the name of the Bahriya Oasis, and there is a question as to whether our lake was situated there. Sometimes, however, *Yam Desdes* is associated with Hermopolis in Middle Egypt and in any case has nothing to do with the parting of the sea nor with the Exodus story (which, according to Jacobovici, occurred more than a millennium earlier). In this inscription, the lake serves as a medium for the magical transformation of the Uraeus (serpent) of the king in order to protect him, legitimize his rule and fortify him against his enemies (the Persians as well as enemies within Egypt).[6] To the non-Egyptologist, the argumentation in the film may look great, but the specialist is left to wonder and scratch his head at what educational value a film like this can provide for the public.

The most incredible part of the film—although very impressive from a visual point of view—is the claim that a group of Israelites separated from Moses, took to their ships (where did they get the ships?) and sailed to Greece! The supposed proof of this contention is a Minoan wall painting from Thera depicting ships traveling between two towns (see photo on p. 43 of this issue). According to the film, one town is Avaris, home of the Hyksos kings; the other is Thera. Another painting from the same building depicts palm trees and felines, suggesting, according to the film, a Nilotic landscape. The suggestion is not new. It has, however, been refuted by several specialists in the subject.[7]

Jacobovici also relies on the fact that paintings depicting bull-leaping and other Minoan motifs have been found at Avaris. In my interview with the film maker, I explained that these paintings cannot be associated with Ahmose (the pharaoh of the Exodus of the film) because the Avaris frescoes date to the time of Tuthmosis III (1479–1425 B.C.E.), not Ahmose (c. 1540–1515 B.C.E.). In the film, however, my words were cut short and, instead, allowed the message of the film to be delivered by Dr. Charles Pellegrino, a fiction writer with experience in the *Titanic* production. Dr. Pellegrino, of course, knows what he has to say, according to the film's script.

Incredibly, the film also suggests that the shaft graves at Mycenae in Greece are the last resting place of the group of Israelites who broke from Moses and sailed to Greece. It is also stated that they were buried at the foot of a pyramid-shaped mountain. The gold found in the Mycenae tombs (see photos on p. 35 of this issue) is supposed to be the gold the Bible says that the Israelites got from the Egyptians when they left Egypt (Exodus 12:35).

Finally, some tiny gold plaques from the Mycenaean tombs, exhibited in the National Archaeological Museum in Athens, depict a typical Aegean Bronze Age feature: a tripartite shrine. In the virtual reality (or unreality) of this film, part of this gold shrine is a replica of the Ark of the Covenant, with the stepped altar popping up from behind. In the film it is admitted that no one knows exactly how the ark looked. How, then, is one able to identify it with part of a tripartite shrine from the Aegean?

From a technical point of view, the film is brilliant. If this film were presented as a work of fiction, it would be engaging and entertaining. But it is not presented as a work of fiction. It makes the public believe it is based on a serious investigation. It is a pity that the theory behind the film has been so superficially researched and does not stand up to close scrutiny.

## Notes

1. This was proposed by Robert Ritner (University of Chicago), Karen Foster (Yale University) and Ellen Davis (Queens College).
2. By James Allen (now of Brown) and Malcolm Wiener (INSTAP).
3. Tell el-Dab'a, Tell Hebwa and Tell el-Ajjul.
4. Atomic Institute of the Austrian Universities, and the special research program SCIEM2000 (The Synchronisation of Civilizations in the Eastern Mediterranean in the Second Millennium B.C.) of the Austrian Academy of Sciences, Vienna.
5. J.C. Darnell, "Die fruhalphabetischen Inschriften im Wadi el-Hol," in *Der Turmbau zu Babel, Ursprung und Vielfalt von Sprache und Schrift,* vol. 3A (Die Schrift: Vienna and Milano, 2003), pp. 165–171. See also the newest study by O. Goldwasser, "For a Late 12th Dynasty Date of the Proto-Sinaitic Script," *Egypt and the Levant* 17 (forthcoming).
6. See Thomas Schneider, "Mythos und Zeitgeschichte in der 30. Dynastie," in A. Brodbeck, ed., *Ein ägyptisches Glasperlenspiel* (Berlin 1998; pp. 207–242). I am grateful to Erich Winter, University Trier, Germany, for consultation.
7. Lyvia Morgan (at present visiting professor at Harvard University and Austrian Archaeological Institute in Cairo) and Nanno Marinatos, professor of classics, University of Illinois, Chicago.

# Holy Family Values

## The world into which Jesus was born and raised has shaped morals for two millennia. How Jewish mores became Christianity's customs.

LISA MILLER

Sometime around the beginning of the Common Era, a nice Jewish girl comes to her fiancé with a problem. She is pregnant; he is not the father. The groom-to-be is understandably enraged. In his world, almost nothing brings more shame on a man and his family than a broken promise of virginity. Her explanation, that the baby was conceived by God, must have sounded implausible, desperate, even insane. On reflection, though, the man, who is profoundly decent—"righteous," as the story goes—decides that he cannot bear to inflict upon the girl the rare (but wholly legal) punishment for such crimes, which is stoning. And so he resolves to handle the matter in his own way. He will "divorce her quietly."

If the story ended there, it would be an ordinary drama about a family in crisis, one familiar in many times and many places. But this story was only beginning. The righteous man, Joseph, goes to sleep and receives a visit from an angel. "Joseph, son of David," the angel says, "do not be afraid to take Mary home as your wife, because what is conceived in her is from the Holy Spirit. She will give birth to a son and you are to give him the name Jesus for he will save his people from their sins." Like all good Jews who had received visits from God or angels before him—Abraham, Moses—Joseph does as he is told. The baby is born in Bethlehem; his human parents name him Jesus.

As the world's 2 billion Christians prepare to commemorate the birth of the figure they believe to be the Son of God, it is important to note that Christianity's origins lie more in the image of the empty tomb on the Sunday after the crucifixion than they do at the crèche. It was their fervent belief in the resurrection of Jesus of Nazareth that convinced his followers he was, as Peter put it, "the Christ, the son of the living God" who had told them of a new way of salvation: that he would die and rise again, thus effecting the forgiveness of sins and offering a portal to eternal life.

But whatever one's personal beliefs, no student of religion or culture should overlook the significance of the world of the Nativity, for the milieu into which Jesus was born—and in which he was raised—has fundamentally shaped the manners and morals of the ensuing two millennia. The Jewish family values that were prevalent in first-century Judea—the values of Mary and Joseph and of the young Jesus—became the values of Christianity, and of the regions of the world in which Christianity has long been a critical force.

> **The harmonious coming together of man and woman and their consummation is figuratively a house. And everything which is without a woman is imperfect and homeless.**
>
> —Philo of Alexandria, Jewish philosopher

It all began with the habits and culture of Judaism. The emphasis on family, on sexual morality, on caring for one's kith and kin—all were (and are) sacred Jewish traditions, and the transmission of those mores from a relative backwater of the Roman Empire in the first years of the Common Era to our own time is the unlikely result of Mary and Joseph's parenting, the disciples' failed apocalyptic hopes and, ultimately, the early Christians' search for a way to survive once they realized the Second Coming was not as imminent as they first believed.

The story of Jesus—and thus the story of Christianity—begins with a common Jewish family. Mary is an innocent; Joseph is generous and protective, even of a child who is not his own. The baby is a baby, miraculous enough; like all happy births, his is cause for gossip, celebration and gift giving. On close inspection, the details of the Nativity don't add up particularly well: the birth narrative appears in just two of the four Gospels, Matthew and Luke, and they differ a great deal. Matthew starts with a genealogy, Luke with the story of the miraculous pregnancy of Mary's cousin Elizabeth. The Christmas story most people know from church pageants and television specials is a conflation of the two Gospels, putting Matthew's Magi together with the shepherds of Luke.

As the Nativity story makes clear, though, Mary and Joseph's era was one rich in moral standards designed to offer stability in an uncertain world, and they would have transmitted those standards to their son as he grew up. A woman's virginity, for example, was a sacred possession, to be given away or stolen at great cost. According to Deuteronomy, a man who violated a virgin had to pay a fine of 50 silver shekels and marry the woman in question; an unmarried woman who willfully had sex with a man other than her fiancé could be put to death. In ancient Israel, this value was probably a matter of pragmatism more than theology; it assured men who lived in a culture that prized family above all that their children were their own. "Because it was encoded in Biblical texts and the texts became sacred, [virginity] took on a moral dimension," says Carol Meyers, editor of "Women in Scripture" and a professor of religion at Duke. "By the time of Christianity . . . any violation was seen as going against God's word."

**To the unmarried and the widows I say it is well for them to remain unmarried as I am. But if they are not practicing self-control, they should marry. For it is better to marry than to be aflame with passion.**

—1 Corinthians 7:8-9

The values of Jewish families were unique given the circumstances of the time. It is true that Romans of the first century had some regard for family, too (in his book "Jewish Marriage in Antiquity," Brown University professor Michael Satlow points out that Roman law esteemed married men with children above married men without children and unmarried men as part of the social order).

But Jewish devotion to family predates the Romans by thousands of years—think of all those begats—and by the time of Jesus, Jewish family values were noticeably different from those of their neighbors. A Roman father could, for any or no reason, choose to kill his newborn infant either by cutting the umbilical cord too close or by leaving the baby outside, and the Jewish refusal to do so was seen as peculiar. "The Jews see to it that their numbers increase," wrote the historian Tacitus around A.D. 100. "It is a deadly sin to kill a born or unborn child, and they think that eternal life is granted to those who die in battle or execution—hence their eagerness to have children, and their contempt for death." Herod himself executed two of his own sons, leading Augustus Caesar to remark that "I'd rather be Herod's pigs than Herod's sons."

**The Jews see to it that their numbers increase. It is a deadly sin to kill a born or unborn child, and they think that eternal life is granted to those who die in battle or execution.**

—Tacitus, A.D. 56–117

In a culture so devoted to children, married sex was a blessing. "The harmonious coming together of man and woman and their consummation is figuratively a house. And everything which is without a woman is imperfect and homeless," wrote the Jewish philosopher Philo of Alexandria (20 B.C.-A.D. 40). Within this context, whether Joseph and Mary, a married Jewish couple, did or did not eventually procreate on their own is a subject of endless scholarly and theological debate. When, in the Gospel of Matthew, the author says that Joseph had no union with Mary "until she gave birth to a son," he implies that a union did occur afterward—a decent explanation for the appearance in Mark and Matthew of Jesus' brothers James, Joseph, Judas and Simon, as well as unnamed sisters. "Some good historians believe that [these brothers and sisters] were part of Jesus' entourage," says Rodney Stark, of Baylor University.

And so the growing Jesus would have come of age in a world that cherished procreation, family ties and the history and theology of Israel, including immersion in the Scriptures and the ancient stories of God's deliverance of his people. According to Luke, when Jesus was 12, he traveled with his parents to Jerusalem from Galilee to celebrate Passover. The family feasted there and when they were done, Joseph and Mary turned around and headed home. After a day, they noticed that their son was missing from their entourage and rushed back to Jerusalem to find him. There, the story goes, they discovered Jesus in the temple, talking to the priests and astonishing the assembled crowds with his wisdom.

But his parents were parents, and they were worried. "Son, why have you treated us like this?" his mother asks. "Your father and I have been anxiously searching for you."

"Why were you searching for me? Didn't you know I had to be in my father's house?" But they did not understand what he was saying.

**Your wife Elizabeth will bear you a son, and you are to give him the name John. He will be a joy and delight to you, and many will rejoice because of his birth, for he will be great in the sight of the Lord.**

—Luke 1:13

It would not, in all likelihood, be the last time. Their son was growing up in a time of great theological and political turbulence in Judea; in the time of Mary and Joseph, some Jews had begun to believe that the end of the world was coming any day. It would be brought about by a warrior king, a messiah from the house of David, who would destroy the wicked and usher in the kingdom of heaven on earth. The Gospels do not say what Joseph and Mary believed about the apocalypse, but John the Baptist believed in one, and when Jesus says, in Luke, "The Kingdom of God is near," an apocalypse is precisely what he means.

In the temple, Jesus is as rude as a 12-year-old can be. But he's also the kind of Jewish son a mother would be proud of: he takes the family values of his childhood and, in his later years, makes a revolutionary leap. Family, he comes to preach, is not in the blood ties and biology his parents' generation so reveres. To him, the end of the world is coming and what matters now is the community of believers, the followers of the Messiah—on earth and in heaven. What matters is the family, as he put it, of man. Throughout the Gospels, Jesus makes this point again and again. "Let the dead bury the dead," he says in Luke. There's no need for sweet goodbyes. The only thing a believer must do is "follow me" and proclaim the Kingdom of God.

The meaning of this message was powerful to his followers, who tended to be laborers and not affluent urbanites. (Though his ministry was apparently funded by relatively wealthy single women.) "For Jesus, family values means treating other people in the community as if they were your biological siblings or your mother, and that's extraordinary," says Amy-Jill Levine, author of "The Misunderstood Jew" and a professor at Vanderbilt. That is why, when the Pharisees come to him and ask him how to punish an adulterer, he takes her side. "If any of you is without sin, let you be the first to throw a stone at her," he says.

With the kingdom at hand—really at hand; Jesus says at one point that there are listeners in his hearing "who shall not taste death" before the coming of the Messiah—practical concerns about the care and feeding of kin were less than critical. Jesus de-emphasized not just earthly family, but also sex and marriage—though he preached strongly against divorce. Unmarried himself, his disciples were also either single or solo, presumably leaving behind parents, children and spouses to follow their new family. In Matthew, he speaks with respect of "eunuchs who have made themselves eunuchs for the sake of the kingdom of heaven. Let anyone accept this who can."

Jesus was not the first Jew to connect ideas of sexual asceticism with spiritual salvation. Around the time of his birth, another group of apocalypse-minded Jews called the Essenes lived together in ascetic community, and the Jewish historian Josephus found their marital customs odd enough to write down. One sect of Essenes, he wrote, shuns marriage and prefers instead to educate other people's children; another has "no intercourse with [their wives] during pregnancy, thus showing that their motive in marrying is not self-indulgence but the procreation of children." The break Jesus and people such as the Essenes made with the values of their youths was predicated on the end of the world.

Then came the Passion, but still nothing happened. Jesus had died and risen again—even appeared to his disciples on numerous occasions shortly after the first Easter—yet the world continued just as it had the day before, without trumpets or angels or fiery battles. The first small band of followers must have felt at least some disappointment; instead of going to heaven, they were going back to their farms, to their fishing or, in cases like Peter and James's, to the work of making sense of the theological thunderbolt that had changed them forever. No matter what they were doing, their parents, their children and their earthly responsibilities were waiting.

As the years passed and the early church took shape, the original followers began, naturally, to die off, and the followers of Jesus' message had a choice to make: would they shape the message for the masses or would they opt, like Paul and the Jewish Essenes, for a more ascetic approach? The decision was urgent, for history was unfolding, the pull of the Roman Empire was strong, and without some kind of family and social structure the movement would be doomed.

It was, then, time to return to the values of the world of the Nativity, to ways of preserving families even in times of crisis. In her 1988 book "Adam, Eve and the Serpent," Elaine Pagels of Princeton University argues that Matthew recalibrated some of Jesus' more radical sayings to accommodate the familial concerns of regular people. Matthew, Pagels points out, provides a loophole for divorce: "Let no man put asunder," Jesus says, except in cases where the wife has committed adultery. Also in Matthew, Jesus reasserts the commandment "Honor your mother and father." Near the end of the first century, Pope Clement argues that Jesus' unmarried state was in no way meant to be an example for everyone: "the reason that Jesus didn't marry was that, in the first place, he was already engaged, so to speak, to the church; and, in the second place, he was no ordinary man."

No matter what one thinks of Jesus of Nazareth—that he was the Son of God, an interesting prophetic figure or a religious provocateur with particularly prolific followers—surely we can agree that he was no ordinary man. Yet at the end, in agony on Golgotha, Jesus affirmed the familial order he had spent so much of his public ministry arguing was about to be disrupted. He saw his mother standing nearby, watching her boy die a criminal's death. In a final act of human compassion, he called to his disciple John. "And he said to his mother 'Dear woman, here is your son,' and to the disciple, 'Here is your mother.' From that time on this disciple took her into his home." At the end of his life, then, Jesus took care of his mother, the penultimate act of a nice Jewish boy—and a blessing of the kinds of values that should endure, as his followers say even now, until his coming again.

---

**Lisa Miller** with Anne Underwood; Julie Scelfo and Joshua Alston

# UNIT 4

# Muslims and Byzantines

## Unit Selections

18. **Adrianople,** Joe Zentner
19. **The Survival of the Eastern Roman Empire,** Sephen Williams and Gerard Friell
20. **Islam's First Terrorists,** Clive Foss
21. **Rediscovering Arabic Science,** Richard Covington

## Key points to Consider

- What were the bad military tactics which resulted in the death of Emperor Valens?
- How was the Eastern Roman Empire able to survive even after the West had fallen? Was this Byzantine civilization merely an extension of the late Roman culture, or was it a new departure?
- Why were the Kharijites influential in Islamic history?
- What do we owe to Islam in the realm of science?

## Student Web Site

www.mhcls.com/online

## Internet References

**ByzNet: Byzantine Studies on the Net**

*http://www.thoughtline.com/byznet/*

**Islam: A Global Civilization**

*http://www.templemount.org/islamiad.html*

After the collapse of the Roman Empire in the west, three ethnic/religious entities emerged to fill the vacuum. Germanic kingdoms arose in central and western Europe. In the Balkans and Asia Minor, the eastern remnants of Rome evolved into the Byzantine Empire. The Near East, North Africa, and much of Spain fell under the control of the Arabs. Each area developed a unique civilization, based in each instance upon a distinctive form of religion—Roman Catholicism in most of Europe, Orthodox Christianity in the Byzantine sphere, and Islam in the Arab world. Each placed its unique stamp upon the classical tradition to which all three fell heir. The articles in this unit concentrate on the Byzantine and Muslim civilizations. The medieval culture of Europe is treated in the next unit.

Western perceptions of Islam and Arabic civilization have been clouded by ignorance and bias. To European observers during the medieval period, Islam seemed a misguided or heretical version of Christianity. In the wake of Arab conquests, Islam increasingly came to represent terror and devastation (see "Islam's First Terrorists"), a dangerous forced loosed upon Christendom. Reacting out of fear and hostility, Christian authors were reluctant to acknowledge the learning and high culture of the Arabs.

Muslim commentators could be equally intolerant. Describing Europeans, one wrote: "They are most like beasts than like men. . . . Their temperaments are frigid, their humors raw, their bellies gross . . . they lack keenness of understanding . . . and are overcome by ignorance and apathy."

The stereotypes formed in the early encounters between Christians and Muslims survived for generations. Centuries of hostility have tended to obscure the extent of cultural exchange between the Arab world and the West. Indeed, as historian William H. McNeil has observed, "Muslims have been written out of European history."

The lands of Islam encroached at too many places for the two cultures to remain mutually exclusive. In Western Europe Islam swept over Spain, crossed the Pyrenees, and penetrated France; in the central Mediterranean, it leaped form Tunis to Sicily and then into southern Italy; and in Eastern Europe, Islam broke into Asia Minor, the Balkans, and the Caucasus. In its expansion, early Islam was exposed to Jewish, Christian, and classical influences. History and geography determined that there would be much cross-fertilization of Islam and the West.

Yet there is no denying the originality and brilliance of Islamic civilization. The religion of Muhammad is unquestionably one of the world's most influential faiths. Additional evidence of Arab creativity can be found in the visual arts, particularly in the design and decoration of the great mosques. The Arabs also made significant contributions in philosophy, history, geography, science and medicine (see "Rediscovering Arabic Science").

Aramco Photo

The medieval West borrowed extensively from the Arabs. The magnificent centers of Islamic culture—Baghdad, Cairo, Cordoba, and Damascus outshone the cities of the West. Their administration of Andalusia was a model of successful governance. Islamic scholars surpassed their Christian counterparts in astronomy, mathematics, and medicine—perhaps because the Arab world was more familiar than medieval Europe with the achievements of classical Greece. European scholars eventually regained access to the Greek heritage, at least partially, through translations from Arabic.

As for the Byzantine Empire, it was for nearly 1,000 years a Christian bulwark against Persians, Arabs, and Turks. Stephen Williams and Gerard Friell recount the reasons for its success in "The Survival of the Eastern Roman Empire". It also made important cultural contributions. The beautiful mosaics and icons of Byzantine artists set the pattern for later visualizations of Christ in the West. Byzantine missionaries and statesmen spread Orthodox Christianity, with its unique tradition of Caesaropapism, to Russia. While Byzantine scholars and lawmakers preserved much of the classical heritage. Even hostile Islam was subject to a constant flow of ideas and traditions from the Byzantines.

# Adrianople

## *Last Great Battle of Antiquity*

**Emperor Valens' haste to come to grips with the Goths cost him his life and Rome its last predominantly Roman army.**

JOE ZENTNER

The annals of the later Roman empire are scarred by events that took place near the Thracian city of Adrianople on the afternoon of August 9, AD 378. By that evening, the eastern Roman Emperor Valens was dead along with tens of thousands of irreplaceable warriors, in a defeat that signaled the beginning of the end of Rome's ability to resist external pressure and prevent penetration of its defenses. According to the contemporary historian Ammianus Marcellinus, himself a Roman officer, "No battle in our history except Cannae [Hannibal Barca's great victory in 216 BC] involved such a massacre."

After the death of Emperor Constantine in AD 337, the Roman empire saw the return of sibling struggles for total control. Constantine had hoped that his three surviving sons would be satisfied with one-third of the empire each—western Europe, southeastern Europe and the eastern provinces—but such was not to be. After his three sons were killed, they were followed not by blood relations but by a succession of generals from their armies.

The general who finally secured the imperial purple on February 26, 364, was Flavius Valentinianus, a man of humble birth but considerable military skill. As Emperor Valentinian I, he focused on shoring up the frontier along the Danube River. To keep the eastern part of the empire in friendly hands, on March 28 Valentinian appointed his brother, Flavius Julius Valens, to the position of co-emperor and placed him in Constantinople. Valentinian died in 375 and was succeeded by his 16-year-old son, Flavius Gratianus, or Gratian. Contemporaries described Gratian as "a young man of remarkable talent: eloquent, controlled, warlike, yet merciful." During his short life, he fought successfully against Rome's enemies and vigorously attacked the last vestiges of paganism. At the time he became emperor in the west, however, Gratian was much too inexperienced to hold any sway over his uncle, Valens.

In contrast to his brother, Valens did not join the Roman army until 360, and thanks to Adrianople he has gone down in history as an ineffective military leader. In actuality, he was not without skill as a commander. His earlier offensive campaign against the Goths, from 367 to 369, was conducted with vigor and skill. In spite of difficulties in carrying out operations against elusive enemies in their home territory, he was able to bring his Goth foes to battle and defeat them.

According to their own traditions, the Goths originated in a land called Gothiscandza, identified as southern Scandinavia. Those same traditions cite population pressure as the reason for their move to what would become their long-standing homeland between the Oder and Vistula rivers, in what is now Poland. However, no archaeological evidence exists to support this idea. What seems to have happened was a slow, steady drift from the Oder-Vistula region into Scythia, now known as Ukraine. That region already contained a mixed population, and the Goths would certainly have mixed with other peoples to produce a populace that was far from homogeneous. By the middle of the 3rd century, they had become a formidable power.

The leader of a Visigothic tribe called the Tervingians, Fritigern (derived from the Goth word *frithugairns,* "desiring peace"), was a prominent warrior-king whose followers included a number of Roman subjects as well as Goths. The former ranged from escaped slaves and gold miners to Goth soldiers in the Roman army who, although initially loyal to Rome, had been driven to rebellion by the hostility of the local populace. Fritigern must have been a man of enormous charisma and strength of will. He managed to hold together a confederacy of disparate clans and tribes with no greater authority than their belief in his ability to win. Since Fritigern's followers included Huns, Roman expatriates and Germanic tribesmen, large numbers would have deserted him had they felt better off under someone else's leadership.

Compared to the vast trove of information available on the Roman army of the 4th century, virtually nothing is known of the Goth fighting organization—if there was one. Nevertheless, the Goths were not mere wild men, as popularly portrayed in Roman and later accounts. Many had served in Roman armies and knew how to wield a sword, spear or battle-ax with skill. Such weapons were more of a threat to the Romans than in previous centuries because of changes in the Roman infantry. Due to reductions in available funds for military spending, the Roman soldier wore less metal armor, his shield was smaller and rounder and, to compensate, his short stabbing *gladius* had been replaced by a sword longer than the one he had used in the 1st century. Roman infantry formations were still formidable but had lost some of the invincible aura they had enjoyed in the imperial heyday.

The Goths often fought from laagers, a group of wagons arranged in a circle, from which they would dart out to do battle, then quickly return. This amounted to a mobile fortress that could protect them no matter where they fought.

In the fall of 376, the Romans agreed to help Fritigern's people cross the Danube and settle in the province of Moesia. In 377, however, a famine struck the Roman areas settled by the Visigoths, and their appeals for help went unanswered by the Roman authorities. The *magister militum* (governor-general) of the area, Lupicinus, and his *dux secundae,* Magnus Maximus, treated the Visigoths badly, forcing them to pay exorbitant prices for food and keeping Goth women as concubines.

As the Goths became restive, Lupicinus invited Fritigern, Alaviv and other Visigothic chieftains to a banquet at his headquarters in Marcianople, planning to make them hostages to keep their tribes in line. His plan failed—a fight broke out, the Gothic escorts and Alaviv were killed, but Fritigern escaped.

The Tervingians under Fritigern now rose in open revolt, pillaging the countryside surrounding Marcianople. Lupicinus led a small force to confront them nine miles outside the city, only to be overpowered and massacred.

The crisis continued into 378, with the Visigoths holding sway over much of Thrace, an ancient country in the southeastern part of the Balkan Peninsula, reaching north to the Danube and comprising modern Bulgaria and parts of Greece and Turkey.

Emperor Valens and his army were in Thrace, marching west from Adrianople along the Martisa River valley when news reached him that the Goths were moving south along the Tundzha River. At first he thought it was only a small raiding party, but he soon realized it was a much larger force. He therefore turned back toward Adrianople and established a fortified camp just outside the city.

Located at the western end of the Thracian plain near the Greek border, 130 miles northwest of Constantinople, Adrianople (now Edirne in Turkey) was originally named Hadrianopolis, for the Roman Emperor Hadrian, who built it in AD 125 on the site of the ancient city of Uskudarna. Lying at the confluence of the Martisa, Tundzha and Arda rivers, it had been of geographic and military importance since ancient times.

Holding a conference with his lieutenants during the night of August 8, 378, Valens faced a crucial decision: Should he engage the Goths at once or wait for his young nephew and co-emperor, Gratian, to join him? This caused a rift among his senior officers. The more cautious among them recommended that Valens wait and allow Gratian to arrive with his army. The Romans could then move as a combined force to fight a stronger battle and wipe out the entire Goth threat. Gratian's western contingent was not many days' march away, they argued, and communications between the two armies had already been established.

Another group of officers, led by a general who knew what he was doing, urged immediate action. *Comes* (Count) Sebastianus had been appointed to overall command in the region two months earlier, and in the previous weeks had adopted an aggressive guerrilla-style mode of campaigning. It had proven immensely successful thus far, forcing the Goths to cease raiding in small bands and coalesce into much larger groups for their own protection. That made them vulnerable to a conventional, large-scale Roman attack. Sebastianus had, in fact, caught and destroyed a large column of Goths returning from a plundering expedition to Rhodope in southern Thrace, shortly before joining Valens and being appointed to command his infantry.

Several factors influenced Valens' final decision. First, his scouts reported that the Goth force contained only about 10,000 fighting men. Since Valens had about 15,000 soldiers in his own army, it was tempting to engage the Goths in battle then and there. Moreover, Valens' standing in Constantinople was very low at that time. If he allowed a Goth army to take position between Adrianople and Constantinople, he would not only find his supply lines cut off but also risk the likelihood of the populace in the eastern capital feeling abandoned by their emperor.

Valens' contemporary, Ammianus, and many later historians believed that the emperor—jealous of his young nephew—decided on an immediate battle to gain personal glory. Though that was perhaps true, it would not have been the only reason for Valens' hasty actions. He may have underestimated the Goths' strength, for he had defeated them on the Danube nine years earlier. In any case, Valens seemed confident of an easy victory on the morning of August 9, as he led the field army of the east from Adrianople to attack the Goths, who were camped 12 miles from the city.

The Romans marched rapidly under a blazing sun, coming upon the Goth camp at about 2 that afternoon. The Goths were encamped in a secure position, probably on high and easily defensible ground. The imperial troops were hastily drawn up into battle formation while the Goths broke into savage howls, as they were accustomed to do just before an engagement.

Either because of unfamiliarity with the terrain or by mistake, the right wing of the Roman cavalry came within sight of the Goths while the left was still a considerable distance away, with many of the horsemen on the left wing scattered along roads leading up to the Goth camp. Some historians assume that the Goths fought from behind their wagon laager at Adrianople, but that would have been unlikely. Their usual procedure was to engage their enemies in the open and fall back on the camp only when an encounter was not going well. Had they remained behind the laager, they would have not only surrendered the initiative to the Romans but also would have been unable to use their preferred fighting tactic of charging into hand-to-hand combat with spears, swords and shields. On several occasions Ammianus' descriptions of the battle explain that one part of the Roman line managed to fight its way forward as far as the wagons, clearly indicating that the fighting took place primarily in the open, beyond the wagon laager.

Riding boldly into the Roman right wing, the Goth cavalry scattered the surprised Roman cavalry line and then turned to attack the Roman left wing. Within moments, all the Roman horsemen had been driven from the field, leaving the weary infantry exposed.

Fritigern chose that moment to burst from the laager at the head of his own infantry. Ammianus d scribed the Roman soldiers' plight: "The different companies became so huddled together that hardly anyone could pull out his sword, or draw back his arm, and because of immense clouds of dust, the heavens could no longer be seen. . . . Hence Goth arrows whirling death from every side found their mark with fatal effect, since they could not be seen beforehand nor guarded against."

Hemmed in from all sides, the Roman foot was packed together too tightly to create any effective battle formation. The slaughter was frightful as Fritigern's infantry closed in, while his cavalry kept any Romans who broke out from getting very far. The battlefield ran red with blood, most of it Roman. Men slipped on the bloody ground and many died after falling on their own weapons. Heaps of bodies littered the field, including *Comes* Sebastianus.

There are two stories concerning Valens' fate. One claims that an arrow struck him while among the ranks of his army, and his body was never found. The other claims that, wounded by an arrow, he was taken by his guards to a nearby peasant dwelling, which the Goths subsequently attacked. The Roman defenders initially managed to drive back the Goths with arrows, but they soon returned, piled up brushwood and straw against the house and set fire to it. One Roman soldier jumped from a window and was captured by the Goths, but the others, including the emperor, perished in the blaze. The prisoner later escaped to tell the story.

Ammianus stated that two-thirds of the Roman army died at Adrianople. His comparison of the massacre to Hannibal Barca's tactical masterpiece at Cannae is apt because in both battles Roman horsemen were driven from the field, leaving the infantry to be encircled, hemmed in and destroyed.

The outcome at Adrianople shocked the Western world. The Romans had lost battles before, but never so decisively. Nor had barbarians made Roman commanders look so utterly incompetent at the art of war. From beginning to end, Valens and his generals had been outguessed, outsmarted and outmaneuvered by Fritigern's Goths.

Various explanations have been offered for this improbable victory by an ad hoc force of refugees and deserters over the best organized, equipped and disciplined army in the world. Some observers claimed that, contrary to Valens' faulty appraisal, the Goths enjoyed a numerical superiority of as many as 200,000 warriors. In fact, given the logistical difficulties of feeding and sustaining so many men, Fritigern would have been lucky to muster one-tenth that number. Other historians claimed that the battle proved the superiority of cavalry over infantry. The truth is that while a timely cavalry charge sealed the battle's ultimate outcome, it was primarily a clash of infantry with infantry.

The Roman defeat at Adrianople can be attributed to both strategic and tactical reasons. At the strategic level, the Romans were unable to assemble enough high-quality troops to deal rapidly and decisively with the Goth threat. Although the empire had some 500,000 men under arms at that time, they were committed to guarding imperial borders from Britannia to Syria. There was a real danger that if a significant number were moved from one point to another, a potential enemy would take advantage of the weakened border segment to attack. Moreover, while Roman field armies were supposedly mobile and rapidly deployable, orders to move to a new area of operations often resulted in mass desertions that critically thinned their ranks.

When it came to using the force at their disposal, the Roman commanders at Adrianople acted with an arrogance typical of leaders of a well-equipped "civilized" army faced with what they perceived as rabble. Those commanders allowed themselves to be drawn into battle without proper reconnaissance and without ensuring that the odds were stacked in their favor before committing their forces to a fight.

It is also probable that the quality and morale of eastern Roman soldiers were low before the campaign began. Only 13 years earlier, Valens had led them on a rigorous but reasonably successful campaign against the Sassanian Persians, only to abandon the effort and leave Armenia in Persian hands. In any case, it was an overwhelmingly hot August day when Valens' soldiers had marched hurriedly from Adrianople to the plain near where the Goths had been reported. Consequently, they were exhausted and thirsty before the fighting began. It would be unjust, however, to cite the Roman failings without crediting the strategic skill shown by Fritigern; in spite of his logistic problems, the Goth commander managed to dictate the terms and tempo throughout the campaign.

Gratian was well advanced in his march to assist Valens at Adrianople when he learned that his impatient co-emperor had been killed and most of his army destroyed. In light of this setback and distracted by his own affairs in the western empire, he believed that imperial administration in the east would require undivided attention that he would be unable to give. Gratian therefore placed Flavius Theodosius, the son of a distinguished general and himself a commander of some experience, in charge. On January 19, 379, Theodosius was proclaimed co-emperor and officially assigned to rule the eastern provinces.

Fritigern's victory at Adrianople gave the Goths control of nearly the entire Balkan Peninsula. They raided Greece, leaving only the city of Athens and other small areas of that country unravaged.

Theodosius' plan for pacifying the Goths proved to be as damaging as Valens' original decision to let them cross the Danube. He would grant them the right to occupy Thrace if they would swear loyalty to the empire and become Roman soldiers. Peace was restored, but at a tremendous cost. With the empire lacking the human resources to replace its losses in the wake of Adrianople, the Roman army was transformed into an army of Goths fighting for the emperor. As the fourth century ended, the Goths bloodlessly gained control of the army. For the first time in its history, the Roman army was no longer composed primarily of Romans.

Scholars have given a variety of dates for the fall of Rome, the latest being 1453, when Constantinople, capital of the eastern Roman empire, fell to the Ottoman Turks, but that was a new, Byzantine, Greek-speaking empire far removed from the Caesars. The fall of the western empire is set at 476, when its last emperor, Romulus Augustulus, surrendered to the Ostrogoths. That, however, was just the coup de grâce following a succession of disasters, such as the murder of Valentinian III in 455, the loss of the African provinces to the Vandals in 429 and Alaric's sack of Rome in 410.

It might be argued that ancient Rome received its mortal blow in 378, and simply took almost a century to die. The empire had been in bad shape before, but not so bad that a single strong leader could not have saved the situation. After Adrianople, however, Rome's decline became irreversible. Once the Romans had to rely on the Goths to fight their wars for them, the emperor's power collapsed, and the new Goth-dominated army was unable to fend off other marauding peoples who spilled over the eastern frontiers.

It may be stretching the point for military historians to pronounce Adrianople a victory of cavalry over infantry that ushered in the era of the medieval knight. After that battle, however, Roman armies lost their classical character. Cavalry came to predominate and because horsemen, especially those from the east, were also archers, their ability to attack at long range severely limited the power of infantry formations. Not until the 15th century did weapons such as the longbow and crossbow begin to overturn the effectiveness of cavalry on the battlefield.

As the reliability of the native Roman army declined after Adrianople, emperors, generals and even private citizens began to hire bands of retainers, usually Germanic in makeup. By the mid-fifth century, Roman field armies had evolved into large bands of mounted warriors owing their allegiance directly to powerful warlords rather than to the state. Those armies had more in common with a feudal host than with Rome's republican or imperial legions of classical times.

Although it was fought in the east, the Battle of Adrianople had its most direct effect on the affairs of Rome's western provinces. It initiated a huge influx of Germanic peoples who continued their migrations to overrun the western Roman empire within the next century. In ironic contrast, the eastern Roman empire, with its capital at Constantinople, would survive the fall of Rome itself and, adapting to the eastern environment in which it was isolated amid a sea of barbarians, endure for another 1,000 years.

# The Survival of the Eastern Roman Empire

STEPHEN WILLIAMS AND GERARD FRIELL

The old attitude still prevails in some quarters that what we know of as the Roman Empire was dismembered in the fifth century, and that what survived in the East was something different—Byzantium, Greek and Christian; fascinating, no doubt, but no longer the real Rome. This quite misleading picture is often accompanied by another: that the survival of the Eastern half in the terrible fifth century, when the West went under, was a more or less natural development—even unconsciously anticipated by Constantine's wise foundation of his new capital in the wealthier, more urbanised East.

The reality of course was very different. Despite the administrative division into East and West, which predated Constantine, the empire was everywhere seen as one and indivisible. At the beginnings of the fifth century both halves faced similar chronic problems: immature or inept emperors, rebellious armies, external barbarian invaders and the large and dangerous settlements of barbarian 'allies' within imperial territories. By difficult expedients and innovations the East was eventually able to overcome these problems, while the West was not. After several attempts, Constantinople accepted that it had not the strength to save the West, but it still treated it as a group of temporarily lost provinces to be recovered when the situation permitted—a view that the emperor Justinian in the sixth century took entirely literally.

After the disastrous defeat by the immigrant Visigoths at Adrianople (Edirne) in 378, the new Eastern emperor, Theodosius, was eventually able to fight and manoeuvre them into signing a treaty in 382, settling them in the Balkans as 'allies' (*foederati*), since they could not possibly be expelled. They were obliged to support the emperor, militarily, on request, but this was nonetheless a radically new departure in foreign policy, the result of Roman weakness. Instead of mere farmer-settlers under Roman administration, this was an entire armed Germanic nation established deep within Roman territory under its own tribal leaders. It could not help but be a precedent for other land-hungry barbarians. Theodosius, however, had no option but to hope that in time the Goths could be assimilated as others had been.

After Theodosius's death in 395, his two young sons, Arcadius (377–408) and Honorius (384–423), inherited the thrones of East and West respectively. Both boy-emperors were immature and incapable (Honorius was practically retarded), and although strong loyalty to the dynasty kept them on their thrones, they were entirely managed by individuals or factions within the two courts. Instead of the cooperation that was badly needed, the two governments of East and West intrigued and manoeuvred against each other like hostile states for over ten years, with damaging consequences.

On Theodosius's death the Visigoths immediately broke out of their assigned territories and ravaged the Eastern provinces, under their leader Alaric, who now declared himself king. Temporarily without their main army, the Eastern government, dominated by the eunuch chamberlain Eutropius, was able to deflect Alaric westwards by granting him a top military command in Illyricum (Yugoslavia). The combined status of Roman general and tribal warlord created yet another dangerous precedent. Alaric was able to exploit the deep hostility between the two governments, becoming a destabilising force over the next fifteen years.

In the West, real power was legitimately in the hands of the commander-in-chief Stilicho, of Vandal origin, who had been appointed guardian of the boy-emperor Honorius. He was resented and feared by the ruling circles at Constantinople, who had him declared a public enemy. Stilicho, hoping in vain to force Alaric back into his former alliance, was able to defeat him several times but not destroy him. He had to crush a revolt in Africa (encouraged by Constantinople) and then defeat an Ostrogothic invasion of Italy itself. He was by now forced to buy barbarian fighting men from any source and on any terms, often with personal promises, and even grants of land.

To defend Italy, Stilicho had to strip Britain and the Rhine frontier of troops, and at New Year 407 multiple barbarian invaders crossed the frozen Rhine into Gaul virtually unopposed, never to be expelled again. For this, Stilicho's political enemies in the Senate contrived to have him condemned and executed on the weak emperor's orders, where upon thousands of his loyal barbarian troops, fearing for themselves and their families, fled over to join Alaric. With Stilicho removed, nothing could prevent Alaric from besieging and finally sacking Rome in 410.

The East had rid itself of the menace of Alaric by propelling him westwards, but this did not free it from other barbarian dangers. What Alaric's Visigoths could do, others could imitate. A new revolt broke out in 399 among the recently-settled Ostrogothic federates. Gainas, the general sent to suppress it, mistrusted the government and was himself of Gothic origin and the commander of other Gothic federate troops. The two Gothic groups joined forces, marched on Constantinople and occupied it, with Gainas dictating his terms to the emperor. However, he was met by a violent anti-Gothic, popular backlash and total hostility from the civil government. Having achieved nothing, he attempted a clumsy withdrawal from the capital in which many Goths and their families were massacred by the mob. Those that escaped were later defeated by loyal units (also commanded by a Goth).

These events had a profound effect on the civilian ruling circles in Constantinople. Henceforth they were determined to keep a firm grip on imperial power and curb ambitious generals, especially those of Gothic origin, even though many were entirely loyal. For several years Goths were excluded from top commands, armies were thinned in numbers, and care was taken to avoid any new settlements of barbarian federates. The Praetorian Prefect, Anthemius, the acknowledged leader of the state, invested instead in strengthening the defences on the Danube frontier, building a new and massive belt of land walls to protect Constantinople, its emperor and government, from both barbarian invasions and its own potentially dangerous armies.

The exclusion of Gothic generals did not last long. With the federate crises past, and a growing external threat from the Huns, able professional commanders such as Plinta, Aspar and Areobindus once again rose to the top *Magister* posts. The fact that they were divorced from any federate or tribal power base (unlike Alaric and Gainas) made them acceptable. They remained what they had been in the previous century—loyal members of the Roman ruling class.

The really farsighted achievement of the Eastern empire during this period was not so much the weakening of the power of the army, as the institutionalising of it within a central ruling establishment at Constantinople, which included the palace and civil bureaucracy. The Eastern field army, about 100,000 strong, was already divided into five regional mobile groups, and the commands carefully balanced between men of Gothic and Roman origin. Two of these groups—the Praesental armies—were stationed in the vicinity of Constantinople and their commanders, of whatever background, were senior members of the senate and members of the emperor's inner council of state, the Consistory.

Any successful, ambitious general was faced with a choice and a temptation. He could use external military violence to try to dominate the emperor at Constantinople, perhaps even making himself emperor, or at least military dictator. Or he could use the army's indispensability and natural leverage within the legitimate, established power structure where there was a place for him at the top table.

Gainas had attempted the first option and had been ruined. Other military leaders overwhelmingly chose the second. Though politically powerful, the army was only one of several competing, but also interlocking, forces around the throne. To break out of this careful web of power risked losing everything. Certainly, there were bitter conflicts within the Constantinople establishment. For many years the deficiencies of the pious and bookish emperor Theodosius II (408–450) were heavily compensated by his dominating sister Pulcheria, who did everything possible to keep power within the palace and the imperial family rather than the civil ministers and generals. But even she had to negotiate with these other power centres.

The solidarity of the inner establishment was strikingly demonstrated when confronted by the end of an imperial dynasty, when all the old threats of factional coup, military violence and even civil war, reared their heads in the struggle to place a new emperor on the throne. Aware of what each stood to lose, palace, bureaucracy, army and, later, church found ways to fight their conflicts behind closed doors and then present an agreed imperial choice to be acclaimed by the senate, the troops, the people and the wider world.

This orderly transmission of imperial power was achieved in the elevation of Marcian in 450, Leo in 457 and Anastasius in 491, all of them dynastic breaks. Through these precedents, buttressed by an increasingly elaborate ceremony of emperor-making, violent coups and civil wars became the exception. Even if a declared rebel succeeded in gaining wide support outside, he still had to cash in his imperial claims in the capital itself, in the face of the central establishment and the city's virtually impregnable defences: if he did not already enjoy powerful allies within the city this was a daunting task.

Thus, an important factor in the durability of the establishment was simply the acknowledged geographical concentration of power and authority in a single capital, Constantinople, which was in every sense what Rome had once been. The emergence of a viable, rival power base was made very difficult, and this, as much as the city's strategic position and fortifications, contributed heavily to the stability and Survival of the Eastern state.

Of all the elements in the establishment, stability was most steadfastly provided by the civil bureaucracy, which provided experience, statecraft and continuity. They kept the impersonal, administrative machine functioning even during violent conflicts within the palace, or purges of this or that faction. These senatorial mandarins, in fact, represented a new service aristocracy created by Constantine. Frequently of modest origins, they owed their power and status not to birth or landed wealth, but entirely to government service. Consequently, regardless of whether a particular emperor was strong or weak, they took great care to uphold and strengthen the imperial authority itself, since their careers, and hence their prosperity, completely depended on it.

In contrast, the great Western senatorial clans such as the Anicii and Scipiones were only concerned to husband their already huge accumulated family wealth, and treated high state positions as no more than honorific perquisites. Part of the East's undoubtedly greater financial muscle, therefore, was due not just to its inherently greater wealth but also to these mandarins' more honest management of the tax machine, even when it bore on their own aspiring social order.

In the West, the response to the problem of a weak unmilitary emperor was quite different. Real power was concentrated in a military strongman such as Stilicho who ruled on his behalf

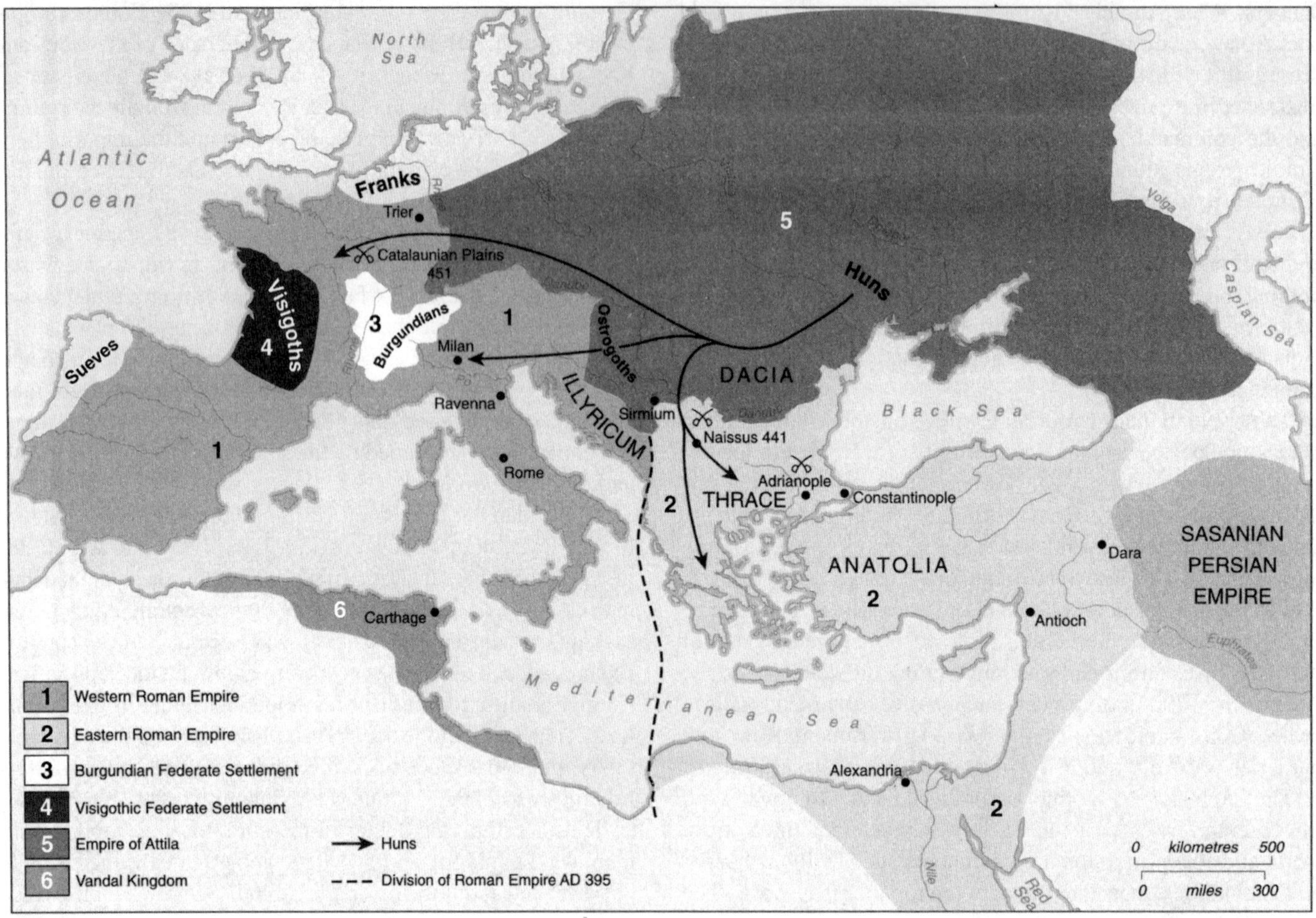


By 450, the Western empire was already a patchwork of barbarian settlements whereas the East retained its integrity.

and enjoyed extraordinary authority, making appointments and issuing laws in the emperor's name. The long reign of the feeble Honorius, the multiple military emergencies and the need to raise and move armies rapidly made this new ruling figure indispensable. Alter a few years of turmoil the general Constantius stepped into this new position, now vaguely designated 'Patrician' and perhaps better described as military dictator or *generalissimo.* After him came Aetius. Both were patriotic and energetic rulers but had no legally acknowledged position beyond their monopoly of military force, and no regular way of transferring their power to a successor. Each had to intrigue or fight his way to dominant power, which was destructive and destabilising.

Inevitably they came to depend more on their personal popularity and prestige among the troops, whom they recruited and paid. A gulf steadily grew up between the real power of the warlord with his army, and the symbolic, legal authority with the emperor in his palace. During the invasion of Italy, Stilicho had persuaded Honorius to shift the imperial capital from Milan to the safe refuge of Ravenna, creating a geographical split in addition to the political one.

Constantius achieved a degree of stability in the West, but at enormous cost. Visigoths, Burgundians, Franks, Suevi and Vandals were all settled as federates on large tracts of Gaul and Spain, and were evolving into Germanic kingdoms under only the most nominal Roman overlordship. Constantius and Aetius skilfully exploited their rivalries to maintain some ascendancy. But having relinquished control of so much taxable land and its populations, the regular Roman armies were only one force among many, and no responsible leader could do more than hold the balance, and avoid risking this force if possible.

The Hun menace took on an entirely new dimension with Attila, who had unified them under a single king and subjected all the remaining tribes to Hun rule. His object was not land to settle, but plunder, tribute and glory, and once again the blow fell initially on the East. His hordes ravaged the Balkans three times in the 440s, sacking and ruining many major cities and enslaving their populations. The Roman armies that met him in the field were repeatedly beaten by his cavalry, but he was always deterred by Constantinople whose defences he could not storm. After each invasion he had to be bought off by an increasingly ignominious 'treaty' and larger annual payments, involving heavier taxation of the senatorial classes. In all, the East paid him about nine tons of gold, until the new emperor Marcian finally tore up the treaties and defied him.

Yet here, the two great resources of the East came to the rescue: the impassable fortifications of Constantinople and the enormous taxable wealth of the Asiatic provinces—Anatolia, Syria, Palestine, Egypt. So long as this great land gate was kept shut and so long as these provinces remained secure—meaning peaceful relations with Persia—Attila could always be bought off and much of the Balkan territories temporarily lost without mortal damage to the empire.

Relations with Persia were always a crucial consideration if the empire was to avoid the perils of fighting on two frontiers simultaneously. Unlike other potential enemies, Persia was a centralised, sophisticated state, and both empires were continually involved in a chess game of military and diplomatic manoeuvres which at intervals broke down into open war. In set battle the Romans could usually win, but at quite huge logistical costs. The 1,400-mile frontier zone along the Euphrates was already the most expensive in terms of providing troops and resources. The danger was not so much that Persia would conquer the Roman provinces, as that they would disrupt the whole delicate defensive system of Arab alliances and force the empire to a great commitment of forces, imperilling other frontiers.

But, although Persia tried to take advantage of the empire's difficulties elsewhere, its war aims were limited and it was usually amenable to negotiation. After nearly twenty years of peace, a brier Persian attack in 441 was halted and led to a new treaty involving Roman payments. At the same time, Persia's ambitions were severely checked by pressure from their own northern enemies, the Ephthalite horse peoples, akin to the Huns, who were tacitly encouraged by Constantinople. Whatever martial propaganda they still broadcast to their peoples, the two empires gradually came to accept the advantages of avoiding costly and unrewarding wars, and sought if possible to resolve conflicts by other means. As a result, a mature and structured diplomacy became as important as the military strategy.

Finally, after suffering heavier casualties in battle for diminishing returns of plunder, Attila decided to cut his losses and invade westward. Here Aetius, with all his carefully cultivated barbarian friendships, performed a diplomatic miracle in uniting and commanding the mutually hostile Germanic kingdoms in a great coalition to stop Attila in 451. After a huge and bloody battle on the Catalaunian plains of northern Gaul, Attila was forced for the first time to retreat. The next year he mounted an abortive invasion of Italy. Soon afterwards, he died suddenly in a drunken stupor. Within a short time his always personal and charismatic 'empire' collapsed.

In the West, Aetius was immediately concerned to disperse the more numerous and powerful Germanic armies as quickly as possible. But now that the main barbarian threat seemed removed, he was treacherously murdered by the emperor Valentinian III (425–455) who had long hated him. In revenge, Aetius's partisans assassinated Valentinian shortly afterwards, ending the Theodosian dynasty.

The next *generalissimo* figure, Ricimer, was himself a barbarian and naturally well-qualified to deal with the overwhelmingly barbarian army and allies. He was related both to the Visigoth and Sueve royal houses, and very willing to allow more federate settlements. Ricimer was a leader spanning two worlds. He saw the Roman empire more as a prestigious, unifying symbol than a political reality, and he set up and deposed puppet emperors at will. In the end it was only logical that a barbarian king should step into the ruling role of patrician and *generalissimo.* When that happened there was no need to retain even a figurehead emperor in the West. In 476 the barbarian king Odovacer forced the emperor Romulus Augustulus to abdicate, and sent an embassy to Constantinople declaring that he would henceforth rule as the viceroy of the Eastern emperor. The fiction of a single united Roman empire was still retained.

The East had tried, and partially succeeded, in arranging the fragments of Attila's old empire to its advantage, but it had been forced to accept two large blocs of Ostrogoths, formerly subjects of Attila, as federates in Illyricum (Yugoslavia) and Thrace (Bulgaria-Romania). These were a destabilising element, each too strong to be defeated by a single Roman field army. In the confused reign of Zeno (474–491) all the dangerous elements erupted again: open conflict in the imperial family, civil wars for the throne, rebellion by the Gothic federates. At one point there was fighting within the capital itself. There seemed a real danger that the Ostrogoths would carve out permanent kingdoms for themselves in the way this had happened in the West.

For a time, the central establishment lost control, but they had several strong advantages. There was always a strong core of regular Roman troops to balance the federates, and they continued to be steadily recruited. All the soldiers, Roman or federate, could only be paid from the central treasuries, which were a potent lever in negotiations, as were timely bribes of gold. The Goths also suffered periodic food shortages which the imperial government, with its network of cities and supply depots, naturally exploited. The two Gothic blocs were often in competition and could easily be played off against each other. Their aims were opportunistic and their long-term goals uncertain. One king, Theoderic (471–526), wanted larger, more secure territories for his people, while the other, Strabo, aimed at a top Roman command and a seat at the centre of government.

By the time Zeno had managed to crush or conciliate his other domestic enemies, by adroit and unscrupulous manoeuvring, Strabo was dead and all the Goths followed Theoderic. In 488, with only one king to deal with, Zeno played the masterstroke. Instead of poor and precarious lands in the Balkans, he invited Theoderic to take Italy from Odovacer. Theoderic did so, finally freeing the East of the federate problem.

It was left to the next emperor Anastasius (491–518) to consolidate these gains. Himself a civil bureaucrat who knew the government machinery intimately, he overhauled and improved the entire fiscal system to produce considerably greater sums for the treasury without injuring the mass of taxpayers. With these funds he expanded the armies by raising pay, built new defences, revived and repopulated much of the Balkans, and fought a successful war against Persia, still leaving a healthy surplus. It was with these great resources that Justinian was soon to embark on his ambitious schemes of reconquest.

The East had certain long-term advantages: a strategically placed capital, shorter vulnerable frontiers, a wealthier agricultural base. But it demanded a high order of statecraft to overcome all the external and internal threats of the fifth century. Individually, its leaders were no more skilful than their Western counterparts, but they managed to evolve institutions and practices which applied these skills and perpetuated them. The Constantinople establishment; the constitutional rituals of imperial succession; the integration of the top army commands; the opposition to federate settlements; the centralised pool of administrative, fiscal and diplomatic experience—all these enabled the East to avoid the unravelling process of diminishing control which occurred in the West.

## For Further Reading

A.H.M. Jones, *The Later Roman Empire* (2 vols, Oxford University Press, 1990); J.B. Bury, *History of The Later Roman Empire,* (Dover paperbacks, 1958); R.C. Blockley, *East Roman Foreign Policy* (ARCA, 1992); J.H.W.G. Liebeschuetz, *From Diocletian to the Arab Conquest,* (Oxford University Press, 1990); J.H.W.G. Liebeschuetz, *Barbarians and Bishops: Army, Church and State in the Age of Arcadius and Chrysostom* (Oxford University Press, 1991); C. Mango, *Byzantium. The Empire of New Rome* (London, 1980).

**Stephen Williams** and **Gerard Friell** are also the authors of *Theodosius: the Empire at Bay* (Batsford, 1994).

*Article 20*

# Islam's First Terrorists

CLIVE FOSS

Before dawn on the seventeenth day of the holy month of Ramadan in the year 40 of the Hegira (January 24th, An 661), the Caliph AH entered the great mosque of Kufa to prepare for the day's prayers. A conspirator lurking in the shadows sprang at him and plunged a poisoned sword into his head. The Caliph died later the same day. He was the third of the Prophet's four successors to be assassinated, but the first to fall victim to religion. The murderer, who was soon caught, was part of a conspiracy to kill all the leaders of the Islamic community: Ali himself, Muawiya, governor of Syria, and Amribn al-As, governor of Egypt. It only succeeded in the case of Caliph Ali.

The plotters belonged to a new sect, the Kharijites, who had only come into existence four years previously. When the Caliph Othman had been assassinated in 656, Ali, who was the Prophet's cousin and son-in-law, was recognized in Medina as the new head of the Islamic community—but not by everyone. He soon faced the opposition of Muawiya, who demanded revenge for the murder of his cousin Othman (both were members of the powerful Umayyad family that was to found the first dynasty of Islam after Ali's death). War soon followed. The course of its only armed conflict, the battle of Siffin in 657, was indecisive but apparently going against the Syrians, when they raised the Koran on their lances and brought the fighting to a stand-still, demanding instead arbitration by the authority of the sacred text. AH agreed, but the result of his agreement turned out to be fatal.

One party of Ali's followers, numbering some 12,000, refused to accept the idea of arbitration by humans, on the grounds that only God could decide. They proclaimed la hukma illa li-llah, 'judgment belongs to God alone', and withdrew from the field. Although Ali managed to persuade them to return peacefully to his basc of Kufa in Iraq, resentment took a more serious turn when the results of the arbitration, which was unfavourable to Ali, were announced in 658. A hard core of intransigents, joined by supporters from Basra, then left Kufa, elected their own caliph or spiritual leader, and took a stand in central Iraq. They became known as the 'withdrawers' (Arabic khariji, pl. khawarij from kharaja 'withdraw'). On their way, they murdered Muslims who did not support their uncompromising position, considering them worse than infidels. Ali's army attacked the rebels in July, killed their leader and destroyed the majority of their forces. However, this marked not the end but the beginning of a movement that was to cause turmoil in the Islamic world for centuries.

Ever since the death of the Prophet in AD 632, the Islamic community had faced a serious, and as it turned out insoluble, problem: who was to be their head? Muhammad himself had revealed a religion that provided a new basis for forming a community and a nascent state. When he emigrated from Mecca to Medina in 622, he became head of both state and religion, creating a position that had to be filled. No one of course could be another prophet, but Islam needed a Commander of the Faithful who would lead it in prayer, war and government. There was no idea of separating religion from statecraft. The Prophet's first two successors had been his close associates, and the third, Othman, had been chosen by a council, but he represented the old ruling classes of Mecca who had opposed the Prophet in the beginning and only converted to Islam at the last moment.

The civil war that broke out between the Umayyad Muawiya and Ali reflected two irreconcilable points of view: should a powerful family lead Islam, or should it be in the hands of the Prophet's relatives and descendants? Muawiya's followers came to be called the Sunnis (those who follow the example, sunna, of the Prophet), while the champions of AH were the Shi'ites (from shi'at Ali, the party of Ali). Long after the Umayyads were gone from the scene, the difference remained to inspire a sectarianism that became perpetual and often hostile. The Kharijites had their own point of view on this question.

After Ali's assassination, the remnants of the Kharijites began to organize, choosing leaders who usually took the caliph's title amir almu'minin, 'Commander of the Faithful'. Their radical doctrines attracted a large following, especially in Iraq. They were egalitarians who tolerated non-Muslims and looked favourably on converts, whom many of the pure Arabs regarded with disdain. Islam had begun in a purely Arab milieu but the great conquests of the generation after the prophet had incorporated vast populations of foreigners, principally Syrians, Egyptians, and Persians, into its realm. How to deal with them? The new state left them alone as a subject population paying taxes, but as foreigners began to convert to Islam, questions arose about their status. The Arabs accepted the new converts as 'clients', which usually implied an inferior position in society and limited rights.

The Kharijites believed in the absolute equality of all believers, maintaining that any Muslim who followed the precepts of the Koran, even if he were an Abyssinian slave, was qualified to head the community. Any leader who deviated from the true faith, though, or indulged in corruption or tyranny, had to be removed. This was against the normal Islamic doctrine that rulers, however bad, had to be obeyed unless they ordered the sacred law to be violated. Kharijiles rejected any principle of heredity or supremacy based on ethnic, tribal or family origin. This meant they spurned equally the claims of the Quraysh (Muhammad's own tribe) and of the Umayyads. Their views, reflecting an ancient tribal system based on consensus, were far more democratic than any prevailing in the greater Muslim community. Consequently, the Kharijites became a focus for discontented elements and those opposed to any form of established authority. They attracted the young, the obscure and many ex-slaves and converts.

The Kharijites had a particular idea of who was a Muslim. Strictly following the Koranic injunction to 'command the good and forbid the evil', they were uncompromising puritans for whom a Muslim was defined not only by his faith but his practice. Anyone who deviated from what the Kharijites considered the path of righteousness was an apostate, worse than an infidel and deserving any punishment. The more extreme were prepared to sacrifice their lives for their faith, and to kill any Muslims they considered as sinners or heretical, even with their wives and children. They recognized only the first two caliphs, Abu Bakr and Omar, and proclaimed their own leaders as heads of the entire Muslim community. By so doing, they implied that all others who claimed supremacy were illegitimate.

Opposition to Caliph Ali was easily transferred to his successor Muawiya (r.660–80), against whom the Kharijites continually rebelled in Basra, Kufa and the surrounding regions; sixteen outbreaks are recorded during his reign. They usually formed small bands adopting guerrilla tactics, striking suddenly and unexpectedly at cities and towns, then retiring to the safety of the marshes around Basra or the hill country east of the Tigris. Muawiya's governors in Iraq reacted with ferocity, killing thousands, driving them from Kufa altogether, and restoring stability. As a result, many Kharijites in Basra went underground, maintaining their beliefs in secret and creating a new stream of Kharijite development.

When Yazid, Muawiya's son and chosen successor, died suddenly in 683, he was succeeded by a young son who only lasted a few weeks. Supreme power lay open to be claimed. Abd Allah ibn Zubayr was proclaimed caliph in Arabia, but he had to face the opposition of the Umayyads in Syria, led by their caliph Abd al-Malik (r.685–705). The ensuing decade of civil war gave the Kharijites the opportunity to rise up in a series of devastating revolts. The main centres were in Arabia, Iraq, and northern Mesopotamia. In 683, two leading Kharijites, Nafi ibn al-Azraq and Najda ibn Amir went to Mecca to join ibn Zubayr, at the time when Umayyad forces were besieging the city. They soon realized, however, that ibn Zubayr was far from sharing their point of view, so they departed in hostility and returned to Basra—where the two leaders themselves fell out and came to head two separate movements.

In 684, one group of Kharijites left Mecca to settle in north central Arabia. Najda ibn Amir joined them and was chosen as their caliph. He rapidly took over a vast region including Bahrain, the Yemen and Hadramawt. Everywhere he went, he appointed governors and collected taxes, becoming a serious rival to Ibn Zubayr, whose control of Arabia was fatally weakened. Consequently, the pilgrimage to Mecca of 687 featured no fewer than four prospective leaders of the Islamic umma (community) and their followers: ibn Zubayr, the Umayyad Abd al-Malik, ibn al-Hanifiyya (a son of Ali) and Najda ibn Amir. The Kharijites were claiming equal authority with the two rival caliphs.

By this time, Najda had sent one of his followers, Atiyya ibn al-Aswad, to subjugate Oman. Although temporarily successful there, he soon broke with Najda and moved his base to eastern Iran, which he dominated during the 690s.

Najda's success, however spectacular, did not last long, for reasons typical of the Kharijites. Followers even stricter than he revolted in 691 and chose a new leader, who gained Bedouin support. But the next year the Kharijites of Arabia were crushed by a combined force from Kufa and Basra. The followers of Najda survived in obscurity, but with a real peculiarity: unlike other Islamic communities, they did not believe in a powerful leader. Their secular head was chosen by the whole community, with a mandate that could be revoked at any time; rule was basically by consensus. Nor did they need an imam, or religious leader, for all Najdis were equally qualified so long as they knew and followed the precepts of the Koran. No free man was to be subject to another, in what has been described by historian Patricia Crone as the 'most radical affirmation of intellectual and political freedom in the formative centuries of Islam'. Such a doctrine, though suitable to a small homogenous community, was never conducive to the formation of a powerful state.

Meanwhile, Nafi ibn al-Azraq, who had returned from Mecca to Basra, he started a revolt in the spring of 684. His followers, known as Azraqites, assassinated the governor and seized the city. They publicly announced the policy that identified them as the most extremist and violent wing of the Kharijites: that all Muslims—even other Kharijites—who disagreed with their strict interpretation of doctrine and practice were worse than unbelievers and worthy of immediate death. They held Basra until ibn Zubayr's forces drove them into southwestern Iran where they were defeated and Nafi' ibn al-Azraq killed in January 685. From there, the surviving Azraqites spread far to the east, making use of the excellent horses, weapons and chain-mail that they stripped from Iran. In 687, they descended once more into the heart of Iraq, attacking and devastating al-Mada' in, the ancient Sasanian capital. They slaughtered women and children of the opposing parties, and were even accused of ripping open pregnant women. When an army approached from Kufa, however, they again withdrew to Iran (for they were always too few to face a regular army), where their leader was killed. In 688 or 689, the Azraqites chose a new caliph, Qatari ibn al-Fujaa, who was to be their most formidable champion.

Qatari used loot and taxes from southern Iran to increase the forces which he led toward Iraq, facing and often defeating the militias of the local governors for four years. By now, however, the wider civil war was at an end and Abd al-Malik firmly in charge of the vast Islamic realm. In 694, his ferocious governor of Iraq, al-Hajjaj, moved against the Azraqites, pushing them back and securing the country with a series of fortified camps.

Although Qatari gained some victories in surprise night attacks, he had to abandon central Iran by 697 and retreat into the southeast, where he successfully held out for eighteen months. His power finally succumbed not to the caliphal army but to the typical Kharijite penchant for disunion. When his forces split over a quarrel about the murder of a fellow Kharijite, Qatari was doomed. Al-Hajjaj sent a Syrian army against Qatari who had stirred the resentment of the local population by his rigid collection of the poll-tax on non-Muslims; he was caught in an ambush, and killed in 698 or 699. His head was sent to the Caliph in Damascus, visible witness of the defeat of this ferocious enemy. His followers were soon mopped up and the threat from the Azraqites finally brought to an end. By this lime, terrorism had made the Kharijites deeply unpopular with mainstream Islam. In 686, a Shi'ite described them as 'the worst religion amongst us' and three years later a Kharijite who proclaimed la hukma illa l-illah during the pilgrimage in Mecca was killed on the spot by the people.

The last great Kharijite uprising of this period began in 695 in northern Mesopotamia, when the Sufris rose in revolt. These were the moderate Kharijites who (unlike the extremist Azraqites) regarded other Muslims not as infidels to be killed but as misguided people with whom it might be possible to compromise. Their revolt was provoked by the persecutions of al-Hajjaj, who had no tolerance for any kind of Kharijite. After their forces were defeated by al-Hajjaj, the Sufris resorted to guerrilla tactics.

Their leader Shabib ibn Yazid al-Shaybani gained stunning success in Iraq thanks to the swift and unexpected moves of his small forces and the help he received from the local Christians. Victory followed victory, culminating in 696, when Shabib entered Kufa in al-Hajjaj's absence, banged an iron bar against the door of his palace, attacked the mosque and killed the people he found praying there. He then withdrew into the mountains where he was joined by many who opposed the harsh regime of al-Hajjaj. When he came down again into the plain, Shabib not only defeated the armies sent against him but even seized the city of al-Madain. Al-Hajjaj, who was occupied at the same time with the struggle against the Azraqites, finally called on 'Abd al-Malik who sent him a force of battle-trained Syrian troops. This army forced Shabib to retreat to Iran, where he drowned in a river late in 097 having terrorized Iraq for more than a year.

Al-Hajjaj had worked so thoroughly that the Caliphate enjoyed a half-century of respite from serious Kharijite troubles. When Umayyad power began to break up in the mid-eighth century, however, revolts spread, two of them led by Kharijites who enjoyed spectacular if momentary success in Mesopotamia and Arabia. In both cases, the religious element became merged with the revolutionary, and the Kharijites found themselves at the head of considerable armed forces. These revolts were the products of the two moderate Kharijite sects, the Sufris and the Ibadis. The Sufris had survived in Mesopotamia, and the Ibadis were the real quietists, who believed in peaceful accommodation with other Muslims, among whom they were willing to live, concealing their true beliefs.

The greatest Sufri outbreak began in 744. Under the leadership of the religious scholar Dahhak ibn Qays al-Shaybani, the Sufris moved from Mosul against the Arab bases in Iraq, reinforced by thousands of armed followers from Kurdistan and the north, where their doctrine had taken root. Dahhak commanded the largest force Kharijites had ever put into the field. In April 745 he took Kufa and appointed his own governor, then besieged the main military base of Wasit whose governor, to universal astonishment, pledged allegiance to him. The next year, Dahhak returned to Mosul and raised a huge force from the local inhabitants. By now, though, the Umayyad Caliph Marwan II (r.744–50) had subdued his opponents in Syria and could turn his attention to Dahhak, whom he defeated and killed late in 746. Although Sufris continuously rebelled through the ninth century, they were never again a major threat to the central government.

The future belonged to the Ibadis, who had lived peacefully in the Muslim community, enjoying friendly relations even with al-Hajjaj. After the death of Abd al-Malik in 705, however, al-Hajjaj began to persecute them, driving many into exile in Oman and arresting others. Among these was the scholar and (as it turned out) great organizer Abu Ubayda Muslim, who became leader of the Ibadis of Basra when he was freed in 714. Not willing to risk the adventurous Azraqite policy of withdrawing to build an army outside Basra, he raised money from rich sympathizers and used it to create a network of missionaries who would spread the sect and preach revolution at the same time.

His ideal was to establish bases for revolts that would destroy the Umayyad caliphate and lead to a universal Ibadi state. Secretly trained teams spread through the Islamic world and enjoyed great success. One team reached Arabia, where they helped the rebel Abd Allah ibn Yahya to organize a regime, thus founding the first Ibadi state in 746. Abd Allah soon look of all southern Arabia. He set up a regular administration incorporating many officials of the previous regimes, and proclaimed that Kharijites and other Muslims could live at peace. Many Kharijites from other regions came to join his movement. His forces participated in the pilgrimage of that year, and even seized the holy cities of Mecca and Medina. However, his threat to the heartland of the caliphate provoked a strong response: Marwan II sent a tough Syrian army that re-established Umayyad control by the end of 748.

Another centre of successful missionary activity was North Africa, where the Ibadis took root in the eighth century and spread to the Berbers, making great headway among tribes who were hostile to Arab rule. After a bitter conflict with the local Sufris, the Ibadis established their own Rustamid dynasty (776–909) whose domain stretched from Algeria to Tripolitania, with much of southern Tunisia. Imams, or religious leaders, ruled this state which was noted for its tolerance—Christians rose to high positions—and its network of merchants who spread the Ibadi doctrine far and wide in North Africa and south of the

Sahara. True to their principle of equality, the Ibadis chose leaders who were not Arabs. The Rustamids eventually succumbed to the dynamic Shi'ite Fatimids (who later conquered Egypt), ending any hope of setting up an Ibadi imamate in the Maghreb, though sporadic revolts sometimes managed to occupy small territories into the late tenth century.

Although Abd Allah's regime in Arabia was extinguished, his followers had great success in Oman, where in 793 they established an independent state that became the headquarters of the Ibadi movement. They chose their leaders by a complex electoral system, rejecting the demands of heredity. Although subdued by the Abbasids in 893, the Ibadis retained real local control and regained independence as the central caliphate declined. From Oman, they spread their doctrine to East Africa, where it still flourishes.

The modern Ibadis of Oman, East Africa and the Maghreb have evolved far from the violence and hostility of their Khanjite forebears. Instead of regarding Muslims of other sects as unbelievers worthy of death, they consider them as ungrateful to God and to be kept at arm's length. That means avoiding friendship but not association with them. Ibadis and others can pray in the same mosques. The Ibadis are generally regarded as peaceful members of the community, and far from fanatical. They have substantial differences with other Muslims, however: they condemn the memory of the caliphs Othman, Ali and Muawiya and believe that there is no possibility of redemption from eternal punishment in hell for those who deserve it. Like the early Kharijites, they follow a democratic principle in choosing their leader who is named by the community elders according to his morals, religion and leadership ability. Their imam, Ahmad ibn Said (r.1754–83) united all Oman under his religious leadership, founding the currently ruling Bu Sa'id dynasty, though its rulers now claim secular leadership only. In the late nineteenth century, the tribes of the interior broke with those of the coast, establishing a ruler whom they call Imam of the Muslims; they remained independent until the 1950s, forming the last purely Kharijite state. The sultanate that the Omanis established in Zanzibar in 1832 also became a major seat of Ibadi doctrine and learning, though its rulers did not claim to be imams.

The Kharijites, then, have a history almost as long as that of Islam itself. They erupted on the scene spectacularly in the late seventh century, and caused widespread chaos during the Arab civil wars of the late seventh and mid-eighth century. They flourished in times of instability, attracting large followings and undermining existing rulers. In some instances, they set up regular states, with a caliph and an army that controlled a territory from which they collected taxes. This was the case of Najda ibn Amir in Arabia and Qatari in the east. Qatari and Atiyya ibn al-Aswad even struck coins, a sure symbol of claimed sovereignty, as did Dahhak in Mesopotamia and some of the ephemeral states of North Africa. But none of these states lasted; they could exploit turmoil and civil war, but their harsh, demanding extremism was of limited appeal in times of peace. Their very democracy undermined strong leadership, while their fanaticism often led to splits within the community, with factions continually breaking away or rising in revolt if their leader failed to maintain the high standards the community demanded. An even more extreme potential leader was usually lying in wait. The extremists attracted all kinds of followers, especially from non-Arab Muslims, but never appealed to an entire class of the population, and so never managed to take root in a region. Only the Ibadis, who learned to bide their time and to compromise, lasted into the present. Terrorism and extremism failed; the future belonged to those who could adapt and cooperate.

## For Further Reading

Julius Wellhausen, *The Religio-Potitical Factions in Early Islam* (North Holland, 1975); Abd al-Ameer Dixon, *The Umayyad Caliphate* (S. Illinois University Press. 1971); Michael Morony, *Iraq after the Muslim Conquest.* (Princeton, 1984); Patricia Crone, *God's Rule: Government and Islam* (Columbia University Press, 2004).

**Clive Foss** is Professor of History at Georgetown University in Washington DC.

# Rediscovering Arabic Science

RICHARD COVINGTON

You have to hand it to Ahmed Djebbar: The science historian certainly knows how to draw a crowd. As we circulate among the astrolabes, maps and hydraulic models of an eye-opening Paris exhibition on medieval Arabic science, curious museum-goers gather around us.

"Did you know that the Egyptian doctor Ibn al-Nafis recognized that the lungs purify blood in the 13th century, nearly 350 years before the Europeans?" he asks, standing in front of an anatomical drawing of the human body. "Or that the Arabs treated the mentally ill with music therapy as early as the ninth century?"

Examining a case of rare manuscripts, the dapper Lille University professor launches into a mini-lecture before the rapt group. The 13th-century Persian astronomer Nasir al-Din al-Tusi, the author of one of the yellowing Arabic-language texts, upended the geocentric Greek view of the universe, Djebbar explains, by declaring Ptolemy's model of planetary motion flawed and creating his own more accurate, but still Earth-centered, version. Three centuries later, the Polish astronomer Nicholas Copernicus borrowed al-Tusi's model to make the shocking proposition that the Earth revolves around the sun. "Al-Tusi made his observations without telescopes or even glasses," says Djebbar, removing his own spectacles and waving them theatrically in the air. "Even though the Arabs possessed the knowledge to make lenses, they probably thought it was an idiotic idea. God made us like this; why hang something on our noses to see better?" he jokes, placing his glasses back on his nose with a flourish. His audience erupts into laughter as Djebbar, who was curator of "The Golden Age of Arabic Sciences"—the Paris exhibition, which ran from October 2005 through March 2006 at the Arab World Institute—tries to quiet them down.

For most westerners, and indeed for many Arabs, the spectacular achievements of Arabic-language science from the eighth through the 16th centuries come as a startling discovery, as if an unknown continent had suddenly appeared on the horizon. In mathematics, astronomy, medicine, optics, cartography, evolutionary theory, physics and chemistry, medieval Arab and Muslim scientists, scholars, doctors and mapmakers were centuries ahead of Europe. Centers for scientific research and experimentation emerged across Muslim lands—in Baghdad, Cairo, Damascus, Samarkand, Shiraz, Bukhara, Isfahan, Toledo, Córdoba, Granada and Istanbul.

Generations of science historians once rejected Islamic accomplishments. One critic, the French physicist Pierre Duhem, even accused Muslims of trying to destroy classical science in his 1914–1916 historic survey *Le Système du Monde (The System of the World)*. Others asserted that the Arabic language itself was not suited for science, contends Roshdi Rashed, the dean of Islamic science in France. "Otherwise well-respected scholars like Ernest Renan and Paul Tannery excluded even the possibility of an Arabic contribution to science," says Rashed, a former fellow at the Institute for Advanced Studies in Princeton, professor emeritus at the University of Paris and editor of the three-volume *Encyclopedia of the History of Arabic Science.*

**For most Westerners, and indeed most Arabs, the spectacular achievements of Islamic science from the eighth through the 16th centuries come as a startling discovery, as if an unknown continent had suddenly appeared on the horizon.**

Although an alternative spectrum of science historians, beginning with the 19th-century European Orientalists Jean-Jacques Sédillot and Eilhard Wiedemann and including the 20th-century Harvard professor George Sarton, staunchly promoted the pivotal Arab/Muslim role in science, the general public has remained largely unaware of Arab discoveries. The 1300-year period between the Greek golden age of science (from the fifth century BC to the second century of our era) and the 15th-century Italian Renaissance was perceived as a scientific desert. If Arab scholars were acknowledged at all outside academia, they were seen merely as useful messengers, conduits who preserved the classical Greek knowledge of Euclid, Aristotle,

## Arabic Science: The Language

A thousand years before English emerged as the international language of science in the latter half of the 20th century, the Arabic language unified scholars across the Muslim world, generating a lively market of ideas from Samarkand to Córdoba. "A book published in Central Asia could be read in southern Spain less than a year later," explains Roshdi Rashed, an eminent Egyptian-born historian of science, in his office near Paris. "Islamic learning was not like Greek science, which was limited principally to the eastern Mediterranean, but was spread across most of the known world."

One celebrated example is the *Kitab al-Istikmal,* a treatise on geometry by Yusuf al-Mu'taman, the 11th-century king of Sarakusta (today's Zaragosa in northern Spain). The Jewish philosopher Maimonides brought it from Córdoba to Cairo and copies were soon circulating in Baghdad. The work was eventually republished in the 13th century in Central Asia.

Among the babel of scientists and scholars who crisscrossed the polyglot Muslim empire, the common language was Arabic. "Besides Maimonides, you have the great mathematician and physicist Alhazen (Ibn al-Haitham) moving from Basra to Cairo," says Rashed, "and the astronomer Nasir al-Din al-Tusi journeying every year from Khorasan in northern Iran through Iraq and on to Aleppo to teach." Even if scholars spoke Persian or another language at home, they wrote their papers in Arabic so that their colleagues in Baghdad, Toledo and elsewhere could understand them, he adds. Omar Khayyam may have penned his quatrains in Persian, but he explicated his mathematical concepts in Arabic. Correspondence among scientists—typically carried by caravan messenger or carrier pigeon—was nearly as far-reaching in the 11th and 12th centuries as it was in the 17th, Rashed maintains.

But despite its ultimate ascendancy, scholarly Arabic had a slow start. "Before the advent of science, Arabic was the language of poetry; it soon became the language of the new religion of Islam, but paradoxically, it did not become the language of power right away," explains French science historian Ahmed Djebbar. Although the Umayyad caliph 'Abd al-Malik decreed at the beginning of the eighth century that government institutions, schools, courts and communications conduct their business in Arabic, it took another 50 to 100 years before the translation of scientific texts from Greek, Syriac, Persian and Indian languages into Arabic got under way in earnest, with some 100 translators at work over the course of the ninth and 10th centuries, according to the 10th-century bibliographer Ibn al-Nadim of Baghdad.

Baghdad's Bayt al-Hikmah ("House of Wisdom") became a vibrant center of translation. Works like Ptolemy's *Almagest* and Dioscorides' *De Materia Medica* were translated numerous times as scholars perfected Arabic terminology. The Greek word *parabola* was initially Arabicized phonetically as *barabula,* then subsequently refined to *qat za'id,* which literally means "thick section." *Diabetes* was first rendered as *diyabita* then transformed to *da as-sukkar* ("sugar sickness"). Over time, Arabic scientific terms and star names were adopted into other languages, a list that includes *alkali, alcohol, algebra, algorithm, alembic, alchemy, azimuth, elixir, nadir, zenith,* Betelgeuse, Aldebaran, Rigel and Mizar.

After some seven centuries in which Arabic dominated scientific discourse, it began to be eclipsed in the 15th century by Turkish as Ottoman rule expanded. Ghiyath al-Kashi's 1427 mathematical treatise *Risala al-Muhitiya (Treatise on the Circumference),* in which he calculated the value of *pi* to 17 decimal places, was one of the last significant scientific texts in Arabic. By the time Taqi al-Din, the director of the Istanbul observatory, wrote his books in Arabic on light and marvelous machines in the second half of the 16th century, Latin had largely supplanted Arabic as the universal language of science. Unlike Arabic, however, which was understood by all classes and gave ordinary Muslims access to scholarly knowledge, Latin was used principally by academics and clergy, fencing science in as the preserve of an educated elite.

---

Hippocrates, Galen, Ptolemy, Archimedes and others through Arabic texts.

True enough, much of ancient science came back to Europe via Arabic translations, which were subsequently translated into Latin and other languages. (See "Lines of Transmission"). Some key texts, like Ptolemy's *Planisphere,* Galen's commentary on Hippocrates' treatise *Airs, Waters, Places* and the final chapters of the third-century BC mathematician Apollonius' book on conic sections exist only thanks to the Arabic translations, since the original Greek manuscripts have all disappeared.

But according to astrophysicist Jean Audouze, director of the French National Center for Scientific Research in Paris, the Arabs were not simply transmitters of Greek concepts; they were creators in their own right. Like Djebbar and Rashed, Audouze is one of a small number of dedicated scholars—fewer than 150 in France, Germany and Britain, but also scattered through the US, Arab countries, Asia and Latin America—who are struggling to give Arabic science the long overdue respect it deserves.

"One of the more drastic consequences of the dismissal of the vast Islamic contribution is that you cannot understand classical science without it," argues Rashed. "If you reduce the distance between Greek science and 17th century science, you are going to say, for example, that Apollonius first conceived algebraic geometry. But he has nothing of the kind in his writings."

"Either you push Apollonius to invent ideas he did not have or you pull back 17th-century scholars closer to Greek levels of understanding. This results in very serious errors of perspective. But if you take into account Arabic science, you are better able to understand what is truly new in the 17th-century outlook and the steps that led from Greek classical science."

**Drawing principally from Greek texts, but also Persian and Indian sources, medieval Islamic scientists made a staggering number of breakthroughs.**

Tunisian geologist Mustafa El-Tayeb, director of science policy and sustainable development for the United Nations Education, Scientific and Cultural Organization in Paris, is another impassioned advocate for Islamic science. He believes that reclaiming a proper place for medieval Arab achievements is vital for encouraging future generations of Arab and Muslim researchers.

"When I hear reactionaries preaching to young Muslims that science is not good for Islam, I want these students to realize that it's a crucial part of their heritage and not something to be rejected, or seen as alien," says El-Tayeb. "As it is, the history of Islamic science is barely taught at all in universities across the Middle East."

In fact, the discipline is everywhere in a deepening crisis, warns George Saliba, professor of Arabic and Islamic science at Columbia University. "The most urgent need now for the study of Islamic science is to train people who can edit and publish the hundreds of scientific texts that are still lingering in world libraries with almost no one aware of their existence, let alone their contents," he says. "But despite this need, Islamic science historians are becoming an endangered species." To make his point, Saliba cites the 200 to 300 Muslim treatises on planetary theories that he's tracked down. Only two have been translated into European languages—one into Latin centuries ago and the other, in modern times, into English.

Yet the duty to promote the Arab intellectual legacy has never been greater, argues Rashed, underscoring the philosophical alliance between science, which strives for unity in the natural world, and religion, which seeks a similar balance in the realm of the spirit. "Muslim science demonstrates that there has always been a profoundly rational base to Islamic civilization," he explains.

Drawing principally from Greek texts, but also Persian and Indian sources, medieval Islamic scientists made a staggering number of breakthroughs. The brilliant ninth-century Baghdad mathematician Muhammad ibn Musa al-Khwarizmi invented algebra, initially to resolve property disputes (even though countless generations of high school students wish he hadn't bothered). He also solved linear and quadratic equations using algorithms, the basis of computer programming; the term itself is derived from his surname, testimony to al-Khwarizmi's enduring gift to mathematics.

**Skilled at determining the precise location of Makkah from anywhere in the Muslim empire, Islamic astronomers were unsurpassed. Many mosques engaged a full-time astronomer, called a *muqqawit*.**

Reversing the false Greek notion that light is emitted from the eye, the 11th-century physicist Alhasan ibn al-Haitham, known in the West by his Latinized first name as Alhazen, correctly asserted in Cairo that light rays travel in the opposite direction, reflecting off the surface of objects to enter the eye. Devising the first rudimentary pinhole camera, or *camera obscura,* Alhazen demonstrated that light emanates from an object in straight lines, establishing the principle of linear perspective essential to the art of Leonardo da Vinci and other Renaissance masters. (Alas, the Basra-born scientist did not invent film for his primitive camera; civilization would wait until the 19th century for the first photograph.) By putting his concepts to various tests, using the camera obscura and other tools, Alhazen also introduced the experimental method of proof, insisting that theories had to be verified in practice, a key element to modern science that was missing from the less empirical Greek tradition.

"Arab science succeeded as much in pragmatic applications as it did in theoretical concepts," Audouze maintains. "Islamic scholars distinguished themselves from their Greek predecessors, who were more inventive in ideas than in practical matters." Arab scholars also introduced the practice of peer review and citations to confirm their source material.

Although the Babylonians, Indians and Egyptians had astronomical observatories, those founded under Islamic rulers in Maragha (in present-day Iran), Samarkand and Istanbul were far more sophisticated, equipped with an impressive array of astrolabes, sundials, sextants, celestial globes and armillary spheres to track the movements of the planets and constellations.

Skilled at determining the precise location of Makkah from anywhere in the Muslim empire, Islamic astronomers were unsurpassed in their calculations and predictions. Many mosques engaged a full-time astronomer, called a muqqawit, to determine the hours of prayer and consult lunar calendars to fix the dates for Ramadan and other religious events.

Persian astronomer Muhammad ibn Ahmad al-Biruni (973–1048), a protean intellectual figure who wrote in Persian, Arabic, Greek, Hebrew and Sanskrit, and lived in Kath (in present-day Uzbekistan), corresponded with Abu al-Wafa, another astronomer 2000 kilometers (1242 mi) west in Baghdad, to coordinate the simultaneous observation of a lunar eclipse. On May 24, 997, according to al-Biruni's book *Al-athar al-baqiyah an al-qurun al-khaliyah (Vestiges of Bygone Days,* usually shortened to *The Chronology),* they got their eclipse, measuring its duration and the moon's angle in the sky to calculate the longitude of Kath with unprecedented exactitude.

Arab astronomers and cartographers strove for—and frequently achieved—uncanny accuracy. To ascertain the distance separating degrees of latitude for a projected global map, the ninth-century Baghdad caliph al-Ma'mun dispatched 70 scientists into the Syrian Desert. Using astrolabes, measuring rods and stretched lengths of cord, the teams walked until they observed a change of one degree in the elevation of the polestar, the equivalent to a degree of latitude. Reckoning the distance traveled at 562 2/3 Arab miles (64.5 statute miles or 103.8 km), they computed the Earth's circumference, which is 360 degrees, as 23,220 statute miles, or around 37,380 kilometers, a respectable error only about seven percent less than the true figure of 24,800 miles (40,000 km). (However, around 200 BC the Alexandrian geographer Eratosthenes handily beat their estimate, calculating the Earth's circumference at 39,690 km.)

Arabic/Muslim achievements in medicine were also impressive. The ninth-century Persian doctor Muhammad ibn Zakariya al-Razi, known in Latin as Rhazes, penned the first treatise on smallpox in his *Kitab al-tajarib (Book of Experience),* which probed some 900 cases of various maladies. Another Persian doctor, Abu Ali ibn Sina, or Avicenna (980–1037), compiled *Qanun fi 'l-tib (Canon of Medicine),* a five-volume compendium of Greek and Islamic healing that became one of the principal textbooks in European universities centuries later.

Abu al-Qasim al-Zahrawi (Abulcasis in Latin), a 10th-century surgeon in Córdoba, composed Al-Tasrif, a 30-chapter medical encyclopedia describing dozens of operations, complete with graphic illustrations of surgical instruments, including scalpels, cauterizing tools, feeding tubes and cupping glasses. (A 15th-century Turkish edition added instructively terrifying depictions of doctors treating patients.) Some 300 years after al-Zahrawi, another Andalusian doctor, Ibn al-Baitar, published *Al-jami li mufradat al-adwiyya wa l-aghdhiyya (Book of Simple Medications and Alimentations),* adding more than 400 medicines and curative plants to the 1,000 catalogued by the first-century doctor Dioscorides and other Greek botanists.

**Arab scholars even theorized about evolution, arriving at conclusions that anticipated Darwin.**

Arab scholars even theorized about evolution, arriving at conclusions that anticipated Darwin. In 1377, nearly half a millennium before the 1859 publication of *On the Origin of Species,* the Tunisian-born historiographer Ibn Khaldun, renowned as one of the founders of sociology, asserted in *Al-Muqaddimah (Prolegomena),* "The animal kingdom was developed, its species multiplied, and in the gradual process of Creation, it ended in man & arising from the world of the monkeys."

The period from the ninth through the 16th centuries was also a golden age for hydraulic technology, with Muslim engineers devising underground canals, dams, waterwheels and water-lifting machines to modernize agriculture and provide fresh water to rapidly growing cities from Córdoba to Samarkand. Intricate water clocks, pumps and piston-driven machines were the forerunners of mechanisms that would not appear in Europe until the Italian Renaissance and later with the development of steam and internal-combustion engines in the 18th and 19th centuries.

The importance of *all* branches of learning, including science, is emphasized in the Qur'an itself, which reads, in Chapter 58, Verse 11, "God will raise up in rank those of you who have been given knowledge." The value placed on scholarship by Muslims at large is underscored by two sayings popularly linked to the Prophet Muhammad: "Search for learning even if it be in China," and "The quest for learning is a duty for every Muslim." Although these sayings cannot be traced to authentic *hadiths* (traditions) of the Prophet, they reflect the general feeling of esteem in which the Muslim community holds learning, based on the Qur'an's emphasis on the importance of knowledge and reason, and respect for learned persons.

To Djebbar, early theological debates over the meaning of the words in the Qur'an, interpretations of hadith and etymological arguments on the Arabic language itself all nurtured the questioning spirit of rationalism necessary for scientific development. "These [religious and linguistic] critiques are the true departure point for the Arabic scientific tradition," he asserts in his 2001 book, *Une histoire de la science arabe (A History of Arabic Science).*

Although Umayyad princes filled libraries in Damascus with Greek scientific texts from Spain, beginning in the early eighth century, and commissioned Arabic translations, the main push for scientific inquiry arose in Baghdad around the time of the city's founding in 762.

Beginning with the first Abbasid caliph, al-Mansur, the victorious dynasty promoted science for ideological and political reasons. "The new rulers needed capable astronomers and geographers to measure the recently conquered empire under their control and to demonstrate to their subjects that Abbasid power was a force for good," Djebbar explains. As rural populations migrated to the cities, creating a highly diverse, socially volatile mix of peoples, the demand for competent doctors, engineers and scientists exploded. Baghdad had a population of more than 800,000 inhabitants by the 10th century, and was, after Constantinople, the largest city on Earth.

**Drawing principally from Greek texts, but also Persian and Indian sources, medieval Islamic scientists made a staggering number of breakthroughs.**

At the end of the eighth century, Harun al-Rashid, the grandson of al-Mansur and the caliph whose court inspired *The Thousand and One Nights,* erected Baghdad's first paper mill, the second in the empire. (The first mill had been constructed in Samarkand by Chinese engineers captured in the Battle of Talas in Central Asia around 750, according to Djebbar. The Chinese, who had been making paper since at least the second century BC, had kept the process a jealously guarded secret.) Shortly after the Baghdad plant opened, paper mills cropped up in virtually all the major Muslim cities. By the end of the 12th century, the Moroccan capital Fez sustained some 400 paper-making workshops.

The introduction of paper into the Middle East was a key technological breakthrough and a critical innovation for the spread of science. Paper gradually supplanted parchment and papyrus, making publication of manuscripts far cheaper and providing access to ideas for a much broader range of the educated public. Feather-light but sturdy paper was developed for use in correspondence by carrier pigeon. Since al-Biruni's Chronology mentions an exchange of letters with Abu al-Wafa to measure an eclipse, Djebbar suggests that the two astronomers used carrier pigeon "air mail" to speed up their 2000-kilometer correspondence between Kath and Baghdad.

Around the same time that Harun al-Rashid ushered in the paper mill, he also founded Baghdad's first hospital and a separate scientific academy known as Bayt al-Hikmah ("House of Wisdom"). Initially little more than the caliph's private library, the House of Wisdom became a full-blown research and translation center and astronomical observatory under al-Rashid's son, Caliph al-Ma'mun, who ruled from 813 to 833. It was here that the versatile al-Khwarizmi developed algebra and, turning his hand to cartography, drafted an elaborate map tracing the meanders of the Nile River.

According to Ibn al-Nadim, a local 10th-century bibliographer, al-Ma'mun had a prophetic dream of the white-bearded Aristotle seated on a throne in which the Greek philosopher advised the caliph on the path to wisdom through reason, law and faith. Al-Ma'mun took this vision as a sign to amass knowledge and shortly afterward sent a cohort of academics to Byzantium to bring back reams of scientific and philosophical texts to be translated into Arabic. Gradually, scholars acquired manuscripts from state archives and private collections in Alexandria, Damascus, Antioch, Harran and other cities. Although most of the books were in the original Greek, many volumes had already been translated between the fifth and seventh centuries into Syriac, the western Aramaic tongue used in ancient Syria. This massively ambitious initiative to translate Greek, Syriac, Persian and Indian treatises into Arabic lasted more than 200 years, from the middle of the 700's until the end of the 10th century, according to Djebbar. (See "Arabic Science: The Language").

Al-Ma'mun's patronage set an example, prompting princes, merchants, doctors and well-to-do scholars to finance research with charitable endowments, known as awqaf (waqf in the singular). "Scientists were always close to the courts; there was no such thing as independent science," explains Rashed. "One had to eat and for that the scholars needed a patron, either the caliph, a wealthy merchant or a nobleman."

The support of powerful benefactors became a vital element for the development of science across the Muslim empire. In Córdoba, the 10th-century caliph al-Hakam II sponsored extensive scholarly missions to scour manuscript collections in the eastern capitals to stock a library that soon rivaled the best in the world. In the early 11th century, the Fatimid ruler al-Hakim invited the renowned mathematician and physicist Alhazen to teach in his court, greeting him in person at the gates of Cairo, an extraordinary honor that gave a tremendous boost to the prestige of science in Egypt. That honeymoon ended abruptly, however, when Alhazen failed to realize the caliph's scheme to regulate Nile flooding. Feigning madness to avoid execution, the scholar was placed under house arrest, taking advantage of the solitude to churn out a flood of treatises, biding his time until al-Hakim's death in 1021.

Generally, scientists worked without religious constraints, Djebbar maintains, with Nestorian Christians, Jews and Muslims collaborating in relative harmony. The sort of persecution that inflamed the Spanish Inquisition in the 15th century and later fired the 1633 heresy trial of Galileo in Rome did not occur in Islamic countries at the time, he says.

"It was not because Muslims were nicer people than Christians," the professor explains. "It was a matter of timing. In Christian countries, there was a scientific renaissance at a period when religion had already locked the doors of experimentation and speculation. In Arab countries, science arose shortly after Islam was established, creating its own secular space without reference to religion."

There were, however, isolated instances of repression. Shortly after al-Hakam II's death in Córdoba in 976, the prime minister Abu Amir al-Kahtani, who assumed power as regent for the underage prince Hisham, burned many of the manuscripts the caliph had acquired at such great cost, claiming that the teachings of the Greeks, particularly in astronomy and philosophy, contradicted the Qur'an. Only works of medicine and arithmetic were spared. Some 150 years later, in the 12th century, the Baghdad theologian and mystic Muhammad al-Ghazali branded theoretical mathematics and physics as dangerous, claiming that they bred a rationalistic philosophy that led to atheism, according to Djebbar.

## Arabic Science: Lines of Transmission

Long before Dan Brown's *Da Vinci Code* popularized the Fibonacci sequence as an early clue to his murder mystery, the 13th-century Italian mathematician who gave his name to that number series was learning the principles of advanced arithmetic from Arab teachers in Bejaia, in present-day Algeria. In the Fibonacci sequence, every number after 0 and 1 is the sum of the previous two numbers, so that the sequence runs: 0, 1, 1, 2, 3, 5, 8, 13, 21, 34, 55, 89, 144, 233, 377, 610, 987, 1597, 2584, 4181, 6765, 10,946 and so on. The series appears in nature in many forms, including the spiral arrangements of sunflower seeds, pineapple fruitlets and pinecone scales; it appears in geometry, where, starting with the number 5, every *other* Fibonacci number is the length of the hypotenuse of a Pythagorean right triangle with integral sides; it recurs in mathematics, where the ratio between successive Fibonacci numbers approaches the classical "golden ratio" of 1:1.618033. . . .

Like the Polish astronomer Copernicus and the Spanish physician Michael Servetus in the 16th century, Fibonacci, who was one of the founders of western mathematics, constructed a substantial portion of his pioneering scientific research on the foundations laid by his Arabic-speaking predecessors. Using Latin translations of Muhammad ibn Musa al-Khwarizmi's treatises on algebra and algorithms, Fibonacci, also known as Leonard of Pisa, wrote the *Liber abaci,* the first widely available book on Arabic numerals and arithmetical problems, expanding Indian-based concepts that had arrived in Spain starting in the 10th century.

On an expedition to Catalonia around 967 in search of unknown manuscripts, Gerbert, a Benedictine monk from Aurillac in Provence who later became Pope Sylvester II, came across Latin texts explaining Arabic numerals. He later taught about them, in Rheims and Rome, using a rudimentary abacus. From these modest beginnings, ancient Greek knowledge preserved in Arabic texts, as well as original Muslim science, was translated principally into Latin, Hebrew and Castilian Spanish to blossom gradually across Europe. In the courts of Toledo, Palermo and London, and the universities of Salerno, Padua, Paris and Oxford, a network of intellectual cross-pollination arose that spanned more than half a millennium, ushering in a European scientific renaissance.

Translators such as Gerard of Cremona from Italy, Adelard of Bath from England, Constantine the African, who brought an entire library of Muslim medicine to Salerno, and Michael Scot, a Scotsman who studied in Spain and Sicily, crisscrossed Europe. These itinerant scholars disseminated critical Arab revisions of Greek learning and popularized the revolutionary innovations made by generations of Islamic astronomers, physicians, mathematicians and physicists. Roger Bacon, the 13th-century proponent of the experimental method, astronomers Tycho Brahe in the 16th century and Galileo in the 17th, English physician William Harvey, who formulated his theory of blood circulation on Arab models in the 17th century, and many others owe a direct debt to Muslim knowledge brought to the West in this period.

Occasionally, there was a distinctly personal link between East and West. Journeying to Aleppo and elsewhere around the Middle East, the 17th-century Dutch Orientalist Jacobus Golius, who spoke and read Arabic, brought back the tracts of Alhazen. Since his son was secretary to Descartes in the Dutch city of Leiden, Golius excitedly showed his acquisitions to the exiled French mathematician, who incorporated the Muslim physicist's findings on optics and geometry into his own writings, according to French science historian Roshdi Rashed.

The transmission of Islamic science to Europe was not a fixed event like the delivery of a package whose contents launched the Renaissance. It was an ongoing, fluid exchange over time, a transfer that traveled in both directions, although it flowed mostly from East to West. Once Christian armies began to retake Spain in the 11th century and Crusaders returned from the Middle East over the course of the 12th and 13th centuries, western scholars began a dogged search for Arabic texts. Some key Arab and Persian documents, such as Alhazen's *Kitab al-Manazir (Book on Optics)* and al-Khwarizmi's *Book on Indian Calculation,* lost in their Arabic editions, have survived thanks only to Latin translations.

"The translators were very important, but there was also a great deal of direct contact among the scientists themselves," points out Rashed. "This explains why you find the same information in Arabic and Latin texts even though they are not exact translations; there was also verbal transmission of the knowledge."

The Castilian city of Toledo, which was reconquered by King Alfonso vi in 1085 after nearly four centuries of Arab rule, became a magnet for scholars intent on harvesting Arab and Greek science. According to science historian Ahmed Djebbar of the University of Lille, more than 100 major scientific and philosophical essays were translated in Toledo from Arabic into Latin and Hebrew between 1116 and 1187. In a typical example illustrating the cosmopolitan nature of this mountaintop city, the English philosopher Daniel of Morley recounts meeting the Italian linguist Gerard of Cremona near the banks of the Tagus River. The two foreigners were awestruck by the vestiges of several monumental water clocks built by Ibrahim ibn Yahya al-Zarqali (Azarchel in Latin) shortly before the city fell to Alfonso.

By far the most prolific translator of the era, Gerard had left Italy chiefly in quest of Ptolemy's *Almagest,* which existed only in Arabic and Syriac, a pre-Islamic language of ancient Syria. Uncovering an Arabic transcription in Toledo, he stayed there 30 years, making Latin translations of Ptolemy, Ibn Sina's *Canon,* astronomical coordinates by al-Zarqali that became known as the "Toledan tables," and al-Zahrawi's manual on surgery, featuring a tonsillectomy technique as gruesome as it was efficacious.

Around the same time, Adelard of Bath, who had spent seven years traveling as far as Antioch seeking learning based on "reason rather than authority," as he wrote in *Quaestiones Naturales,* returned to the court of English King Henry I. There he introduced Muslim research on trigonometry, botany, falconry and other subjects. Soaking up Muslim mathematics and astronomy in Córdoba and Toledo, his compatriot Daniel of Morley later lectured his Oxford students that they should "not despise the simple and clear opinions of the Arabs, but should note that Latin philosophers make heavy weather of these subjects quite unnecessarily." Although Daniel of Morley's books from Spain were destroyed in English religious wars, Oxford's Bodleian Library later built up one of the most important collections of medieval Arabic manuscripts and 12th- and 13th-century Latin texts translated from Arabic sources.

Landing in southern Italy around 1060 from Qayrawan, in today's Tunisia, Constantine the African became a Benedictine monk at the abbey of Montecassino, 130 kilometers (80 miles) south of Rome. He transcribed numerous Arabic books, including Hunayn ibn Ishaq's versions of discourses by Galen and Aristotle, Ibn Ishaq's manual on ophthalmology and the physicians' encyclopedia of Ali ibn Abbas al-Majusi. Rapidly adopted by doctors at Salerno's medical school, Constantine's translations eventually filtered into France, England and Germany.

Even the Crusades failed to slow the pace of intellectual discourse—quite the contrary, argues Roshdi Rashed. "The Crusaders brought back a great deal of science, medicine, foods and so forth from the Middle East," he explains. In the first half of the 13th century, in fact, the Arabic-speaking Holy Roman Emperor Frederick II maintained a thriving correspondence with Muslim philosophers and scientists from his court in Palermo, Sicily, and even during his occupation of Jerusalem. "When you consider the two sides were in the middle of fighting one another, this is fairly astonishing," marvels Rashed.

Frederick enthusiastically encouraged Muslim scientists, an enlightened policy of Arab–Christian cooperation begun by his grandfather, Roger II, who had sponsored the geographer Muhammad al-Idrisi. (See "The Third Dimension".) In addition, Frederick financed translations of Arabic works, enlisting the services of Michael Scot, the astronomer-alchemist-wizard who later earned a place in Dante's *Inferno.* Scot had achieved renown in Toledo for transcribing Nur al-Din ibn Ishaq al-Bitruji's astronomical treatises on planetary motion and Averroes' commentaries on Aristotle into Latin, according to French science historian Danielle Jacquart. Both texts represented heretical challenges to Catholic doctrine, and hiring such a subversive character no doubt contributed to the emperor's ongoing problems with the church, which ultimately excommunicated Frederick II not once, but twice.

Around 1277, Toledo again became the focus of Muslim science, as King Alfonso X commissioned the first renditions of Arabic texts into Castilian Spanish instead of Latin. Apart from sponsoring the *Libros del saber de astronomía (The Books of Astronomical Knowledge),* which incorporated Thabit ibn Qurra's revision of the *Almagest* and translations of Abd al-Rahman al-Sufi's *Suwar al-kawakib al-thabit (Treatise on the Fixed Stars),* Muhammad ibn Ahmad al-Biruni's text on the spherical astrolabe and other Muslim texts, the king also promoted research into astrology, magic and philosophy.

Astrology also provoked a heated polemical debate that lasted for centuries. "Critics argued that astrology lied to people by claiming to predict the future when only God can see the future," says Djebbar, "but no Muslim astrologer—and there were many at the various courts—was ever put to death because of his predictions."

Although the first astronomical tables for calculating the positions of stars and planets arrived in Baghdad from Persia and India in the eighth century, the chief reference for Islamic astronomy was Ptolemy's *Almagest,* or *The Great Book,* initially translated into Arabic by al-Hajjaj around 828. Contrary to a common misperception, the second-century scholar from Alexandria did not believe the Earth was flat. Like his Arab successors, however, he was convinced that the sun, moon and planets revolved in celestial spheres around the Earth. In an attempt to match this geocentric theory with the actual movement of heavenly bodies, Ptolemy posited an eccentric model that depended on off-center orbits that were "physically impossible," according to Saliba of Columbia University. Struggling to reconcile the Greek universe with their own observations led a number of Islamic astronomers to challenge Ptolemy's faulty concepts of celestial motion.

The Syrian astronomer Muhammad ibn Jabir al-Battani, who worked in Raqqa from the late 10th century through the early 11th century, amended Ptolemy's figures for the inclination of the Earth's axis and was later praised by Copernicus as a source for his own heliocentric theory of the solar system. Around the same time, al-Biruni, who had been captured by Sultan Mahmud and hauled away to his court in Ghazni, in present-day Afghanistan, observed that the sun's apogee, its highest point in the heavens, was mobile, not fixed, as Ptolemy had maintained. In his comprehensive encyclopedia of astronomy, *Kitab al-qanun al-Mas'udi,* or the *Canon Mas'udicus,* dedicated in 1031 to Mahmud's son and successor, Mas'ud, al-Biruni also observed that the planets revolved in apparent elliptical orbits, instead of the circular orbits of the Greeks, although he failed to explain how they functioned. It was not until the 13th century that al-Tusi conceived a plausible model for elliptical orbits.

While parts of the *Almagest* underwent extensive revision by Arab and Persian scholars, much of this fundamental text was adopted intact. Commissioned by the Buwayid sultan Adud al-Dawla in Isfahan, the 10th-century astronomer Abd al-Rahman al-Sufi created a magnificently illustrated catalogue of the 1017 stars in 48 constellations enumerated by Ptolemy. It was a measure of the great value that medieval Muslim society placed on astronomy that this work was the first Islamic manuscript to contain figurative drawings. Al-Sufi's elegant sketches in his *Suwar al-kawakib al-thabit (Treatise on the Fixed Stars)* are filled with whimsical lions, fanciful serpents and mythological characters representing constellations and zodiacal signs. Tracing the outline of Perseus (also called Farsawus, or Hamil Ra's al-Ghul in Arabic) in red-painted stars, one dramatic scene depicts nearly identical facing images of the Greek hero, with Oriental features and flowing black hair, each brandishing a sword aloft and holding the head of a grimacing Medusa.

While some astronomers devoted themselves to illustrating or improving Ptolemy's science, others ventured forth on new tacks, designing more exact calendars, measuring eclipses and refining astronomical tables. In Cairo, the 10th-century scholar Ibn Yunus perfected tables used to calculate planetary motion to a number-crunching nine figures after the decimal point.

Three centuries later in Baghdad, the Persian polymath Zakariya al-Qazwini, a doctor, jurist, geographer and amateur astronomer, issued the first cosmography in the Muslim realm. This "layman's guide to the universe" covered everything celestial—solar cycles, weather forecasting and ruminations on the comportment of angels—and terrestrial, with fanciful illustrations depicting animal, vegetal and mineral kingdoms. Some editions of his 1270 *Kitab aja'ib al-makhluqat wa ghara'ib al-mawjudat (Book of Marvelous Creatures and Rare Things)* contain movable paper levers with the sun at one end and the moon at the other, pivoting on the Earth in the center to demonstrate how the Earth casts a shadow on the moon during a lunar eclipse—"the first interactive book," writes Parisian historian Danielle Jacquart.

One of the most forward-thinking scientific geniuses of the age was the astronomer-mathematician-theologian-physician al-Tusi. He was a Benjamin Franklin figure who persuaded the 13th-century Mongol conqueror Hulagu Khan to finance a boldly experimental observatory in the northwest Persian city of Maragha. Staffed by the most experienced astronomers in the empire, the new observatory set about educating a rising generation of stargazers. It was here that the scholar from Khorasan, who wrote more than 100 works of science, philosophy and poetry, contrived an ingenious model of heavenly motion that came tantalizingly close to explaining away the inconsistencies in Ptolemy's theories.

"Al-Tusi's couple" consists of one large circle representing the orbit of the moon and, inside it, a smaller circle, half the radius of the larger circle, that represents the orbit of a planet. Both circles, the "couple," revolve in tandem around the Earth. As the couple orbits the Earth, the moon rotates in the same direction on its own orbit and the planet spins twice as fast on its inside orbit in the opposite direction. Using this model, both the moon and the planet appear to revolve around the Earth in elliptical orbits with oscillating centers. In this mind-bending way, al-Tusi tried to reconcile the irregular movements of the sun, moon and planets, yet preserve Ptolemy's geocentric circular orbits.

Although Maragha, with its library and copper foundry for manufacturing astronomical tools, constituted one of the first astronomy schools in Islamic civilization, the observatory at Samarkand, inaugurated a century and a half later in 1420 by the ruler Ulugh Beg, the grandson of Timur (Tamerlane), was positively palatial. With its three-story tower 48 meters (156') in diameter, encircled by dozens of lofty arched niches decorated with blue, gold and green faience tiles, the observatory prided itself on its giant sextant—two stone circles dug 20 meters (66') into the ground that were used to gauge the height of the sun and the stars.

Here, more was definitely more, and size mattered enormously. "[The astronomers] considered that the instruments of grand dimension were the best adapted [for their work] for the simple reason that they allowed them to obtain more precise measurements," writes Saliba in the catalog for the Arab science exhibition at the Arab World Institute. The celebrated Persian scholar Ghiyath al-Kashi (1380–1429), reputed for calculating the value of *pi* to 17 decimal points, was so impressed by their scale that he penned a letter to his father describing the techniques and materials employed to produce bigger—and presumably more exact—astronomical equipment.

After Maragha and Samarkand, another major observatory was built near the present-day site of Taksim Square in Istanbul around 1576, supplanting an earlier installation in the Galata Tower financed by Süleyman the Magnificent in 1557. Coming from Cairo, Taqi al-Din persuaded Sultan Murad III to found the best-equipped facility in the Muslim world. Some of the observatory's exceptional instruments are depicted in a vivid painting from the manuscript *Sama'ilnama* in the library of Istanbul University. Here, 16 astronomers sporting flamboyant white turbans engage in animated discussion as they demonstrate astronomical clocks, updated globes and newfangled compasses (one shaped like a stick tripod as big as a man) to enhance star readings.

Unfortunately, Taqi al-Din's success goaded jealous rivals to convince the sultan that the observatory was intended for un-Islamic astrology, not astronomy, according to Turkish-born Fuat Sezgin, director of the Institute for the History of Arabic-Islamic Sciences at the Goethe University in Frankfurt. Other scholars maintain that Taqi al-Din incurred the sultan's wrath when the man of science tried to play fortuneteller, interpreting a comet's passage as an omen of Ottoman victory over the Persians. (The Turks won the battle, but suffered a devastating plague and other setbacks that were blamed on the comet.) In any event, Murad ordered the magnificent edifice destroyed in 1580, dealing a significant blow to Islamic astronomy and helping to usher in a period of stagnation across all the sciences, says Sezgin. (See "The Third Dimension").

**Like astronomy, which evolved from the practical necessities of finding the directions and hours for prayers, Islamic mathematics was very much a hands-on affair at the beginning, a product of the marketplace and of the need for pragmatic legal precedents.**

Like astronomy, which evolved from the practical necessities of finding the directions and hours for prayers, Islamic mathematics was very much a hands-on affair at the beginning, a product of the marketplace and of the need for pragmatic legal precedents. Both algebra and the use of zero had the same end in mind—streamlining computations for business deals. Al-Khwarizmi had a hand in the development of both.

In his *Kitab al-jabr (Book of Algebra)*—the word comes from the Arabic word *jabara,* "to restore"—the Baghdad mathematician spells out his no-nonsense intent: "It's a summary encompassing the finest and most noble operations for calculations which men may require for inheritances and donations, for shares and judgments, for commerce and all sorts of transactions that they have among them such as surveying tracts of land, digging canals and other aspects and techniques."

In another treatise, the *Book on Indian Calculation,* which was lost in the Arabic original and only survived due to its Latin translation, al-Khwarizmi introduces the nine integers borrowed from the Indian system (1 through 9) and explains how zeroes are used to create multiples of ten, a hundred, a thousand and so on. Unlike archaic numerical systems, which were based on multiples of five, 12 or even 60, or cumbersome Roman numerals, the Indian–Arabic decimal system made arithmetic vastly simpler and more rapid.

Using the geometry of Euclid and Apollonius as starting points, Muslim mathematicians went much farther than their Greek predecessors. While al-Biruni promulgated the first book on trigonometry in the 10th century, it was not until the 13th century that the Maragha astronomer al-Tusi developed trigonometry into a separate discipline. After absorbing Apollonius' book on conic sections such as circles, parabolas, ellipses and hyperbolas, and deliberating over what was contained in the lost eighth chapter, Alhazen, the inventor of the camera obscura, proposed his own version of the book's ending, adding solutions for computing the volume of a three-dimensional parabolic shape.

In 10th-century Baghdad, the mathematician-astronomer Abu Sahl al-Quhi formulated a life-saving use of trigonometry by employing it to determine the height and position of lighthouses and to gauge distances of ships at sea from hidden shoals. The resourceful scholar also invented the so-called "perfect compass," a hand-held mechanical tool with an adjustable arm pivoting around a fixed arm, to trace ellipses and other conic sections.

Enlarging on Indian notions of the sine (the ratio of the length of the side of a right triangle opposite an acute angle to the length of the hypotenuse), the ninth-century mathematician Habash al-Hasin developed the concept of tangents (straight lines and planes touching arcs, circles and conic sections) to facilitate geometrical calculations.

When the multi-talented 11th-century Persian poet Omar Khayyam was not rhapsodizing in *The Rubaiyat* and other verse, he kept busy revising solar calendars for the Seljuk sultan Jalal al-Din and drafting geometrical proofs for cubic equations by intersecting parabolas with circles. The mathematical bard also circulated a visionary critique of Euclid's theories on parallel lines that prefigured non-Euclidean geometry, to come some 800 years later.

In several other areas, Arab mathematicians were centuries ahead of European theorists. The 13th-century scholar Ibn Munim from Marrakech used Khayyam's earlier studies to plot a triangular numerical grid that allowed him to figure permutations and combinations. This exercise yields, for example, the maximum number of words that can be created with the 28 letters of the Arabic alphabet. Four hundred years later, the 17th-century French mathematician Blaise Pascal reinvented Ibn Munim's numerical grid.

The famous last theorem by Pascal's colleague, Pierre de Fermat, offers another example of Muslim scholars presaging European discoveries. Some 600 years before Fermat posited his mathematical riddle—that there are no non-zero integers x, y and z such that $x^n + y^n = z^n$ where n is an integer greater than 2—Muslim scientists Alhazen, al-Sizji, al-Khazin and others were grappling with a similar conundrum. Fermat's enigma would remain unsolved until 1994, when British mathematician Andrew Wiles at last provided a definitive proof.

While Islamic mathematicians outstripped their Greek and Indian predecessors, Muslim doctors used Hippocrates and Galen as springboards for their own expanded findings about medicine and anatomy. In his seminal *Canon,* Ibn Sina expanded on Hippocrates' influential fifth-century BC work, *Airs, Waters, Places,* by enumerating the effects that clean air and water and salubrious mountain and coastal environments have on health. Some Arab critiques of Greek physicians were pointedly specific. Writing about a famine in Egypt around 1200, Abd al-Latif al-Baghdadi recounts his observations of the skeletons of starvation victims, noting that the lower jaw consisted of a single bone, instead of two articulated bones, as Galen had wrongly concluded. Neither Galen nor al-Baghdadi was able to dissect human bodies, due to religious taboos that lasted until the 17th century.

Even before the consolidation of the Islamic empire, the Arabs sought to raise the abysmal standards of public health, with the first Muslim hospital opening in Damascus in 706. "One of the great successes of Arabic medicine was the organization of hospitals at a level that far surpassed Greek, Roman or Persian models," says Djebbar.

Beginning in the late eighth century when Caliph Harun al-Rashid established a Baghdad hospital, doctors made daily rounds with their students, setting a precedent used in medical schools ever since. Typically, there was one courtyard wing for physically ill patients, another for those with moderate mental health problems and a third for those suffering from more severe psychological disorders. "In addition to music therapy, the courtyards all had fountains, trees and warbling birds so that the sounds of nature were part of the healing process," notes the Lille professor.

A handful of institutions boasted incredibly luxurious circumstances. According to Ahmed Issa Bey in his 1928 book *The History of Hospitals in Islam,* the 12th-century Almohad ruler Abu Yusuf Ya'qub al-Mansur provided the fortunate patients of his Marrakech facility with running water in every room, wool blankets, silk sheets, free medicines and 30 dinars a day for food and other necessities. When indigent patients got well enough to leave, they received a small sum of money to ease their reentry into working society.

A few of these medieval hospital buildings still exist intact, even though they now serve different purposes. Aleppo's 14th-century Argun Maristan is a dramatic backdrop for folk dance, and a 12th-century stone hospital in Damascus houses the National Museum of Arabic Medicine and Science. Cairo's Qalawun hospital, which treated some 4000 patients a day when it was constructed in the 13th century and accommodated lecture halls, a mosque and doctors' residences, is currently one of the top ophthalmology clinics in Egypt.

Although physicians had to be certified, scores of uncertified barbers and itinerant surgeons practiced bloodletting, tooth extraction and more dangerous operations with few anesthetics or antiseptics. Surgery was so chancy in the 10th century that even the adventurous doctor Rhazes refused to allow ophthalmologists to remove his cataracts. But by the 14th century, the situation had improved dramatically. Persian surgeon Mansur ibn Ilyas produced sophisticated anatomical drawings tracing nerves, veins, arteries, muscles and complex organs like the heart and brain that aided him immensely in conducting effective operations.

Al-Zahrawi and other healers sang the praises of herbal cures, recommending the *duhn,* or oil, of laurel, wheat, sweet and bitter almonds, mustard and other plants. Wild mint purportedly relieved fatigue when used as a compress and drove out colds if taken as nose drops. "It will also cure the sting of a scorpion," the 10th-century Córdoban doctor promised patients. One look at the fearsome arsenal of surgical tools in al-Zahrawi's *Al-Tasrif* made quick converts to less intrusive herbal nostrums.

**While Islamic mathematicians outstripped their Greek and Indian predecessors, Muslim doctors used Hippocrates and Galen as springboards for their own expanded findings about medicine and anatomy.**

Chemistry, a word derived from the Arabic *al-kimya,* was vigorously promoted, fostering a rigorous routine of trial-and-error experimentation that did not become widespread in Europe until the 18th century with Joseph Priestley, Antoine Lavoisier and other empirical researchers. According to the 10th-century bibliographer Ibn al-Nadim, Arab chemists manufactured waterproof fabrics, invisible inks and mosquito repellents. Around the same time, the Fatimid caliph al-Mu'izz designed a primitive pen with a self-contained ink cartridge nearly nine centuries before the Romanian student Petrache Poenaru invented the fountain pen in Paris in 1827.

The distillation of rosewater and other perfumes evolved into a Muslim specialty, with scents used medicinally to treat migraines, epilepsy and melancholy. In *Kitab kimya al-'utoor w' al-tas'idat (Book of the Chemistry of Perfumes and Distillations),* the ninth-century scientist Abu Yusuf al-Kindi lists formulas for preparing some 107 perfumes.

In his survey of optics, the 10th-century Baghdad scholar Ibn Sahl observed that light passing through crystals, water and other translucent substances slows down and is bent at different angles according to the density of the material—the basic principle of refraction. According to Rashed, this was reformulated in the 17th century by Dutch scholar Willebrord van Roijen Snell and French mathematician René Descartes as the Snell-Descartes law, or the law of sines. In the early 14th century, more than 300 years after Ibn Sahl, Maragha astronomer-mathematician Kamal al-Din al-Farisi experimented with a glass sphere filled with water to analyze the way sunlight breaks into the spectrum colors of a rainbow.

The 12th-century Persian physicist Abdur Rahman al-Hazini incorporated Archimedes' findings on the density, buoyancy and specific gravity of objects to perfect "the balance of wisdom," an ingenious scale that resembled a miniature Calder mobile. Originally invented by Abu Hatim al-Isfizari, the device consisted of five hanging trays, one of which was immersed in water to verify precise amounts of gold, silver and other precious metals in coins, jewelry and other materials.

Even as gold and silver mining expanded, the fabrication of artificial rubies, sapphires and other gems grew into a lucrative industry. Poring over the works of Egyptian and Greek alchemists, a handful of Muslim scientists employed their expertise in minerals to dabble in the elusive quest for an elixir, a magical "philosopher's stone," capable of transforming lead to gold. All failed, of course. The eighth-century Persian scientist Jabir ibn Hayyan (Geber in the West), however, turned these experimental dead ends to advantage, concocting an array of previously unknown compounds, including sulfuric acid, caustic soda and nitric oxide, Djebbar explains.

Far more useful than the alchemists' hunt for gold were al-Biruni's pioneering treatises on mineralogy and geology. In one work, the Persian scholar, who spent much of his career in Ghazni in Afghanistan, asserted that the desert was once covered by the sea. He supported this controversial thesis with detailed descriptions of perfectly preserved fossils of fish and other aquatic creatures, paving the way for paleontology.

**The first crippling blow to Islamic science occurred with the Mongol invasions.**

Despite centuries of innovation, Islamic science ultimately went into an irreversible decline with the eclipse of Arab political and economic power, marked in the West by the fall of Granada in 1492 to the Castilian monarchs Ferdinand and Isabella, and in the East by the muscular expansion of the Ottoman Empire in the 16th century under Süleyman the Magnificent. But this slide into decadence was a slow process.

Surprisingly, perhaps, the Crusades in the 12th and 13th centuries did more to energize Muslim science than retard it, according to Rashed. (See "Lines of Transmission"). "The Crusades encouraged Muslims and to find out the secrets of their enemies' forces," he contends.

The first crippling blow to Islamic science occurred with the Mongol invasions, culminating in the devastating sack of Baghdad in 1258, when two million Muslims were massacred, libraries, laboratories, hospitals and the landmark House of Wisdom were destroyed, and the Tigris ran red with the blood of scholars and black with the ink of their books. "Even after the Mongol invasions, there was still a substantial amount of scientific investigation," Rashed observes, "but scholars had to spend more time and energy preserving knowledge instead of pushing ahead with new explorations."

Another long-term reversal began in the 15th century, as Portuguese and Spanish navigators in heavily armed vessels exploited sea-trade routes between East and West. The slow-moving caravans of the Silk Road were gradually abandoned, breaking the Arab monopoly on commerce with the Orient and further undermining scientific progress, according to Rashed.

"Arabic science had arrived at a critical turning point where a cognitive revolution was needed in order to continue," the French science historian explains. In mathematics, for example, complex equations became so cumbersome they required 50 pages to articulate. "Creating new symbols to condense these equations required a conceptual leap that's possible in a society in expansion, but not in a society in decline," says Rashed.

With the rise of Ottoman hegemony, the heyday of Islamic science drew to a close, he argues, since Turkish rulers were far more interested in pursuing military goals and piling up layers of bureaucracy than in encouraging research.

But the lessons of Islamic science have yet to be fully appreciated, even in the Arab world, Audouze maintains, where the unprecedented accomplishments of generations of medieval scholars should inspire contemporary Muslims to rebuild the foundations for a new round of discoveries.

"Science only develops in cultivated societies where the economy and commerce are in good health," says the French astrophysicist. "And it creates a virtuous circle where the economy favors science which in turn generates profits and wealth of all kinds, spiritual as well as material."

Paris-based author **Richard Covington** writes about culture, history and science for *Smithsonian, The International Herald Tribune, U.S. News & World Report* and the *London Sunday Times.*

# UNIT 5
# The Medieval Period

## Unit Selections


22. **A Turbulent Reputation,** Michael Staunton
23. **What Did Medieval Schools Do For Us?,** Nicholas Orme
24. **Lackland,** Nick Barratt
25. **The Fourth Crusade and the Sack of Constantinople,** Jonathan Phillips
26. **East Meets West in Venice,** Richard Covington
27. **Genghis Khan,** Timothy May
28. **How a Mysterious Disease Laid Low Europe's Masses,** Charles L. Mee Jr.


## Key points to Consider

- What are the various interpretations of the life of Thomas Becket?
- What changes occurred in education during the Middle Ages?
- Why did the English create the Magna Carta in 1215?
- Why was the Fourth Crusade so devastating to the Byzantine Empire?
- What made Venice the most prosperous city in Europe during the Middle Ages?
- How did Genghis Khan and his Mongol army conquer such a vast territory?
- What were the effects of the "Black Death" on medieval civilization?

## Student Web Site

www.mhcls.com/online

## Internet References

**EuroDocs: Primary Historical Documents from Western Europe**
*http://eudocs.lib.byu.edu*

**Feudalism**
*http://www.fidnet.com/~weid/feudalism.htm*

**The Labyrinth: Resources for Medieval Studies**
*http://www.georgetown.edu/labyrinth/*

**The World of the Vikings**
*http://www.worldofthevikings.com*

In the aftermath of barbarian invasions, Western civilization faced several important challenges: to assimilate Roman and Germanic people and cultures, to reconcile Christian and Pagan views, and to create a new social, political, and economic institutions to fill the vacuum left by the fall of the Roman order—in sum, to shape a new unity out of the chaos and diversity of the post-Roman world. The next millennium (550–1500) saw the rise and demise of a distinctive phase of Western experience—medieval civilization.

Medieval culture expressed a uniquely coherent view of life and the world. In theory, medieval society provided a well-ordered and satisfying life. The Church looked after people's souls, the nobility maintained civil order, and a devoted peasantry performed the work of the world. Ideally, as historian Crane Brinton explains, "a beautifully ordered nexus or rights and duties bound each man to each, from the swineherd to emperor and pope."

Of course, medieval society, like our own, fell short of its ideal. Feudal barons warred among themselves. Often the clergy was ignorant and corrupt. Peasants were not always content and passive. And medieval civilization had other shortcomings too. During much of the Middle Ages, there was little interest in nature and how it worked. While experimentation and observation were not unknown, science (or "natural philosophy") was subordinate to theology, which generally attracted the best minds of the day. An economy based on agriculture and a society based on inherited status had little use for innovation. Aspects of Medieval society are treated in the articles such as "A Turbulent Reputation", "What Did Medieval Schools Do For Us?," while "Genghis Khan" and "The Fourth Crusade and the Sack of Constantinople" explore facets of foreign and medieval warfare.

All this is not to suggest that the medieval period was static and sterile. Crusaders, pilgrims, and merchants enlarged Europe's view of the world. And there were noteworthy mechanical innovations: the horse collar, which enabled beasts of burden to pull heavier loads; the stirrup, which altered mounted combat; mechanical clocks, which made possible more exact measurement of time; the compass, which brought the age of exploration closer;

Pixtal/age FotoStock

and the papermaking process that made feasible the print revolution, which in turn played a key roles in the Reformation and the Scientific Revolution. And the commercial encounter between the two faiths produced cross-cultural influences that contributed to fundamental economic, military, and political changes in the West as seen in "East Meets West in Venice."

The medieval order broke down in the fourteenth and fifteenth centuries. Plague, wars, and famines produced a demographic catastrophe that severely strained the economic and political systems. Charles Mee's article, "How a Mysterious Disease Laid Low Europe's Masses," explains how the Black Death affected many aspects of medieval life. During this period, social discontent took the form of peasant uprisings and urban revolts. Dynastic and fiscal problems destabilized England and France. The Great Schism and the new heresies divided the Church. Emerging capitalism gradually undermined an economy based on land. Yet, these crises generated the creative forces that later gave birth to the Renaissance and the modern era. The nation-state, the urban way of life, and the class structure, and other aspects of modern life existed in embryonic forms in the Middle Ages. It was in medieval Europe that the West prepared itself for its modern role as "chief disturber and principal upsetter of other people's way."

# A Turbulent Reputation

MICHAEL STAUNTON

In 2001 Thomas Becket (1120?–70) was named by the Daily Mail as one of history's 100 'Great Britons'. Four years later he came runner-up to Jack the Ripper in a BBC History magazine poll of 'Worst Britons'. Such a disparity of opinion is nothing new. Becket's brutal murder in Canterbury Cathedral in December 1170 unleashed an outpouring of grief and outrage which quickly developed into an extraordinarily successful and dynamic cult of St Thomas. But even as crowds flocked to his tomb, hailing him as the greatest saint of his age, or even the greatest in Christian history, criticism lingered. Not everyone had revised their impression of Becket as an arrogant troublemaker whose life had shown little evidence of sanctity and whose actions had been harmful not only to the King but to the interests of the Church he claimed to represent. In 1538, Henry VIII ordered the destruction of Canterbury's shrine to their martyr, and since then opinion on Thomas has often divided along Catholic/Protestant lines. But criticism and support for Becket have not always come from predictable quarters, or for the reasons one might expect. He has been championed by kings and hated by churchmen, and criticism has not only been acknowledged by his supporters, but employed as part of the construction of his sanctity.

The man who lay dead on the floor of Canterbury Cathedral on December 29th, 1170, was, according to his murderers, a 'traitor to the king and the kingdom'. After six years of exile in France he had returned to England with the goodwill of Henry II, only to disturb the peace, as he had done so many times before. It was the King's furious outburst against his Archbishop that had incited the four knights to set out for Canterbury, but his enemies were by no means confined to the secular world. Henry's rage had been sparked by a visit from the archbishop of York and the bishops of London and Salisbury, exasperated by Becket's decision to excommunicate or suspend them from office for crowning the King's son in his absence. These were long-standing enemies who had frequently clashed with their archbishop.

After his murder, their criticisms of Thomas were largely silenced, but there survives an eloquent and lacerating critique of Becket from the pen of one, Gilbert Foliot, bishop of London. Gilbert was everything that Becket was not: an austere Cluniac monk from a noble family, and a distinguished scholar. Passed over for the position of Archbishop of Canterbury in 1162 in favour of Becket, his views on the dispute are coloured by bitterness, and his letter to Thomas of 1166, Multiplicem nobis, in which he reviewed the archbishop's career, stands as a damning verdict on Becket's policies and an indictment of the man himself.

'It is difficult', writes Gilbert, 'for things begun with bad beginnings to be carried through to a good conclusion'. For an archbishop of Canterbury, Thomas's beginnings were certainly unorthodox. The son of a London merchant, his training had been first as clerk to a city accountant, then as clerk to Archbishop Theobald of Canterbury, before serving the King as royal chancellor for seven-and-a-half years. He showed no great intellectual distinction, and he did not become a priest until the day before his consecration as archbishop on June 3rd, 1162. Above all, his behaviour as chancellor was far from what might have been expected of a future archbishop. His love of feasting, hunting and display are well attested. Once he led an embassy to Paris accompanied by hundreds of attendants, eight wagons carrying silver dishes, changes of clothing and large quantities of ale, each wagon accompanied by a fierce dog and drawn by five horses, and on top of each horse a monkey. On another occasion he led an army of thousands into battle on the Norman frontier against the French, and himself unseated a famous knight from his charger. He was also a loyal servant and close friend of the King, and this fact at once makes more sense of his appointment and also left it open to criticism, making it appear as uncanonical and blatantly royalist. Gilbert claims that Becket had paid money for the office of chancellor and once he had achieved that position used it as a route towards his elevation to Canterbury, where 'fresh from the enjoyment of birds and hounds and the other delights of the court' he now stood before the altar as the spiritual leader of the kingdom. And he recalls how, at Becket's consecration, a passage was plucked from the gospels at random and read out, as was customary, as a prophesy of the archbishop's term. To the horror of those present they heard Jesus's words to the bitter fig-tree: 'May no fruit ever come from you for ever again!' (Matt. 21: 19).

Within a year of his consecration, Becket began to throw off his loyalty to the King, and tension between the former friends escalated with Henry's demand that the Church approve his 'ancestral customs' regarding relations between Church and the crown. Thomas first gave a verbal assent to the customs—known to history as the Constitutions of Clarendon—but when Henry had them put in writing he rejected them. This rejection of the

Constitutions intensified the king's hostility and entrenched their divide, but it was on Becket's initial acceptance that Gilbert Foliot focused his attack. He presents a picture of a united clergy, standing firm against any encroachment upon Episcopal rights and abandoned by their leader:

> Let the Lord judge between us . . . Let him judge who fled, who was a deserter in the battle . . . The captain of the army himself turned tail; the leader of the camp fled.

He recalls how, after submitting to trial at Northampton in October 1164, Becket escaped to France secretly and by night, with no one in pursuit, thereby abandoning his flock: Now from the safety of exile, the archbishop postures as a martyr while urging his fellow bishops to their death, and for what cause?

For Gilbert, there was no great issue at stake between King and archbishop. This was a matter which could have been settled easily by means of a more tactful approach but instead Thomas had acted as a doctor who cures one wound by inflicting another more dangerous, destroying the peace of the Church and kingdom.

Gilbert was not simply an apologist for the royalist cause: he shared Thomas's core principles but condemned his approach. For Gilbert, Becket's strident actions were damaging above all to the Church's cause which he claimed to espouse, and the crises which had beset relations between the Church and the crown were the direct result of Thomas's personal unsuitability for the job. As he put it more succinctly and dismissively during Thomas's trial at Northampton, 'the man's a fool, and always will be'.

After years of tortuous negotiations, Thomas returned from exile to his church in December 1170, amid joy and recrimination. Within a month he was dead. The murder, of course, changed everything. The brutal slaying of the leader of the English Church in his own cathedral, surrounded by the shrines of his saintly predecessors, and numerous bystanders, by men claiming to act in the King's name, was bound to provoke profound shock and horror. But the change to Thomas's reputation was not immediate, universal or consistent.

Even as the bystanders in the cathedral, the monks of Christ Church Canterbury and the clerks of Becket's household, reeled from the sacrilegious act they had witnessed, their emotions must have been mixed. The Canterbury monks had never warmed to their non-monastic archbishop whose extended exile had led the King to confiscate their lands. Now, as the knights threatened further reprisals, it seemed as if in death he would bring ruin upon them. Among the clerks were those such as John of Salisbury who had often upbraided his master during his life, and even moments before his murder had rebuked him for provoking the knights. Fearing further violence by the murderers, the monks hastily stripped the body for burial, whereupon they made a discovery which would form a crucial pillar in the establishment of his sanctity: that beneath his pontifical vestments Thomas had worn a monastic habit, and beneath that a coarse hairshirt riddled with lice and vermin. As one of their number later recorded,

> . . . the monks looked at each other, and were astonished at this view of hidden religion beyond what could have been believed, and with their sorrow thus multiplied, so were their tears.

But if the monks of Canterbury did indeed immediately recognize Thomas as a saint, they were slow to advertise the fact. The initiative was taken instead by the poor and the sick of Canterbury and the surrounding area who hailed Becket as a saint and claimed his miraculous intervention. From Easter 1171, as fear diminished and miraculous cures spread to a wider geographical area and extended their social reach, the monks began their tentative steps towards embracing the cult by allowing access to the tomb, and then placing the body in the cathedral behind the altar of the Virgin Mary. Becket's overwhelming popular acclaim demanded official recognition, and fast. On February 21st, 1173, the monks of Canterbury, now enthusiastic supporters of Thomas's highly profitable cult, got their wish when he was canonized by Pope Alexander III (1159–81).

Within little over two years, then, Thomas had gone from a traitor to the King and the realm to England's martyr, hailed by the people and the Church. In the same year as his canonization, Henry submitted to the Church and promised to make recompense. The transformation seemed complete when, in July 1174 as he was fighting off the rebellion of his sons, the King himself made a pilgrimage to Thomas's tomb, barefoot and fasting, and made a statement of atonement for his role, if inadvertent, in the murder, voiced by none other than the bishop of London, Gilbert Foliot.

But just because Thomas had been hailed as a saint in spectacular manner did not mean that his sanctity was unproblematic, or that criticism had been forgotten. In the thirteenth century Caesarius of Heisterbach wrote of a debate among theologians at Paris in the aftermath of the murder over whether Thomas merited the title of a martyr. 'Some said that he was a damnable traitor to his kingdom', and that 'he had been worthy of death', and one can be sure that murmurs of this kind were not restricted to such elevated discussions. According to Caesarius, 'Christ himself answered the question when he glorified him with so many signs'. But to many, it was necessary to explain that it was not only the posthumous miracles, or even the martyrdom that distinguished Thomas, but that he was a saint in life as in death.

Becket attracted a remarkable number of posthumous biographers, and one of the main reasons that so many Lives were written—at least seven in the first four years after his murder—was to explain the sanctity of his life, and how it seamlessly blended with that of his death. To claim Thomas as a saint in this way was to advance an argument, and it involved taking on his controversial reputation. The biographers did not deny the sumptuousness and worldliness of Thomas's earlier life as a 'pastor of hawks and hounds', but focused on the 'conversion' which followed his elevation to Canterbury. This was the beginning of an ongoing process of spiritual development hidden to all but a few, symbolized by the hairshirt against his skin, developed during his exile and consummated in the martyrdom. Specific aspects of his career are addressed: his capitulation to the King's customs at Clarendon is acknowledged by most as a lapse, but blamed on the manoeuvres of his rivals. The flight from England is presented as a justified retreat from danger in accordance with canon law, and a journey towards martyrdom. His vigorous defence of ecclesiastical rights was in the mould of the prophets, the martyrs and Christ himself. The King is associated, if obliquely, with Old Testament tyrants, his opponents within the Church as their evil counsellors, or the scribes, pharisees and High Priests of the New Testament. In reflecting on the murder, parallels came readily to hand, not only from the Acts of the Christian Martyrs but from the Gospels. Thomas's cry to spare his men was as Christ saying 'Let these men go'; the knights' plunder of the archbishop's palace was as the division of Christ's garments. In some accounts, and in early visual representations, the murder was placed erroneously before the great altar, the archbishop presented simultaneously as priest and sacrificial victim.

Some writers reveal an awareness that such a portrayal might be too much for many of those who had known Becket in the flesh. Particularly notable in this respect is an anonymous Life preserved in a single manuscript in Lambeth Palace Library. Writing before 1173, the Lambeth Anonymous, as it is known, cites at length many of the criticisms that had been expressed about Thomas during his lifetime and that, one suspects, continued to be made. Many have said that Thomas was driven more by desire for glory, zeal for his own vindication and pride than by righteousness, the Anonymous states. As love of God cannot exist with hatred of one's neighbour, and many have seen Becket's behaviour as pompous, arrogant, grasping, cruel and terrible, such a man could not have had true virtue or deserved the reward of martyrdom, 'for when such an array of vices is present, one cannot have accompanying virtue'. But the Anonymous goes on to counter this position, arguing that after his elevation to Canterbury, and his atonement for his early life, he did indeed live a life of virtue. And citing the reading 'Judge not, that you be not judged', he writes that where the intention of a man's deeds is unclear, he should be given the benefit of the doubt. Writing before his canonisation, primarily, it seems, for a London audience, the message seems to be that Thomas had evident and well-known faults, but that this does not deny his sanctity, and should not prevent observers from praising and imitating his virtues.

A few years later, in 1176, the Canterbury monk Alan of Tewkesbury completed a collection of the Becket correspondence. Not only did he include many letters critical of Thomas but he prefaced the collection with a narrative largely consisting of reported speeches adapted from those letters, both for and against Becket's policies. One of those letters included was Foliot's Multiplicem nobis. Though some historians have wondered at this decision, reasons immediately present themselves. It is clear that the case against the archbishop could not be erased, and it required answers. Furthermore, the survival of such criticism could be of benefit to Thomas's legacy. Foliot gave a number of hostages to fortune. His letter repeatedly accuses Thomas of physical cowardice—the good shepherd lays down his life for his sheep—and mocks his posturing as a martyr. Now he who had risen from the royal court was a martyr of the Church; the archbishop who had capitulated to the King's customs had died for ecclesiastical liberty; the exile who had deserted his flock had now laid down his life for his sheep. The 'barren tree' on which no fruit would grow had blossomed.

This perhaps marks the high point of Becket's cult. In the following decade the custodians of his shrine continued to add to the collection of miracles, and more Lives of Thomas appeared, but little new was said. Becket's sanctity was well established, and reconciliation with the King remained firm. Thomas was succeeded as Archbishop of Canterbury by men who were keen to promote his sanctity but had no enthusiasm about following in his footsteps. In the late 1180s Becket's clerk and confidant Herbert of Bosham, now an old man, composed a sprawling Life of Thomas, far longer and more difficult than any other, and embodying a more exalted view of Becket than is found anywhere else. Echoing John the Evangelist, Herbert describes himself as 'the disciple who saw and heard these things', and his work is self-consciously a Gospel of St Thomas. For him, it was not the miracles that distinguished his master, nor even so much his secret asceticism. Rather, it was his defence of the Church's rights:

> Thomas fought against the world on the stage of the world, a spectacle for men and for angels.

This is argued in intricate theological detail, with Herbert haranguing Thomas's successors to emulate the martyr. But the times had changed, and few were interested in the finer points of the dispute or such analogies with Christ and the saints. In many ways closer to the spirit of the times were the views expressed in William of Newburgh's History, written towards the end of the century, that Thomas was a saint, but that all his actions did not need to be followed. This attitude allowed Thomas's memory to be appropriated ever more widely, by the Church, by kings, and as a symbol of concord between them.

In 1194 Richard I (r.1189-99) was captured in Germany on his return from crusade and only released upon the payment of a substantial ransom. One of his first actions on his return to England was to visit Becket's tomb at Canterbury. His brother John did likewise immediately after his coronation in 1199. In 1220 Thomas's body was 'translated' to a new golden casket adorned with precious stones atop a marble altar in Canterbury Cathedral, lavishly rebuilt after a fire thanks to the newfound wealth of the community. Presided over by Archbishop Stephen Langton, in the presence of the young Henry III, this was not only a celebration of the saint but an act of national reconciliation after the civil war which had ended King John's reign. Becket's defence of the Church was acknowledged, but so too was the re-establishment of royal authority in the person of Henry III, under the protection of the papal legate, and the restoration of order to the kingdom.

In the following centuries Thomas remained a draw for pilgrims, most famously those depicted by Chaucer in the Canterbury Tales. His name was linked to opponents of the crown, whether such ecclesiastics as Stephen Langton (in his dispute with King John) and Edmund Rich, or such laymen as Simon de Montfort and Thomas of Lancaster. But successive kings were also keen to associate themselves with the memory of the martyr. Henry III's successor Edward I paid an annual visit to the tomb, as did his grandson Edward III. The unluckier kings of the fourteenth century, Edward II and Richard II, tried to appropriate Thomas's patronage, attempting unsuccessfully to be anointed with 'the holy oil of St Thomas', a bottle containing oil which had supposedly been given to Becket by the Virgin Mary, and which would, according to legend, guarantee the recovery of lost territories to the rightful king anointed with it. It was with this oil that Henry IV was anointed in his coronation of 1400, a significant act in the legitimation of his succession, and upon his death he was buried in the Trinity Chapel at Canterbury, close to the body of the martyr.

Any reputation takes on a life of its own, and it is not surprising that different people have chosen to read different things into Thomas Becket. He was a complex character, and the availability of so much material about him—more than for any other Englishman of the Middle Ages—allows us to appreciate this complexity in a way impossible with many of his contemporaries. He may be neither the greatest nor the worst Briton in history, but he will remain one of the most fascinating.

## For Further Reading

F. Barlow, Thomas Becket (Guild Publishing, 1986); A. Duggan, ed., The Correspondence of Archbishop Thomas Becket, Archbishop of Canterbury, 1162-70, 2 vols (OUR 2000);A. Duggan, Thomas Becket (Hodder Arnold, 2004); A. Morey and C.N.L. Brooke, Gilbert Foliot and his Letters (CUP, 1965); J. C. Robertson and J. B. Sheppard, Materials for the History of Thomas Becket, 7 vols (1875-85); B. Smalley, The Becket Conflict and the Schools (Oxford, 1973); M. Staunton, ed., The Lives of Thomas Becket (MUP, 2001); M. Staunton, Thomas Becket and his Biographers (Boydell & Brewer, 2006).

---

**Michael Staunton** is Lecturer in Medieval History, School of History and Archives, University College Dublin.

# What Did Medieval Schools Do For Us?

NICHOLAS ORME

There are few worse insults than 'medieval', or safer ones, because those who might be offended are no longer with us! Where education is concerned, independent schools, old school buildings, unfashionable subjects like the classics, or strict regimes, can all be dismissed as 'medieval' without imagining what medieval schools might have been like. If anyone does imagine them, it is probably as few in numbers, poorly equipped, with unimaginative teaching, and pupils kept in order by vigorous corporal punishment—altogether different from what good modern schooling should be.

The history of schools in England begins a long way back, probably soon after the Romans came in AD 43. The Romans used reading and writing for a wide range of purposes, and many signs of these survive today. There are milestones and tombstones carved with inscriptions, and words stamped onto pottery and tiles. There are the wooden tablets from Vindolanda near Hadrian's Wall containing letters and inventories, and the metal plates with prayers and curses found in the waters of Bath. These writings were in Latin, and if you wished to learn to read or write in Roman Britain, you did so in that language.

Little is known of how schools functioned in Britain. In the Roman empire as a whole, however, it was common to find elementary teachers of reading in towns, and the major cities supported more learned schoolmasters who would teach grammar and rhetoric (how to write and speak Latin correctly and read the best classical authors). While only the noblest and wealthiest in Britain would have studied these subjects, mostly boys at that, many others must have learnt to read and write at a basic level since the bits of Latin that have survived on everyday objects are often crudely spelt and expressed.

When Roman control in Britain evaporated soon after AD 400, the western half of the country reverted to rule by native British kings. The eastern half became infiltrated by Anglo-Saxons, who established kingdoms of their own. One might have expected Latin literacy to have dried up also. It did not—any more than literacy in English or French disappeared when colonialism ended in Africa. By AD 400 Britain was becoming Christian, and Christianity is a religion of books and writings: the Bible, prayer-books, letters, laws, and non-Christian Latin scholarly works. British Christians–clergy and the more important laity–needed to go on learning Latin to read or write it. As soon as the Anglo-Saxons were converted to Christianity, which happened after 597, they followed this path as well.

There were, however, two big educational changes in the post-Roman era. One was a change in where schooling took place. By 400 the towns in Britain were in decline. They no longer contained enough literate people to support schoolmasters teaching the public. The centres of literacy in Britain moved from the towns to monasteries, and it was monks who now provided schooling, primarily for boys and youths intending to be monks but not invariably so. It was to be a long time before free-standing teachers appeared again in the towns of what by then would be England.

The other change involved how schooling was done. In Roman times, when a good deal of Latin was spoken even in Britain, you went to school to learn the Latin alphabet, but after that you could pick up much of your knowledge of Latin from Latin speakers around you. The advanced teachers of grammar and rhetoric assumed that you had a basic knowledge of Latin already, and sought to polish and improve it.

After 400, when there were far fewer Latin speakers in Britain, learning it informally became difficult. One solution was to learn the Latin alphabet but to use it to write in your local language, and from about the fifth or sixth century this was done In Welsh and Irish, and later on (by the seventh century) in English. But although these languages were suitable for composing poetry and local laws and customs, you still needed Latin to access religious and learned writings and to communicate with people in France and Italy.

The Romans had hardly thought how to teach Latin to non-Latinists. Roman grammars, the most popular of which was by Donatus who lived in the mid-fourth century, were rather like Fowler's English Usage. They took it for granted that you knew basic Latin, and told you how to write it correctly. This wasn't good enough for non-Latinists. Latin is a complicated language. There are five major types of nouns and four major types of verbs, and unlike English nouns and verbs they have many 'paradigms' or forms, depending on the roles they play in a sentence.

So, in the post-Roman period, Irish, British, and eventually Anglo-Saxon teachers, compiled new grammars, based on those of the Romans, but expanded to help learners who knew no Latin already and whose own language worked in different ways. These teachers developed an important tool of education: the foreign-language grammar. The texts they produced are the direct ancestor of the ones that we use for learning French,

German, or any other language, which expect their readers to have difficulties with an unfamiliar language and take them into it by gentle stages.

Along with Latin grammars came Latin word-lists, eventually with English translations, and Latin dialogues imagining scenes of everyday life and helping you to converse about them. These works too anticipated modern phrase-books and foreign language readers. At first the books that taught you Latin were in Latin themselves. But in the 990s a monk named Ælfric, teaching at Cerne Abbey in Dorset, produced the first-known Latin textbook in English, and this was widely used in England up to and even beyond the Norman Conquest.

For most of the 'Anglo-Saxon period', then, from the seventh century to the mid-eleventh, schooling shared much in common with schooling today. It set out to give you access to all knowledge, which at that time required reading and studying Latin. Increasingly, from about the ninth century onwards, there was knowledge available in English too, and having learnt the Latin alphabet you could use your literacy to access English as well as Latin.

The Anglo-Saxons were also modern in that their schooling was, in principle, suitable for anyone. Although it took place chiefly in monasteries of monks or nuns, or later on in minsters (churches staffed by more worldly clergy), it soon attracted boys and even girls who did not intend to become clergy (or did not end up in that life). The Venerable Bede makes it clear that the great northern bishops of the seventh century like Aidan of Lindisfarne and Wilfrid of York had lay youths in their households, as well as young clerics, who were learning the scriptures and even going on to careers as warriors.

Some of the Anglo-Saxon kings of Bede's day were literate in Latin. He tells us that Aldfrith of Northumbria was 'most learned in the scriptures' and was given a book on the holy places in Palestine by the abbot of Iona. Bede also reports a story about a warrior in Mercia, who died between 704 and 709 after seeing a vision of angels and demons. They showed him books in which his good and bad deeds had been written, and in each case he was given the book 'to read' and did so.

Women's education is less clear. They certainly learnt to read basic Latin in the nunneries, in the sense of being able to pronounce the Latin of the services, and by the time of King Alfred (871–99) lay noblewomen were learning to read. Alfred's daughter Ælfthryth is said to have learnt the Latin psalter and to have read books in English, especially poetry. Edith, the daughter of Earl Godwine and wife of Edward the Confessor, who spent part of her childhood with the nuns of Wilton Abbey in the 1030s and 40s, was later credited with having known music, grammar, and languages, which she had presumably learnt in the abbey.

By the time of the Norman Conquest there were dozens of places in England where schooling could be had. They included monasteries, cathedrals and minsters, and possibly some royal and noble households like Alfred's. Before 1066, however, schools are not recorded as independent bodies. Schooling was an activity within some other body, and teaching was a task rather than a vocation. The teacher, when not in the class, was a monk, a nun, or a cleric, not a professional instructor.

By 1100 this situation was changing. In the 1070s, soon after the Norman Conquest, we start to hear of schools as distinct institutions and, in the twelfth century, of school teaching as a distinct occupation. How far these changes were due to the Normans is hard to say. They were reformers who may have tried to make schools more effective, but other forces were tending to separate schooling from church institutions.

One was the revival of towns. Once again, as in Roman times, there were sizeable settlements of people who needed and practised literary skills: clergy, merchants, and administrators. It was becoming feasible again for a teacher to make a living from charging fees to boys from the neighbourhood. Another factor was to be found in the Church reforms of the twelfth century, by which the monasteries and many of the minsters became stricter and more enclosed in their way of life. It was less easy for them to admit children and youths to their premises and provide a cleric to teach them. The increasing demand for education, in itself, dictated that it needed a teacher's full-time attention.

As a result, during the twelfth century, schools in England began to achieve two other features that we take for granted as modern. First of all, many schools moved out of churches and acquired separate identities. They occupied their own buildings, usually in a street accessible to the public. Their schoolmasters became full-time teachers, rather than doing the job along with religious duties. Monks stopped teaching schoolboys, and teachers from now on were either laymen or chaplains akin to parish clergy.

Secondly, there was an explosion in the number of schools. We can't easily say how many there were in England and Wales before the nineteenth century, because no one kept lists and they tend to be recorded only by chance. Currently we know of free-standing schools in about forty places during the twelfth century, seventy-five in the thirteenth, and two or three hundred by the fourteenth and fifteenth. There would have been many more than we know of, and new ones emerge in records all the time.

They occur from Norham on the Scottish border to western Cornwall where Cornish was spoken, and from Haverfordwest to Ipswich. There were other schools in Scotland and Ireland. By the thirteenth century it seems likely that all cities and market towns had them, and we hear of them even in villages like Awre in Gloucestershire, Kinoulton in Nottinghamshire, and Rudham in Norfolk. The schools in the larger towns were relatively grand organizations with impressive buildings, graduate teachers, book collections, and a good record of continuity. Others were small private ventures that came and went, possibly leaving places without a school for a time.

Some schools, known by contemporaries as song or reading schools, concentrated on elementary education. They took in boys from about the age of five. You started by learning the Latin alphabet from a small tablet held in the hand or from a small prayer-book, known as a primer. Once you could pronounce the letters, you learnt how to read Latin words from basic prayers. 'The Paternoster' (Lord's Prayer), 'Ave Maria' (Hail Mary), and 'Apostles' Creed' were commonly used for this purpose. Then you went on to read psalms, again in Latin, and learnt how to chant them in plainsong.

Up to this point you did not know what the words meant. Chaucer's 'Prioress's Tale' describes two small boys in a song school, one of whom confesses that he cannot translate what he is singing because 'I learn song, I know but little grammar'. Grammar—understanding how Latin worked and what it meant—came next, for those between the ages of seven and ten. Sometimes you left the song school at this stage for a specialized grammar school, but in small towns schoolmasters often taught the whole range of learning in a single school.

In the grammar school, where you stayed for four or more years depending on your career ambitions, you learnt—as you had done in Anglo-Saxon times—how Latin worked grammatically and how to write and to speak it. You wrote your notes and exercises on tablets that could be wiped, and after 1400 you did so on paper, which became cheap at about that time. Some pupils' paper notebooks still survive. To improve your style, and to teach you knowledge and wisdom, you read Latin poetry. Two popular school authors were Cato, who wrote wise advice in couplets, and Theodulus, whose poem gave a brief guide to classical mythology and compared it with some of the main historical episodes in the Bible.

The school year started in September and occupied three terms, ending in about June. This familiar arrangement goes back as early as we know, to the thirteenth century, reflecting the custom of taking holidays in June and then concentrating on getting in the harvest during August. The school day mirrored the working day, starting at day-break and ending in the late afternoon, with a break for breakfast and a long interval of an hour or so for midday dinner. In school the master presided from a large chair, and the pupils sat around the edge of the room on benches. The master did not move about but sat like a king or the lord of the manor, and called out boys for questioning or punishment as necessary.

If you stayed there long enough, you left school with a thorough knowledge of Latin and an ability to read, write, and speak it, and to understand other people speaking it. This was essential for going to university, where lectures and books would be entirely in Latin. Most schoolboys did not go to university, however, and became gentlemen, merchants, parish clergy, or secretarial clerks. For them it was sufficient to know enough Latin to read documents and financial accounts, or to do fairly simple writing in the language. Practical studies, like arithmetic, accountancy, and law were not taught in grammar schools. You learnt them 'on the job' or, if necessary, went to a specialist teacher after leaving school.

This was the infrastructure that produced the great shift in English culture that Professor Michael Clanchy has called the change 'from memory to written record'. In the time of William the Conqueror and even Henry II, a dispute about land, for example, would be decided on the evidence of what witnesses could remember about the ownership. By the reign of Henry III (1216–72), in the mid-thirteenth century, the parties were likely to produce written documents–charters–to establish their claims. Even the serfs of Peterborough Abbey acquired and disposed of bits of land with charters by this date, and the charters were kept as evidence.

By about 1250 English society was not yet totally literate. Many people, perhaps most, were still illiterate. But it was literate in a collective sense. Nearly everyone was dependent on writings to some extent and could access these through other people, if not personally. The schools trained the people who wrote and read these records and not only records, of course, but church service-books, private prayer books, letters, accounts, and works of literature.

Not enough of the growing literate population could cope with Latin. Many boys continued to learn it in school, but other boys and many girls, once they could read, soon deviated to reading in English or, up to the fifteenth century, French. By 1400 schoolmasters were once again producing Latin textbooks in English as Ælfric had done. This was a recognition that their pupils were reading English more easily than they were Latin.

In 1382 William Wykeham founded Winchester College–the first school to be a fully-endowed and self-governing institution. It provided education, board, and lodging for seventy scholars. Previous schools had been largely (though not totally) dependent on charging fees. Winchester offered teaching free of charge, but it was not available to everyone. The scholarships at the college were reserved for the founder's family, the sons of tenants on the college estates, and boys who lived in the counties where the estates were situated.

Wykeham laid down that the scholars must have no private income greater than £3 6s. 8d. per annum. In practice (perhaps on the grounds that boys or youths have no real income of their own) the places soon came to be taken by the sons of gentry, merchants, or wealthy yeomen farmers who had some connection with the college or influence in it. In consequence Wykeham's foundation was the ancestor of modern public schools rather than of state schools today.

But Winchester was also an unusually large and rich foundation, untypical of its period and for a long time matched only by Henry VI's imitation of it, Eton College founded in 1440. The model for free schools in the later Middle Ages was not Winchester but a more modest foundation contemporary with it, situated in a small Cotswold town: the grammar school of Wotton-under-Edge.

Wotton School was founded in 1384 by Katherine Lady Berkeley, a wealthy baron's widow. She planned it on a modest scale with an endowment to pay for the salary of a single schoolmaster teaching grammar without charge to anyone who came to the school. No arrangement was made for boarding, and the pupils were drawn from the town and its neighbourhood. In these respects Wotton was more like a modern state school than was Winchester.

Many free grammar schools like Wotton were founded during the fifteenth century and, indeed, down to the nineteenth century when state education arose. Though called 'grammar schools', they often taught reading as well as Latin and gathered in boys at any age for any part of the process. Most of them were day schools, catering for the local community. Perhaps inevitably they came, like Winchester, to be taken over by the local elites. People already literate and wealthy had a better understanding of the value of schooling, and could better afford the extra charges that even free schooling entails, like decent clothes, books and payments for school activities. There is nothing new in middle-class parents seeking out the best available schools for their children!

Girls' education, even in 1500, was less formal. The new free grammar schools were for their brothers. Girls who learnt to read did so chiefly at home from literate mothers, siblings, or clergy, or at the top of society from nuns. Their studies did not reach so high as those of boys. They learnt Latin in the sense of pronouncing it correctly and being able to do so at sight from a prayer-book, but rarely learnt the grammar of Latin to unlock the meaning. They did not spend hours in class writing exercises, and so their handwriting skills were less developed.

Nevertheless, there were plenty of literate women at the level of the nobility, the gentry, and the merchant class–women able to read fluently in French or English. And, in a shy and unobtrusive way, the first schools for girls and the first schoolmistresses were making their appearance. So unobtrusive was this development that no one commented on it.

In 1335 there is a casual reference to a certain Margaret Skolmaystres in Oxford. A similar woman, Matilda Maresflete, occurs in Boston in 1404 with her occupation given in Latin (magistra scolarum), and two others, E. Scolemaysteresse and Elizabeth Scolemaystres, turn up in London in 1408 and 1441 respectively. A fifth women with a similar title, Agnes 'teacher of girls' (doctrix puellarum), is recorded in London before 1449.

Nothing is known about them but their names point to the likelihood that they taught reading at home to girls or small boys. Yet the fact that four of them were called 'school mistress' shows that people were familiar enough with women teachers to develop a standard term to describe them. This suggests that such teachers were common, yet so lowly that nobody tried to regulate or record them. Even for girls, education was beginning to move out of the home to a school and to a specialized teacher.

If we stop the history of education in 1500, when, roughly speaking, we cease to talk of the Middle Ages, the achievements of medieval school founders, schoolteachers and pupils turns out to have been impressive. They were anything but 'medieval' in the modern dismissive term. They were modern in being free-standing, self-governing institutions. They were extremely common all over the country. They had recognizable fulltime schoolmasters and mistresses.

Education was free in some places. It had some of the same aims that it does today. It gave children knowledge of the world of learning and the skills to navigate in that world. It used sophisticated methods, like the Latin textbook written for a non-Latinist in his own language. It tried to empathize with pupils through humour and references to everyday life. That is not to deny that schools were smaller in buildings and pupil numbers than most modern ones, and that books were scarcer (though not absent). They also used corporal punishment in a way that we would find unacceptable, but one that was taken for granted down to the twentieth century, both in home life and in the judicial system.

Our understanding of schooling is that you start it at about four or five and follow it until you are about eighteen. The school year falls into three terms, divided by Christmas and Easter holidays, with a long holiday in the summer. You start by learning to read and go on to more complicated studies. The teacher tries to gain your interest, rather than just communicating facts. You get an education that is not narrowly vocational, but fits you for a wide range of careers.

None of these is a modern invention. They all developed in the schools of the Middle Ages, and we have kept them because they work. They are what medieval schools did for us.

## For Further Reading

N. Orme, Medieval Schools (Yale UP, 2006) and Medieval Children (Yale UP, 2001). Anglo-Saxon education: P. Riché, Education and Culture in the Barbarian West, Sixth through Eighth Centuries (University of South Carolina Press, 1976); M. Lapidge, Anglo-Latin Literature 900-1066 and Anglo-Latin Literature 600-899 (Hambledon Press, 1993 and 1996). History of the study of Latin: Vivien Law, The History of Linguistics in Europe from Plato to 1600 (Cambridge UP, 2003). History of literacy: M.T. Clanchy, From Memory to Written Record: England 1066-1307, 2nd ed. (Blackwell, 1993).

---

**Nicholas Orme** is Professor of History at the University of Exeter. His new book Medieval Schools was published by Yale University Press in May, price £25.

# Lackland

## *The Loss of Normandy in 1204*

Nick Barratt

Britons are drawn to events when their independence and freedom have been under threat, yet overwhelming odds have been defied. The Second World War brought the evacuation of the Dunkirk beaches, the Battle of Britain and D-Day. Victories at Trafalgar and Waterloo safeguarded Britain from Napoleon. The defeat of the Spanish Armada cemented the reputation of Queen Elizabeth. The dates we remember most are usually linked with triumph, or at least the aversion of disaster. In contrast one of the most important dates in English history—one which represents one of the greatest catastrophes ever to befall an English monarch—has been airbrushed from national consciousness.

Eight hundred years ago, in 1204, the political map of Western Europe was redrawn in the space of a few months when John, king of England and ruler of territories covering roughly two-thirds of modern France, was expelled from most of these continental lands by the French king, Philip Augustus. The consequences of this humiliating defeat still reverberate, particularly in relations between the English and their neighbours in the British Isles, attitudes to continental Europe, lingering concepts of British imperialism, and the significance of Magna Carta as a symbol of human rights. I believe this humbling defeat should be seen as a key turning point.

The kings of England from 1066 considered themselves first and foremost as landowners in Normandy and nominal subjects of the King of France but who, as a result of William the Conqueror's invasion, had also acquired a royal title and access to England's riches. The relative unimportance of England to them is illustrated by William's division of his lands before his death in 1087; his eldest son Robert received the Duchy of Normandy, while his second son William Rufus took the secondary prize, becoming William II of England. Nevertheless, the fledgling Anglo-Norman realm was re-united under one ruler, when the Conqueror's third son Henry I inherited England after Rufus's death in 1100 and then defeated and imprisoned his brother Robert at the battle of Tinchebrai in 1106. A cross-Channel aristocracy developed, holding lands in both territories and having a vested interest in keeping them united in one ruler. The wars of Stephen's reign (1135–54) emphasised this; he failed to win over the Norman aristocracy and thereby made the task of hanging on to England much harder. Unification was achieved under Henry II (r. 1154–89), but now the Anglo-Norman realm became part of an even larger accumulation of titles.

Henry II, son of the Empress Matilda and Geoffrey of Anjou, was the nominal ruler of lands stretching from the borders of Scotland to the Pyrenees. He inherited England partly through conquest, partly through his mother's birthright as daughter of Henry I; Normandy had been conquered by his father and Henry was invested as duke of Normandy some time between November 1149 and March 1150; Anjou also passed to him on Count Geoffrey's death in 1151. Perhaps the most audacious acquisition was the strategically important duchy of Acquitaine when Henry married its heiress Eleanor in 1152. This was a gamble; not only was Eleanor eleven years older than the nineteen-year-old Henry, but also she was the repudiated wife of Louis VII, king of France. One of the grounds for the annulment was that she had failed to produce a male heir, a serious issue when dynastic continuity depended on a brood of healthy sons.

Thus, through dynastic accident and shrewd marriage, within five years Henry had gained control of unprecedented resources, often referred to as the Angevin Empire. In 1158 he added lordship of Brittany, and claimed lordship of Ireland following an invasion in 1171 and subsequent settlement by English adventurers. To secure the borders of these lands, Henry forged a complicated network of alliances, paid for by a steady flow of money from England's treasury. Indeed a cynic might argue that money from England's cash-rich economy was more important to Henry than the prestige that its royal title brought.

Thus Henry was an international figure with multiple calls on his time; England was only a constituent part of this territorial jigsaw and it is not surprising that he spent most of his reign abroad. He was a French lord several times over; his place of birth was Le Mans in the province of Maine; his education was as a French nobleman, his first language was French and his leading advisers and courtiers were all French. He was naturally more concerned with affairs on the continent, and spent most of his life defending his acquisitions against external foes such as the King of France, and ambitious sons.

Henry had no intention of keeping the lands together, yet his policy of partially handing the governance of key territories to each of his sons without fully releasing control, led to bitter resentment and open warfare amongst his offspring. On Henry's death in 1189 the vast conglomeration passed virtually in tact to his son Richard, but this was down to the untimely deaths of Richard's brothers Henry and Geoffrey. Only one brother remained—Henry's youngest son John, unkindly described by historians as the runt of the Angevin litter, whom Henry had only entrusted with the lordship of Ireland, still a frontier land in the Angevin territories. Henry's last few years had been spent in open warfare with Richard, who was never a favourite of his father; it was the news that John had joined Richard's revolt in 1189 that broke the old king's heart. Wearied by old age and treachery, Henry was forced to acknowledge Richard as his heir. His last words to his estranged son had a prophetic ring: 'May the Lord spare me until I have taken vengeance upon you.' Henry's time had run out—he died a few days later on July 6th, 1189, but Richard had inherited a poisoned chalice.

Arguably, Richard I was an even more famous figure than his father, winning renown and the nickname 'Lionheart' as a Crusader in the Middle East and locking horns with Saladin. Whilst Richard's fame as a warrior and general has endured, his reputation as a competent ruler has come under scrutiny, particularly in the context of the loss of Normandy, the traditional heartland of the Anglo-Norman realm. The Duchy was fundamentally destabilised during Richard's reign on a number of levels—financial, political and structural—through the excessive militarisation of Normandy's frontiers. Furthermore the French king Philip Augustus, 1179–1223, one of Western Europe's most astute and opportunist monarchs, had constantly sought to exploit his position as Henry and Richard's feudal overlord to undermine their position as Duke of Normandy. He had often acted as catalyst in the arguments between father and son. Despite little material success in the ensuing conflicts, the effects on the duchy of Philip's constant military, political and diplomatic barrage was further to destabilise relations between the leading barons and their Angevin princes. The ambivalence of the Norman barons can be traced back to Geoffrey of Anjou's conquest of Normandy, which had forcibly ended many years of open enmity between the two territories. For as long as Henry II and Richard remained successful, the Norman aristocracy proved loyal, albeit grudgingly. However, during Richard's captivity on his way back from Crusade (1193–94), Philip forged an alliance with Prince John, who handed over key castles such as Evreux to the French king, allowing Philip to seize large sections of the French-Norman frontier. Richard spent the rest of his life trying to win them back, whilst the Norman aristocracy never forgot John's treachery.

In the face of Philip's aggression, Richard embarked on a massive programme of fortification along a disputed section of the Norman border called the Vexin. Castle after castle was constructed to provide a strategic network, at the heart of which was Château Gaillard—literally the 'saucy castle'. Built on Les Andelys, an island in the Seine, Château Gaillard was personally designed by Richard, who boasted that its defences were so well conceived that he could defend the castle even if its walls were made of butter. It protected strategic routes to the ducal capital of Rouen: whilst Château Gaillard stood intact, Normandy was safe.

Richard's castle-building programme came at an enormous cost. The duchy's finances were pushed to breaking point, and large drafts of cash from England were required to complete the construction. Norman ducal revenues were insufficient to meet even the cost of garrisoning its defences and so, to fund Richard's seemingly never-ending wars against Philip, England was subjected to unprecedented levels of financial exaction. Worst of all, Richard fatally undermined England's fiscal base, namely revenue from royal demesne lands, at a time when Philip Augustus was vastly expanding the French royal demesne.

On Richard's death in 1199, the new king John faced an unenviable position—committed to unsustainable levels of expenditure in Normandy that could only be funded by huge cash injections from England, drawn largely from politically sensitive sources. Contemporary chroniclers reveal a hitherto unrecognised level of resentment directed against Richard, and in contrast, the first years of John's reign saw praise heaped on the new king as the bringer of peace to a people wearied from heavy taxation and constant warfare. Yet within a few years, John's reputation was in tatters.

Amongst English monarchs, perhaps only Richard III can claim to have been vilified at a level similar to John. There are so many low points of John's reign it is difficult to know where to begin. Here was a man who was alleged to have murdered his nephew with his own bare hands; who lusted after and married a thirteen-year-old heiress, much to the disgust of her fiancé, a key ally; who lost territories that had been in his family's possession for centuries; whose actions in England brought the wrath of the Pope onto his God-fearing subjects during the great Interdict of 1208–14, when all church doors were locked; who managed to alienate so many leading English subjects that they declared war on him, having first attempted to tie him to written guidelines for good-government; and who was so disliked that a foreign prince—Louis, son of Philip Augustus—with no legitimate claim to the throne was preferred as a potential monarch by the rebels, who offered him the throne. Even taking into account the difficult political and financial situation bequeathed to him, John was indisputably the architect of his own misfortune.

A chain of events was set in motion by John's marriage in 1200 to Isabella d'Angoulême, betrothed at the time to one of his leading vassals in Acquitaine, Hugh le Brun, Lord of Lusignan. The ensuing squabble quickly turned to full-scale revolt, and as supreme overlord of both John and Hugh, Philip Augustus was provided with an easy opportunity to intervene directly in Angevin affairs. His demands for John to grant justice to Hugh were ignored; and thus, as a disobedient vassal, in 1202 John was formally stripped of all lands held of Philip except Normandy. Philip handed them to Arthur, John's nephew, and promptly embarked on raids against Normandy's borders. In an astonishingly decisive response, John won a victory more stunning than any achieved by his father or brother, and at the castle of Mirabeau captured Arthur along with all the leading Lusignan rebels. All were imprisoned, Arthur at Falaise; but in the words of the Margam chronicler, 'after King John had captured Arthur and kept him alive in prison for some time, at length, in the castle of Rouen, after dinner on the Thursday before Easter [April 3rd, 1203], when he was drunk and possessed by the devil, he slew him with his own hand, and tying a heavy stone to the body cast it into the Seine.' Rumours of this barbaric act, and the treatment of other noble prisoners, sealed John's fate.

The erosion of Norman confidence in their duke had been growing during Richard's last years, but under John, loyalty sank to a new low. Sensing this, Philip continued his assault on John's lands throughout 1203, and quickly seized control of Anjou, Maine and large sections of Acquitaine. More significantly, he made heavy inroads into the Norman defences, seizing castle after castle. John acted like a rabbit caught in headlights and, (correctly) fearing treachery from the Norman nobles, fled the duchy on December 5th, 1203. Philip had already begun his assault on Château Gaillard in August. In one sense Richard's boasts about the defensive capability of Château Gaillard were proved accurate; while opposition to Philip had melted away like butter, the walls of this key defence held out until March 1204. For as long as Château Gaillard held there was hope, as control of Normandy depended on its possession. However, John continued to cower in England, and by the time he had begun to make preparations for a return, it was too late. After a lengthy siege during which local residents were condemned to a horrific existence of depravation and starvation, trapped between the castle walls and the besieging army, Philip Augustus stormed the fortress on March 6th, 1204. He then mopped up resistance in the south and west of the duchy, taking the symbolically important towns of Falaise and Caen, before heading east. He reached Rouen, the ducal capital, in May; with the rest of Normandy in French hands and with no realistic hope of relief from John, resistance seemed futile and the city surrendered on June 24th, 1204. The heart had been ripped out of the Angevin Empire.

John devoted the remainder of his reign to the recovery of his lands. The next ten years were spent frantically gathering resources to mount a campaign of reconquest. Trapped in England, he traversed his kingdom selling royal justice, privilege and office, raising heavy taxes and imposing massive financial penalties on leading magnates to secure the King's 'goodwill'. This was particularly odious given the arbitrary nature of the exactions; and John's treatment of William de Braiose, who was hounded out of his lands and his wife and children starved to death in the dungeons of Windsor Castle on John's orders, left few in doubt of the need for compliance. By 1214 John's arbitrary exactions had secured an enormous war chest. He was risking everything on a military gamble to recover his lost lands. Succeed, and the means would justify the ends; fail, and the consequences were unthinkable.

The funds bought an impressive array of allies, including John's nephew and Holy Roman Emperor, Otto of Brunswick. John had planned a two-pronged assault, and led the southern attack himself. Predictably, he made little headway and, deserted by his Poitevin vassals, he was forced to withdraw. Nevertheless, a momentous encounter took place on July 27th, 1214, at Bouvines in Flanders, where Philip squared up to Otto and John's northern allies. In a pitched battle fought on a hot summer's day, Philip's victory was crushingly decisive; God had delivered his verdict on the battlefield, and John slunk back to England to face the consequences.

The date of the battle of Bouvines deserves to be as famous as Hastings, mainly because it decided the direction of England's future development as a nation. First and foremost, the floodgates of political protest in England were opened, leading directly to the creation of Magna Carta in 1215. Although large sections of the document simply attempted to limit the financial exactions of the Crown, several key clauses still have significance as defining civil liberty: 'No freeman shall be arrested or imprisoned or 1 disseised or outlawed or exiled or in any way destroyed, neither will we set forth against him or send against him, except by the lawful judgement of his peers and by the law of the land'; and 'To no one will we sell, to no one will we refuse or delay right or justice.' These statements of justice and the rule of law are enshrined in constitutions around the world, and have been used as rallying cries against oppression. Without John's actions after the loss of Normandy, it is entirely possible that Magna Carta would never have materialised.

Secondly, Bouvines confirmed the end of the Anglo-Norman realm. The cross-Channel aristocracy were forced to choose on which side of the fence they belonged. Thus for the first time the English nobility focused solely on the acquisition and consolidation of possessions within England. Their attention to their English estates led to greater political and social integration, as well as the development of a sense of Englishness that hitherto had been largely absent. Within forty years, John's son Henry III found himself facing a political crisis of his own because he had surrounded himself with non-English courtiers. Although the kings of England retained some continental lands, most importantly Gascony, they were now for the first time resident rulers, with a greater role to play in England's development.

More ominously, the severance of the Anglo-Norman reign had left John free to turn his attention to Wales and Ireland. After successful campaigns, one chronicler remarked that 'Ireland, Scotland and Wales all bowed to his nod—a situation which, as is well known, none of his predecessors had achieved—and he would have thought himself as happy and successful as he could have wished, had he not been despoiled of his continental possessions and suffered the Church's curse.' Although the Angevin monarchs no longer had most of their Angevin lands, their grand dynastic visions had not diminished. John's grandson Edward I undertook the conquest of Wales (complete with a castle-building programme of which Richard I would have been proud), and an abortive attempt to establish sovereignty over Scotland. Similarly, the gradual extension of English rule in Ireland continued. Thus the tone for English imperialism within the British Isles was set in the early years of the thirteenth century.

Finally, the events of 1204 and the battle of Bouvines had created an enmity between the kings of England and France that remained until the nineteenth century. Although Henry III recognised the loss of Normandy, Anjou and Acquitaine under the terms of the Treaty of Paris in 1259, the terms by which he was permitted to hold on to Gascony stored up problems for future generations. The impractical nature of one sovereign having to perform homage as a vassal to another, with ties of fealty that theoretically prevented an independent foreign policy, were unworkable and was a major cause of the Hundred Years War. It was only in 1801 that the British monarchy formally relinquished its claim to the French throne.

Thus without the ineptitude of King John, no modern debate that takes in British devolution, British sovereignty and role within Europe, trial by jury, civil liberty, or even sporting rivalry with the French would be possible. We owe much to the humiliating events of 1203–4, and should celebrate this, one of the least glorious chapters in our history.

## For Further Reading

J. Gillingham *The Angevin Empire* 2nd edition, (Arnold, 2001); S.D. Church, ed., King John: *New Interpretations* (Boydell, 2003); J. Holt, *The Northerners* (Oxford UP, 1961); D. Bates and A. Curry, eds., *England and Normandy in the Middle Ages* (Woodbridge, 1994).

**Nick Barratt** has written numerous articles about the reigns of Richard I, John, Henry III and Edward I. He currently works as a historical consultant and researcher to the media.

# The Fourth Crusade and the Sack of Constantinople

Jonathan Phillips

The capture of Constantinople by the armies of the Fourth Crusade was one of the most remarkable episodes in medieval history. One of their number wrote, 'No history could ever relate marvels greater than those as far as the fortunes of war are concerned'. On April 12th, 1204, an army of perhaps 20,000 men and a fleet of about 200 ships crewed by Venetian sailors and warriors, broke in and began to loot the greatest metropolis in the Christian world. Constantinople's mighty walls had resisted numerous onslaughts as the Avars, Persians and Arabs had tried to assail its defences over the centuries. Yet always 'the queen of cities', as the Byzantines described their capital, had survived. What had brought the crusaders to attack their fellow Christians and how did they manage to succeed? The crusaders understood their success as a manifestation of God's will. One commented, 'There can be no doubt that the hand of the Lord guided all of these events'.

There was a history of difficulties between the two parties, dating from the 1054 Schism between the Catholic and Orthodox churches. This concerned matters of doctrine, religious practice and papal authority and gave an added sharpness to future disputes. The advent of the crusades in 1095 brought further tensions often created by large and sometimes ill-disciplined armies passing through the Byzantine Empire en route to the Holy Land. Greek purges of the Venetian (1171) and western (1182) communities in Constantinople added to this record of troubles.

Relations between Byzantium and the West at this time were often characterised as a clash of cultures. The Greeks viewed themselves as civilised superiors to the barbaric and violent westerners; the people of Europe regarded the Byzantines as unwarlike, effeminate and duplicitous. In the fullest sense, of course, these stereotypes were inaccurate: the Latin West produced thinkers of the calibre of Anselm of Bec and St Bernard of Clairvaux; magnificent buildings such as the 531-feet long abbey of Cluny testify to practical and artisitic qualities as well. Equally, brutality was not exclusive to the westerners; the Byzantines were capable of extraordinary unpleasantness. The death of Emperor Andronicus I Comnenus in 1185 bears witness to this. With one eye gouged out, his teeth pulled out and his right hand severed, he was paraded through the streets of Constantinople, pelted with excrement before being hung upside down, having his genitals hacked off and finally killed by sword thrusts into his mouth and between his buttocks.

Nonetheless, however unsubtle or partial these respective viewpoints were, they can cast some light on the events of 1203-4 because, though other issues were involved, one key factor was the contrast between the westerners' military power and the Greeks' lack of fighting ability.

By the start of the thirteenth century the chivalric culture gripped the knightly classes of northern Europe. The intensive internecine warfare of the early twelfth century had become subsumed under an all-encompassing code of conduct that fell under the banner of chivalry. This included notions of honour and service, the patronage of *chansons de geste,* ideas of courtly love and, most pertinently to the crusades, the popularity of tournaments.

At the time of the Fourth Crusade, tournaments were not yet orderly contests between two individuals facing each other across the lists in front of ordered ranks of spectators. Rather, they were fast-moving, brutal struggles, sometimes involving hundreds of men. Contests ranged over many acres of lands with the 'arena' designated by particular fortresses or villages. Spectators were confined to the safety of castle walls to watch the fighting. On the herald's signal, two teams would charge each other; the thundering of hooves and the shouts of men were followed by a terrible impact as the combatants began with a lance charge. Then, hand-to-hand fighting broke out and victory was usually achieved by the side that preserved best order. The idea was to capture opponents, rather than to kill or harm them, although in such a heated atmosphere accidents were frequent. In 1186, for example, Richard the Lionheart's younger brother, Geoffrey of Brittany—a man famed for his fighting prowess—perished at a tournament. In spite of the dangers, many knights took part in a circuit of such events across northern Europe. The co-ordination of groups of knights and the violent ebb and flow of a tournament provided by far the most realistic preparation for actual warfare that could be imagined. Alongside the military aspect of these gatherings there were also splendid feasts. Castles might be specially decked out in bright banners, minstrels and entertainers hired and long evenings spent celebrating the deeds of warriors past—some of whom included the heroes of the First Crusade.

Churchmen viewed tournaments in a darker light because, alongside the promotion of violence, they appeared to encourage the vices of pride, envy, gluttony and lust. Prohibitions of such occasions were largely in vain, however, because by the time of the Fourth Crusade they had become an integral part of the knightly culture of the West. Ironically, among the leading patrons were the nobility of Champagne and Flanders—the two areas most associated with the crusades at this time. The counts of Flanders had been on crusades to the Holy Land in 1099, 1108, 1139, 1147, 1157, 1164, 1177 and 1191—an unequalled commitment to the cause of Christ.

When Pope Innocent III (1198–1216) launched recruitment for the Fourth Crusade he was unable to enlist the kings of the West; Richard I was killed in 1199, King John was too preoccupied fighting Philip II Augustus of France, and the German empire was the subject of a bitter succession dispute. It fell to the leading noble families of northern Europe to take the cross, including Count Baldwin of Flanders, his brother-in-law Count Thibaut of Champagne, Count Hugh of St Pol and Count Louis of Blois. Alongside the extensive crusading traditions in these men's blood, a number of them—such as Louis of Blois—had taken part in the Third Crusade (1189–92). The most important addition to their number was the northern Italian, Marquis Boniface of Montferrat, another veteran of the tournament scene and member of a family that had been twice married into the ruling dynasty of Jerusalem over recent decades. The men at the core of the Fourth Crusade, therefore, were tough, highly experienced fighters.

In tandem with this formidable force came the Venetian fleet. The northern Europeans had decided that the most effective way to regain Jerusalem was through the conquest of Egypt. The Nile delta would provide the financial and strategic strength for a long-term tenure of the Holy Land, but to capture it would require a huge naval force. The crusaders approached the acknowledged master mariners of the day and contracted the Venetians to supply a fleet. In the autumn of 1202, around 200 ships, adorned with brightly coloured pennants, set sail. As the crusaders sang hymns to fortify themselves ('Come Holy Ghost, our souls inspire and lighten with celestial fire') an eyewitness wrote of 'the finest thing to see that has ever been since the beginning of the world.'

These ships represented the most advanced naval technology of the day and were crewed by expert sailors, accompanied by many Venetian warriors who had also taken the cross. While the Venetians were among the leading commercial powers of the time they were, as was the entire Latin West intensely religious and had been involved in earlier crusades. On this occasion they were led by the remarkable Doge Enrico Dandolo, who was probably in his early nineties, and had been blind since the 1170s. One of the most charismatic leaders of any military campaign, the doge was commended by his allies as 'a maxi who is prudent, discreet and skilled in hard decision-making'.

A combination of the powerful knights of northern Europe and the excellent Venetian navy formed a potent threat. Yet the forces of Christian Europe had only a patchy military record and could be defeated for a variety of reasons, some self-inflicted and others a reflection of their opponents' strengths.

The overriding difficulties that faced the Fourth Crusaders in particular were a lack of men and money. In April 1201, the leaders made a contract with the Venetians to transport to the Holy Land and provision 33,500 men for a year, in exchange for 85,000 silver marks. The Venetians would also take part as an equal crusading party. By the summer of 1202, however, only around one-third of the provisional number of crusaders had reached Venice and these men could not hope to find the sum of money outstanding. To forestall the payment Doge Dandolo suggested an attack on the port of Zara (now Zadar in Croatia), a settlement that, until recently, had been under his control. There was, however, a serious problem with this idea: Zara was a Catholic city and its new overlord, King Emico of Hungary, was also signed with the cross. Emico was, therefore, under the protection of the papacy and to take Zara would be to invite almost certain excommunication. Some of the crusaders could not stomach the idea of fighting their fellow Christians and left to seek other ways to travel to the Holy Land, but the remainder—who argued that, without the help of the Venetians, the expedition would collapse immediately—stayed to capture the city, taking it on November 24th, 1202. Innocent III was furious and issued a bull of excommunication, although this was soon withdrawn from the French crusaders after a penitent delegation persuaded him that the liberation of the Holy Land was best served by such a move. The Venetians, however, saw the Zarans as rebels and refused to apologise. Their excommunication remained in place, although the crusade leaders suppressed it for fear of' inciting further discontent.

In early 1203, another ingredient was added to the mix. Envoys from Prince Alexius Angelos, a claimant to the Byzantine imperial title, arrived in the crusaders' camp at Zara. Well aware of the westerners' lack of men and money he made a persuasive offer: if they helped to reinstate him in Constantinople he would pay them 200,000 marks, give them all the supplies they needed and provide an army of 10,000 men. He would also place the Greek Orthodox Church under the authority of the papacy. But once again, the prospect of turning their weapons against their Christian brothers appalled many of the crusaders and another body of men chose to leave. Those who remained were convinced that joining with the Prince presented the most effective way of achieving the means to their goal.

Prince Alexius had assured the westerners that he would be welcomed back by his people. Unfortunately, these hopes were unfounded and by June 1203 it was evident to all in the crusader army that they would have to fight to get him re-instated. The mere sight of' Constantinople's massive walls put fear into their hearts; they had 'never imagined there could be so fine a place in the world', yet 'there was indeed no man so brave and daring that his flesh did not shudder at the sight'. What hope did such a small force have against the mighty Byzantine Empire?

In fact, by the early thirteenth century, the Byzantine world was in a fragile condition, corroded by two decades of internal feuding. The death of Emperor Manuel Comnenus (1143–80), presaged a series of regencies, usurpations and coups. Between 1180 and 1204 no fewer than fifty-eight rebellions or uprisings took place across the empire. Prince Alexius's father, Isaac Angelos (1185–95), had come to power by such means, but was deposed and blinded by his brother, Alexius III. Coupled with this chaos in leadership, external and internal forces had also imposed serious pressure on the Greeks. In 1176 the Seljuks of Asia Minor had heavily defeated a large Byzantine army at the Battle of Myriocephalum. In 1185, the Sicilians had sacked Thessalonica, the empire's second city. Five years later, an alliance with Saladin brought the Greeks into conflict with the huge crusading army of Emperor Frederick Barbarossa of Germany (1152–90) and the Byzantines were swiftly pushed to one side. With the decline in central authority the provinces sought advantage too. In 1184, Cyprus broke away, the following year the Bulgarians revolted, and in 1188 the city of Philadelphia in Asia Minor seceded.

Amid such chronic instability, it is not surprising that the Byzantines' military strength declined, most alarmingly in the navy. In 1169, the Greeks had sent a splendid fleet of 150 ships to help the Crusader States fight the Egyptians. By the time of the Fourth Crusade, however, Niketas Choniates, an eyewitness, observed that only twenty half-rotten vessels could be mustered to face the invaders. The Greeks' land forces, were not so feeble. At their core was the Varangian Guard, an elite unit made up of foreign mercenaries (often Scandinavians) armed with fearsome double-headed axes. Furthermore, the sheer size of Constantinople's population gave the Byzantines numerical superiority.

In July 1203 the crusaders staged an amphibious landing. Capturing the suburb of Galata, they broke through into the harbour of the Golden Horn and took a section of the sea walls. The Venetian mariners were able to brush aside Greek opposition and use their skills to adapt their vessels to take siege towers, bringing the ships up to the sea walls to disgorge safely the armed men necessary to continue the assault.

In contrast, the Greek resistance was patchy and usually relied on the presence of contingents of the Varangian Guard. There was a glaring difference between the two forces in quality of leadership. When Dandolo sensed that his men were making insufficient progress during the assault he threatened dire punishment for any that shirked the fight and demanded that the sailors land him on the shore. The crew obeyed and propelled his vermilion vessel forwards; Dandolo on the prow, the winged lion on the banner of St Mark flying before him. As the doge calculated, the other Venetians were shamed by the old man's bravery in landing—they could not abandon their venerable leader. Instead they rushed to join him. This sudden onslaught had the desired effect and the Venetians took a length of the walls.

Dandolo's boldness contrasts with the actions of Emperor Alexius III later the same day. Realising that he needed to make some kind of response he led his men onto the plains outside the land walls to confront the crusader knights. As line after line of Greek troops strode out of the city the sheer size of the Byzantine army daunted Geoffrey of Ville-hardouin: 'you would have thought that the whole world was there assembled'. Another witness believed that the Greeks had seventeen divisions of men compared to the crusaders' seven, but the westerners' mounted men, who probably numbered around 1,000, took the initiative and advanced. The Byzantine army seemed to cover the plain, flanked to one side by the walls of Constantinople which were also crammed with troops. As the Greeks moved forwards too, the westerners seemed briefly on the verge of losing formation—one group wanted to keep going and, in chivalric fashion, viewed the pause proposed by the others as a loss of honour. Fortunately, the moment passed and the battle line held: the crusaders waited for the onslaught, yet, incredibly, it never came. The Emperor ordered a retreat back into the city and the bemused and relieved westerners watched their opponents march away. Whatever tactical reasons lay behind this move, psychologically it appeared to all as a devastating admission of defeat. The crusaders wrote that 'astounded at our steadfastness (given our small number), he ignominiously turned his reins and retreated'; the Byzantine writer Niketas Choniates wrote that Alexius 'returned to the city in utter disgrace'. That same night the emperor fled into exile and the following day the crusaders and Prince Alexius entered the city in triumph.

Ten months later, the crusaders had to break into the city a second time. In the interim, their hopes of receiving the support promised by the Prince (now Emperor Alexius IV) had evaporated. The Byzantines resented his 'barbarian' allies and suspected the Venetians of being motivated by a desire to secure commercial privileges. When Alexius IV started pressurising his people for the money he owed the crusaders, they began to turn against him; equally, the westerners were increasingly angry at the Emperor's failure to fulfil his side of the bargain. Eventually, Alexius IV's position became untenable and he was murdered by the virulently anti-western noble known as Murtzuphlus, a name that denoted his huge eyebrows that joined together on his forehead. Murtzuphlus intensified aggression towards the crusaders and they began to struggle to find sufficient food supplies.

Thus, by March 1204, the westerners were camped outside a deeply hostile city, thousands of miles from home, with only limited provisions and facing increasingly frequent assaults from a man who had murdered their ally, the rightful ruler of Byzantium. Their position desperate, they felt compelled to attack Constantinople, and justified in doing so. As the crusade progressed, Pope Innocent III had issued edicts forbidding attacks on Christian lands, but by this stage the churchmen in the crusader army argued that they had sufficient cause to fight the 'heretics'. The longstanding effects of the schism were brought to bear and the Byzantines were described as 'the enemies of God' in a sermon delivered to the troops. In opposing the crusade they might also be seen to be hampering God's work, which was another reason to incur divine disapproval.

On April 9th, 1204, therefore, the crusaders launched an attack on the sea walls along the Golden Horn. Once again their ships were topped with huge and unwieldy siege towers. Some bore walkways, made from ships' yard-arms 110 feet long, lashed high on the masts, 95 feet above deck. Handrails and fire-resistant coverings of hide were added to protect those inside as they prepared to try to get a foothold on the walls.

This time, however, the Byzantines were well prepared. Murtzuphlus had ordered enormous wooden constructions, some six or seven storeys high according to contemporaries, to be erected on top of the existing walls to prevent the crusaders from gaining access. The crusaders began their assault, but the

Greeks stood firm and they were forced to withdraw. Murtzuphlus and his people were jubilant; they mocked and jeered at their enemies and some dropped their trousers and exposed their backsides in contempt.

The crusaders were despondent. Their expedition, which had set out in such splendour almost two years previously, appeared to be foundering on the shores of the Bosphorus. They would either face death or imprisonment at the hands of the Greeks, be forced to return home in disgrace, or else struggle on to the Levant where, penniless and tired, they could hope to achieve little. The leadership steeled the men for one final effort, and on April 12th, another attack was launched.

All through the morning the bat tie raged and it seemed as if the Byzantines were poised to gain the upper hand again. Then, just after midday, the crusaders received a crucial stroke of good luck: the wind began to blow from the north and their ships, which had been unable to reach the walls along the Golden Horn, were able to move up close. Two of the largest vessels, the *Paradise* and the *Lady Pilgrim,* had been tied together to create a larger fighting platform and the great siege equipment reached out to embrace one of Constantinople's towers.

The first man across, a Venetian, was killed, but the second, Andrew of Dureboise, managed to survive and enable a tower to be taken. Further along, Aleaumes of Clari squeezed through a small hole created in the walls and fought off enough Greeks to allow his comrades to follow him in. This astonishing feat was the trigger to the collapse of Byzantine resistance and the crusaders began to pour into the city. The toughness acquired on the tournament fields of Europe, the shared bond of their long expedition and the skills of the Venetian sailors enabled them to exploit the favourable elements and to capture the city.

That same night Murtzuphlus fled. Over the next few days the westerners began to put the city to the sword. Many of its citizens were slaughtered and women of all ages were raped as the crusaders ruthlessly despoiled the metropolis. The great cathedral of the Hagia Sophia was stripped of its priceless relics and the hundreds of churches and palaces of Constantinople were pillaged.

To the crusaders, God had approved their actions by granting them victory and many returned home proudly bearing precious relics. At first, Pope Innocent III was delighted but, as news of the atrocities became clear, he changed his view and began to express anger and disgust at the westerners' actions. He accused one senior noble of 'turning away from the purity of your vow when you took up arms not against Saracens but Christians . . . preferring earthly wealth to celestial treasures'.

On May 16th, 1204, as the crusaders gathered in the Hagia Sophia to acclaim Baldwin, Count of Flanders, the first Latin Emperor of Constantinople, some may have reflected how fate had conspired to bring them to the Bosphorus. An expedition of warriors sworn to liberate the Holy Land had created a new outpost of the Catholic Church, yet it was at the expense of fellow-Christians. In pursuing their attempts to sustain the crusade to the Holy Land, they had become tragically sidetracked. Until the murder of Alexius IV their hopes might have been realised, but after this they were trapped. Ironically, in the long run, the need to support the new Latin Empire of Constantinople against Byzantine counter attacks proved a drain on the crusading resources of the West, and by 1261 Constantinople was again in Greek hands. Yet it was the unleashing of the tensions generated through arduous months camped outside Constantinople, coupled with longstanding problems between Byzantium and the West, that was to leave a legacy of ill-feeling. To the Greeks, the barbarians of Europe had lived up to their reputation.

---

**Jonathan Phillips** is Senior Lecturer in History at Royal Holloway, University of London.

# East Meets West in Venice

## Venice's Grand Canal curves east at its mouth and opens toward the Mediterranean—and the world. It served as Europe's maritime gateway to Turkey, the Levant and North Africa for more than a millennium.

RICHARD COVINGTON

Through binoculars, I can barely make out the palm trees, gazelles, camels and other Middle Eastern images on the Palazzo Zen, ancestral home of one of the most prominent Venetian families involved in diplomacy and trade with the Islamic world.

"The entire façade was once covered with frescoes recounting the Zen family's contributions to the Venetian Republic," says Concina. "The frieze was a memento of Caterino Zen the Elder's mission in the 15th century to the Turkmen *khan* Ozun Hasan in Persia."

What an amazing family it was! Nicolo Zen explored Greenland and the Orkney Islands in 1393–1395. In 1398, his brother Antonio made it as far as Nova Scotia—or so claim Frederick Pohl and other historians. Daragon Zen traded in Arabia in the 15th century. In the 16th century, Pietro Zen was vice-consul in Damascus and voted unsuccessfully against war with the Ottomans in 1537. Pietro's son Francesco wrote the earliest western book praising Turkish architecture, and another son, Nicolo, compiled a history of the Abbasids. The Zen chapel in the Basilica of St. Mark was constructed in the 16th century as the funerary chapel for Cardinal Giovanni Battista Zen.

Venice's fortunes, like those of the Zen family, have been inextricably linked to the Islamic world at least since the eighth century, when her merchants began trading with Alexandria. In this long-running tale of interdependence, the Adriatic city was a gateway to the Middle East, giving Muslims a taste of Europeans as businessmen rather than Crusaders.

The Venetian Republic was "an entrepôt for the importation into Europe of profitable luxury goods such as carpets and textiles, and opened a European door to the Islamic cultures that created those goods," writes Walter Denny, an art professor at the University of Massachusetts in Amherst, in the catalogue for "Venice and the Islamic World." This landmark exhibition of art, ceramics, metalwork and fabrics ran at the Arab World Institute in Paris, the Metropolitan Museum of Art in New York and Venice's own Palazzo Ducale last year.

From the cupolas, pointed arches and gilt mosaics of the Basilica of St. Mark to the labyrinth of winding streets that Cambridge University architectural historian Deborah Howard compares to a "colossal *souk,*" Venice has borrowed liberally from Muslim architecture and urban design. (See "Seeking Islamic Venice.")

Inside the Muslim cities of Alexandria, Constantinople (later renamed Istanbul), Damascus, Acre, Aleppo, Trebizond and Tabriz, the Republic created mini-Venices, commercial enclaves overseen by a *bailo,* or consul, complete with churches, priests, merchants, doctors, barbers, bakers, cooks, tailors, apothecaries and silversmiths.

"Abroad, Venetian diplomats and merchants traveled throughout the Islamic world, from the Nile Delta to Syria to Constantinople to Azerbaijan," notes Denny, "and their *relazioni* or reports to the Venetian authorities still serve as important documentation of Islamic politics, history, economics and art."

Without Muslim trade, Venice would simply not have existed. Instead of the powerful maritime republic, "La Serenissima," that dominated Mediterranean commerce from the 12th to the 16th century, the lagoon settlement would likely have remained a fishing village.

But of course, there was trade—arguably the greatest the world had known. Silk, spices, carpets, ceramics, pearls, crystal ewers and precious metals arrived in Venice from the East, while salt, wood, linen, wool, velvet, Baltic amber, Italian coral, fine cloth and slaves went to Egypt, Anatolia, the Levant and Persia.

"Who could count the many shops so well furnished that they also seem warehouses," marveled the Milanese priest Pietro Casola on a 1494 visit to Venice's Rialto, "with so many cloths of every make—tapestry, brocades and hangings of every design, carpets of every sort, camlets of every color and texture, silks of every kind; and so many warehouses full of aromatics, spices and drugs, and so much beautiful white wax!" (Presumably, the priest was happy to locate wax suitable for votive candles.) It was a somewhat one-sided business, since trade with Venice was a relatively minor aspect of the Mamluk and Ottoman economies. Nonetheless, the Republic was important enough to be the only Christian city to appear on Ibn Khaldun's 14th-century world map. Yet for Venice, on the other hand, Muslim trade represented fully half the Republic's revenues.

Christian pilgrims flocked to the city from across Europe to sign on for package tours to the Holy Land. These visitors were so critical to Venice's economy that they were invited into the Palazzo Ducale to be individually embraced by the doge himself, and sailings were sometimes delayed on purpose to force the faithful to linger longer, and spend more money, before departing for Jaffa. On separate galleys, Venetian merchants collected Muslim pilgrims in Tunis, Djerba and Alexandria and brought them to the Levant en route to Makkah.

The 13th-century Venetian Marco Polo brought back tales of the fabulous Middle and Far East, of course. But there were other, less famous travelers, such as 23-year-old Alessandro Magno, whose 16th-century diary portrays daily life in Alexandria and Cairo with ink sketches of typical house interiors and sights like the Sphinx and pyramids at Giza. (Like Venice, each city had around 150,000 residents.) Although Magno was a tourist, many young Venetian noblemen spent years at a time learning Arabic and bookkeeping in their homeland's far-flung commercial outposts. Other visitors were bowled over by Muslim craftsmanship. After inspecting pieces of delicately incised inlaid metalware in Damascus, 14th-century merchant Simone Sigoli breathlessly declared, "If you had money in the bones of your leg, without fail you would break it to buy these things."

Numerous Arab words were absorbed into Italian, including trade terms such as *doana* (customs) and *tariffa* (duty) and the names of luxury goods such as *sofa, divan* and *damasco.* A gold ducat was a *zecchino,* taken from the Arabic word *sikka,* or mint.

As the chief European center for publishing, Venice also printed many Arabic texts in Latin and Italian translation, including the *Canon,* the standard medical reference book by Persian physician Ibn Sina (called Avicenna in the West), and commentaries on Aristotle by 12th-century Córdoban philosopher Ibn Rushd (known in the West as Averroës). Even the first printed text of the Qur'an was published in Venice in 1537–1538 by enterprising local booksellers aiming to crack Arabic-speaking markets. Riddled with errors, the edition proved a dismal failure, but it did inspire translation into Italian in 1547, according to Stefano Carboni, the curator for the Met exhibition.

"From the last years of the 15th century onward, Venetian publishers printed Muslim treatises on medicine, philosophy, astronomy and mathematics," explains Giandomenico Romanelli, the director of the city's Correr Museum, an extensive repository of art, ceramics, maps and manuscripts. Elaborately tooled leather bookbindings made in Venice were modeled after those of Istanbul, Tabriz and elsewhere in the Muslim world, he notes. In publishing, trade, diplomatic relations and pilgrimages, "Venice was the hinge between East and West," says Romanelli.

The connection is deeply entrenched in myth and history. According to legend, two Venetian merchants spirited away the bones of St. Mark from Alexandria in 828, hiding them in a basket beneath a shipment of pork. Images of the episode appear in mosaics on the façade and ceiling of St. Mark's Basilica, which was built to house the saint's remains.

To Venetians, possessing the relics of St. Mark gave the city a holy status to rival Rome, the seat of western Catholicism. The Republic set about establishing its reputation as the new Alexandria, where the evangelist had preached and been martyred. In the 15th century, a campanile tower was erected at the Basilica of San Pietro Castello in homage to the famous Pharos, Alexandria's ancient lighthouse. Paintings by Gentile Bellini, Giovanni Mansueti and Vittore Carpaccio mingle Venetian and Alexandrian backdrops in scenes depicting St. Mark.

The recent exhibition was designed to illustrate Venice's status as a "privileged partner" of the Islamic world, says Carboni, who was himself born near the Rialto and has devoted the past two decades to studying the artistic exchanges between Venice and the East."Venice is usually associated with Byzantium, not the Islamic world," he explains. "But I wanted to surprise the public with the breadth of artistic, cultural, mercantile and diplomatic connections."

## A Very Brief History

Fleeing Gothic and Lombardic tribes in the fifth century, settlers from the Italian mainland took refuge on the Adriatic lagoon islands that would become Venice. Driving piles into the seabed, the refugees gradually enlarged the islands and built bridges linking them. Lacking arable land, the earliest Venetians relied on fishing and trade, declaring an independent republic in 726 and erecting the first fortress for the *doge,* or duke, and the government in the ninth century. After sacking Constantinople in 1204, the Venetians adorned their city with loot from the Byzantine capital, ushering in a golden age of commerce with the Middle East and the Orient that lasted some four centuries. By the 16th century, the population of Venice was around 150,000, roughly the same as Cairo's, and the city was filled with artistic and architectural masterpieces. As Portuguese, Spanish and English explorers shifted the balance of trade away from the Mediterranean to the Indian and Atlantic Oceans, Venice lost its dominance of the merchant routes to the East. After Napoleon abolished the Republic in 1797, the once-proud city went into a prolonged decline. Today, tourism buoys the economy, and a project to save the sinking city from flooding, under discussion for at least 40 years, may finally be getting underway.

Carboni is quick to point out that the key to the pragmatic Venetians' trading success was that they never regarded themselves as superior. "Muslims were understood simply as figures in the wider world with whom it was necessary to do business," he says. "Also, the Venetians were far more tolerant from the religious point of view than the rest of Europe."

For centuries, the Christian Republic carried on a diplomatic high-wire act, balancing competing allegiances to Muslim rulers and the Catholic Church, essentially doing whatever was necessary to keep commerce as free and unhindered as possible.

Even during the Crusades, the Venetians continued trading with Islamic partners. The Fourth Crusade, in fact, famously turned into an opportunity for Venice to attack the Byzantine empire, not Muslims. After the sack of Christian Constantinople in 1204, Venetians brought back incalculable treasures, including the four bronze horses now in the basilica museum. (The ones on the roof are copies.) From time to time, the Vatican placed restrictions on trade with Muslims. But the Venetians, eager to assert their independence from papal authority, circumvented the bans by trading surreptitiously through Cyprus and Crete.

The Mamluks, who ruled a vast stretch of territory from Egypt to Syria from 1250 till 1517, relied on the Venetian navy to protect their coasts, according to Deborah Howard. Although diplomatic relations were generally warm, the sultan Qansuh al-Ghuri personally placed chains on vice-consul Pietro Zen in 1511 and imprisoned him in Cairo for holding secret talks with Shah Ismael, the first Safavid ruler of Persia. The Venetians were seeking a Persian alliance to contain the expanding Ottoman empire, which did indeed end Mamluk power six years later, in 1517.

Carboni acknowledges that Venetians had a "love-hate relationship" with the Ottomans, who, unlike the land-locked Mamluks, nurtured aspirations to usurp Venetian control of the eastern Mediterranean. Despite several bitterly fought conflicts—notably over Corfu in 1537, Cyprus in 1571, Candia (Crete) from 1646 till 1669 and Morea between 1684 and 1716)—overall there were many more years of peaceful trading than war, he says, and it was Napoleon, not the Ottomans, who finally conquered Venice in 1797.

Like the ambitious French emperor, the Ottoman sultan Mehmet II, who conquered Constantinople in 1453, had a hunger for world recognition. "He wanted to be acknowledged by the European powers as the equal of emperors and kings," says Carboni. To spread his fame, Mehmet requested that the Venetian government send an artist to immortalize him in portraits and a sculptor to forge medallions with his image.

The Venetians thought it would be in their interest to please the conqueror of Constantinople, so they selected Gentile Bellini, the most prominent painter of the time, and sent him off in 1479. In the nearly two years he resided at the Ottoman court, Bellini painted numerous portraits that ultimately left their marks on local artists and miniaturist painters in Istanbul and as far away as Isfahan and Tabriz. Mehmet's publicity campaign succeeded beyond his dreams. The Bellini portraits have spawned so many copies on everything from book covers and posters to banknotes, stamps and comic books that, according to the Turkish Nobel Prize–winning author Orhan Pamuk, "any educated Turk must have seen them hundreds, even thousands, of times." They embody the iconic image of an Ottoman sultan "the way Che Guevara's portrait incarnates that of a revolutionary,"

Pamuk observes in the French magazine *Connaissance des Arts*. After Mehmet's death, his son and successor, Bayezid II, who warred with the Venetians over their southern Greek territory of Morea, sold Bellini's portraits in the Istanbul bazaar to help finance the construction of a mosque complex.

When it came to Muslim artists and craftsmen settling in Venice, however, the locals wanted to limit the competition; they allowed in very few artisans. Instead, the city imported impressive quantities of luxury goods made overseas, including Mamluk and Persian carpets, Syrian and Egyptian glass, Iznik porcelain and incised metal bowls and ewers from Syria.

From Venice, carpets were sold throughout Europe. Cardinal Wolsey, first minister to the English King Henry VIII, was "a pathological carpet collector," who pressured diplomats to give him dozens as gifts, says Denny. Venetians bought raw silk from the shores of the Caspian Sea in northern Persia, manufactured elegant velvet caftans with Ottoman-style floral designs and sold them in Constantinople and elsewhere in the Muslim world. To combat the Venetian monopoly on luxury textiles, the 16th-century Grand Vizier Rüstem Pasha promoted new techniques to produce silk brocades and velvets that are "among the supreme artistic achievements of Ottoman art," according to Denny.

Ultimately, the development of the pedal-powered loom and spinning wheel in Europe led to the export of so much cheap cloth that it constituted what one economist called an early example of product dumping in Islamic markets. In the 15th century, Cairo historian Taqi al-Din al-Maqrizi exhorted Muslims to abandon low-quality European fabrics and wear local clothing instead.

A similar give-and-take process occurred in glass production. Recognizing that the glassmakers of Syria and Egypt had no serious rivals in Europe, the Venetians began importing raw glass, as well as broken glass (cullet) and plant soda ash from the Levant around the 13th century to copy Muslim designs at home. So successful was the transfer that certain enameled and gilt beakers, decorated with camels and desert plants and once believed to have originated in Syria, turned out to be Venetian-made. By the middle of the 15th century, Venetian glassmakers had perfected a technique to produce *cristallo* glass, a clear, colorless creation, free of defects, that successfully imitated expensive rock crystal. Ottoman artisans soon adapted the technique in the manufacture of Iznik porcelain. Thus a process that had begun with Venetians borrowing styles and materials from Islamic craftsmen came full circle with Ottoman ceramists building on Venetian expertise.

As cargoes of carpets, glass, silks and porcelains filled the harbor, it was obvious how Venetian fortunes and spirits faced East. The sheer energy of the commerce driving the city was a spectacle and entertainment to behold. The scale of trade was staggering; the sight of countless ships coming and going was breathtaking. From his quayside house overlooking the Riva degli Schiavoni, the 14th-century poet Petrarch, on a three-month visit from Florence, marveled at ships the size of "floating mountains," the square-rigged, round-hulled cogs that boasted five decks and a hold. Four centuries later, the 18th-century painter Canaletto found the harbor just as vibrant, filling his canvasses with dozens of ships at anchor and a forest of masts.

Convoys of galleys, two-masted lateeners and cogs set sail for Constantinople, Alexandria, Tripoli and Beirut carrying wool, wood and metals. By the 15th-century, they were also laden with such manufactured goods as textiles, soap, paper and glass. In return, cotton, spices, dyes, aromatics and salt arrived from Syria and Egypt, and silk, slaves and furs from the Tartar regions of Central Asia.

"On board the ships were sailors, soldiers, merchants, as well as doctors, priests and master carpenters," Concina explains. Trumpeters and bagpipers were on hand to herald arrivals into ports of call; some captains even had them announce mealtimes. A diary compiled in the 1440's by the trumpeter Zorzi da Modon that is now in the British Library describes life aboard ship and includes musical notations for leading crew and passengers in songfests. The outward journey to Alexandria took around a month and the return trip against the wind at least six weeks, notes Howard. Pilgrim voyages to the Holy Land were far shorter, taking around three weeks each way.

The state-run *mude* system, an immense trading network lasting for nearly 200 years from the early 14th century to the early 16th century, dispatched armed convoys to destinations as far north as England and Flanders and as far east as the Black Sea, according to Concina.

Overseas, trading posts known as *fondacos* (*funduqs, khans* or *wakalas* in Arabic) served as home bases for Venetian merchants. First mentioned by Herodotus in the fifth century BC, these caravanserais eventually stretched from Spain to China and are illustrated in the *Maqamat,* a 13th-century compendium of travelers' tales by Muhammad Ali al-Hariri. Constructed around a large square courtyard with a well, the two-or three-story structure had colonnaded arcades with storage rooms for goods and stables for pack animals on the ground floor and rooms for travelers on the upper levels. Typically, the fondaco's single great gate was locked at night, both to protect merchants from robbery and to keep close watch on them. Although most of the fondacos decayed or were destroyed long ago, Acre's Khan al-Ifrani, with its huge Gothic arches, is one that still exists; it has been converted into private residences.

Over the centuries, Venetian enclaves expanded around the fondacos. In Constantinople, where the Venetian quarter was located near the spice market, the residents built three churches over the course of 400 years from the 11th to the 15th century. The former house of the bailo is now—still—the Istanbul residence of the Italian consul-general. In Trebizond on the Black Sea, the Venetians built a church, houses, warehouses, quay and loggia.

Despite treaties intended to protect them, the Venetians were occasionally held prisoner in their fondacos, and one 17th-century bailo was hanged in Istanbul. Instead of retaliating with sanctions, the Venetians continued business as usual. "The boundlessly cynical Venetians never let morality, religion or ideology get in the way of making money," Romanelli dryly observes.

In contrast to the extensive Venetian settlements in cities of the Muslim world, there were no permanent Muslim embassies in Venice. Ambassadors generally came for brief annual stays ranging from several days to a few weeks, according to Maria Pia Pedani, a specialist on Ottoman history at the University of Venice. When Mamluk envoy Taghribidi arrived from Cairo with his retinue of 20 attendants for an unusual 10-month round of treaty negotiations in 1506 and 1507, he caused a sensation as he was escorted around the city by pages and macebearers. Taghribidi and other Muslim diplomats were housed on the Venetian island of Giudecca so they could be controlled and watched, says Pedani.

Before the creation of a temporary funduq for Muslims in the late 16th century, merchants visiting Venice and a handful of artisans stayed at inns near the Rialto. But even when the Fondaco dei Turchi opened in 1621 in the Santa Croce quarter, across the Grand Canal from the Jewish ghetto, it housed fewer than 100 merchants, including Turks, Bosnians, Albanians and Persians. An imposing, three-story building with two tiers of colonnaded arcades surrounding an inner courtyard, the Fondaco dei Turchi had been modeled after Middle Eastern funduqs. Above the ground-floor warehouse were living rooms, a bath and a prayer room. Muslim visitors were free to come and go during the day, but were locked in at night. The former fondaco now houses the city's natural history museum.

"We have accounts of Turks having coffee at the Piazza San Marco and exchanging news from Turkey," Concina explains. "Despite frequent wars with the Ottomans, Turkish merchants were figures of respect."

When I meet Giampiero Bellingeri, a leading authority on Venetian–Turkish relations from the University of Venice, at the 18th-century Caffé Florian, a landmark institution on St. Mark's Square, the professor reminds me that the Caffé was modeled after coffee houses in Istanbul.

"The Ottoman authorities banned cafés from time to time because they were seen as places where subversive ideas circulated," he explains. "Poets exalted coffee as 'the black angel' that inspired them."

While Venetians respected Turkish merchants, they could not admit that the Ottomans possessed a well-developed culture of their own. "It was only after the Ottomans were defeated at Vienna in 1683 that we could begin to acknowledge that the Turks were not barbarians and had produced literature and art of great finesse and profound reflection," says Bellingeri. "Once the Ottomans ceased to be a military threat, we could begin seeing them as equals."

And, occasionally, as objects for ridicule. Carlo Goldoni, the 18th-century Venetian playwright, wrote a number of works poking fun at Turks and Persians—yet mocking Venetians in equal measure. In "The Impresario of Izmir," an unwitting Turk comes to Venice to organize an opera company and becomes so embroiled in the quarrels of backbiting divas and a nasty castrato that he returns home in frustration without a troupe.

Around the corner from the Florian.

Bellingeri takes me to the Biblioteca Nazionale Marciana to inspect a masterpiece of Venetian forgery. Inside the library, we slip quietly past scholars poring over books and manuscripts at long tables and enter a back room where the so-called "mappamundo," the 1559–1560 map of the world created for the Ottoman market, is displayed on one wall. In the center of the map, intricately detailed drawings of western and eastern hemispheres are joined in the shape of a heart, surrounded by cramped scrawls of miniscule Ottoman script that describe cities, states and empires of the known world.

The text purports to have been written by "poor, powerless, indigent Hajji Ahmed from Tunis," says Bellingeri. He allegedly studied in Fez and was captured by "the Franks," but allowed to continue practicing his religion. In compiling the map, Ahmed explains that he consulted Socrates, Plato and Abu al-Fida, the last a Syrian geographer-prince who lived from 1273 to 1331 and was greatly respected by Venetian scholars, Bellingeri explains.

Where did the mapmaker live, I ask.

"Good question," the professor replies. "He never says, and for good reason. In fact, Ahmed was a fictional creation by the Venetian scholars who made the map. They thought that having a Muslim author would make it sell better in Islamic lands, but their ruse didn't work."

It certainly couldn't have helped the map's authenticity that the true authors made several glaring errors. "When my colleague, the late Giorgio Vercellin, and I saw mistakes in writing the words Islam and Allah, we figured the authors had to be Venetian, not Muslim," says Bellingeri with a wry grin. Even though there's no proof, the professor is positive the forged map was a collaboration by Giovanni Battista Ramusio, a noted cosmographer and naval historian, and Michel Membré, a former ambassador to Persia and the Republic's senior dragoman, or interpreter.

Apart from the counterfeit map, the Biblioteca Marciana contains one of the most extensive collections of Islamic manuscripts, incunabula and later printed books in the world. The day after meeting Bellingeri, I have an appointment with Marino Zorzi, the library director, to view a remarkable pair of books. One, the *Iskandarnama* or *Book of Alexander,* is an illustrated manuscript dated 1430 from Edirne, the Ottoman capital before Mehmet II conquered Constantinople; the other, *Diverse Dressing Habits of the Turks,* is a 17th-century volume devoted to Ottoman clothing.

Inside his corner office across from the Doge's Palace, Zorzi is obliged to partially close the heavy wooden shutters to block out the dazzling sunlight and his breathtaking view across the water to the Palladian church of San Giorgio Maggiore. Pushing aside exhibition catalogues and books scattered on an enormous table, the director makes room to pore over the two books.

"The *Iskandarnama* is probably the most important Islamic work of art in Venice today," Zorzi explains. "It's one of the few illustrated manuscripts we have from the Ottoman empire."

Acquired by the library in 1797 as part of an extensive collection of Greek manuscripts, Arabic and Islamic books, coins and objects donated by Giacomo Nani, Venice's chief superintendent of naval affairs, the *Iskandarnama* is a curious East-meets-West cultural grab-bag. It contains not merely the highly embellished exploits of a legendary Muslim version of Alexander the Great, but also an account of the Prophet Muhammad's journey to heaven, episodes from the Persian *Book of Kings,* or *Shahnama,* the signs of the zodiac and the planets as well as conversations between the book's poet-author Taj al-Din Ibrahim ibn Khidr Ahmadi and a friend.

The costume book, donated to the library by the patrician bibliophile Giralamo Contarini in 1843, could not be more different. Bound in inexpensive cardboard and about the size of a trade paperback, this popular edition was published in Istanbul but features Italian captions, indicating it was published for export. It presents a cross-section of Ottoman society with 62 realistic portraits of individuals characterized by the vividly colored clothes they wear.

The turbaned sultan Bayezid I, "the Thunderbolt," strikes an unusually meditative pose in a blue robe and sleeveless purple tunic. Regally attired in a dark pink tunic dress with gold belt and brocaded cape, the unnamed wife of a sultan sports red lipstick, painted eyebrows and a crown surmounted by a broad fan. There's a court page in a long orange caftan and domed hat, a head gardener all in green, a hunter with rifle, horn, axe and plumed hat. On one page, a barefoot Hindu pilgrim with a wispy beard and fringed cape carries a stick to support him on his begging rounds; another illustration shows a sword-bearing soldier with a leopard skin slung around his shoulders and a human head dangling from his belt. In addition to the court treasurer in sober brown caftan and a pair of eunuch harem guards, there's also a jaunty idyll of three women in a rowboat.

As modest as the Iskandarnama is opulent, the costume book strikes me as yet one more means through which the Venetians were bent on acquiring knowledge, culture and wealth from the Islamic world. Collectors like Contarini and Nani, mapmakers like Ramusio and Membré, explorers and diplomats like Marco Polo and the Zen family, all depended on Muslim trade to make their fortunes. As Zorzi reopens the shutters on one of the world's most glorious perspectives, with black gondolas bobbing in the silvery water, I wonder how much of this image would have remained a mirage without the matchless Venetian ambition to embrace the risks and possibilities of trading goods and ideas with the strangers of the East.

## Seeking Islamic Venice

Tracking down Islamic influences and Muslim connections in Venice is not hard if you know where—and how—to look. If you stand on the square in front of St. Mark's Basilica, signs are all around. To the right is the Doge's Palace with its distinctive three-tiered merlons, modeled on crenellations on Cairo's Ibn Tulun Mosque. To the left is the Torre dell'Orologio, the 1498 clock tower with a giant blue zodiac dial identical to the clock face in al-Ghazari's 13th-century treatise on robots. (Twelfth-century historian Ibn Jubayr mentions a similar clock with descending weights at the Great Mosque in Damascus.) At your back is the Caffé Florian, an 18th-century institution patterned after coffee houses in Istanbul. Straight ahead, the tall cupolas of the basilica resemble mosque domes in Cairo's City of the Dead and across the Arab world. Stone window grilles resemble the decorative tracery abundant in Muslim religious architecture. On the basilica's facade is a glittering 13th-century gold mosaic depicting the theft of St. Mark's body from Alexandria in 828. Venetians built the first church, a precursor to the present 11th-century basilica, to house the saint's relics. Inside the basilica's atrium, Biblical mosaics with scenes of banquets, bedside miracles and camels traversing deserts were modeled on similar scenes in illustrated Arabic texts such as al-Hariri's *Maqamat* and the Persian epic, the *Shahnama,* according to Cambridge University architectural historian Deborah Howard.

Within the main sanctuary, which is covered floor to roof with opulent mosaics, the entrance to the treasury is surmounted by a pointed arch with a Fatimid-style relief of peacocks and the gap-toothed decorative border called billet molding, common in Jerusalem and other cities of the Levant. The treasury itself showcases stunning Arab pieces, including a rock-crystal ewer that belonged to the 10th-century Fatimid caliph al-'Aziz, a 10th-century Abbasid glass bowl carved with lions and a delicately beautiful, silver gilt and niello casket incised by Arab craftsmen in 12th-century Sicily with images of women playing a lute and a harp.

Upstairs in the basilica museum are five 16th-century gold-and-silver brocaded carpets from Isfahan. Another well-preserved Persian carpet measuring 150 by 275 centimeters (5′ × 9′) is woven with ducks and flowers surrounding bright blue, interlacing designs in the center. A third carpet was donated by the Safavid Shah Abbas I in the 16th century, with instructions that it be used to present items from the basilica's treasury during religious celebrations.

Next to the basilica, the 14th-century Doge's Palace is completely without fortification, virtually unique for the time in Europe. Instead, the two levels of colonnaded arches make for a blessedly open and airy ground floor and second-story loggia. Howard maintains that the Venetian envoy Nicolo Zen brought home this bold architectural plan after his 1344 visit to Cairo, where he saw the Iwan al-Kabir, the official hall of justice, and the Citadel Mosque of Sultan al-Nasir Muhammad. The exterior design of the Doge's Palace bears a striking resemblance to both buildings.

Upstairs inside the Doge's Palace, the walls of the Shields Room, where visiting envoys gathered, are covered with giant, vividly colored maps of the Mediterranean, Italy and Arabia. They were drawn by 16th-century geographer Giovanni Battista Ramusio, who used numerous Muslim sources, including maps by the 13th-century prince Abu al-Fida. In a nearby room, the Sala della Quattri Porte, is Gabriel Caliari's 1603 painting of Doge Mario Grimani flanked by turbaned emissaries from Shah Abbas I, dressed in blue and white silk. In the foreground, black-robed Venetians admire a magnificent cloak, velvet brocade and a silk rug threaded with gold, perhaps the very one that's in the basilica museum.

While this painting delivers a pointed lesson on the benefits of diplomacy, the vast murals in the Sala del Scrutinio, dramatizing the murderous chaos of the naval Battle of Lepanto and other Venetian victories, are reminders that the peace-loving Serenissima could fight when provoked. Elsewhere in the palace are various spoils of war: an enormous red Ottoman banner, gorgeous ships' lanterns bearing crescent moons and *tughs* or standards, two-meter (7′) poles decorated with horse tails. The more tails, the higher one's rank in the Turkish court; the sultan had seven.

Across the Grand Canal from the San Marco quarter, the Accademia gallery concentrates a number of masterpieces with Muslim references. In Giovanni Mansueti's painting of scenes from the life of St. Mark, Mamluk figures wearing conical red *zamt* hats and the white "horned" judicial turbans crowd an Alexandrian cityscape that evokes Venetian architecture. In a Tintoretto painting from between 1562 and 1566, St. Mark reaches down from the heavens to lift up a drowning Saracen sailor. In Gentile Bellini's detailed account of a religious procession through St. Mark's Square, housewives proudly drape Turkish carpets from balconies lining the north side of the piazza. In Paris Bordone's 1534 painting of a fisherman returning the doge's ring, Andrea Gritti, the Venetian chief of state from 1522 to 1538, is enthroned on a western Anatolian "star ushak" carpet with red, green and gold arabesque designs.

Back outside, simply wandering the streets is an education in Islamic influence on Venetian architecture. Christopher Wren, the 17th-century architect of St. Paul's Cathedral in London, wrote about Islamic elements in Gothic art and architecture—from ogive windows to the resemblance of flanking church towers to minarets. John Ruskin, the 19th-century art critic and philosopher, went even further, arguing in *The Stones of Venice* and other works that much of Venice was directly copied from the Near and Middle East.

Cambridge scholar Deborah Howard maintains that the city's labyrinth of streets, patios and secret gardens, and its saturated colors and ornamentation, were inspired by Muslim urban design. Venetian palazzos—with their inner courtyards surrounding underground cisterns, winding open staircases, flat-roofed terraces and balcony verandas that resemble *mashrabiyyah* windows—imitate floor plans in the Levant, she says. Exterior windows are based on scale models of *mihrabs*—prayer niches—brought back from the East.

Impressed by Islamic architecture, Venetian merchants wanted to adapt elements of the style at home, partially for esthetic reasons and partially to advertise their trading success. Two of the more striking Muslim-influenced palaces are the Ca' Dario and the Ca' d'Oro. On a mission to Cairo, 15th-century diplomat Giovanni Dario so admired Amir Bashtak al-Nasiri's magnificent palace that he incorporated its distinctive "telephone-dial" motif in marble decorations for his own palace, down the Grand Canal from the Accademia. On the opposite side of the serpentine Grand Canal past the Rialto bridge, the Ca' d'Oro is one of the most lavishly decorated palaces in the city, with its ogive windows, cream-colored Gothic tracery and Egyptian-style pinnacles. Originally, the façade was painted in gold leaf and ultramarine like the interior of a Persian palace, says Howard. The Ca' d'Oro now houses a museum of paintings, sculpture and furniture, and contains a medallion portrait of Mehmet II by Bellini.

Walking from the Rialto back to St. Mark's Square, I try to imagine what the shops were like in the 15th and 16th centuries, when storekeepers inflated prices to take advantage of visiting eastern dignitaries and merchants. Glass, silk and tapestries are still on sale, but nowadays, the boutiques are also filled with Furla bags and dresses, watches, sneakers, gianduja chocolates and La Perla lingerie. Chinese immigrants sell me a souvenir bag printed with a painting of St. Mark's Square.

Inside the Correr Museum at the opposite end of the square from the basilica, I have a look at Jacopo de Barbari's panoramic 1500 map of Venice, showing dozens of ships jostling for space in the harbor.

These days, instead of the round-bellied cogs in de Barbari's map, the waterside Riva degli Schiavoni is lined with water buses, called *vaporetti,* car ferries and cruise ships. A two-story ocher-brown building with Mamluk crenellations midway up its façade was a 15th-century bakery that produced long-lasting ships' biscuit for voyagers. Nearby were houses for pilgrims awaiting departure for the Holy Land.

Across a small bridge, the Naval History Museum displays elaborately carved side panels from wooden galleys, the figure of a Turkish prisoner from the stern of a warship, large models of galleons, triremes and galleys, and a full-sized boat rigged like a Nile felucca.

Up the broad Via Garibaldi with its working-class cafés and shops, I make my way to the Basilica of San Pietro Castello, the city's principal cathedral until 1807, when the Basilica of St. Mark's became Venice's primary church. An immaculately white stone campanile rises from the grassy park surrounding the basilica. Constructed from 1482 to 1488 by Mario Codussi, the bell tower was erected at the eastern tip of the city as a Venetian version of Alexandria's Pharos lighthouse. Inside the magnificent cathedral is the so-called "Throne of St. Peter," donated by the Byzantines to thank Venice for its help wresting Sicily from the Arabs in the 13th century. In fact, it is not a throne at all, but a stone chair with a back fashioned from a 12th-century Islamic funerary stele inscribed with Qur'anic verses around a six-pointed star.

Elsewhere, Near and Middle Eastern references pop up in unexpected places across the city. At a museum of Greek icons next to the church of San Giorgio dei Greci, I stumble across a page from a 14th-century copy of *The Alexander Romance* with Arabic writing in the margins. Nearby, at the Scuola di San Giorgio degli Schiavoni, paintings by Vittore Carpaccio from the early 16th century portray Mamluk musicians and judges against Near Eastern backdrops as St. George slays a dragon and baptizes converts. On the wide square in front of the church of Santi Giovanni e Paolo, schoolchildren play noisy games of soccer and tag in front of 1489–1490 stone panels by Tullio Lombardo, one representing St. Mark healing the cobbler Anianus in Alexandria, the other of the evangelist baptizing him. In one of those historical juxtapositions peculiar to Venice, I find myself seeking out the first printed copy of the Qur'an at the church of San Francesco della Vigna. Legend has it that St. Francis embarked from the site in the 13th century, on his way to Egypt to try to convert the sultan.

Out in the Cannaregio district, about as far north as you can get in the main city without swimming, lies a Moorish mystery—four statues of Muslims in the Campo dei Mori. This theatrical quartet, "dressed up like characters from the cast of a comic opera," as Howard writes, probably once graced the nearby Palazzo Camello, which still sports a charming stone frieze of a turbaned man gazing up at a camel with a bulky pack strapped to its back. The most prominent of the figures leans awkwardly in his niche next to the birthplace of 16th-century artist Jacopo Robusti, or Tintoretto. The poor fellow is weighed down by an outsized turban, probably added a century or more after the image was originally carved in the late 13th or early 14th century. Some historians once thought that the stone "moors" belonged to a *fondaco* created for Arab merchants, but Howard disagrees, speculating that the statues may have something to do with the Moro family and its role in the spice trade. No one really knows.

And I like it that way. In a city where the minutiae of the past have been pored over for centuries, it's reassuring that some links of the Republic's DNA, and aspects of its East–West trade in particular, remain a question mark for future generations of scholars.

## Venice and the Printed Page

Move over Marco Polo. The massive, 58-volume diary by Marin Sanudo the Younger, a 16th-century Venetian senator equipped with unparalleled access to the Republic's secrets and a refreshing candor, is an unsurpassed account of life at home and abroad during the city's heyday. Unlike the peripatetic Polo, who spent a quarter of a century on the road, Sanudo stayed put, letting the East come to him, recording the activities of Muslim envoys in Venice and anecdotes by Venetian merchants returning from overseas. A political insider with a well-honed esthetic sensibility, he writes of the Persian envoy Ali Bey showing off magnificent decorated leather boxes and launching a fad for reproductions of them in Venice. He reveals that the Senate pretended a narwhal horn had been stolen from St. Mark's Treasury rather than admit that the potent amulet, reputed to detect poison, had been offered as a secret gift to Sultan Süleyman the Magnificent. When news arrives that the Ottomans defeated the Safavids at the 1514 battle of Çaldiran, Sanudo dryly notes that "we know through the grapevine that the Ottomans got the short end of the stick," despite their victory.

"He was a very witty observer, detailing important meetings in the Ducal Palace and commenting on secret documents in the archives," explains Stefano Carboni, curator of the 2007 exhibition "Venice and the Islamic World" at the Metropolitan Museum of Art in New York. It was not until the early 20th century that the diaries were published in full. "Because he wrote in Venetian dialect, translating them will be a huge enterprise," says Carboni, but they represent an invaluable and largely untapped wealth of information about East–West trade and the period when Venetian artisans were busy creating a vogue for Islamic-style textiles, inlaid metalwork, lacquered wood, enameled glass and other crafts.

Venice's link to the East has produced an extraordinary wealth of literature, philosophy and travelogue. In the 13th century, Polo recounted the sack of Baghdad, the "villainy" of Isfahan and the pearls and spices of Hormuz en route to Cathay. The maritime republic became a conduit for ancient Greek dialectics and Islamic discoveries in astronomy, mathematics and medicine. Between the 14th and the 17th centuries in particular, Venice was "an island of relative intellectual freedom," according to Michael Barry, a curator in the Islamic art department of the Metropolitan Museum of Art and lecturer in Near Eastern studies at Princeton University.

After the reconquest of much of Muslim Spain in the 13th century, the University of Padua (a city that was annexed to Venice around the same time) became the chief European center for the study of Ibn Rushd (Averroës) and his interpretations of Aristotle. Dante himself turned to the 12th-century Andalusian scholar to make sense of the Greek philosopher's difficult teachings. Ibn

Rushd's speculations on the predominance of reason over faith had profound effects on the evolution of religious doctrine in the West, prompting the 13th-century theologian Thomas Aquinas to repudiate Ibn Rushd as "a corrupter of Aristotelian philosophy."

In Europe's centuries-long assimilation of Islamic science, a 1521 Latin translation of *The Canon,* the medical reference text by Persian doctor Ibn Sina (Avicenna), who lived from 980 to 1037, supplanted Gerard of Sabloneta's 13th-century edition and spread throughout Europe.

The influence of Arab philosophy and science persisted longer in Venice than most other cities in Europe. Fresh editions of Ibn Sina's writings were being published in Latin as late as the 16th century and *The Canon* was still part of the curriculum at the University of Padua until the 17th century, Barry observes.

One of the earliest and most ardent observers of Islamic influence on Venice was the 19th-century English art critic John Ruskin. "The Venetians deserve especial note as the only European people who appear to have sympathized to the full with the great instinct of the Eastern races," Ruskin declared in his masterpiece, *The Stones of Venice,* a three-volume paean to the city published from 1851 to 1853. With thoroughgoing and often lyrical analysis of arabesque ornamentation, pointed windows and arches, ornate molding and other architectural details, Ruskin outlined the transition of Venice from a Byzantine city to one that borrowed heavily from Islamic models. In a poetic rumination on the ways the city mimicked the patterns of nature, he claimed that even the flowing curves of Veneto–Moorish architectural decoration echoed the design of a galley's hull and the swirl of waves along it.

European novelists fell in love with the city partly for its exotic Muslim elements, popularizing the image of Venice as a romantic mirage, an escapist hold-out against the belching smokestacks and dehumanizing mass production of the industrial age. The 19th-century French novelist Emile Zola famously claimed that "the Orient begins in the Merceria [of Venice], with its streets so narrow," and Charles Dickens said the city evoked *The Thousand and One Nights.* "Opium couldn't build such a place, and enchantment couldn't shadow it forth in a vision," the English novelist wrote in a 1844 letter to his friend and biographer, John Forster. Marcel Proust made numerous Moorish allusions in Venetian scenes in his seven-volume, fictional opus *Remembrance of Things Past.* In *The Sweet Cheat Gone,* the sixth novel of the series, he wrote, "My gondola followed the course of the small canals, like the mysterious hand of a Genie leading through the maze of this oriental city,". . . passing "tall houses with their tiny Moorish windows."

Other authors draw inspiration from Venice for works that take place in the East. Set in 16th-century Istanbul, *My Name is Red* by Orhan Pamuk, the recipient of the 2006 Nobel Prize for Literature, is a mystery about the murders of a pair of court artists commissioned by the sultan to create Venetian-style illustrations for a book intended to glorify his reign. Apart from the crime and a romantic subplot, the novel reflects on the tension between Islamic and western traditions in art.

---

Paris-based author **Richard Covington** writes about culture, history and science for *Smithsonian, The International Herald Tribune, U.S. News & World Report* and *The Sunday Times of London.*

# Genghis Khan

## *Secrets of Success*

**Widely feared for extreme brutality, the Mongols also mastered more subtle and sophisticated tactics.**

TIMOTHY MAY

In Bukhara, one of the great cities of the Khwârazmian Empire, the Friday mosque was filled one day in the year 1220, the throng gathering to listen to the man who had just captured their city. The warrior who climbed into the pulpit after dismounting from a small horse was a foreigner, with clothing and armor indicating that he had come from a distant land. The audience of religious leaders, doctors, scholars and other eminent men waited for the strange warrior to speak. Finally he did, speaking through a translator:

> *O people, know that you have committed great sins, and that the great ones among you have committed these sins. If you ask me what proof I have for these words, I say it is because I am the punishment of God. If you had not committed great sins, God would not have sent a punishment like me upon you.*

The self-styled scourge of God, however, did not come simply to lecture the citizens of Bukhara. His soldiers had plundered the city in a highly organized fashion. Then the people were herded into groups, and those who were not killed immediately were forced to march with the conquerors. These events bewildered the inhabitants, for many of those assembled in the mosque had little idea of who the warrior was or why his army had appeared before the walls of Bukhara. Shortly afterward, their conqueror and his army of Mongols would conquer the rest of the region, and much more. He was called Chinggis Khan.

The Mongol Empire founded by Chinggis Khan (also known as Genghis Khan in the West) became the largest contiguous empire in history, stretching from the Sea of Japan to the Mediterranean Sea and the Carpathian Mountains. At its peak, more than a million men were enrolled in the armies of the khan, or emperor of the Mongol Empire. The Mongol khans were determined to conquer the world, and indeed, with the resources at their disposal, there was little reason for them to fail. The empire did eventually collapse, partially under its own weight, but for more than a century the Mongol khans came close to conquering the world, thanks to their leadership and to the efficacy of their tactics, weapons and strategies.

## Tactics

While many of the tactics used by the Mongols were common on the steppe, the Mongols transformed them into sophisticated operational concepts that were characteristic of a permanent army. The tactics and strategies they developed enabled them to fight on several fronts and allowed a planned, steady expansion of the Mongol Empire rather than haphazard conquests over vast territories. As the Mongols' methods of war and conquest became increasingly well-organized, the Mongol army evolved from a tribal force into a true army.

Like most steppe armies, the Mongols were primarily light horse archers. Their tactics exploited their abilities with archery and their mobility: They usually stayed out of reach of their opponents' weapons and used hit-and-run tactics in waves while showering the enemy with arrows. Like the Turkic troops the Crusaders encountered in Anatolia, the Mongols initiated combat at bowshot range. They closed for combat only for the decisive encounter once the enemy's formation had broken. Often they retreated before the enemy, utilizing the famous "Parthian shot" (a shot fired during a feigned retreat). At the right moment, normally when the enemy forces were drawn out, the Mongols wheeled around and annihilated them. These methods of war were augmented with surprise attacks, ambushes and encirclements, and such tactics ensured the Mongols did not require superior numbers to gain victory.

## Arrow Storm and Rolling Barrage

The arrow storm was the most common tactic practiced by the Mongols: They enveloped their enemy, then shot a hail of arrows in such numbers that it seemed a phenomenon of nature. The range at which they attacked in this way varied: At 200 or

300 yards their shooting was still accurate enough to disrupt an enemy formation, and once it broke, the Mongols charged. In the course of an arrow storm, archers did not aim at a specific target, but loosed their arrows at a high trajectory into a predetermined "killing zone" or target area. While this practice probably caused few mortal wounds, it undoubtedly impacted morale as soldiers had to watch arrows wound their comrades while being unable to retaliate.

## Concentrated Firepower

While the practice of concentrating firepower certainly existed prior to the Mongols, they were perhaps the first to use it to maximum effect in all aspects of war, from the arrow storm to batteries of siege weapons. At the siege of Nishapur in 1221, the Mongols amassed enough weaponry to overawe its defenders, who were reportedly defended by 300 ballistae and catapults, along with 3,000 crossbows. While those numbers are probably exaggerated, they indicate that the Mongols deployed a large number of siege weapons to demolish walls and pound cities or fortresses into submission.

## Caracole Tactics

The Mongols combined the arrow storm with hit-and-run tactics: Approximately 80 men in each *jaghun,* or company, participated; the remaining 20 acted as heavy cavalry. Each *jaghun* sent 20 men per wave of attackers. The waves fired several arrows as they charged and then circled back to the Mongols' lines after completing their charge. They loosed their final shot roughly 40 to 50 meters from the enemy lines before wheeling around. This distance was close enough to pierce armor, but distant enough to evade a countercharge. While circling back, the Mongols often used the aforementioned Parthian shot. They changed horses frequently to keep their mounts fresh. Since each man was equipped with 60 arrows, the Mongols could maintain this barrage for almost an hour, and perhaps longer.

They used this technique throughout their era of dominance, as Marco Polo observed in the late 13th century:

> When they come to an engagement with the enemy, they will gain the victory in this fashion. [They never let themselves get into a regular medley, but keep perpetually riding round and shooting into the enemy. And] as they do not count it any shame to run away in battle, they will [sometimes pretend to] do so, and in running away they turn in the saddle and shoot hard and strong at the foe, and in this way make great havoc.

## Feigned Retreat

The feigned retreat was a classic tactic of steppe warfare practiced since ancient times: A token force charged the enemy and then retreated, pulling the enemy after them in pursuit. The retreat might extend a great distance in order to stretch the enemy's ranks and formations. Then at a prearranged location, other Mongol forces attacked from the flanks while the initial force wheeled around and attacked the enemy's front.

Perhaps the most renowned use of the feigned retreat took place in 1223, when Mongol generals Jebe and Sübedei encountered a combined army of Kipchak Turks and Rus' along the Dnieper River. The Mongols retreated, luring the Kipchaks and Rus' several days deeper into the steppe until they reached the Kalka River. Here the main Mongol force waited and promptly destroyed the allied force.

Marco Polo also remarked on the effectiveness of the feigned retreat:

> *Thus they fight to as good purpose in running away as if they stood and faced the enemy, because of the vast volleys of arrows that they shoot in this way, turning round upon their pursuers, who are fancying that they have won the battle. But when the Tartars see that they have killed and wounded a good many horses and men, they wheel round bodily and return to the charge in perfect order and with loud cries; and in a very short time the enemy are routed.*

## Fabian Tactics

At times the Mongols avoided combat with the enemy until they found an ideal location for battle or had regrouped far-flung forces to confront their opponent. This tactic differed from the feigned retreat; Fabian tactics involved the avoidance of all direct contact with the enemy. The Mongol army often divided into small groups to avoid being surrounded, but then they regrouped and launched a surprise attack on the enemy at a more opportune time. Fabian tactics also exhausted the enemy through avoidance of combat, particularly when the enemy forces maintained a strong defensive posture, whether in the open or in a fortress. As long as the Mongols remained in the vicinity, the constant stress of anticipating an attack wore down the enemy.

When the Mongols were confronted by an enemy who, for instance, planted spears in the ground to prevent cavalry charges, they responded by withdrawing the bulk of their forces, leaving behind a few detachments to harass the enemy. Eventually, their enemy—having either decided that the main Mongol force had withdrawn for strategic reasons or had moved away because of hunger or thirst—emerged from their defenses. Then the main Mongol force would return to destroy them.

## Flanking Tactics and Double Envelopment

Chinggis Khan used encircling tactics on several occasions. He sought to encircle his enemies, especially if their flanks and rear were exposed or, in the case of sieges, if the defenders were weak. When he was confronted by an enemy army that was using features of the terrain—a river, for instance—to its advantage, he attempted to encircle it on both sides of the riverbank.

The Mongols sometimes confused their enemy by feinting at the front and then unleashing the main attack on their rear. By attacking from several directions, the Mongols gave the enemy the impression that they were surrounded. By leaving a gap in the encirclement, the Mongols allowed the enemy what looked like a means of escape. In reality, the gap served as a trap. In their panic and desire to get away, the enemy rarely maintained their discipline and often discarded their weapons to flee faster. The Mongols then attacked from the rear much like they did to the Hungarians at Mohi in 1241. Mongol scholar Dalantai called this the "Open-the-End Tactic" and noted that the Mongols used it if the enemy seemed to be very strong and might fight to the death when trapped.

The practice of double envelopment or even encirclement, while a traditional method employed on the steppe, also stems from the Mongols' training in the *nerge* or the *battue* style of hunting. Just as in the *nerge,* the warriors gradually tightened their circle around their prey, forming a dense mass from which it was difficult to escape. The Mongols did not always require large numbers of troops to achieve this; their archery skills and mobility allowed them to encircle an enemy force even when they were outnumbered.

The *nerge* used in military operations essentially served as a double envelopment tactic, in which the wings of the Mongol army would wrap around an opposing army. At times the Mongols used it as a strategy on a broader front during an invasion, as they did when they attacked the Rus' lands. After the capture of the city of Vladimir in 1237, "They turned back from there and held a council, deciding that they would proceed *tūmān* by *tūmān* in *jārge* formation and take and destroy every town, province and fortress they came to." In this fashion the Mongols encircled an area, then gradually closed in so that avenues of escape narrowed as they would in a battle.

In some instances, the Mongols sent a force of prisoners and conscripted levies to attack the enemy front, backed of course by Mongol troops to ensure the levy performed its duty. Meanwhile, Mongol columns marched out of sight until they reappeared on the flanks or in the rear of the enemy.

## Siege Warfare

In the early days of the Mongol conquests, siege warfare was a weakness that Chinggis Khan and his generals had to overcome if they were to hold territory. As their success grew against their sedentary opponents, the Mongols incorporated engineers—either conscripted or volunteers—into their armies. For the entire existence of the Mongol Empire, they were dependent on Muslim and Chinese engineers who manned and manufactured artillery and other siege equipment.

The Mongols delayed sieges until the later part of a campaign. They began a campaign with the reduction of smaller outlying places before concentrating their armies on a greater target. Thus they ensured that they had sufficient manpower to besiege the larger towns. When they came up against an inaccessible city or fortress, the Mongols set up a blockade in order to starve an enemy into surrendering. They also dealt with strongholds by bypassing them, once these were isolated, they lost their strategic importance. If the Mongols found they could not reduce the city or fortress, they often built a counter fortress to blockade it and waited until the enemy succumbed to hunger or agreed to a diplomatic settlement.

Prior to a siege, the Mongols collected numerous captives and conscripts from previously conquered cities and villages. These people served as forced labor and arrow fodder. After seizing a city, town or village, the Mongols divided the population into units of 10, and each Mongol soldier received a unit. These levies gathered grass, wood, earth and stone. If any of the captives fell behind during the march, the Mongols executed them. When the levies arrived at the city that was to be attacked, they filled the moat or defensive trench quickly with stones and other materials they carried—bundles of straw, wood and debris—so the Mongols could reach the walls. Captives were also forced to dig trenches and erect defenses and to undertake any other tasks that were necessary.

During a siege, the Mongols compelled prisoners to build siege engines, presumably under the direction of their Chinese or Persian engineers. With these engines and their own bows, the Mongols maintained a constant barrage on the city in order to prevent the enemy from resting. The Mongols also used naphtha and possibly Greek fire, and the Franciscan friar John de Plano Carpini noted a more gruesome fuel. According to him, "They even take the fat of the people they kill and, melting it, throw it on to the house, and wherever the fire falls on this fat, it is almost inextinguishable."

Prisoners were forced to take an active part in the sieges. They carried battering rams which were operated under the cover of a canopy or perhaps a more hardened shelter. If the captives tried to run away, they were put to death. Thus they had a choice of certain death at the hands of the Mongols or probable death at the hands of the defenders of the city.

In addition to using catapults and rams to weaken the walls of a city, the Mongols dug tunnels to undermine them. If a river ran near a city—as in Xixia, for instance—they would dam it and flood the streets. The conscripted levies did most of the dangerous work, and the Mongols only exposed themselves when they were required to engage in combat. During a siege they tended to stay out of the range of fire from the city, thereby conserving their own troops while letting auxiliaries and local levies perform the most perilous jobs. Finally, once the wall was breached, the Mongols donned their armor and attacked, often at night.

These tactics were standard operating procedure for the Mongols throughout their conquests. The campaign in Russia demonstrated the sophistication and efficiency of their siege-warfare techniques; the siege of Vladimir is a particularly good example: The Mongols isolated the city by surrounding it with a wall before bombarding it with catapults, arrows, fire arrows and attacks by levies with battering rams. Once they had breached a city wall, they mounted a quick assault at night to reduce casualties.

## Psychological Tactics and Means of Deception

The Mongols realized it was more efficient to convince a city or fortress to surrender without resistance rather than to be drawn into a siege. As a consequence, the Mongols gained a notorious reputation for massacres. According to some chroniclers, most notably Jûzjânî and the Rus' chroniclers, the Mongols rarely left a living soul wherever they conquered. Their massacres generally were not carried out in wanton blood lust—but served several purposes: The first was to discourage revolts by hostile populations behind the Mongol armies. Second, as news of the massacres spread, particularly in cases where the defenders had put up a determined resistance, other cities and peoples were intimidated and chose to surrender to the Mongols. Finally, a massacre served as a powerful deterrent to rebellion. According to anthropologist Thomas Barfield, the Mongols

> *. . . were extremely conscious of their small numbers and employed terror as a tool to discourage resistance against them. Cities . . . that surrendered and then revolted were put to the sword. The Mongols could not maintain strong garrisons and so preferred to wipe out whole areas that appeared troublesome. Such behavior was inexplicable to sedentary historians for whom conquest of productive populations was the goal of warfare.*

In addition, the Mongols used propaganda and often spread rumors in advance that exaggerated the size of their army. In 1258 Möngke invaded Szechuan with 40,000, but spread rumors of 100,000. The Mongols resorted to other subterfuges to confuse and intimidate their enemies. When he fought the Naiman in 1204, Chinggis Khan ordered his soldiers to set up camp on the Sa'ari Steppe in western Mongolia, and in order to hide the true size of his army, he commanded that each soldier should light five campfires, giving the impression of a more numerous army. When confronting numerically superior forces, the Mongols often sent troops back to stir up dust behind their own lines by means of branches tied to the tails of their horses, to create the illusion of approaching reinforcements. They also mounted dummies on their spare horses, and rode in single file to mask their numbers at a distance.

The Mongols sought to weaken their opponents by promoting discord or rebellion and by courting the support of oppressed minorities (or majorities). While the Mongols made good use of their reputation for extreme brutality, they also took pains to portray themselves as liberators when circumstances warranted. They also played rivals off against one another. As the French knight Jean de Joinville once wrote, "Whenever the Mongols wish to make war on the Saracens, they send Christians to fight against them, and on the other hand employ Saracens in any war against Christians."

## Supernatural Tactics

The Mongols resorted to supernatural means to assure their success. They asked Tenggri, or Heaven, for favor on the battlefield in the same way Muslim and Christian armies appealed to their god before battle. The Mongols also employed other supernatural tactics, the most important of which was weather magic conducted by a shaman known as the *jadaci*. The *jadaci* used special rocks, thought to be imbued with the power to control weather and known as "rain stones," in order to summon rainstorms, or even snowstorms in the summer, which caught the enemy ill-prepared. During the storm, the Mongols, who had lured their opponents away from their base, would take shelter and then attack while the enemy was disoriented.

## Strategy

The most effective strategies in war exploit the strengths of the army, and for the Mongols this meant a strategy of high mobility. The horses used by the Mongols were surpassed in strength and speed by those of sedentary armies, but they were superior in endurance, and the Mongols had more of them. The average trooper in the Mongol army possessed three to five mounts, so he could remain mobile even if one or two of his mounts were lost or exhausted. In consequence the Mongols engaged in a highly mobile style of warfare that was not employed again until the 20th century, when armies were mechanized.

## Timing

When preparing for war, the Mongols took several steps. First, they conducted a census in order to organize the mobilization of their troops. They also accumulated intelligence on their opponents. Only after sufficient intelligence had been obtained did they make a declaration of hostilities. The declarations of war varied, but by the peak of the empire, they outlined why the Mongols were invading and gave the enemy a few options such as surrendering and providing tribute and troops when requested—or facing destruction. At a *quriltai,* or Mongol assembly, the strategy for the upcoming war was agreed on and the commanders were chosen. Points of rendezvous were established, and mobilization began in earnest.

According to Denis Sinor:

> *Mongol strategy at its best was based on a very careful planning of the military operations to be performed, and the essence of it lay in a very rigid timetable to which all Mongol commanders were expected to adhere strictly.*

While timetables were important to Mongol armies, they were not afraid to alter their plans in order to take advantage of favorable weather and other environmental conditions. They sought to attack when their enemies least expected it, even when their own horses were lean or weak, or in the middle of winter. Although campaigns were meticulously planned, the Mongol generals maintained a high degree of independence. They could fulfill their objectives in their own way so long as they abided to the overall timetable.

## Travel by Columns

Invading Mongol armies usually followed several routes of advance. Against the Khwârazmian Empire, Chinggis Khan used at least four and perhaps five routes, one of which ran through the Kyzyl Kum desert. During the invasion of Russia, generals Sübedei, Batu and Möngke approached from three directions. Ultimately, as in modern warfare, these columns converged upon a single target, usually the center of power. Against the Khwârazmian Empire it was Samarqand; in Europe, Budapest. With their pre-planned schedules and their skillful use of scouts, the Mongols marched divided, but fought united. Because their forces marched in small detachments, their advance was not slowed by large columns that stretched for miles, and their opponents were not able to concentrate their forces before the Mongols appeared on many fronts at the same time. While the Mongols were quite capable of concentrating their forces at a critical point in an enemy's defenses, such as at a strategic fortress or a field army, instead they often overwhelmed their opponents by applying pressure to several points simultaneously.

## Annihilation of Field Army

A multi-pronged invasion plan suited the Mongols' favored method of engaging the enemy—that is, to destroy the opposing field army before moving deep into enemy territory. Screens of scouts ensured that the Mongols could rapidly locate enemy armies. After defeating an army, the Mongols pursued it until it was destroyed. Assaults on enemy strongholds were often delayed by this effort to put the enemy field army out of action. Of course, small fortresses and ones that could be surprised easily were taken in the course of the advance. The Khwârazmian campaign is perhaps the best example of this—smaller cities and fortresses were taken before the capital Samarqand was captured. This strategy had two obvious advantages. First, it prevented the principal city from communicating with other cities that might have come to its aid. Second, refugees from the smaller cities fled to the last stronghold. Reports from the defeated cities and the stream of refugees not only reduced the morale of the inhabitants and the garrison of the principal city, but also strained its resources of food and water. Upon destruction of the field army, the Mongols were then free to lay siege without interference.

## Pursuit of Leaders

Once an enemy field army had been defeated, the Mongols concentrated on destroying their opponent's capacity to rally. They targeted all the enemy leaders and harried them until they were killed. Chinggis Khan first pursued this policy during the wars of unification in Mongolia. In his first few campaigns his failure to eliminate the opposing leaders allowed them to regroup their forces and start the conflict anew. He learned from this experience, and in his later campaigns the merciless pursuit of the enemy commanders evolved into a standard operational procedure.

## Key to Success

Altogether, the Mongols possessed a highly developed and complex military structure. This provided them an edge in warfare over their opponents, but a key to Mongol success in war and conquest was the melding of traditional and still effective steppe tactics with new tactics and forms of warfare they encountered. Throughout the expansion of their empire, the Mongols remained pragmatic and open to incorporating new methods of waging war and adopting new weapons and tactics. They ensured their soldiers were properly trained to execute the appropriate tactics when ordered. Finally, due to their extensive planning, the Mongols were better informed about their opponents than most medieval armies. The outcome was that for more than 150 years of conquest from Asia to Europe they suffered no serious defeats.

Appeared in *Military History,* July/August 2007. From *The Mongol Art of War* by Timothy May, (Westholme Publishing, 2007. 

Article 28

# How a Mysterious Disease Laid Low Europe's Masses

## In the 1300s, a third of the population died of plague brought by fleas, shocking the medieval world to its foundations.

CHARLES L. MEE JR.

In all likelihood, a flea riding on the hide of a black rat entered the Italian port of Messina in 1347, perhaps down a hawser tying a ship up at the dock. The flea had a gut full of the bacillus *Yersinia pestis.* The flea itself was hardly bigger than the letter "o" on this page, but it could carry several hundred thousand bacilli in its intestine.

Scholars today cannot identify with certainty which species of flea (or rat) carried the plague. One candidate among the fleas is *Xenopsylla cheopis,* which looks like a deeply bent, bearded old man with six legs. It is slender and bristly, with almost no neck and no waist, so that it can slip easily through the forest of hair in which it lives. It is outfitted with a daggerlike proboscis for piercing the skin and sucking the blood of its host. And it is cunningly equipped to secrete a substance that prevents coagulation of the host's blood. Although *X. cheopis* can go for weeks without feeding, it will eat every day if it can, taking its blood warm.

One rat on which fleas feed, the black rat *(Rattus rattus),* also known as the house rat, roof rat or ship rat, is active mainly at night. A rat can fall 50 feet and land on its feet with no injury. It can scale a brick wall or climb up the inside of a pipe only an inch and a half in diameter. It can jump a distance of two feet straight up and four horizontally, and squeeze through a hole the size of a quarter. Black rats have been found still swimming days after their ship has sunk at sea.

A rat can gnaw its way through almost anything—paper, wood, bone, mortar, half-inch sheet metal. It gnaws constantly. Indeed, it *must* gnaw constantly. Its incisors grow four to five inches a year: if it were to stop gnawing, its lower incisors would eventually grow—as sometimes happens when a rat loses an opposing tooth—until the incisors push up into the rat's brain, killing it. It prefers grain, if possible, but also eats fish, eggs, fowl and meat—lambs, piglets and the flesh of helpless infants or adults. If nothing else is available, a rat will eat manure and drink urine.

Rats prefer to move no more than a hundred feet from their nests. But in severe drought or famine, rats can begin to move en masse for great distances, bringing with them any infections they happen to have picked up, infections that may be killing them but not killing them more rapidly than they breed.

Rats and mice harbor a number of infections that may cause diseases in human beings. A black rat can even tolerate a moderate amount of the ferocious *Yersinia pestis* bacillus in its system without noticeable ill effects. But bacilli breed even more extravagantly than fleas or rats, often in the millions. When a bacillus finally invades the rat's pulmonary or nervous system, it causes a horrible, often convulsive, death, passing on a lethal dose to the bloodsucking fleas that ride on the rat's hide.

## The Ultimate Bacillus Breeder

When an afflicted rat dies, its body cools, so that the flea, highly sensitive to changes in temperature, will find another host. The flea can, if need be, survive for weeks at a time without a rat host. It can take refuge anywhere, even in an abandoned rat's nest or a bale of cloth. A dying rat may liberate scores of rat fleas. More than that, a flea's intestine happens to provide ideal breeding conditions for the bacillus, which will eventually multiply so prodigiously as finally to block the gut of the flea entirely. Unable to feed or digest blood, the flea desperately seeks another host. But now, as it sucks blood, it spits some out at the same time. Each time the flea stops sucking for a moment, it is capable of pumping thousands of virulent bacilli back into its host. Thus bacilli are passed from rat to flea to rat, contained, ordinarily, within a closed community.

For millions of years, there has been a reservoir of *Yersinia pestis* living as a permanently settled parasite—passed back and forth among fleas and rodents in warm, moist nests—in the wild rodent colonies of China, India, the southern part of the Soviet Union and the western United States. Probably there will always be such reservoirs—ready to be stirred up by sudden climatic change or ecological disaster. Even last year, four authentic cases of bubonic plague were confirmed in New Mexico and Arizona. Limited outbreaks and some fatalities have occurred in the United States for years, in fact, but the disease doesn't spread, partly for reasons we don't understand, partly because patients can now be treated with antibiotics.

And at least from biblical times on, there have been sporadic allusions to plagues, as well as carefully recorded outbreaks. The emperor Justinian's Constantinople, for instance, capital of the Roman empire in the East, was ravaged by plague in 541 and 542, felling perhaps 40 percent of the city's population. But none of the biblical or Roman plagues seemed so emblematic of horror and devastation as the Black Death that struck Europe in 1347. Rumors of fearful pestilence in China and throughout the East had reached Europe by 1346. "India was depopulated," reported one chronicler, "Tartary, Mesopotamia, Syria, Armenia, were covered with dead bodies; the Kurds fled in vain to the mountains. In Caramania and Caesarea none were left alive."

Untold millions would die in China and the rest of the East before the plague subsided again. By September of 1345, the *Yersinia pestis* bacillus, probably carried by rats, reached the Crimea, on the northern coast of the Black Sea, where Italian merchants had a good number of trading colonies.

From the shores of the Black Sea, the bacillus seems to have entered a number of Italian ports. The most famous account has to do with a ship that docked in the Sicilian port of Messina in 1347. According to an Italian chronicler named Gabriele de Mussis, Christian merchants from Genoa and local Muslim residents in the town of Caffa on the Black Sea got into an argument; a serious fight ensued between the merchants and a local army led by a Tartar lord. In the course of an attack on the Christians, the Tartars were stricken by plague. From sheer spitefulness, their leader loaded his catapults with dead bodies and hurled them at the Christian enemy, in hopes of spreading disease among them. Infected with the plague, the Genoese sailed back to Italy, docking first at Messina.

Although de Mussis, who never traveled to the Crimea, may be a less-than-reliable source, his underlying assumption seems sound. The plague did spread along established trade routes. (Most likely, though, the pestilence in Caffa resulted from an infected population of local rats, not from the corpses lobbed over the besieged city's walls.)

In any case, given enough dying rats and enough engorged and frantic fleas, it will not be long before the fleas, in their search for new hosts, leap to a human being. When a rat flea senses the presence of an alternate host, it can jump very quickly and as much as 150 times its length. The average for such jumps is about six inches horizontally and four inches straight up in the air. Once on human skin, the flea will not travel far before it begins to feed.

The first symptoms of bubonic plague often appear within several days: headache and a general feeling of weakness, followed by aches and chills in the upper leg and groin, a white coating on the tongue, rapid pulse, slurred speech, confusion, fatigue, apathy and a staggering gait. A blackish pustule usually will form at the point of the fleabite. By the third day, the lymph nodes begin to swell. Because the bite is commonly in the leg, it is the lymph nodes of the groin that swell, which is how the disease got its name. The Greek word for "groin" is *boubon*—thus, bubonic plague. The swelling will be tender, perhaps as large as an egg. The heart begins to flutter rapidly as it tries to pump blood through swollen, suffocating tissues. Subcutaneous hemorrhaging occurs, causing purplish blotches on the skin. The victim's nervous system begins to collapse, causing dreadful pain and bizarre neurological disorders, from which the "Dance of Death" rituals that accompanied the plague may have taken their inspiration. By the fourth or fifth day, wild anxiety and terror overtake the sufferer—and then a sense of resignation, as the skin blackens and the rictus of death settles on the body.

In 1347, when the plague struck in Messina, townspeople realized that it must have come from the sick and dying crews of the ships at their dock. They turned on the sailors and drove them back out to sea—eventually to spread the plague in other ports. Messina panicked. People ran out into the fields and vineyards and neighboring villages, taking the rat fleas with them.

When the citizens of Messina, already ill or just becoming ill, reached the city of Catania, 55 miles to the south, they were at first taken in and given beds in the hospital. But as the plague began to infect Catania, the townspeople there cordoned off their town and refused—too late—to admit any outsiders. The sick, turning black, stumbling and delirious, were objects more of disgust than pity; everything about them gave off a terrible stench, it was said, their "sweat, excrement, spittle, breath, so foetid as to be overpowering; urine turbid, thick, black or red. . . ."

Wherever the plague appeared, the suddenness of death was terrifying. Today, even with hand-me-down memories of the great influenza epidemic of 1918 (SMITHSONIAN, January 1989) and the advent of AIDS, it is hard to grasp the strain that the plague put on the physical and spiritual fabric of society. People went to bed perfectly healthy and were found dead in the morning. Priests and doctors who came to minister to the sick, so the wild stories ran, would contract the plague with a single touch and die sooner than the person they had come to help. In his preface to *The Decameron,* a collection of stories told while the plague was raging, Boccaccio reports that he saw two pigs rooting around in the clothes of a man who had just died, and after a few minutes of snuffling, the pigs began to run wildly around and around, then fell dead.

"Tedious were it to recount," Boccaccio thereafter laments, "brother was forsaken by brother, nephew by uncle, brother by sister and, oftentimes, husband by wife; nay what is more and scarcely to be believed, fathers and mothers were found to abandon their own children, untended, unvisited, to their fate, as if they had been strangers. . . ."

In Florence, everyone grew so frightened of the bodies stacked up in the streets that some men, called *becchini,* put themselves out for hire to fetch and carry the dead to mass graves. Having in this way stepped over the boundary into the land of the dead, and no doubt feeling doomed themselves, the *becchini* became an abandoned, brutal lot. Many roamed the streets, forcing their way into private homes and threatening to carry people away if they were not paid off in money or sexual favors.

## Visiting Men with Pestilence

Some people, shut up in their houses with the doors barred, would scratch a sign of the cross on the front door, sometimes with the inscription "Lord have mercy on us." In one place, two lovers were supposed to have bathed in urine every morning for protection. People hovered over latrines, breathing in the stench. Others swallowed pus from the boils of plague victims. In Avignon, Pope Clement was said to have sat for weeks between two roaring fires.

The plague spread from Sicily all up and down the Atlantic coast, and from the port cities of Venice, Genoa and Pisa as well as Marseilles, London and Bristol. A multitude of men and women, as Boccaccio writes, "negligent of all but themselves . . . migrated to the country, as if God, in visiting men with this pestilence in requital of their iniquities, would not pursue them with His wrath wherever they might be. . . ."

Some who were not yet ill but felt doomed indulged in debauchery. Others, seeking protection in lives of moderation, banded together in communities to live a separate and secluded life, walking abroad with flowers to their noses "to ward off the stench and, perhaps, the evil airs that afflicted them."

It was from a time of plague, some scholars speculate, that the nursery rhyme "Ring Around the Rosy" derives: the rose-colored "ring" being an early sign that a blotch was about to appear on the skin; "a pocket full of posies" being a device to ward off stench and (it was hoped) the attendant infection; "ashes, ashes" being a reference to "ashes to ashes, dust to dust" or perhaps to the sneezing "a-choo, a-choo" that afflicted those in whom the infection had invaded the lungs—ending, inevitably, in "all fall down."

In Pistoia, the city council enacted nine pages of regulations to keep the plague out—no Pistoian was allowed to leave town to visit any place where the plague was raging; if a citizen did visit a plague-infested area he was not allowed back in the city; no linen or woolen goods were allowed to be imported; no corpses could be brought home from outside the city; attendance at funerals was strictly limited to immediate family. None of these regulations helped.

In Siena, dogs dragged bodies from the shallow graves and left them half-devoured in the streets. Merchants closed their shops. The wool industry was shut down. Clergymen ceased administering last rites. On June 2, 1348, all the civil courts were recessed by the city council. Because so many of the laborers had died, construction of the nave for a great cathedral came to a halt. Work was never resumed: only the smaller cathedral we know today was completed.

In Venice, it was said that 600 were dying every day. In Florence, perhaps half the population died. By the time the plague swept through, as much as one-third of Italy's population had succumbed.

In Milan, when the plague struck, all the occupants of any victim's house, whether sick or well, were walled up inside together and left to die. Such draconian measures seemed to have been partially successful—mortality rates were lower in Milan than in other cities.

Medieval medicine was at a loss to explain all this, or to do anything about it. Although clinical observation did play some role in medical education, an extensive reliance on ancient and inadequate texts prevailed. Surgeons usually had a good deal of clinical experience but were considered mainly to be skilled craftsmen, not men of real learning, and their experience was not much incorporated into the body of medical knowledge. In 1300, Pope Boniface VIII had published a bull specifically inveighing against the mutilation of corpses. It was designed to cut down on the sale of miscellaneous bones as holy relics, but one of the effects was to discourage dissection.

Physicians, priests and others had theories about the cause of the plague. Earthquakes that released poisonous fumes, for instance. Severe changes in the Earth's temperature creating southerly winds that brought the plague. The notion that the plague was somehow the result of a corruption of the air was widely believed. It was this idea that led people to avoid foul odors by holding flowers to their noses or to try to drive out the infectious foul odors by inhaling the alternate foul odors of a latrine. Some thought that the plague came from the raining down of frogs, toads and reptiles. Some physicians believed one could catch the plague from "lust with old women."

**Most Christians believed the cause of the plague was God's wrath at sinful Man.**

Both the pope and the king of France sent urgent requests for help to the medical faculty at the University of Paris, then one of the most distinguished medical groups in the Western world. The faculty responded that the plague was the result of a conjunction of the planets Saturn, Mars and Jupiter at 1 P.M. on March 20, 1345, an event that caused the corruption of the surrounding atmosphere.

Ultimately, of course, most Christians believed the cause of the plague was God's wrath at sinful Man. And in those terms, to be sure, the best preventives were prayer, the wearing of crosses and participation in other religious activities. In Orvieto, the town fathers added 50 new religious observances to the municipal calendar. Even so, within five months of the appearance of the plague, Orvieto lost every second person in the town.

There was also some agreement about preventive measures one might take to avoid the wrath of God. Flight was best: away from lowlands, marshy areas, stagnant waters, southern exposures and coastal areas, toward high, dry, cool, mountainous places. It was thought wise to stay indoors all day, to stay cool and to cover any windows that admitted bright sunlight. In addition to keeping flowers nearby, one might burn such aromatic woods as juniper and ash.

The retreat to the mountains, where the density of the rat population was not as great as in urban areas, and where the weather was inimical to rats and fleas, was probably a good idea—as well as perhaps proof, of a kind, of the value of empirical observation. But any useful notion was always mixed in with such wild ideas that it got lost in a flurry of desperate (and often contrary) stratagems. One should avoid bathing because that opened the pores to attack from the corrupt atmosphere, but one should wash face and feet, and sprinkle them with rose water and vinegar. In the morning, one might eat a couple of figs with rue and filberts. One expert advised eating ten-year-old treacle mixed with several dozen items, including chopped-up snake. Rhubarb was recommended, too, along with onions, leeks and garlic. The best spices were myrrh, saffron and pepper, to be taken late in the day. Meat should be roasted, not boiled. Eggs should not be eaten hard-boiled. A certain Gentile di Foligno commended lettuce; the faculty of medicine at the University of Paris advised against it. Desserts were forbidden. One should not sleep during the day. One should sleep first on the right side, then on the left. Exercise was to be avoided because it introduced more air into the body; if one needed to move, one ought to move slowly.

By the fall of 1348, the plague began to abate. But then, just as hopes were rising that it had passed, the plague broke out again in the spring and summer of 1349 in different parts of Europe. This recurrence seemed to prove that the warm weather, and people bathing in warm weather, caused the pores of the skin to open and admit the corrupted air. In other respects, however, the plague remained inexplicable. Why did some people get it and recover, while other seemed not to have got it at all—or at least showed none of its symptoms—yet died suddenly anyway? Some people died in four or five days, others died at once. Some seemed to have contracted the plague from a friend or relative who had it, others had never been near a sick person. The sheer unpredictability of it was terrifying.

In fact, though no one would know for several centuries, there were three different forms of the plague, which ran three different courses. The first was simple bubonic plague, transmitted from rat to person by the bite of the rat flea. The second and likely most common form was pneumonic, which occurred when the bacillus invaded the lungs. After a two- or three-day incubation period, anyone with pneumonic plague would have a severe, bloody cough; the sputum cast into the air would contain *Yersinia pestis*. Transmitted through the air from person to person, pneumonic plague was fatal in 95 to 100 percent of all cases.

The third form of the plague was septocemic, and its precise etiology is not entirely understood even yet. In essence, however, it appears that in cases of septocemic plague the bacillus entered the bloodstream, perhaps at the moment of the fleabite. A rash formed and death occurred within a day, or even within hours, before any swellings appeared. Septocemic plague always turned out to be fatal.

Some people did imagine that the disease might be coming from some animal, and they killed dogs and cats—though never rats. But fleas were so much a part of everyday life that no one seems to have given them a second thought. Upright citizens also killed gravediggers, strangers from other countries, gypsies, drunks, beggars, cripples, lepers and Jews. The first persecution of the Jews seems to have taken place in the South of France in the spring of 1348. That September, at Chillon on Lake Geneva, a group of Jews were accused of poisoning the wells. They were tortured and they confessed, and their confessions were sent to neighboring towns. In Basel all the Jews were locked inside wooden buildings and burned alive. In November, Jews were burned in Solothurn, Zofingen and Stuttgart. Through the winter and into early spring they were burned in Landsberg, Burren, Memmingen, Lindau, Freiburg, Ulm, Speyer, Gotha, Eisenach, Dresden, Worms, Baden and Erfurt. Sixteen thousand were murdered in Strasbourg. In other cities Jews were walled up inside their houses to starve to death. That the Jews were also dying of the plague was not taken as proof that they were not causing it.

**Very rarely does a single event change history itself. Yet an event of the magnitude of the Black Death could not fail to have an enormous impact.**

On the highways and byways, meanwhile, congregations of flagellants wandered about, whipping themselves twice a day and once during the night for weeks at a time. As they went on their way they attracted hordes of followers and helped spread the plague even farther abroad.

The recurrence of the plague after people thought the worst was over may have been the most devastating development of all. In short, Europe was swept not only by a bacillus but also by a widespread psychic breakdown—by abject terror, panic, rage, vengefulness, cringing remorse, selfishness, hysteria, and above all, by an overwhelming sense of utter powerlessness in the face of an inescapable horror.

After a decade's respite, just as Europeans began to recover their feeling of well-being, the plague struck again in 1361, and again in 1369, and at least once in each decade down to the end of the century. Why the plague faded away is still a mystery that, in the short run, apparently had little to do with improvements in medicine or cleanliness and more to do with some adjustment of equilibrium among the population of rats and fleas. In any case, as agents for Pope Clement estimated in 1351, perhaps 24 million people had died in the first onslaught of the plague; perhaps as many as another 20 million died by the end of the century—in all, it is estimated, one-third of the total population of Europe.

Very rarely does a single event change history by itself. Yet an event of the magnitude of the Black Death could not fail to have had an enormous impact. Ironically, some of the changes brought by the plague were for the good. Not surprisingly, medicine changed—since medicine had so signally failed to be of any help in the hour of greatest need for it. First of all, a great many doctors died—and some simply ran away. "It has pleased God," wrote one Venetian-born physician, "by this terrible mortality to leave our native place so destitute of upright and capable doctors that it may be said not one has been left." By 1349, at the University of Padua there were vacancies in every single chair of medicine and surgery. All this, of course, created room for new people with new ideas. Ordinary people began wanting to get their hands on medical guides and to take command of their own health. And gradually more medical texts began to appear in the vernacular instead of in Latin.

## An Old Order Was Besieged

Because of the death of so many people, the relationship between agricultural supply and demand changed radically, too. Agricultural prices dropped precipitously, endangering the fortunes and power of the aristocracy, whose wealth and dominance were based on land. At the same time, because of the deaths of so many people, wages rose dramatically, giving laborers some chance of improving their own conditions of employment. Increasing numbers of people had more money to buy what could be called luxury goods, which affected the nature of business and trade, and even of private well-being. As old relationships, usages and laws broke down, expanding secular concerns and intensifying the struggle between faith and reason, there was a rise in religious, social and political unrest. Religious reformer John Wycliffe, in England, and John Huss, in Bohemia, were among many leaders of sects that challenged church behavior and church doctrine all over Europe. Such complaints eventually led to the Protestant Reformation, and the assertion that Man stood in direct relation to God, without need to benefit from intercession by layers of clergy.

Indeed, the entire structure of feudal society, which had been under stress for many years, was undermined by the plague. The three orders of feudalism—clergy, nobility and peasantry—had been challenged for more than a century by the rise of the urban bourgeoisie, and by the enormous, slow changes in productivity and in the cultivation of arable land. But the plague, ravaging the weakened feudal system from so many diverse and unpredictable quarters, tore it apart.

By far the greatest change in Western civilization that the plague helped hasten was a change of mind. Once the immediate traumas of death, terror and flight had passed through a stricken town, the common lingering emotion was that of fear of God. The subsequent surge of religious fervor in art was in many ways nightmarish. Though medieval religion had dealt with death and dying, and naturally with sin and retribution, it was only after the Black Death that painters so wholeheartedly gave themselves over to pictures brimming with rotting corpses, corpses being consumed by snakes and toads, swooping birds of prey appearing with terrible suddenness, cripples gazing on the figure of death with longing for deliverance, open graves filled with blackened, worm-eaten bodies, devils slashing the faces and bodies of the damned.

Well before the plague struck Europe, the role of the Catholic Church in Western Europe had been changing. The Papacy had grown more secular in its concerns, vying with princes for wealth and power even while attempts at reform were increasing. "God gave us the Papacy," Pope Leo X declared. "Let us enjoy it." The church had suffered a series of damaging losses in the late 1200s—culminating in 1309 when the Papacy moved from Rome to Avignon. But then, the Black Death dealt the church a further blow, for along with renewed fear and the need for new religious zeal came the opposite feeling, that the church itself had failed. Historical changes rarely occur suddenly. The first indications of change from a powerful catalyst usually seem to be mere curiosities, exceptions or aberrations from the prevailing worldview. Only after a time, after the exceptions have accumulated and seem to cohere, do they take on the nature of a historical movement. And only when the exceptions have come to dominate, do they begin to seem typical of the civilization as a whole (and the vestiges of the old civilization to seem like curiosities). This, in any case, is how the great change of mind occurred that defines the modern Western world. While the Black Death alone did not cause these changes, the upheaval it brought about did help set the stage for the new world of Renaissance Europe and the Reformation.

As the Black Death waned in Europe, the power of religion waned with it, leaving behind a population that was gradually but certainly turning its attention to the physical realm in which it lived, to materialism and worldliness, to the terrible power of the world itself, and to the wonder of how it works.

# UNIT 6

# Renaissance and Reformation

## Unit Selections

29. **The Guns of Constantinople,** Roger Crowley
30. **Joan of Arc,** Kelly DeVries
31. **The Luther Legacy,** Derek Wilson
32. **Explaining John Calvin,** William J. Bouwsma
33. **The Third Way,** Phillip E. L. Greene
34. **Vlad Dracula's War on the Turks,** Will Romano
35. **Women in War,** John A. Lynn
36. **Will the Real Henry VIII Please Stand up?,** Eric Ives

## Key points to Consider

- Why were the cannons so helpful to Ottoman Sultan, Mehmed II for capturing Constantinople?
- How was Joan of Arc helpful to French Nationalism?
- How is our opinion of John Calvin as a cold and inflexible moralist a mistaken view?
- How did the Anabaptists differ from other reformists of the 16th century?
- Why can we view Vlad Dracula both as a hero and as a vicious madman?
- Why were women important in wars during the 16th century?
- What are the various aspects of Henry VIII's personality? Why is he one of the most famous Tudor monarchs?

## Student Web Site

www.mhcls.com/online

## Internet References

**Burckhardt: Civilization of the Renaissance in Italy**
*http://www.idbsu.edu/courses/hy309/docs/burckhardt/burckhardt.html*

**Elizabethan England**
*http://www.springfield.k12.il.us/schools/springfield/eliz/elizabethanengland.html*

**1492: An Ongoing Voyage/Library of Congress**
*http://lcweb.loc.gov/exhibits/1492/*

**History Net**
*http://www.historynet.com/*

**The Mayflower Web Pages**
*http://www.mayflowerhistory.com/*

**Sir Francis Drake**
*http://www.mcn.org/2/oseeler/drake.htm*

**Society for Economic Anthropology Homepage**
*http://sea.org.ohio-state.edu/*

The departure from medieval patterns of life was first evident in the Italian Renaissance. There, the growth of capital and the development of distinctly urban economic and social organizations promoted a new culture. This culture, which spread to other parts of Europe, was dominated by townsmen whose tastes, abilities, and interests differed from those of medieval clergy and feudal nobility.

The emerging culture was limited to a minority—generally those who were wealthy. But even in an increasingly materialistic culture, it was not enough just to be wealthy. It was necessary to patronize the arts, literature, and learning, and to demonstrate some skill in a/any profession. The idea Renaissance man, as Robert Lopez observes (in *The Three Ages of the Italian Renaissance,* University of Virginia Press, 1970), "came from a good old family, improved upon his status through his own efforts, and justified his status by his own intellectual accomplishments."

The new ideal owed much to the classical tradition. Renaissance man, wising to break out of the otherworldly spirituality of the Middle Ages, turned back to the secular naturalism of the ancient world. Indeed, the Renaissance was, among other things, a heroic age of scholarship that restored classical learning to a place of honor. It was classical humanism in particular that became the vogue. And in the new spirit of individualism, however, humanism was transformed.

Civic humanism was another Renaissance modification of the classical heritage. It involved a new philosophy of political engagement, a reinterpretation of political history from the vantage point of contemporary politics, and the recognition that men would not simply imitate the ancients but would also rival them.

Renaissance art and architecture reflected the new society and its attitudes. Successful businessmen were as likely as saints to be subjects of portraits. Equestrian statues of warriors and statesmen glorified current heroes while evoking memories of ancient Rome. Renaissance painters rediscovered nature, which generally had been ignored by medieval artists, often depicting it as an earthly paradise—the appropriate setting for humanity in its new image. And in contrast to the great medieval cathedrals, which glorified God, the Renaissance structure focused on humanity.

Some of these developments in art and architecture indicate the changes in the role of Christianity and the influence of the Church, which no longer determined the goals of Western civilization as they had during the medieval period. Increasingly, civil authorities and their symbols competed with churchmen and their icons, while Machiavelli and other writers provided a secular rationale for a new political order. Nonetheless, most Europeans, including many humanists retained a deep and abiding religious faith.

The Reformation, with its theological disputes and wars, is a powerful reminder that secular concerns had not entirely replaced religious ones, especially in northern Europe. The great issues that divided Protests and Catholics—the balance between individual piety and the Church's authority, the true means of salvation—were essentially medieval in character. Indeed, in their perceptions of humanity, their preoccupation with salvation and damnation, and their attacks upon the Church's conduct of its affairs, Martin Luther, John Calvin, Ulrich Zwingli, and other Protestant leaders echoed the views of medieval reformers. These Protestant reforms are treated in the articles, "The Luther Legacy," "Explaining John Calvin," and "The Third Way."

The Palma Collection/Getty Images

Taken together, then, the Renaissance and the Reformation constituted a new compound of traditional elements—classical and medieval, secular and religious—along with elements of modernity. The era was a time of transition, or as Lynn D. White describes it, "This was a time of torrential flux, or fearful doubt, making the transition from the relative certainties of the Middle Ages to the new certainties of the eighteenth and nineteenth centuries.

# The Guns of Constantinople

## History's first great artillery barrage, in 1453, shattered the Byzantine capital and changed warfare forever.

ROGER CROWLEY

Early in 1452, a Hungarian cannon founder by the name of Orban arrived in Constantinople, seeking his fortune at the imperial court. One of a growing band of technical mercenaries who plied their trade across the Balkans, he offered Emperor Constantine XI one of the most highly prized skills of the age: the ability to cast large bronze guns.

For Constantine and the Christian empire of Byzantium that he ruled, these were dark days. For 150 years the Byzantine frontier had been crumbling before the advance of the Ottoman Turks. By the time Constantine assumed the throne in 1449, his impoverished kingdom had shrunk to little more than the footprint of the city, surrounded on all sides by Ottoman land. The new sultan, Mehmed II—young, ambitious and hungry for conquest—was making ominous military preparations in his European capital, Edirne, 140 miles to the west. It was clear he was intent on capturing the prize that had eluded previous Ottoman rulers: Constantinople.

Constantine was extremely interested in Orban's offer and authorized a small stipend to detain him in the city. But Constantine had few funds available for the construction of new weapons. Bronze cannons were ruinously expensive, well beyond the means of the cash-strapped emperor. Orban's tiny allowance was not even paid regularly, and as the year wore on, the master craftsman became destitute. So later that same year he decided to try his luck elsewhere. He made his way to Edirne to seek an audience with the young sultan.

At the time, Mehmed was racked by indecision over Constantinople. The city was the ultimate prize; it would provide a fitting capital for the Ottoman Empire, and its capture was the subject of ancient Muslim prophecies, attributed to Muhammad himself, that predicted great honor for its eventual conqueror. However, Constantinople had repulsed repeated Muslim assaults from the 7th century onward. Its triangular site made it all but impregnable: Two sides were surrounded by sea, and the third landward side was commanded by the great Walls of Theodosius, a defensive line four miles long, the greatest bastion in the medieval world. In a thousand years the city had been besieged some 23 times, but no army had found a way to crack open those land walls.

Accordingly, Orban's arrival at Edirne must have seemed providential. The sultan welcomed the master founder and questioned him closely. Mehmed asked if he could cast a cannon to project a stone ball large enough to smash the walls at Constantinople. Orban's reply was emphatic: "I can cast a cannon of bronze with the capacity of the stone you want. I have examined the walls of the city in great detail. I can shatter to dust not only these walls with the stones from my gun, but the very walls of Babylon itself." Mehmed ordered him to make the gun.

During the autumn of 1452, Orban set to work at Edirne, casting one of the largest cannons ever built, while Mehmed stockpiled substantial quantities of materials for guns and gunpowder: copper and tin, saltpeter, sulfur and charcoal. Workers excavated an enormous casting pit and melted scrap bronze in the brick-lined furnaces, superheating it with bellows and pouring it into the mold.

What finally emerged from Orban's foundry once the molds had been knocked off was "a horrifying and extraordinary monster." It was 27 feet long. The barrel, walled with 8 inches of solid bronze to absorb the force of the blast, had a diameter of 30 inches, enough for a man to enter on his hands and knees and designed to accommodate a stone shot weighing something over half a ton. In January 1453, Mehmed ordered a test firing of the gun outside his royal palace. The mighty bombard was hauled into position near the gate and primed with powder. Laborers lugged a giant stone ball to the mouth of the barrel and rolled it back to sit snugly against the gunpowder chamber. A lighted taper was put to the touchhole. With a shattering roar and a cloud of smoke, the mighty projectile hurled across the countryside for a mile before burying itself six feet into the soft earth.

**'Mehmed asked Orban if he could cast a cannon large enough to smash the walls at Constantinople'.**

Mehmed now addressed the challenge of transporting the gun the 140 miles to Constantinople. Two hundred men and 60 oxen were detailed for the task. The immense barrel was loaded onto several wagons chained together and yoked to the ox teams. The great gun rumbled toward the city at a speed of two and a half miles a day, while another team of engineers worked ahead, leveling roads and building wooden bridges over rivers and gullies. Orban's foundry continued to turn out barrels of different sizes; none was as large as the first supergun, though some measured more than 14 feet.

It took six weeks for the guns to lurch and jolt their way to Constantinople. By the time they arrived, in early April, Mehmed's army—a huge force of 80,000 men—was dug in along the length of the land walls. Sappers had cut down orchards and vineyards outside the Walls of Theodosius to provide a clear field of fire. Others dug a ditch the length of the walls and 250 yards from them, with an earth rampart to shield the guns. Within the city walls, a mere 8,000 men awaited the inevitable assault.

Mehmed grouped the cannons into 14 or 15 batteries along the walls at key vulnerable points. Orban's supergun, which the Greeks called the Basilica cannon—"the royal gun"—was positioned in front of the sultan's tent so he could critically appraise its performance. Each large cannon was supported by a cluster of smaller ones in a battery the Ottoman gunners named "the bear with its cubs." They could fire stone balls ranging from 200 pounds up to a colossal 1,500 pounds, in the case of Orban's monster gun. Though eyewitnesses spoke of "innumerable machines," Mehmed probably had about 69 cannons, a huge artillery force by the standards of the day. They were augmented by more traditional technologies for hurling stones, such as the trebuchet. The latter had been effective in the Muslim capture of crusader castles 300 years earlier, but now it looked like a device from another age.

Installing and readying the cannons was a laborious process. Workers had to erect a massive block-and-tackle system to lower the barrels into position on a sloping wooden platform. Shielding the cannons from enemy fire were a wooden palisade and a hinged door that could be opened at the moment of firing.

The logistical support for this operation was immense. Ships transported loads of black stone balls mined and shaped on the north coast of the Black Sea. The cannons also required substantial quantities of saltpeter. Founders who worked with Orban at Edirne doubled as gun crews, positioning, loading and firing the cannons—even repairing them on site.

Preparing the big cannon to fire required time and attention to detail. Crews would load gunpowder, backed by a wooden or sheepskin wad pounded tight into the barrel. Next they manhandled a stone ball to the muzzle and eased it down the barrel. Each ball was designed to be a good fit, though an exact caliber match was often elusive. Crews set their aim by "certain techniques and calculations" about the target—i.e., trial and error—and adjusted the angle of fire by chocking the platform with wooden wedges. Great timber beams weighted down with stones acted as shock absorbers. Crews then poured priming powder into the touchhole.

On April 12, 1453, lighted tapers were put to the touchholes of the sultan's guns along a four-mile sector of the front line, and the world's first concerted artillery barrage exploded to life.

If there is any single moment in the history of warfare at which an authentic sense of awe at the exponential power of gunpowder could be palpably felt, it is here in the accounts of those firing these great guns in 1453. The taper ignited the powder:

> *And when it had caught fire, faster than you can say it, there was first a terrifying roar and a violent shaking of the ground beneath and for a great distance around, and a din such as has never been heard. Then, with a monstrous thundering and an awful explosion and a flame that illuminated everything round about and scorched it, the wooden wad was forced out by the hot blast of dry air and propelled the stone ball powerfully out. Projected with incredible force and power, the stone struck the wall, which it immediately shook and demolished, and it was itself shattered into many fragments, and the pieces were hurled everywhere, dealing death to those standing nearby.*

When the huge stone balls struck the walls at an advan-tageous spot, the effects were devastating. "Sometimes it destroyed a complete portion of wall," an eyewitness reported, "sometimes half a portion, sometimes a greater or smaller part of a tower, or a turret, or a parapet, and nowhere was the wall strong enough or sturdy enough or thick enough to withstand it, or to hold out totally against such a force or the velocity of the stone ball." It must have seemed to the defenders that the whole history of siege warfare was unraveling in front of their eyes. The Walls of Theodosius, the product of two millennia of defensive evolution, crumbled wherever it was hit. The defenders were amazed and horrified by what they saw.

Balls from the superguns that cleared the walls traveled up to a mile into the heart of the city, shattering with devastating force against houses or churches, mowing down civilians or burying themselves in orchards and fields within the walls. According to eyewitnesses, the ground was shaken for two miles around, and even the galleys tied up in the harbors felt the explosions through their wooden hulls.

The psychological effects of the artillery bombardment on the defenders were even more severe than its material consequences. The noise and vibration of the massed guns, the clouds of smoke, the shattering impact of stone on stone dismayed seasoned defenders. To the civilian population, it seemed a glimpse of the coming apocalypse. It sounded, according to one Ottoman chronicler, "like the awful resurrection blast." People ran out of their houses, beating their chests and crossing themselves. Women fainted in the streets. Churches were thronged with people voicing petitions and prayers.

The defenders tried different methods to mitigate the shock of the stone balls. Some poured a mortar of chalk and brick dust down the walls' outer face as a hardened coating; others padded the walls with suspended bales of wool, leather sheets and even precious tapestries. These measures made little difference. The defenders also tried to knock out the big guns with their own few cannons, but they were short of saltpeter, and the palisades effectively screened the Ottoman cannons. Worse, the walls and towers proved unsuitable as gun platforms—neither wide enough to accommodate the recoil nor strong enough to withstand the vibrations, which "shook the walls, and did more damage to them than to the enemy" Their largest cannon soon exploded, enraging the harassed defenders so much that they threatened to put the gun master to death for being in the pay of the sultan. Regardless, it was clear that in this new age of warfare, the Walls of Theodosius were inadequate.

Mehmed's strategy was attritional—and impatient. He decided to breach the walls with artillery fire and launch unpredictable skirmishes to wear down the defenders prior to a final attack. "The assault continued night and day, with no relief from the clashes and explosions, crashing of stones and cannonballs on the walls," reported a defender, "for the sultan hoped in this way to take the city easily, since we were few against many, by pounding us to death and exhaustion, and so he allowed us no rest from attack."

Managing the great cannon remained difficult work. Loading and aiming were such laborious operations that the Basilica could only be fired seven times a day. The guns could be unpredictable and deadly to their teams. In the spring rain, they proved hard to keep in position, recoiling with the slam of a charging rhino and frequently slipping from their cradles into the mud. The possibility of being crushed to death was only exceeded by the risk of being blown to pieces by the shrapnel of disintegrating gun barrels. The Basilica quickly became a cause for concern to Orban; casting on this scale was extremely demanding, and the intense heat of the explosions started to exploit hairline fractures in the impure metal. After each shot, crews soaked the barrel in warm oil to prevent cold air from penetrating and enlarging the fissures.

**'Dust and cannon smoke obscured the front line, but Ottoman troops were quickest into the breach'.**

Their stopgap measure failed. The Basilica soon "cracked as it was being fired and split into many pieces, killing and wounding many nearby." Strengthened with iron hoops and pressed back into service, it soon cracked again, to Mehmed's intense anger. The supergun simply exceeded the tolerances of contemporary metallurgy.

In the end, it didn't matter. Though the supergun inflicted great psychological trauma, the slightly smaller yet still formidable bombards would do the real damage.

In the early days of the bombardment, a deputation of Hungarians visited the sultan's camp. One observed the firing of the great cannons with interest. Watching a shot strike the walls at a certain point, he laughed to himself as the gunners aimed a second shot at the same point. He advised them to aim their second shot "about 30 to 36 feet from the first shot, but at the same height" and to position a third shot between the two "so that the shots form a triangular shape. Then you will see that portion of wall collapse." Soon the "bear and cubs" were working as coordinated teams. Smaller guns would make the two outer hits, then one of Orban's great guns would complete the triangle in the now weakened central section, "the shot being carried by such devilish force and irresistible impetus that it caused irreparable damage."

The bombardment continued unabated for six days. Despite aiming difficulties and a slow rate of fire, gunners managed to launch about 120 shots a day at the city, concentrating their heaviest fire on the central section of wall. Inexorably, the walls began to crumble. Within the week a section of the outer wall had fallen, as had two towers and a turret on the inner wall.

However, after their initial terror at the bombardment, the defenders had regained heart and now worked unceasingly to repair the damage. They devised an effective ad hoc solution to shore up the outer wall, constructing a makeshift replacement of stakes reinforced with any material that came to hand, including stones, timber, brushwood, bushes and large quantities of earth. The defenders placed barrels full of soil at regular intervals to create firing positions that would absorb Ottoman arrows and bullets. At dusk men and women came up from the city to work all night, carrying timber, stones and earth to rebuild smashed defenses. The resulting earthworks provided a surprisingly effective counter to the devastating impact of the stone balls. Like stones thrown into mud, the cannonballs were smothered, their force neutralized.

As their own artillery was poorly situated for firing heavy balls, the defenders reinvented the pieces as huge shotguns, packing each cannon with five or 10 lead balls the size of walnuts. Fired at close range, the effect was appalling:

> *[They had] immense power in penetrating and perforating, so that if one hit a soldier in armor, it went straight through both his shield and body, then through another behind who was in the line of fire, and then another, until the force of the powder was dissipated. With one shot, two or three men could be killed at the same time.*

Hit by this withering fire, the Ottomans suffered terrible casualties. But to Mehmed, men were a cheap and expendable resource.

On April 18, the sultan judged that his gunners had punched enough holes in the walls to launch a major assault. It failed, with a huge loss of life, but there was no respite; his big guns went on firing. Cannons had been used in siege warfare before, but what was unprecedented about Mehmed's bombardment was its intensity and duration. No other army in the world possessed the materials required to mount a continuous artillery bombardment on this scale. The guns blasted away day and night, and chunks of wall continued to collapse.

For the defenders, the unceasing cycles of bombardment, attack and repair began to blur. Like later diaries of trench warfare, the chroniclers' accounts become repetitive and monotonous. "On the 11th of May," recorded a defender, "nothing happened either by land or at sea except a considerable bombardment of the walls from the landward side. . . . On the 13th of May, there came some Turks to the walls skirmishing, but nothing significant happened during the whole day and night, except for continuous bombardment of the unfortunate walls." This pattern gradually drained the defenders of energy and morale. By May 28, the guns had been firing continuously for 47 days, expending 55,000 pounds of gunpowder and delivering an estimated 5,000 shots. Gunners had blasted nine substantial holes in the outer wall, only to be replaced piecemeal by the earth stockade. Both sides were exhausted.

Mehmed knew the time had come: On May 29, 1453, he ordered a climactic full-scale assault. At 1:30 in the morning, to the beating of drums and clashing of cymbals, the Ottoman army rolled forward along the whole four-mile sector. Behind them the cannons put up a withering fire. Volleys of stone shot sprayed the walls, peppering the defenders and felling Ottoman troops from behind. The extraordinary noise of the battle was so deafening that, according to one defender, "the very air seemed to split apart. . . . It seemed like something from another world."

After several hours of confused fighting, one of the big cannons landed a direct hit on the stockade and opened a hole. Dust and cannon smoke obscured the front line, but Ottoman troops moved quickly into the breach. Mehmed's men soon overwhelmed the defenses and sacked and burned the city in a few hours of terrible massacre.

Mehmed had succeeded where all previous Ottoman attempts had failed, and it was the big guns that made the difference. The fall of Constantinople symbolized the end of outmoded medieval techniques of castle construction and siege warfare and opened a terrible new chapter in military history. The use of massed artillery bombardment would prevail all the way to the battlefield of the Somme and beyond.

Mehmed lies buried in a mosque complex in the city he captured. At the door of his tomb stands a stone cannonball.

---

For further reading, **Roger Crowley** recommends his own *1453: The Holy War for Constantinople and the Clash of Islam and the West* and *The Fall of Constantinople,* by David Nicolle, Stephen Turnbull and John Haldon. Or listen to a radio discussion on the subject in the BBC audio archives at [www.bbc.co.uk/radio4/history/inourtime].

# Joan of Arc

## Forget the gauzy Hollywood saint—she was an inspired battlefield leader.

KELLY DEVRIES

The most famous woman writer of the Middle Ages, Christine de Pisan, wrote her last treatise about the most famous woman in the Middle Ages, Joan of Arc. De Pisang Ditié de Jehanne d'Arc was a paean to the French military leader whose victories were turning the tide of the Hundred Years' War and would lead to the crowning of Charles VII on July 17, 1429. Her account is also a contemporary recognition that Joan's mission was not an act of heresy but had come from God, just as Joan had declared.

Addressing herself to the English and Burgundians then fighting against Joan, de Pisan poses the questions they were afraid to have answered:

> Oh, all you blind people, can you not detect God's hand in this? If you cannot, you are truly stupid, for how else could the Maid who strikes you all down dead have been sent to us? And you do not have sufficient strength! Do you want to fight against God?

Christine de Pisan was well positioned to ask those questions. She had lived through the military resurgence of France at the end of the 14th century, and she had witnessed its many defeats at the hands of Henry V since 1415: Harfleur, Agincourt, Caen and Rouen. Ultimately, nearly all of northern France had fallen into his hands. She had watched her former patron, John the Fearless, duke of Burgundy (head of a faction of French nobles that had wrested control of the throne from King Charles VI, whose madness had rendered him unable to rule), lead the conquering English king into Paris and then into a marriage with Catherine of Valois, Charles' daughter. For his part in this intrigue, John was later assassinated by men under the command of Catherine's brother, Charles, the disinherited Dauphin—the very man Joan would crown king. And, following Henry's early death in 1422, de Pisan had also seen the English armies push French forces across the Loire River, far to the south of Paris. Indeed, by 1429 and the advent of Joan of Arc, the English occupied some two-thirds of France, their Burgundian allies controlling even more.

The 1415 Battle of Agincourt had been a resounding English victory An estimated 6,000 Englishmen defeated a force that may have numbered more than 25,000 (although, one authority on that battle, Anne Curry, has recently suggested closer numbers: 7,000 English against 12,000 French). French losses, especially among knights and nobles, had been high. The French had been not only militarily defeated, but also profoundly demoralized. After Agincourt, French resistance to their conquerors was light and ineffective. Fearing other embarrassing and costly losses, les armées grew cautious and avoided open confrontations. Leadership problems, recruitment woes and logistical troubles multiplied on the French side, while the smaller English army, under the dynamic leadership of Henry V, went on to conquer Normandy, Brittany, Le Maine and Île-de-France with unprecedented speed during between 1415 and 1422. The English had also capitalized on a civil war that raged throughout France, dividing the kingdom and making allies of the Burgundians, led after 1419 by Duke Philip the Good.

Such setbacks prompted many French towns to surrender to the English and Burgundians without even being attacked. They sought to avoid any punishment that might follow a failed defense. Often, the English didn't even assign garrisons to the surrendered towns, enabling them to disperse their limited forces and cover even more threatened territory.

But through these years of setbacks, pockets of French resistance did hold out, largely unsupported by the Dauphin or his generals. The successful defenses at Mont-Saint-Michel, Tournai, Vaucouleurs and Orléans gave hope to many French patriots who thought the occupiers of their lands were vulnerable to a concerted, aggressive military effort. Such leaders as Jean, duc d'Alençon; Robert de Baudricourt; Étienne de Vignolles, dit La Hire; Louis de Culen; and Jean Poton de Xaintrailles, not to mention many anonymous French soldiers, believed that the English could be defeated, but that the French needed inspiring leadership. The Dauphin had certainly not provided any such thing. Nor was he likely to, as his favorites, Georges de la Trémoille and Archbishop Renault de Chartres, were counseling him to proceed with caution against the English and Burgundians. That the spark of inspiration for more aggressive military action was to arise in the person of a peasant female was probably not anticipated by any of those willing French warriors. However, when Joan of Arc appeared, they felt her confidence and determination and soon followed her with a fervent loyalty few soldiers in history have given their leaders. Joan responded by leading them to victory.

Joan's approach to military action was simple. In this regard, some of her detractors are correct: Joan did not appear to possess the kind of strategic or tactical cleverness in campaign and battlefield maneuvers that would have impressed classical theorists like Xenophon or Frontinus. But because she believed God had sent her on a mission to save France, and had even provided her with a means of fulfilling that mission by arranging for the Dauphin to give her leadership within the French army (Joan was never appointed as the leader of the French army, only one of several leaders), her strategy and tactics reflected her belief that she could do nothing wrong, and that direct and aggressive action was the means to victory. Joan's convictions further meant that anyone who died in her army, while doing God's bidding, was a martyr for a righteous cause, destined for heaven.

Joan best demonstrated effective leadership in her relief of the Siege of Orleans, although her pre-Orléans history had forecast her battlefield successes. Indeed, her confidence in confronting Robert de Baudricourt at Vaucouleurs, the Dauphin at Chinon, the ecclesiastical leaders in Chinon, the officials in Poitiers and, finally, Charles' mother-in-law, Yolande d'Aragon, queen of Sicily, in Poitiers, brought her prominence and a devoted following even before she reached the French camps at Orléans. Her early reputation also elicited animosity from the other French leaders she encountered upon her arrival at the besieged Loire holdout. But who could blame them? Sending a peasant girl to assist them in their struggles to relieve the English siege of Orléans—regardless of whether she had received this mission directly from God—was an indictment of their military leadership.

Joan would have none of such negative attitudes; she had neither the time nor the patience for their hurt feelings. She was anxious only to engage the enemy. At their first meeting, on April 29, 1429, the following exchange occurred (later recalled in a deposition by Jean, the Bastard of Orleans, commander of the French armies at Orléans):

> Then Joan spoke to him those words which follow: "Are you the Bastard of Orleans?" He answered her: "Yes, I am so and I rejoice at your coming." Then said she to him: "Did you give counsel that I should come here, to this side of the river, and that I should go not straight there where Talbot [Lord John Talbot, head of the English army] and the English are?" [Joan had been led around the English army.] He answered that he and others, wiser on this matter, had given this counsel, believing that they were doing the best and surest. Then Joan said to him, "In the name of God, the counsel of our Lord God is surer and wiser than yours. You thought to deceive me, but it is you who are deceived, for I am bringing you better help than ever came from any soldier or any city, because it is the help of the King of Heaven. It does not come through love for me, but from God himself, who, on the petition of Saint Louis and Saint Charlemagne, has had pity on the town of Orleans and has refused to suffer the enemy to have [this] city."

Jean was not used to enduring such a direct affront to his authority. But then, neither was he prepared to attack the English. In fact, there is evidence he intended to pull away from the town, in effect surrendering it to the English force of some 5,000, then led by the Earl of Suffolk. Joan took that intention as an insult to herself, to the people of Orleans and to God. She also had difficulty understanding why the Bastard would do this, as the English did not even have sufficient troops on hand to surround Orléans. Instead, they had manned only four strongholds, or "boulevards," along the east side of town, one on an island in the Loire River farther east, one more to the north, and another on the road from Orleans to Jargeau. Each held few English troops. Indeed, in coming to Orleans, Joan and her relatively large retinue had passed one English stronghold, the Boulevard of Saint-Loup, without notice. (Joan and a few Orléanais would later capture that same boulevard with ease.) The English had more soldiers on the south bank of the Loire, most of them concentrated at Les Tourelles, the fortification beside the single bridge into Orléans, and in the adjacent Boulevard Augustin, amid the ruins of an Augustinian monastery. The bridge no longer spanned the river, having been destroyed by the Orléanais at the beginning of the siege the previous October, but it remained the defensive hub for the English. To relieve the siege, the French would have to concentrate their efforts on that fortification.

Perhaps this is what frightened the Bastard of Orléans. A boulevard was one of the most daunting fortifications of the later Middle Ages, despite being constructed simply out of earth and wood. Defended by soldiers with gunpowder weapons, however, it could hold out seemingly forever against almost any size force. Most military leaders, unwilling to sacrifice a large number of their men in attacking such a position, simply left the boulevards alone. Complicating matters, the English troops at Les Tourelles could directly support the Boulevard Augustin. It was also rumored that an English force led by the capable Sir John Fastolf was approaching Orleans.

Joan's reaction to the Bastard's withdrawal plans was to be expected. After discovering he had left her out of leadership councils that addressed how to handle Fastolf's arrival, she again rebuked, even threatened, the French leader. Joan's squire, Jean d'Aulon, later recalled her words: "Bastard, Bastard, in the name of God I command you that as soon as you hear of Fastolf's coming, you will let me know. For if he gets through without my knowing it, I swear to you that I will have your head cut off." The count "answered that he did not doubt that, and that he would certainly let her know."

Once firmly established within the French military leadership ranks, Joan devised a plan to relieve the siege before the arrival of the English reinforcements. It was simple and direct: She herself would lead an assault on the Boulevard Augustin. The Bastard and the other French leaders quickly agreed with her plan. They had little choice and after all could only profit from the position in which she had placed herself: If she succeeded, they would share in her victory. If she failed, they could blame her for the incautious attack.

The only potential flaw in Joan's plan was the high number of French casualties likely to result from an attack against such a strong position defended by well-armed men. Fortified by her belief in God's will and presence, Joan didn't seem concerned. Nor were the French soldiers, for they had been drawn to her patriotism and shared her spiritual zeal. It was almost as if they believed they couldn't die in this struggle, and that if they did, they would gain otherwise unattainable salvation.

Many apparently did gain that salvation on May 7, 1429. The bloodiest encounter of the Hundred Years' War since the battle of Agincourt is described in the contemporary Journal du siège d'Orléans:

> Early in the morning on the day after, which was Saturday, the 7th day of May, the French attacked Les Tourelles and the boulevard while the English were attempting to fortify it. And there was a spectacular assault, during which there were performed many great feats of arms, both in the attack and in the defense, because the English had a large number of strong soldiers and had strengthened skillfully all of the defensible places. And also they fought well, notwithstanding that the French scaled the different places adeptly and attacked the angles at the highest of the strong and sturdy fortifications, so that they seemed by this to be immortal. But the English repulsed them from many places and attacked with artillery both high and low, both with cannons and other weapons, such as axes, lances, pole-arms, lead hammers and other personal arms, so that they killed and wounded many Frenchmen.

Despite being wounded herself, Joan persisted in the assault. Delivering a fiery speech "in the name of God," she urged her men forward, claiming that the English "were not a stronger force" than they she promised "to touch the staff of her standard on the boulevard." Her troops responded with shouts and a renewed charge forward. Les Tourelles soon fell. The English defenders fled, and Joan—now bearing her well-earned nickname, the "Maid of Orleans"—entered the city at the head of her victorious army. She had made believers out of those who had doubted her.

Similar direct assaults against other English-held Loire Valley towns brought similar results. Despite Fastolf's attempt to reinforce Jargeau with troops and gunpowder weapons, it fell on June 12. Beaugency succumbed just five days later after an intense bombardment by French guns of the 12th century castle where English troops had holed up. "The English were able to put up only a small amount of resistance," wrote Jean Chartier, a 15th century French monk and historian. That same night the English abandoned the town of Meung-sur-Loire, slipping away under cover of darkness.

English military leaders were not accustomed to such defeats, and Talbot and Fastolf were determined to turn things around. They met the French in battle outside the town of Patay on June 18, 1429. The French were again victorious. Talbot was captured, while Fastolf barely escaped and retreated to Paris. Joan was present, although how much of a role she took in the battle is disputed.

In less than a month, Joan of Arc had relieved the siege of Orléans, retaken the towns of Jargeau, Meung-sur-Loire and Beaugency and participated in the major French victory at Patay And a month later, on July 17, 1429, when the Dauphin was crowned King Charles VII of France at Reims, Joan was by his side. All along their route to Reims, towns that had earlier willingly subjugated themselves to English rule—Auxerre, Châlons, Troyes and even Reims itself—welcomed "liberation" by the Maid.

Paris, however, remained in enemy hands, and thus Joan undertook a new mission: She would recapture the French capital, then under the control of a sizable Anglo-Burgundian army led by John, duke of Bedford, commander of all English troops in occupied France. Again, Joan did not shrink from this challenge. Before the year was out, she conducted minor bloodless skirmishes with the duke of Bedford's force, then attacked and captured the Parisian suburb of Saint-Denis, the basilica of which held the bones of many earlier French kings. The French saw its capture as divine endorsement of their attempts to win back their kingdom.

But when Joan's forces attacked Paris on September 8, it did not fall. "The assault was difficult and long," wrote Percival de Cagny, who rode under the standard of Alençon and later chronicled the conflict, "and it was a marvel how much noise was made by the cannons and couleuvrines, which fired at those outside the walls at such a rate and in such a quantity as to be without number." Still, Cagny insists, because of the Maid's presence with the army and by the grace of God, "no man was wounded or killed." (A more credible eyewitness is French artist Clément de Fauquembergue, who says the guns killed and wounded many French soldiers.) During the fighting, Joan was wounded in the thigh by a crossbow bolt.

Joan cannot be blamed for the failure to retake Paris, declared the Journal du siège d'Orléans: "She wished to attack such a strong town and so well stocked with men and artillery simply because it was the city of Paris." The anonymous author of the journal was undoubtedly accurate in his assessment of the military situation at Paris. But his was not the opinion that prevailed at Charles VII's court: Joan had failed, and her failure cast doubt on the divinity of her mission. It also cast doubt on the tactical methods she had used to gain her Loire victories and assault Paris.

Over the objections of many French military leaders, Charles sought the overly cautious advice of La Trémoille and Chartres. They urged deliberation, to avoid bringing the Burgundians more actively into the fray. They even suggested that the king return to the English some of the towns captured by Joan. This the king refused, but La Trémoille and Chartres did persuade Charles to disband his coronation army and to send Joan—once she had recovered from her wound—to a less significant theater of operations, against a band of mercenaries led by Perrinet Gressart, along the southern Loire River. There she was able to capture the town of Saint-Pierre-le-Moutier by direct assault, despite being woefully undersupplied. But she failed to take heavily fortified La Charitésur-Loire. The reason for her failure at La Charité is suggested in a letter Joan had written on Nov. 9, 1429, to the townspeople of nearby Riom at the outset of the siege:

> Because of the "great quantities of gunpowder, arrows and other equipment of war expended before the said town [Saint-Pierre-le-Moutier], and because the lords who are in this town and I are so poorly provided to besiege La Charité, where we are going presently, I beseech you, that as you love the good and honor of the king and also those others here, that you would instantly send help for this siege, of gunpowder, saltpeter, sulphur, arrows, heavy crossbows and other equipment of war. And do this so that, for lack of the said powder and other equipment of war, the situation will not be prolonged, and that you will not be said to be neglectful or rejecting.

Petitions that winter from her friends at court, including the king's mother-in-law, returned Joan to more pressing military engagements the following spring. She answered by skirmishing with English troops at Senlis, Crépy-en-Valois and Melun. But again her leadership was less than successful in these engagements. Although Joan and her contemporaries considered them victories, they failed to move the English from any of their occupied territory. But her persistence was enough to further irritate the duke of Bedford and to drag Philip the Good, duke of Burgundy, into the fray.

In April 1430, the Burgundians, urged on by the English, attacked the French-controlled town of Compiègne, forcing Joan to move her troops there to thwart a Burgundian occupation. Defense had never been a part of Joan's strategy, and fighting from behind protective walls was certainly not her military style. She frequently sortied out against the attacking Burgundian troops. On May 23, 1430, leading one of these sorties out of Compiègne, Joan got separated from the main body of her force and was captured by the Burgundians, who eventually ransomed her to the English. Some historians believe she was betrayed by Guillaume de Flavy, the garrison commander at Compiègne, but later trial testimony indicates otherwise:

> She crossed over the bridge and through the French boulevard and went with a company of soldiers manning those sections against the lord of Luxembourg's men [Jean de Luxembourg was one of the Burgundian leaders at Compiègne], whom she drove back twice, all the way to the Burgundian camp, and a third time halfway back. And then the English who were there cut her and her men off, coming between her and the boulevard, and so her men retreated from her. And retreating into the fields on her flank, in the direction of Picardy, near the: boulevard, she was captured.

Joan of Arc was burned to death as a heretic in the marketplace of Rouen a little over a year later, on May 30, 1431.

It would be a satisfying end to the story of Joan of Arc if one could say she was the direct cause of the end of the Hundred Years' War and the expulsion of England from most of France. But that war did not end for 23 years after her capture. So if Joan did not directly end the Hundred Years' War, why is she so celebrated? No doubt the character of her trial and execution have much to do with her celebrity. But Joan's renown stems from her military ability, her skill at leading men in battle against great odds and at the risk of death.

Not long after Joan's death, French military leaders began to adopt tactics similar to hers. Her policy of direct engagement and frontal assault was costly, but it ultimately proved more effective than any other military tactic in wresting the English from France. And possibly, as other French generals started to use her tactics, they too began to believe that, should their soldiers die in battle, they might join the Maid who inspired them, the later-to-be Saint Joan of Arc.

---

For further reading, **Kelly DeVries** recommends his book, *Joan of Arc: A Military Leader,* as well as *Joan of Arc: La Pucelle,* edited by Craig Taylor

# The Luther Legacy

DEREK WILSON

Over the centuries Luther (1483–1546) has been variously identified as an advocate of absolute monarchy, democracy, individual freedom, intellectual repression, nationalism, internationalism, spirituality and secularism. The fact that so many later 'movers and shakers' have claimed the monk of Wittenberg as a progenitor of their own convictions is testimony to the stature of the man. Indeed, it would be difficult to identify any other individual who, without wielding political power or leading armies, more decisively changed the course of history. Even our supposedly post-Christian age cannot write him out of the record. Yet, we have to resist the temptation to recreate him in our own image. He was a religious figure; his battles were fought over theological issues that may seem to us obscure but whose implications touched every area of life, individual and corporate.

Jakob Burckhardt was essentially right in identifying the Reformation as an escape from discipline. For centuries the Church had held the monopoly of propaganda: its murals, stained glass, the polychromed paraphernalia of shrines and altars, the pastoral and educational activities of the clergy, all spoke of the awesome need for people to prepare for the world to come. That meant availing themselves of the prescribed means of grace entrusted to their spiritual superiors. The clergy held the keys to eternal bliss or torment. Any who did air doubts or proclaim a rival programme were heretics and were dealt with severely. The only spiritual authority emanated from Rome. Luther, however, insisted that there was another, higher, source of authority: the word of God written in the Bible. In his preaching and teaching—but above all in his public confrontations with spiritual and temporal leaders—he gave people permission to doubt everything the Catholic hierarchy taught; to judge it for themselves against the testimony of the Bible.

Any attempt to assess Luther's impact must begin with his redefining of the individual. His spiritual journey was an intensely personal one. In 1505 he forsook the legal career for which he had been destined and entered the Augustinian monastery at Erfurt, in order to save his own immortal soul. He was following the path of self-denial and holiness as prescribed by the Church for centuries. For at least eight years he gave it his best shot. He failed to find the consolation he sought because, as well as a sensitive conscience, he was blessed with a sharp, logical mind. He could see the flaw in the system of penitence that the Church preached: if contrition and abnegation were practised in the interests of self-preservation then they were selfish, hence sinful. His was not the first earnest soul to find itself on the treadmill of sin, confession, absolution, doubt, confession. It was a terrifying, never-ending predicament. Ever-present was the 'doom' image of Christ separating the sheep and the goats and consigning the latter to the torments of hell. Famously, Luther discovered in Paul's Epistle to the Romans (Romans 1.17) the sword to sever the Gordian knot: 'the righteousness (justice) of God is revealed from faith to faith. . . the just man will live by faith'. Like countless Christians before and since, he experienced an ecstasy of release.

He might have left it there and, as a good monk, preached justification by faith alone as a truth that could somehow be made to fit with the Church's traditional penitential system. But it could not. The maze of scholastic theology seemed to prevent access to the great central truth which he had discovered. His relentless logic persuaded him to suggest, in the 95 Theses by which he publicly challenged the Church in 1517, that the practice of selling indulgences—by which the buyers could secure remission from the penalties of sin in the next world—was a matter for urgent theological debate. When the papal regime refused to grant this debate, the real problem began. Luther defied the Pope, the Inquisition and the corps of Catholic theologians. Called before the Imperial Diet by the Emperor Charles V at Worms in April 1521, Luther refused to recant insisting, 'my conscience is captive to the word of God . . . Unless I am convinced by Scripture *and reason* [my emphasis], I will not recant'.

It is scarcely possible to exaggerate what those words implied. Luther was not just challenging the accumulated teaching of the Church; he was saying that any man or woman possessed of the open Bible could be his or her own theologian. If God had provided the Bible as a lamp to the believer's path, then as many people as possible should be encouraged to read it. So he translated it into German, and had his translation printed (New Testament, 1522, Old Testament, 1534). Within a few years hundreds of untrained lay people were writing devotional and polemical books and pamphlets. Gone was the assumption that people only needed those skills that enabled them to perform their God-given calling in a hierarchical society. Learning was now something to be valued for its own sake. In 1524, Luther wrote to the municipal authorities throughout Germany urging them to establish elementary schools for all children, including girls. The response was not dramatic but by 1580 half the parishes in Electoral Saxony had schools for boys and 10 per cent had made similar provision for girls. As the American historian Steven Ozment has suggested, 'It is not too much to call the early Protestant movement the first Western enlightenment'.

Luther replaced the authority of the Church with that of the Bible. But it was always the Bible *and reason.* With the plain text in his hand everyone could work out his own salvation and no longer needed the ministrations of an intermediary priesthood. This had far-reaching consequences. If truth is the exclusive preserve of a priestly caste, any system built on this foundation will be autocratic. But, if truth is to be found in a book which anyone can read, then authority can be challenged with divine sanction. The way lies open for the development of alternative polities, even democracy. To be sure, Luther himself drew back from the more revolutionary implications of the open Bible. He did not personally initiate debates on such issues as how to establish a godly commonwealth, whether tyrants might be deposed or the balancing of crown and parliament. But his courageous stand against the Pope and the Holy Roman Emperor, the political embodiments of traditional authority, fired the imagination and stiffened the resolve of more radical spirits throughout western Christendom.

Yet Luther never set out to challenge the establishment. That marks him out from most other religious reformers of his day. Wycliffe, Savonarola, Hus and other rebels and charismatic preachers usually had begun from a starting point of popular grievances—oppression, corruption, extortion. Many clothed their message in gaudy apocalyptic language, claiming they had been sent to cleanse the world in preparation for the Second Coming. Not so Luther. He wanted to restore the Church to its New Testament purity. In that desire he was at one with a large swathe of public opinion, including humanist scholars, kings and even the Emperor. There was a clamour for a general council of the Church to initiate reform. It was only when successive popes refused to concede anything which might weaken the power of Rome, that Luther concluded that the papacy must be the Antichrist, subverting the Christian community from within.

In terms of secular politics, an anachronistic but perhaps appropriate label for him is 'right-wing reactionary'. The political theory he found in the New Testament was that God ordained kings to maintain order and that all subjects (including clergy) were to render due obedience to them. It followed that secular rulers were charged with the reformation of the churches in their domains. He therefore advocated such measures as the ending of ecclesiastical jurisdiction in matters matrimonial and the restoration of ex-monastic property to lay ownership.

Luther had an abhorrence of anarchy. He shared the fear of rebellion and chaos that lay close to the surface of medieval life, but for him public disorder was a particularly sensitive issue because politico-religious upheaval in Germany gave his enemies a stick to beat him with. This explains why he reacted so violently to the Peasants' War of 1524–25, a widespread popular rising against secular princes by ordinary people some of whom drew socially radical conclusions from Luther's teaching. By doing so Luther forfeited the support of most of the populace. His notorious invocation of the German nobility to 'smite, slay and stab' any rebel, just as 'one might kill a mad dog' gave rise to the accusation that he was in the pocket of the princes, a taunt that was in large measure justified. Having already enlisted the aid of the German warlords to protect him from the Church and the Emperor, Luther could not prevent his movement becoming hijacked by these men of power, who banded together in 1530 to form the Schmalkaldic League. Over and again Luther warned them not to wage war against the Emperor. If they did, they would have 'no good conscience before God, no legal ground before the Empire, and no honour before the world. This would be dreadful and terrifying.' (1528) But few people were listening. The new Protestant establishment had taken what it wanted from Luther and his politically non-confrontational agenda seemed to them hopelessly out of touch.

This raises the question of whether Luther should be seen as an apostle of absolutism. Some later autocrats certainly claimed him as a founding father. It is no coincidence that memorial statues of the reformer were erected in Worms and Wittenberg during the nineteenth century, a time of German empire-building; nor that Hitler, scrabbling around for anything that would justify his manifesto, claimed Luther as a fellow-traveller in *Mein Kampf.* But what would the man who had set his face against militarism in the service of the Protestant state have had to say to pickelhaubed soldiers who, in 1914, marched to the front singing his own hymn, *Ein feste Burg?* This same 'apostle of absolutism' was also lauded by the German philosopher Johann Fichte in 1793 as the 'patron saint of freedom' who 'broke humanity's chain' and whose shade raised his hand in benediction over Frenchmen overthrowing the *ancién regime.*

Luther was certainly a German patriot. A basic element in his opposition to Rome was his loathing of 'effete Italians'. He shared the resentment of many of his countrymen at benefices and senior clerical appointments held by absentee shepherds who cared not a whit for their flocks and who creamed off Church revenues to finance a luxurious transalpine lifestyle. When Pope Julius II (1503–13) initiated an indulgence to pay for the building of his new basilica of St Peter's in Rome (1506), it was always going to be unpopular in the German states and his successor Leo X (1513–21) waited four years after Julius's death in 1513 before dispatching his agents thither. When Luther expressed his opposition to the project in the 95 Theses, he was echoing a complaint heard in every *bierhaus* and marketplace.

This resentment expressed itself in official protest at the highest level. At the very Diet of Worms where Luther was examined and condemned by the Emperor, the German estates also presented a catalogue of 102 'oppressive burdens and abuses imposed upon . . . the German Empire by the Holy See of Rome'. But a fissure had already appeared two years earlier in 1519 when the Austrian-born Holy Roman Emperor Maximilian I had been succeeded by the Spanish-born Charles V, giving Germany's political leaders another foreign entity against which to define themselves.

In the early sixteenth century the 'Holy Roman Empire of the German Nation', which was described in 1667 as 'a body that conforms to no rule and resembles a monster', was a hotchpotch of electoral, princely and ecclesiastical states and free cities that possessed only the vaguest of yearnings for a cultural identity. But the Reformation set its scholars, artists and historians on a quest for what marked the heirs of Charlemagne as a people distinct from others. Luther himself made one massive contribution to this. Between 1520 and 1546 he was personally responsible for a third of all the vernacular publications that emerged from German print-shops. He wrote in a vigorous vernacular which could be, by turns vulgar and poetic. His greatest achievement was the German Bible (published in 1534), which did more than anything else to merge regional identities. Scarcely less influential were the catechisms Luther wrote for his 'dear German people', which gave them shared versions of the Creed and the Lord's Prayer.

If 1517 and 1521 are important dates in the life of Luther, 1525 is just as significant. In the midst of the Peasants' War and at a time when he was engaged in a theological contest with Erasmus, Luther astonished all his friends and distressed some of them: he got married. When asked why he was taking this step at the age of almost forty-three, he explained that since he had been advising monks and nuns who had left the cloister to espouse matrimony he should set an example. It may have been nearer the truth that the lady made the running. Katharina von Bora was a strong-willed and determined woman, a Catholic nun seventeen years his junior whom Luther helped escape from a convent. The event divided Luther's mature life into two equal halves: it was twenty years since he had entered the cloister and he had just over twenty years left to enjoy family life. But he did not retire into humdrum domesticity. His new status was as much a demonstration of biblical truth as his opposition to indulgences had been. It declared that virginity and celibacy were not superior vocations. It exalted the nuclear family as the essential building block of society. It emphasized the importance of the home for the nurturing of children in the Christian way and for the exercise of hospitality. It involved him in that little world of intimate relationships with its joys and griefs where lay people actually spent their lives. In short, the Luther family which grew up in the old Augustinian convent at Wittenberg became the model Protestant paternalistic *ménage,* a microcosm of the Church, where the head of the household was its bishop, gathering his children and servants around him for daily prayers and leading them to the church building for worship on Sundays. Over the years scores of university students lodged with the Luthers and it is thanks to some of them that we have the celebrated *Table Talk,* a collection of *obiter dicta* on all manner of subjects with which the great man regaled his guests at meal times.

Since the end of the Holy Roman Empire in 1806, Germany has endured successive identity crises that have impacted disastrously on the rest of Europe. The old north-south divide was resolved by Bismarck's Prussification of the new empire but resulted in a nationalist euphoria which the Iron Chancellor was powerless to control. So too the disasters of 1914–18 and 1939–45, which we can now see as a single conflict at the end of which Germany was once more divided, this time between east and west. The achievement of nationhood has cost Germany and her neighbours dear. It is inevitable that partisans of a greater reich have wanted to enlist to their cause one of the greatest and most patriotic of Germans. At the turn of the twentieth century Lutheran leaders had to choose whether or not to support expansionist policies. Those who did so, such as the members of the German-Christian party, unhesitatingly used their founder's name to persuade the electorate that the triumph of the master race was written into the marrow of the German people and that Luther had set the nation on its inevitable course by his defiance of foreign interference. Thus the Luther-to-Hitler myth was born. But the reformer was never a nationalist in the modern sense of the word. He was, above all, a pastor. Many of his convictions were expressed in books and pamphlets written to help people who consulted him about their problems. Thus, for example, when a mercenary soldier came to him with a troubled conscience the result was another pamphlet (1526): *Whether Soldiers, Too, Can Be Saved.* Although he lived to a good age, Luther worked himself to death. It is characteristic of the man that he hastened his end by travelling through atrocious weather to sort out a dispute between a landlord and his neighbours.

Luther, then, touched life at every level—the individual, the family, the church, the state—and he did so not as a dry-as-dust philosopher but as a flesh-and-blood, fallible human being, agonising about the important issues which faced all his contemporaries. He was a theologian who lived his theology.

He put the Bible at the centre of everything and, as well as applying it to every problem of prince and peasant, he tried to live it himself. Indeed, no one more than Martin Luther resembles the flawed hero of which the sacred text affords so many examples. If we do not, now, find him *simpatico* it is probably because we cannot share his biblical world view.

## For Further Reading

Jacob Burckhardt, *Judgements on History and Historians,* (Eng. Trs, 1958); Steven Ozment, *The Reformation in the Cities,* (1975) *Luther's Works* (Eng. Trs, 55 vols, 1955–1986); R.H. Fife, *The Revolt of Martin Luther* (1957); H.A. Oberman, *Luther, Man Between God and the Devil* (Eng trs, 1989); M. Brecht, *Martin Luther,* 3 vols (Eng. Trs, 1985–93).

**Derek Wilson's** *Out of the Storm: The Life and Legacy of Martin Luther* is published this month by Hutchinson.

# Explaining John Calvin

WILLIAM J. BOUWSMA

John Calvin (1509–64) has been credited, or blamed, for much that defines the modern Western world: capitalism and the work ethic, individualism and utilitarianism, modern science, and, at least among some devout Christians, a lingering suspicion of earthly pleasures. During [a] recent American presidential campaign, the two candidates appealed to "values" that recall the teachings of the 16th-century churchman, indicating that what William Pitt once said of England—"We have a Calvinist creed"—still may hold partly true for the United States. But the legend of the joyless tyrant of Geneva obscures both the real man, a humanist as much as a religious reformer, and the subtlety of his thought. Here his biographer discusses both.

Our image of John Calvin is largely the creation of austere Protestant churchmen who lived during the 17th century, the century following that of the great reformer's life. The image is most accurately evoked by the huge icon of Calvin, familiar to many a tourist, that stands behind the University of Geneva. There looms Calvin, twice as large as life, stylized beyond recognition, stony, rigid, immobile, and—except for his slightly abstracted disapproval of whatever we might imagine him to be contemplating—impassive.

Happily, the historical record provides good evidence for a Calvin very different from the figure invoked by his 17th-century followers. This Calvin is very much a man of the 16th century, a time of religious strife and social upheaval. His life and work reflect the ambiguities, contradictions, and agonies of that troubled time. Sixteenth-century thinkers, especially in Northern Europe, were still grappling with the rich but incoherent legacy of the Renaissance, and their characteristic intellectual constructions were less successful in reconciling its contradictory impulses than in balancing among them. This is why it has proved so difficult to pigeonhole such figures as Erasmus and Machiavelli or Montaigne and Shakespeare, and why they continue to stimulate reflection. Calvin, who can be quoted on both sides of most questions, belongs in this great company.

Born in 1509 in Noyon, Calvin was brought up to be a devout French Catholic. Indeed, his father, a lay administrator in the service of the local bishop, sent him to the University of Paris in 1523 to study for the priesthood. Later he decided that young John should be a lawyer. Accordingly, from 1528 to 1533, Calvin studied law. During these years he was also exposed to the evangelical humanism of Erasmus and Jacques Lefèvre d'Étaples that nourished the radical student movement of the time. The students called for salvation by grace rather than by good works and ceremonies—a position fully compatible with Catholic orthodoxy—as the foundation for a general reform of church and society on the model of antiquity.

To accomplish this end, the radical students advocated a return to the Bible, studied in its original languages. Calvin himself studied Greek and Hebrew as well as Latin, the "three languages" of ancient Christian discourse. His growing interest in the classics led, moreover, to his first publication, a moralizing commentary on Seneca's essay on clemency.

Late in 1533, the French government of Francis I became less tolerant of the Paris student radicals, whom it saw as a threat to the peace. After helping to prepare a statement of the theological implications of the movement in a public address delivered by Nicolas Cop, rector of the University, Calvin found it prudent to leave Paris. Eventually he made his way to Basel, a Protestant town tolerant of religious variety.

Up to this point, there is little evidence of Calvin's "conversion" to Protestantism. Before Basel, of course, he had been fully aware of the challenge Martin Luther posed to the Catholic Church. The 95 Theses that the German reformer posted in Wittenberg in 1517 attacked what Luther believed were corruptions of true Christianity and, by implication, the authors of those errors, the Renaissance popes. Luther, above all, rejected the idea of salvation through indulgences or the sacrament of penance. Excommunicated by Pope Leo X, he encouraged the formation of non-Roman churches.

In Basel, Calvin found himself drawing closer to Luther. Probably in part to clarify his own beliefs, he began to write, first a preface to his cousin Pierre Olivétan's French translation of the Bible, and then what became the first edition of the *Institutes,* his masterwork, which in its successive revisions became the single most important statement of Protestant belief. Although he did not substantially change his views thereafter, he elaborated them in later editions, published in both Latin and French, in which he also replied to his critics; the final versions appeared in 1559 and 1560.

The 1536 *Institutes* had brought him some renown among Protestant leaders, among them Guillaume Farel. A French Reformer struggling to plant Protestantism in Geneva, Farel persuaded Calvin to settle there in late 1536. The Reformation was in trouble in Geneva. Indeed, the limited enthusiasm of Geneva for Protestantism—and for religious and moral reform—continued almost until Calvin's death. The resistance was all the more serious because the town council in Geneva, as in other Protestant towns in Switzerland and southern Germany, exercised ultimate control over the church and the ministers.

The main issue was the right of excommunication, which the ministers regarded as essential to their authority but which the town council refused to concede. The uncompromising attitudes of Calvin and Farel finally resulted in their expulsion from Geneva in May of 1538.

Calvin found refuge for the next three years in Protestant Strasbourg, where he was pastor of a church for French-speaking refugees. Here he married Idelette de Bure, a widow in his congregation. Theirs proved to be an extremely warm relationship, although none of their children survived infancy.

During his Strasbourg years, Calvin learned much about church administration from Martin Bucer, chief pastor there. Attending European religious conferences, he soon became a major figure in the international Protestant movement.

Meanwhile, without strong leadership, the Protestant revolution in Geneva foundered. In September of 1541, Calvin was invited back, and there he remained until his death in 1564. He was now in a stronger position. In November the town council enacted his *Ecclesiastical Ordinances,* which provided for the religious education of the townspeople, especially children, and instituted his conception of church order. It established four groups of church officers and a "consistory" of pastors and elders to bring every aspect of Genevan life under the precepts of God's law.

The activities of the consistory gave substance to the legend of Geneva as a joyless theocracy, intolerant of looseness or pleasure. Under Calvin's leadership, it undertook a range of disciplinary actions covering everything from the abolition of Catholic "superstition" to the enforcement of sexual morality, the regulation of taverns, and measures against dancing, gambling, and swearing. These "Calvinist" measures were resented by many townsfolk, as was the arrival of increasing numbers of French Protestant refugees.

The resulting tensions, as well as the persecution of Calvin's followers in France, help to explain the trial and burning of one of Calvin's leading opponents, Michael Servetus. Calvin felt the need to show that his zeal for orthodoxy was no less than that of his foes. The confrontation between Calvin and his enemies in Geneva was finally resolved in May of 1555, when Calvin's opponents overreached themselves and the tide turned in his favor. His position in Geneva was henceforth reasonably secure.

But Calvin was no less occupied. He had to watch the European scene and keep his Protestant allies united. At the same time, Calvin never stopped promoting his kind of Protestantism. He welcomed the religious refugees who poured into Geneva, especially during the 1550s, from France, but also from England and Scotland, from Italy, Germany, and the Netherlands, and even from Eastern Europe. He trained many of them as ministers, sent them back to their homelands, and then supported them with letters of encouragement and advice. Geneva thus became the center of an international movement and a model for churches elsewhere. John Knox, the Calvinist leader of Scotland, described Geneva as "the most perfect school of Christ that ever was on the Earth since the days of the Apostles." So while Lutheranism was confined to parts of Germany and Scandinavia, Calvinism spread into Britain, the English-speaking colonies of North America, and many parts of Europe.

Academic efforts to explain the appeal of Calvinism in terms of social class have had only limited success. In France, his theology was attractive mainly to a minority among the nobility and the urban upper classes, but in Germany it found adherents among both townsmen and princes. In England and the Netherlands, it made converts in every social group. Calvinism's appeal lay in its ability to explain disorders of the age afflicting all classes and in the remedies and comfort it provided, as much by its activism as by its doctrine. Both depended on the personality, preoccupations, and talents of Calvin himself.

Unlike Martin Luther, Calvin was a reticent man. He rarely expressed himself in the first person singular. This reticence has contributed to his reputation as cold and unapproachable. Those who knew him, however, noted his talent for friendship as well as his hot temper. The intensity of his grief on the death of his wife in 1549 revealed a large capacity for feeling, as did his empathetic reading of many passages in Scripture.

In fact, the impersonality of Calvin's teachings concealed an anxiety, unusually intense even in an anxious age. He saw anxiety everywhere, in himself, in the narratives of the Bible, and in his contemporaries. This feeling found expression in two of his favorite images for spiritual discomfort: the abyss and the labyrinth. The abyss represented all the nameless terrors of disorientation and the absence of familiar boundaries. The labyrinth expressed the anxiety of entrapment: in religious terms, the inability of human beings alienated from God to escape from the imprisonment of self-concern.

One side of Calvin sought to relieve his terror of the abyss with cultural constructions and patterns of control that might help him recover his sense of direction. This side of Calvin was attracted to classical philosophy, which nevertheless conjured up for him fears of entrapment in a labyrinth. Escape from this, however, exposed him to terrible uncertainties and, once again, to the horrors of the abyss. Calvin's ideas thus tended to oscillate between those of freedom and order. His problem was to strike a balance between the two.

He did so primarily with the resources of Renaissance humanism, applying its philological approach to recover a biblical understanding of Christianity. But humanism was not only, or even fundamentally, a scholarly movement. Its scholarship was instrumental to the recovery of the communicative skills of classical rhetoric. Humanists such as Lorenzo Valla and Erasmus held that an effective rhetoric would appeal to a deeper level of the personality than would a mere rational demonstration. By moving the heart, Christian rhetoric would stimulate human beings to the active reform of both themselves and the world.

Theological system-building, Calvin believed, was futile and inappropriate. He faulted the medieval Scholastic theologians for relying more on human reason than on the Bible, which spoke uniquely to the heart. The teachings of Thomas Aquinas, and like-minded theologians, appealed only to the intellect, and so were lifeless and irrelevant to a world in desperate need.

As a humanist, Calvin was a *biblical* theologian, prepared to follow Scripture even when it surpassed the limits of human understanding. And its message, for him, could not be presented as a set of timeless abstractions; it had to be adapted to the understanding of contemporaries according to the rhetorical principle of decorum—i.e. suitability to time, place, and audience.

Calvin shared with earlier humanists an essentially biblical conception of the human personality, not as a hierarchy of faculties ruled by reason but as a mysterious unity. This concept made the feelings and will even more important aspects of the personality than the intellect, and it also gave the body new dignity.

Indeed, Calvin largely rejected the traditional belief in hierarchy as the general principle of all order. For it he substituted the practical (rather than the metaphysical) principle of *utility.* This position found expression in his preference, among the possible forms of government, for republics. It also undermined, for him, the traditional subordination of women to men. Calvin's Geneva accordingly insisted on a single standard of sexual morality—a radical departure from custom.

Calvin's utilitarianism was also reflected in deep reservations about the capacity of human beings to attain anything but practical knowledge. The notion that they can know anything absolutely, as God knows it, so to speak, seemed to him deeply presumptuous. This helps to explain his reliance on the Bible: Human beings have access to the saving truths of religion only insofar as God has revealed them in Scripture. But revealed truth, for Calvin, was not revealed to satisfy human curiosity; it too was limited to meeting the most urgent and practical needs, above all for individual salvation. This practicality also reflects a basic conviction of Renaissance thinkers: the superiority of an active life to one of contemplation. Calvin's conviction that every occupation in society is a "calling" on the part of God himself sanctified this conception.

But Calvin was not only a Renaissance humanist. The culture of 16th-century Europe was peculiarly eclectic. Like other thinkers of his time, Calvin had inherited a set of quite contrary tendencies that he uneasily combined with his humanism. Thus, even as he emphasized the heart, Calvin continued to conceive of the human personality as a hierarchy of faculties ruled by reason; from time to time he tried uneasily, with little success, to reconcile the two conceptions. This is why he sometimes emphasized the importance of rational control over the passions—an emphasis that has been reassuring to conservatives.

Calvin's theology has often been seen as little more than a systematization of the more creative insights of Luther. He followed Luther, indeed, on many points: on original sin, on Scripture, on the absolute dependence of human beings on divine grace, and on justification by faith alone. Other differences between Calvin and Luther are largely matters of emphasis. His understanding of predestination, contrary to a general impression, was virtually identical to Luther's; it was not of central importance to his theology. He believed that it meant that the salvation of believers by a loving God was absolutely certain.

In major respects, however, Calvin departed from Luther. In some ways he was more radical, but most of his differences suggest that he was closer to Catholicism than Luther, as in his insistence on the importance of the historical church. He was also more traditional in his belief in the authority of clergy over laity, perhaps as a result of his difficulties with the Geneva town council. Even more significant, especially for Calvinism as a historical force, was Calvin's attitude toward the everyday world. Luther had regarded this world and its institutions as incorrigible, and was prepared to leave them to the devil. But for Calvin this world, created by God, still belonged to Him; it remained potentially His kingdom; and every Christian was obliged to devote his life to make it so in reality by reforming and bringing it under God's law.

Calvin's thought was less a theology to be comprehended by the mind than a set of principles for the Christian life: in short, spirituality. He was more concerned with the experience and application of Christianity than with mere reflection about it. His true successors were Calvinist pastors rather than Calvinist theologians. Significantly, in addition to devoting much of his energy to the training of other pastors, Calvin was himself a pastor. He preached regularly: some 4,000 sermons in the 13 years after his return to Geneva.

Calvin's spirituality begins with the conviction that we do not so much "know" God as "experience" him indirectly, through his mighty acts and works in the world, as we experience but can hardly be said to know thunder, one of Calvin's favorite metaphors for religious experience. Calvin also believed that human beings can understand something of what God is like in the love of a father for his children, but also—surprisingly in one often identified with patriarchy—in the love of a mother. He denounced those who represented God as dreadful; God for him is "mild, kind, gentle, and compassionate."

Nevertheless, in spite of this attention to God's love for mankind, Calvin gave particular emphasis to God's power because it was this that finally made his love effective in the work of redemption from sin. God, for Calvin, represented supremely all the ways in which human beings experience power: as energy, as warmth, as vitality, and, so, as life itself.

Sin, by contrast, is manifested precisely in the negation of every kind of power and ultimately of the life force given by God. Sin *deadens* and, above all, deadens the feelings. Saving grace, then, must be conceived as the transfusion of God's power—his warmth, passion, strength, vitality—to human beings. It was also essential to Calvin's spirituality, and a reflection of his realism, that this "transfusion" be not instantaneous but gradual.

Calvin's traditional metaphor for the good Christian life implied activity: "Our life is like a journey," he asserted, but "it is not God's will that we should march along casually as we please, but he sets the goal before us, and also directs us on the right way to it." This way is also a struggle.

Complex as his ideas were, it is easy to see how the later history of Calvinism has often been obscured by scholars' failure to distinguish among (1) Calvinism as the beliefs of Calvin himself, (2) the beliefs of his followers, who, though striving to be faithful to Calvin, modified his teachings to meet their own needs, and (3) more loosely, the beliefs of the Reformed tradition of Protestant Christianity, in which Calvinism proper was only one, albeit the most prominent, strand.

The Reformed churches in the 16th century were referred to in the plural to indicate, along with what they had in common, their individual autonomy and variety. They consisted originally of a group of non-Lutheran Protestant churches based in towns in Switzerland and southern Germany. These churches were jealous of their autonomy; and Geneva was not alone among them in having distinguished theological leadership. Ulrich Zwingli and Heinrich Bullinger in Zurich and Martin Bucer in Strasbourg also had a European influence that combined with that of Calvin, especially in England, to shape what came to be called "Calvinism."

Long after Calvin's death in 1564, the churchmen in Geneva continued to venerate him and aimed at being faithful to his teaching under his successors, first among them Theodore de Bèze. But during what can be appropriately described as a Protestant "Counter Reformation," the later Calvinism of Geneva, abandoning Calvin's more humanistic tendencies and drawing more on other, sterner aspects of his thought, was increasingly intellectualized. Indeed, it grew to resemble the medieval Scholasticism that Calvin had abhorred.

Predestination now began to assume an importance that had not been attributed to it before. Whereas Calvin had been led by personal faith to an awed belief in predestination as a benign manifestation of divine providence, predestination now became a threatening doctrine: God's decree determined in advance an individual's salvation or damnation. What good, one might wonder, were one's own best efforts if God had already ruled? In 1619 these tendencies reached a climax at the Synod of Dort in the Netherlands, which spelled out various corollaries of predestination, as Calvin had never done, and made the doctrine central to Calvinism.

Calvinist theologians, meanwhile, apparently finding Calvin's loose rhetorical style of expression unsatisfactory, began deliberately to write like Scholastic theologians, in Latin, and even appealed to medieval Scholastic authorities. The major Calvinist theological statement of the 17th century was the *Institutio Theologiae Elencticae* (3 vols., Geneva, 1688) of François Turretin, chief pastor of Geneva. Although the title of this work recalled Calvin's masterpiece, it was published in Latin, its dialectical structure followed the model of the great *Summas* of Thomas Aquinas, and it suggested at least as much confidence as Thomas in the value of human reason. The lasting effect of this shift is suggested by the fact that "Turretin," in Latin, was the basic theology textbook at the Princeton Seminary in New Jersey, the most distinguished intellectual center of American Calvinism until the middle of the 19th century.

Historians have continued to debate whether these developments were essentially faithful to Calvin or deviations from him. In some sense they were both. Later Calvinist theologians, as they abandoned Calvin's more humanistic tendencies and emphasized his more austere and dogmatic side, found precedents for these changes in the contrary aspects of his thought. They were untrue to Calvin, of course, in rejecting his typically Renaissance concern with balancing contrary impulses. One must remember, however, that these changes in Calvinism occurred during a period of singular disorder in Europe, caused by, among other things, a century of religious warfare. As a result, there was a widespread longing for certainty, security, and peace.

One or another aspect of Calvin's influence has persisted not only in the Reformed churches of France, Germany, Scotland, the Netherlands, and Hungary but also in the Church of England, where he was long as highly regarded as he was by Puritans who had separated from the Anglican establishment. The latter organized their own churches, Presbyterian or Congregational, and brought Calvinism to North America 300 years ago.

Even today these churches, along with the originally German Evangelical and Reformed Church, remember Calvin—that is, the strict Calvin of Geneva—as their founding father. Eventually Calvinist theology was also widely accepted by major groups of American Baptists; and even Unitarianism, which broke away from the Calvinist churches of New England during the 18th century, reflected the more rational impulses in Calvin's theology. More recently, Protestant interest in the social implications of the Gospel and Protestant Neo-Orthodoxy, as represented by Karl Barth and Reinhold Niebuhr, reflect the continuing influence of John Calvin.

Calvin's larger influence over the development of modern Western civilization has been variously assessed. The controversial "Weber thesis" attributed the rise of modern capitalism largely to habits encouraged by Puritanism, but Max Weber (1864–1920) avoided implicating Calvin himself. Much the same can be said about efforts to link Calvinism to the rise of early modern science; Puritans were prominent in the scientific movement of 17th-century England, but Calvin himself was indifferent to the science of his own day.

A somewhat better case can be made for Calvin's influence on political theory. His own political instincts were highly conservative, and he preached the submission of private persons to all legitimate authority. But, like Italian humanists of the 15th and 16th centuries, he personally preferred a republic to a monarchy; and in confronting the problem posed by rulers who actively opposed the spread of the Gospel, he advanced a theory of resistance, kept alive by his followers, according to which lesser magistrates might legitimately rebel against kings. And, unlike most of his contemporaries, Calvin included among the proper responsibilities of states not only the maintenance of public order but also a positive concern for the general welfare of society. Calvinism has a place, therefore, in the evolution of liberal political thought. His most durable influence, nevertheless, has been religious. From Calvin's time to the present, Calvinism has meant a peculiar seriousness about Christianity and its ethical implications.

**William J. Bouwsma**, 65, is Sather Professor of History at the University of California, Berkeley. Born in Ann Arbor, Michigan, he received an AB (1943), an MA (1947), and a PhD (1950) from Harvard. He is the author of, among other books, *Venice and the Defense of Republican Liberty* (1968) and *John Calvin: A Sixteenth-Century Portrait* (1988).

# The Third Way

PHILLIP E. L. GREENE

*"They increased so rapidly that the world feared an uprising by them . . ."*

—Sebastian Fraenk, 1531

As the Reformation in Germany focused entirely around the figure of Martin Luther, another religious revolt, simultaneous and close by, swelled about two other men who also came to doubt and challenge the doctrines and practices of Rome. Though in the end neither of the men, Erasmus of Rotterdam and Huldrych Zwingli, were to accept the new religion they had been instrumental in creating, their movement was to spread so rapidly and attract such fervent devotees that it became one of the most persecuted Christian sects in European history.

## Breaking the Grip of Rome

One can debate whether the Renaissance gave rise to technological advances or those advances gave rise to the Renaissance, but the rediscovery and fascination with classical knowledge coupled with the ability to disseminate that knowledge and make it available to the general public initiated a re-examination of almost every aspect of science, art, philosophy and religion that would ultimately result in the fragmentation of the Church. The Enlightenment would break the grip of Rome upon knowledge and, especially, on thought.

Among those who were educated in the early stages of the Renaissance was a boy from Rotterdam named Geert Geertsen (*c.*1466–1536). Although he was almost certainly the illegitimate son of a priest and a young woman, Geertsen was given the best education. In the mid 1480s, Geertsen entered a monastery, where he continued his education and took vows in his mid 20s. However, rather than applying himself to the priesthood, he began travels throughout the major centers of Europe, studying in Paris, Italy and England. Assuming the name Erasmus, he began to make contact with many of the most important minds of his time, including John Colet, Martin Luther, Philip Melancthon, Thomas Linacre, William Grocyn and even Thomas More.

While he took a position with Queen's College at Cambridge University for a period, Erasmus declined many highly prestigious and well paying posts, believing that they would inhibit his intellectual freedom. During his time in England, Erasmus undertook a new Latin translation of the New Testament. Published in 1516, his *Novum Instrumentum omne, diligenter ab Erasmo Rotterdam* became the single most-used source of Biblical study. The second edition, in fact—which substituted the word *Testamentum* for *Instrumentum*—was the book from which the editors of the King James Bible would later work.

## A Troubled Priest

About the same time that Erasmus was corresponding with men such as More, another young priest had begun working in Eisendeln, Switzerland. Huldrych Zwingli had been born in Wildhaus, near Zurich, to parents with close ties to the Church. When his father's brother moved to Wesen in 1487 to take the post of pastor there, young Zwingli went along to study for the cloth. However, both his uncle and his father had decided that the boy would study in accordance with the new ideas and methods that had been growing throughout the land. Zwingli studied at several of the finest schools in Switzerland, including those of Gregory Buenzli and Heinrich Woelfli. He ended up taking his Master's degree from Basel before entering church life.

But from the start Zwingli was troubled by things he had discovered. Like Erasmus, Zwingli had met and conversed with many prominent men who had opened his mind to new ideas. In addition, while in Milan, Zwingli had discovered a 200-year-old liturgical text which he found to differ strikingly from what he'd learned in his studies. Even as he began his service, Zwingli was coming to the conclusion that, from the very beginning, the Church had been teaching different truths in different places.

As early as 1519, Zwingli had preached against abuses and corruption by Church and clergy. With his doubts troubling him, Zwingli had few places to turn. Like most priests of the period, Zwingli had never read the Bible, and instead relied on the lessons of his teachers. Finally, feeling that he had to find some comfort, he decided to read the Bible and search for some reconciliation. The Bible he read was the one translated by Erasmus. This interested Zwingli in other writings of the scholar and he began an exchange of letters with Erasmus.

Over time, Zwingli became known for his excellent mind as well as his rhetorical skills and he was offered the Leut-Priestship of Zurich. It was a position he accepted, even though his doubts about the Roman Church had been steadily growing. He had come to believe above all that the Scriptures, not the Church, were the foundation and source of Christian belief and that Jesus, rather than Mary, was the chief intercedant between the people and God. Even so, Zwingli was well respected and was installed in the Church at Zurich. Therefore, in 1522, when he authored a list of 67 Theses (some scholars number them at 65), enumerating his differences with the Church and its practices, it was not taken lightly.

## The Disputations of Zurich

While Luther was persecuted in Germany for his 95 Theses centering solely on indulgences, Swiss law allowed that before any serious change was made in church practice it must first be granted public debate. On 29 January 1523, Zwingli spoke to an assemblage of clerics from the Swiss cantons detailing those things that he felt must change.

Zwingli based each of his points upon a strict reading of the New Testament and supported his arguments by saying that the Bible was the highest authority on the religion. Chief among his disputes were transubstantiation and infant baptism. The Church taught that during the Eucharist, through a miracle initiated by the priest, the bread and wine of communion became the actual body and blood of Jesus. But Zwingli found no supporting evidence of this in the Scriptures. Additionally, his reading of the New Testament led him to believe that only those who could make a conscious choice to convert to Christianity and to become baptized could be considered true Christians. Because of this, he argued, infant baptism was not only ineffective but also imprisoned the soul of the child and condemned it to hell by misleading the future adult that he or she had been saved.

Two more debates were held, one in October 1523 and the other in January 1524, which amounted mostly to a last-ditch attempt of the old guard to preserve what little of their ways they might. By the last days of 1524, Zwingli had secured the changes he wished within Zurich. Convents for both men and women had been abolished; all manner of decorative arts—including music—had been removed from church buildings and services; and, in perhaps the most drastic change, in 1523, the Great Minster of the Last Supper was observed under a liturgy written by Zwingli himself. In it, men and women sat on opposite sides of a long table that extended down the center aisle of the church. Down the middle of this was passed the bread and wine to be distributed and consumed. This is the single event which many experts acknowledge as the advent of the Swiss Reformation.

## The Internal Division

Sometime prior to 1522, Zwingli had brought together several men in a study group. Among these men were Conrad Grebel and Felix Manz, both knowledgeable in Latin, Greek and Hebrew, and both noted for their intellect. While the original purpose of the group had been to study cultural matters, it found itself increasingly drawn to issues of religion and they had begun a systematic examination of the Bible, leading to the positions taken by Zwingli in his Disputations. But while the group agreed on what was right and wrong concerning the doctrine, they disagreed strongly on how best to effect change.

Both Grebel and Manz were zealots who wanted to aggressively pursue their reforms. Zwingli disagreed, feeling that drastic steps would only bring uproar and trouble. Zurich had already removed itself from Papal authority and declared itself an evangelical city, and Zwingli was cautious about going too far too fast. In fact, Zwingli had become convinced, sometime about 1522–3, that there were those who could not or would not make public confession of their faith and submit to a second baptism and that removing them from the Church was impossible. This, along with the vehemence of Grebel and Manz, caused Zwingli to distance himself from the group and eventually to renounce them. In 1525, Zwingli opposed his former adherents before the Great Council of Zurich and won over the authorities who then pronounced Grebel and Manz radicals. That same year, the Council decreed that it would no longer permit public debate on the issue of infant baptism.

Grebel and Manz had befriended a disillusioned priest named George Blaurock, who wished to sever himself from Rome's authority. He had come to accept what was called "believer's baptism". In defiance of the new statute, he requested it from Grebel and was christened. In turn, he then baptized Grebel, and, owing to the fact that Grebel was not of the clergy, but a lay person, it is Grebel who is noted as being the first Anabaptist.

## The Spread of Faith and Fear

Both Grebel and Manz were strong evangelists and believed in spreading their faith. Calling themselves the Brethren and seeing themselves as the Third Way—the other two being the Reformed church and Lutheranism—the two men began to gather about them others who had become disaffected or disillusioned with the Papal church. In 1527, they met with other leaders of the movement at Schleitheim, Switzerland, to discuss the basic tenets of the new way. The conclusion of this meeting was a Confession of Faith consisting of seven points upon which the assemblage agreed. In addition to adult baptism, the separation of church and state and the rejection of transubstantiation, the Confession also listed beliefs regarding excommunication of errant members, the responsibilities of church leaders and a law prohibiting violence or the holding of public office by any member.

Not only did the new preachers challenge the idea that only the priesthood was capable of interceding with God, challenging the power and influence of the priestly class, the Peasants' Revolt in Germany had brought to light another issue even more troubling to the established authorities. The Peasants' Revolt, which began in 1524, was a bloody and ruthless struggle in which peasants from the southeastern Black Forest region rose up against their masters, in part due to religious reasons and the allegiances required of them. The small group taking shape in Switzerland supported the principles of the commoners and declared that, to be truly holy, no person could be required to take an oath. This, they pointed out, was mandated by the passage in which Jesus told his followers that they could not serve two masters but had to choose between the authority of God and the authority of Man.

To the religious and secular princes of Europe, this was a nightmarish concept. While the feudal system of land bondage had fallen, rulers inside and outside of the Church recognized the dangers of an entire segment of populace who would refuse to swear fealty to them. Fears of anarchy and complete rebellion flooded Europe.

In 1526, the Council of Zurich, the city that had first recognized and accepted the ideas propounded by the new faith, made it illegal under penalty of death to be an Anabaptist. Even Zwingli had begun to speak out vehemently against the very beliefs he had helped formulate, calling the Anabaptist movement a false religion. In his position in that city, he threw many Anabaptists into prison.

While Grebel died in 1526 of the Plague, his companion Manz found himself imprisoned on several occasions because of his refusal to deny his convictions. Finally losing patience, the Zurich authorities sentenced him to death by drowning. This was carried out in January 1527; two years later, the fugitive Blaurock was captured in Tyrol and burned at the stake in Clausen.

Still, many converts flocked to the new sect, and as the belief spread over Europe, so spread the persecutions. Bavaria executed 223 Brethren between 1527–81. In 1529, the nobility of Europe met at Speyers and declared that all Anabaptists were to be executed. In 1530, Zurich went so far as to begin executing anyone convicted of even harboring an Anabaptist. Authorities in the Rhine Valley were so intent on suppressing the new religion that, according to contemporary sources, the night sky was continually lit by those being burned at the stake. And the followers of Grebel and Manz were pursued not only by Rome and the Inquisition; even the newly formed churches of Luther and John Calvin fiercely persecuted them. Some accounts place the number of martyred Anabaptists by 1535 at more than 50,000.

## Refuge and Denial

The idea of simplicity and primitivism in religion was attractive to many common people, but it also had its supporters among the nobility, mostly those of Protestant bent. In 1526, the Brethren were offered refuge in the territory of Moravia, and by 1530, several Swiss cantons began to officially tolerate Anabaptists.

But popular opinion turned further against the Anabaptists following the disastrous Munster Rebellion of 1534–35, a revolt lead by radical Anabaptist John Matthys. After breaking away from the main church, Matthys commanded his followers to set up their own Kingdom of God on earth by, among other things, adopting the practice of polygamy. When his followers defended their hold on the city of Munster with uncharacteristic violence, they were put down in a bloody and short-lived battle with the Westphalian authorities. Although few Anabaptists approved of what happened in Munster, widespread persecution of the sect followed.

William of Orange, the Dutch Protestant leader, was among the first nobles to offer asylum to the Brethren in 1577. In 1579, the Union of Utrecht granted all Dutch citizens freedom of religion and became a haven for many of the Anabaptist sects that were beginning to branch off from the original core. During the years 1527–36, the original group had begun to fragment into other, more narrowly focused sects that, while still essentially Anabaptist, took on their own individualized beliefs in addition. Of these, two major sects were to endure: the Mennonites, named for Dutch founder Menno Simons, who had gathered his own group of followers in 1536, and a later division within that church, led by Jakob Ammann, today known as the Amish.

For nearly a hundred years, the Netherlands remained one of the few sanctuaries for the Anabaptists but gradually, other areas became more lenient. In 1664, the Palatinate granted tolerance and accepted large numbers of Anabaptist immigrants and other pockets of acceptance by different nobles began to develop here and there across northern Europe. Also, by 1735, Amish Anabaptists were appearing on the passenger lists for ships coming to the New World.

However, it was the Russian Empress Catherine the Great who would be the rescuer of the Anabaptist people. Even shortly after her ascension as Catherine II in 1762, the Empress had opened her recently won lands in the Volga region to any and all immigrants who were found acceptable. The offer was especially attractive to religious groups who had been severely repressed in Prussia and parts of Germany and among the first to take up the offer was a group of Moravian Mennonites. Moving into the lands around Saratov, they found not only tolerance, but also a fertile field for evangelizing the native Tartars.

Catherine, after winning the Azov River region from Turkey, offered a special invitation to the Mennonites in the Danzig region. She wanted to enlist the aid of hard-working farmers to set a good example for the nomadic tribes there and the Mennonite sect had gained a reputation for turning even the worst of land into highly productive farms. By 1788, Mennonite Anabaptists were forming colonies around Choritz, Molotschna and, later, Berthgal, Borsenko and Grossfuerstenland, among other areas. In Catherine's Russia, the Anabaptists would enjoy their most peaceful and least harassed period. While exact numbers are impossible to site, the most reliable sources put the total number of Mennonite immigrants to Russia in 1788 at around 8,000. By 1874, those numbers had increased to 45,000, as Anabaptists fled from increasing persecution in the rest of Europe.

The Russians and the Turks engaged in nearly continual warfare through the 18th and 19th centuries. In 1875, Bosnians revolted against their Turkish rulers and Russia supported the rebellion. The Russian military called for more fighting men, and in response Czar Alexander II revoked the Anabaptists' exemption from military service. At first, the Brethren were allowed to serve with alternative services, performing non-violent duties. But as the century drew to a close and the Bolshevik Revolution arose, many more indulgences were taken from the sect causing more and more to flee to other parts of the world. The new regime in Russia brought distrust; suspicion grew toward the Anabaptists and persecutions again began. Many were jailed, exiled or killed and when famine hit in the 1920s, the existence of the Anabaptist community in Russia came to a close. Those who did not die were exiled or immigrated, mostly to either North or South America.

## What Makes an Anabaptist?

Defining Anabaptism can be as difficult as tracing its history. Even though the doctrines were set down in writing as early as 1527, the Anabaptist faith was never a centralized, formal religion in the way that Catholicism and many of the Protestant religions were. Therefore, just as there is some disagreement as to the origins of the sect, so there are disagreements as to what sects were—or are—Anabaptist.

Generally, and literally speaking, a religion is Anabaptist as long as it believes in adult baptism. The name Anabaptist was given the early followers of Zwingli, Grebel *et al* as derision; the Greek prefix ana, meaning again, was meant to suggest that these dissenters were being redundant and foolish. It must be remembered, though, that the Anabaptists did not believe that they were "re-baptizing". It was their belief that the baptism of an infant was invalid and therefore their baptism as an adult was actually the first. It must also be kept in mind that, while this is the area focused on by the opponents of the faith, it was not the only—nor necessarily even the most important—of their beliefs.

The Confessions of Schleitheim sought to set down in a single document of ideas of the Swiss leaders such as Grebel, Manz and others. But this did not stop an evolution and divergence of other sects developing, most of which no longer exist or do so in such small numbers as to be nearly invisible.

There are, today, three main bodies of the original groups of Anabaptist believers. These exist mainly in the United States and Canada, although there are congregations which exist in most other parts of the world. The two best known groups, of course, are the Mennonites and the Amish.

The Mennonites originated in the Netherlands around 1536 when Menno Simons, a follower of Grebel, began his ministry there. Some experts believe that he did so in response to the disastrous Munster rebellion of 1535 when hundreds, if not thousands, of fanatics tried to establish what they believed to be the Kingdom of God on earth. Simons taught a devout pacifism and a complete separation between church and state. He also believed in maintaining a segregation between the followers of his faith and the outside world, which was to lead to perhaps the most vehement suspicions and persecutions during the following centuries.

The Amish branched from the Mennonites under the leadership of Jakob Ammann. The major differences between Ammann's followers and those of Simons is that the Amish do not believe in sustaining that aloofness with outsiders and, in some respects, accept modern ways. Where some more conservative Mennonite communities turn away from electricity, automobiles and other so-called "modern conveniences" the Amish, on at least some level, may make uses of them. But differences exist even within the Amish communities and have resulted in further fragmentation, creating a diversity not unlike those in many Protestant sects and making it nearly impossible to starkly define one from another.

The third, and smallest, of the Anabaptist sects existing today are the Hutterites, a branch that emerged in the 16th century under the leadership of Jakob Hutter. While sharing the basic Anabaptist beliefs, the Hutterites formed their own community based on the communal life suggested in 2 Corinthians and it is this which distinguishes them from the other groups.

All three main bodies share the beliefs of freedom of religion, separation of church and state, the reliance on the Scriptures as the sole authority of Christianity and the rejection of both infant baptism and transubstantiation as the foundation of their faiths.

Similarly, in Nazi Germany, Anabaptists were thrown into concentration camps and executed for their pacifism. Thousands died in the Holocaust.

## A Final Refuge

Those Anabaptists who emigrated to the New World generally did better than those who remained behind. The first Nonconformist leaders in the New World, such as William Penn and George Fox, sent invitations to their fellow Brethren, offering religious freedom and excellent, plentiful farmland. As early as 1683, Brethren were coming to Pennsylvania, settling in the Germantown area.

In the early 1800s, the Napoleonic Wars and the widespread revocation of immunity from conscription brought a second wave of Anabaptist immigrants. However, another war signaled its end. When the Civil War broke out between the Northern and Southern states, the Brethren dedicated to pacifism and non-involvement in political affairs stayed away. While some moved farther west to avoid the war—settling in Iowa, present-day North Dakota and other northwestern territories, or in Canada, overall, immigration to North America slowed to a trickle.

Predictably, given the turmoil of the Crimean War, most of the Anabaptist immigrants in the late 19th and early 20th centuries came from Russia.

Between the years 1873–80, 8,000 Anabaptists settled in the US and 2,000 made their homes in Canada. After the Russian Revolution in 1917, nearly 19,000 Anabaptists fled Russia to find refuge in Canada alone. This mass emigration continued during Hitler's regime in Germany. And while Anabaptists still faced criticism and derision for their refusal to go to war or swear allegiance to a government, for the most part, the different factions found relief from the official pogroms of Europe.

From *History Magazine,* Vol. 6, No. 1, October/November 2004, pp. 39–43. 

# Vlad Dracula's War on the Turks

**Brilliant, complex and unmatched for sheer cruelty, Vlad III Dracula drove the Turks out of his native Wallachia in 1462, only to be deposed from his throne.**

WILL ROMANO

Five and a half centuries after his death, the Turks still equate the name Dracula with evil, and they are not referring to Bram Stokers fictional vampire. In 1462, when the real Dracula retreated from an attack on the Turks in the Danube River valley, he left what history records as "a forest of the impaled"—20,000 Turkish prisoners rotting on large stakes outside the city of Tirgoviste. So cruel was this Dracula that he enjoyed dining while watching mass executions, usually by the slow death of impalement, although he was not averse to watching people skinned or boiled alive. By the time he was deposed, he had killed between 40,000 and 100,000 people. Ironically, he prided himself on his sense of fairness.

Vlad III Dracula came of age during external and internal turmoil that ravaged the Wallachain Danube and Transylvania's Carpathian Mountains. Fifteenth-century Wallachia (now part of Romania) was not strong enough to fend off either the Ottoman Empire or the Kingdom of Hungary. Consequently, Turks forced the principality to pledge a policy of neutrality. More often than not, however, Dracula's father, the Wallachian prince Vlad II Dracul, betrayed treaties for personal or religious reasons.

Vlad Dracula was barely 12 when he became a pawn of his father's political maneuvering. Vlad Dracul gave the young Vlad and his 7-year-old brother Radu to the Ottoman Sultan Murad II in 1442 as human peace offerings, hostages to allay the sultan's fear of further Wallachian attacks.

But Vlad Dracul knew he could not maintain his promise of neutrality. Ten years earlier he had taken an oath to an order—the Order of the Dragon—to protect the Holy Roman Empire. In fact, his very name, Dracul, which meant dragon, was bestowed on him by that order—Dracula means "son of the dragon." Just a year after swearing neutrality to the Turks, Dracul took part in a Bulgarian crusade called for by the pope, though he was still a subject of Murad. The Bulgarian campaign ended with a disastrous defeat of the Christians at Varna in 1444.

Once home from Bulgaria, Dracul and the other Christian leaders feared that the victorious Turks would now dominate Bulgaria, Wallachia and other European countries. Against the better interests of his sons and his own country, Dracul laid siege to Giurgiu, a Turkish stronghold on the Danube. But he failed due to a lack of Hungarian support, having earlier made an enemy of János Hunyadi, a leader and hero in Hungarian service (each blamed the other for the defeat at Varna). This, plus a very harsh winter, brought Dracul's siege of Giurgiu to a stalemate. Then in a sudden change of allegiances, Dracul promised the Turks peace. And as a show of good faith, he returned some 12,000 Bulgarian refugees who had fled into Wallachia seeking asylum from Murad.

Dracul's old enemy from the Bulgarian crusade, János Hunyadi, was incensed at this capitulation to the Turks. As a gesture of his anger, he backed Vladislav Dan II, a member of a rival family, the Danesti, for prince of Wallachia, rather than one from Dracul's own Mircea lineage. The throne of Wallachia was not necessarily passed from father to son. The ruler, or voivode, was elected by the country's boyars, the landowning nobles. The lineage was split into two factions—the Mircea and the Danesti clans. In 1447 Hunyadi killed Dracul and another of his sons.

While their father waged battle, the young Dracula and his brother Radu endured an unhappy captivity at the sultan's palace. The fiery Dracula was frequently reprimanded, sometimes physically, and Radu had to fend off the sexual advances of the sultan's son. Even in those early years one could see that Radu and Dracula were headed in different directions—Radu "The Handsome" was a compromiser, consumed by the pleasures of the palace, whereas Dracula was the defiant one. In spite of, or perhaps because of, their different personalities, the boys would eventually become two distinctly different rulers of Wallachia.

After his father's death, Dracula was released, only to be impressed into the Turkish army. The 17-year-old, having vowed to ascend to the throne of his homeland, got backing from the sultan in 1448 for an invasion of Wallachia. After two months of fighting there, he was driven out by Vladislav Dan. But these were turbulent and shifting times. Not long afterward, during a subsequent political upheaval, Dracula was forced to seek Hunyadi's support. Hunyadi not only refused it, but topped off his rejection with a plot to kill the young Dracula. Tipped off, Dracula slipped away to Brasov.

Then matters took a surprising turn. Relations between Hunyadi and his propped-up prince began to cool, partly because of Vladislav Dan's warming to Murad's son and successor, Mehmed, who was now Sultan Mehmed II. In consequence, Hunyadi championed young Dracula's claim to the Wallachian throne. It may seem odd that Dracula would forge an alliance with the man who was responsible for the deaths of his father and brother, but one must understand that he was driven by two motives—power and revenge. By ascending his father's throne he could achieve both. He therefore swore allegiance to the new Hungarian king, Ladislas Posthumous, and Hunyadi gave him responsibility for guarding the Transylvanian border from Turkish attacks.

Taking what he felt was rightly his, Hunyadi seized the duchies of Amlas and Fagaras in Transylvania, incurring the wrath of Vladislav Dan. When the Turks moved on Belgrade in 1456, Hunyadi ordered Dracula to stay at Sibiu, thus obliging the Turks to split their forces and keep men at Sibiu. Meanwhile, Hunyadi, his professional fighting men and John of Capistrano, a 70-year-old crusading monk who organized a peasant army, plunged into Turkish-held Serbia, routed Mehmed's 90,000-man army and relieved Belgrade.

**Dracula instilled in the common people a feeling of loyalty to a unified country. Some 50 years later, Florentine political theorist Niccolo Machiavelli would help stir those same feelings in Italy with his 1513 book *The Prince,* which some say may be loosely based on Dracula's career.**

Before the end of the campaign, Dracula, with a small band of Hungarians, mercenaries and disgruntled boyars, invaded Wallachia in July 1456, and moved on Vladislav's capital of Tirgoviste. Not much is known of the actual fight, but some historians believe that the invaders won an overpowering victory—at any rate, Vladislav Dan was killed, possibly by Dracula himself.

Just as Christian hopes were riding high in Eastern Europe, Hunyadi and John of Capistrano died of bubonic plague. At the same time the Turkish army was recovering its strength and vigor. The Ottomans' manner of enlisting and training a national army was far superior to that of their enemies. Young Christian males in Turkish-held Europe were inducted into military service, converted to Islam and trained into highly skilled warriors called janissaries (new soldiers). These troops, which first came to prominence about 1330, were in the sultan's service for 20 years and were grouped in units of eight to 12 called *odas.*

As prince of Wallachia for a second time, Vlad III Dracula knew of the sultan's growing might, but he had his own problems. He had to juggle the interests of the Ottoman Empire, Hungary and Wallachia's political infrastructure just to maintain balance. Vlad wished to carry on his father's crusading tradition, but he needed to strengthen his power at home first.

To do that, he employed mercenaries called *armas,* whose duty it was to impale anyone who stepped out of line. Called "Kaziklu Bey" (impaler prince) by the Turks, and Vlad "Tepes" (pronounced Tzepesh) by his own subjects in reference to his favorite form of execution, Dracula would not tolerate subversion of any kind. Because of his harsh leadership, gory stories of Vlad's reign spread from Germany to Russia. Though those accounts were written with various political and religious agendas and cannot be taken as completely accurate, they illustrate how Dracula was feared and despised in his own time, while laying the groundwork for the vampire myth.

"He invited all his principal vassals and the noblemen in his land to a banquet," a manuscript in Nürnberg claimed in 1488. "When the meal was done he turned to the oldest and asked how many princes he remembered who had been rulers in that land. Thus, he asked one after another. They all said as many as each knew. One said fifty, one thirty. So that there were none among them who spoke of seven. Then he had them all impaled. There were five hundred in number."

According to Romanian folklore, when Dracula had discovered that boyars of Tirgoviste had buried his brother alive, he invited those who he felt were responsible to an Easter dinner, and as they were eating, he seized them and marched them, in their Easter clothes, to the site of his future castle, Poienari. According to the story, "They were put to work until the clothes were torn and they were naked."

Much has been made of Dracula's relationship with the boyars. By 1457 there were still three boyars on the 12-man council who had served Dracula's enemy, Vladislav Dan. And there had been as many as 18 princes of Wallachia from 1418 to 1456 alone. No matter how strong Dracula was, could he trust the boyars—or, for that matter, could they trust him?

Dracula also had troubles with the Saxon merchants in the Transylvanian towns of Amlas and Fagaras. Accusing them of unfair trade practices, Dracula pitted himself against the villages and a pretender to the throne, Vladislav II's brother Dan III (Dracula's uncle), whom he later assassinated.

Meanwhile, Dracula was distancing himself from the Ottoman Empire. He forged an agreement with the sultan, in part to stop the Turks from interfering in Wallachian affairs. In 1459, Pope Pius II convened the Congress of Mantua to call for European leaders to embark on a three-year Crusade against the Turks. Holy Roman Emperor Frederick III pledged to fight the infidels, but Dracula was the only ruler to actively respond.

In 1460, Sultan Mehmed II seized the fortress city of Smederevo in Serbia, not far from the Wallachian border. In addition to that city, the sultan commanded two other major points along the Danube, Giurgiu and Nicopolis. Adding salt to an opening wound was the death of Dracula's ally and friend Mihaly Szilagyi, János Hunyadi's brother-in-law and uncle of the new king of Hungary, Matyás Corvinus. While on an exploratory mission in Bulgaria, Szilagyi was caught by the Turks, who pressed him for information on Hungarian military might and Dracula's oath to Corvinus. When Szilagyi would not cooperate, he was sawed in half before the sultan's eyes.

At that point, Dracula, combining megalomania with vengeance, decided that Wallachia should stop paying tribute to the sultan and cease serving as a buffer between Hungary and the Ottoman Empire. If he wanted national independence, however, he would have to fight for it, and fight he did, instilling in the common people a feeling of loyalty to a unified country. Some 50 years later, Florentine political theorist Niccolò Machiavelli would help stir those same feelings in Italy with his 1513 book *The Prince,* which some say may be loosely based on Dracula's career.

Most historians believe that by 1461, if not earlier, Dracula's tribute payments to the sultan were three years in arrears. He owed 30,000 ducats and no longer provided 500 young boys annually for the janissary corps. Mehmed was then on a campaign in Asia Minor, but he ordered Dracula to meet his representative, Hamza Pasha, at Tirgoviste and explain his delinquency. Soon afterward, however, the sultan chanced to obtain intercepted letters, sent by Dracula to Hungary, vowing allegiance to Corvinus against the Turks. Mehmed secretly ordered Hamza Pasha to change the meeting place to the fortress of Giurgiu, where the garrison would be waiting to arrest the Wallachian prince. A second envoy, Hamza Bey, was sent to inform the pasha of Dracula's departure from Tirgoviste. As in the past, Dracula benefited from a tip; instead of being ambushed, he captured both Hamza Bey and Hamza Pasha.

In late 1461, Dracula laid his plans for breaking free of Turkish rule by conquering fortresses along the Danube. Disguised as a Turk, Dracula tricked the garrison at Giurgiu. "As the Turks opened the gates," he wrote to King Matyás in February 1461, "our soldiers mixing with theirs entered the fortress and conquered the city which I then set on fire."

From Giurgiu, Dracula began plundering fortresses and ports along the Bulgarian Danube to the Black Sea, transporting his infantry in barges with Wallachian cavalry riding along the flanks. As he burned cities and villages, ravaged food supplies and impaled Turks, many liberated Bulgarians, Greeks and Serbians sought asylum in Wallachia.

Dracula's letter to Matyás Corvinus recounted the exact number of deaths in each town. In Giurgiu, on both sides of the river, there were 6,414 dead; at Eni Sala, 1,350; at Durostor, 6,840; at Nicopolis and Ghighen, 1,138. He claimed the total to be "23,884 Turks and Bulgarians in all, not including those who were burned in their houses and whose heads were not presented to our officials." Dracula, also known as Vlad the Impaler, even sent two bags of chopped off ears, noses and heads—including the head of Hamza Bey—to Corvinus as proof of his victory. Other unfortunate Turkish prisoners were impaled on long stakes with rounded ends, to prolong the agony of dying, and left to rot in the hills surrounding Tirgoviste. It was said that some Turks were so frightened of "Kaziklu Bey" that they retreated into Asia Minor. Once Dracula reached the Black Sea, however, he halted, knowing that his amphibious army would be overextended and outnumbered.

Mehmed was furious, but did not campaign in the winter when the Danube would be frozen. Knowing that, Dracula appealed to Corvinus for military support. Corvinus had indeed received papal funds for just such crusading, but he was also engaged in a power struggle with the Holy Roman Emperor, so he kept most of the money and released only a small contingent of soldiers to Dracula—just enough to justify his accepting the papal funds.

Mehmed, in the meantime, mustered his forces, which he first dispatched overland through Bulgaria to Braila, where some 18,000 Turkish troops looted and pillaged the Wallachian port and enslaved its populace. To counteract that, according to Italian chronicler Donado de Lezze, Dracula screened his retreat to the right bank of the Danube by launching a series of lightning raids against the Turkish rear guard, killing some 8,000 troops.

Dracula's fighting retreat was successful throughout the winter, but by May 1462 the warm weather had restored safe passage along the Danube. At that point, Mehmed curtailed his Asia Minor campaign and joined his forces in Europe. Though Dracula commanded the river, the Turks could strike anywhere along it. If Dracula miscalculated, there would be dire consequences.

The sultan's troops were equipped with long spears, bows and arrows, an arsenal of firearms, 120 cannons and a wealth of experienced military commanders. The size of his army is still debated, but it probably numbered about 60,000 men, more than a third of them janissaries. Mehmed also employed slave soldiers as advance guards, in what he called his Ceausi Division. They were literally fighting for their freedom, but if someone showed cowardice, he was whipped, beheaded or both.

Dracula's army was largely made up of peasants, with a small number of able-bodied veterans equipped with axes, swords, hammers, scimitars and bows and arrows. Those best prepared for battle were armored boyar cavalrymen who wielded swords, knives and lances. Russian chronicles put Dracula's force at around 30,000 men, including 22,000 foot soldiers, but a letter written by Ven Petrus de Thomasius, the Venetian ambassador to Hungary, stated that Dracula had only 22,000 men in total.

In late May, the sultan led 25 galleys and 150 ships up the Bosporus Strait, the unofficial boundary between Asia and Europe, intending to join a second force assembled at Nicopolis. Ultimately the plan was to reclaim Giurgiu and head to Tirgoviste. Spies informed Dracula of the sultan's plan to cross the Danube at Vidin, near Nicopolis. At first Dracula's archers held off the approaching Turks, but after six days of frustration and heavy Turkish casualties, Mehmed led his soldiers and their weapons across the Danube while his cannons drew the Wallachian army's fire. An Ottoman chronicle stated: "[Dracula] was followed by the Great Sultan with the rest of the glorious army; they inflicted such a merciless punishment on Wallachia that it seemed as if the end of the world had come, shedding much blood with their terrifying swords."

Dracula's retreat northward was interrupted by a few minor skirmishes. Faced with the enormity of what lay before him, he saw only one alternative—a scorched earth policy. Dracula burned villages and crops, killed his own people, slaughtered cattle and poisoned wells as he made his way back through Wallachia, while the surviving population migrated to the island monastery of Snagov and the Carpathian Mountains. Dracula's soldiers, familiar with the vast forest terrain, set traps and ambushed his pursuers. The weather also began to take a toll on the Turks. "There was not a drop of water to quench their thirst," wrote Turkish chronicler Tursun Bey. "The sun was so great that one could cook kebabs on the mail shirts of the [soldiers]."

Dracula's army was also undergoing steady attrition. Reasoning that chopping off the head would confuse the body, he became obsessed with getting at the sultan himself. Through his spies, he learned the location of Mehmed's camp in the mountains south of Tirgoviste and laid his plans to strike.

**He had done considerable damage, but he had failed to get to his primary target, Mehmen. . . . Dracula rewarded men who had been wounded in the front of their bodies, but told any who were wounded in the back, 'You are not a man, but a woman,' and then had them impaled.**

In what the Romanians would remember as the Night Attack of June 17, Dracula slashed his way into the sluggishly guarded Turkish camp. One account of the controversial assault, possibly dictated by Dracula himself, stated that late that evening he "provoked an incredible massacre without losing many men in such a major encounter, though there were many wounded."

According to the account of Asik-Pasa-Zade, the Turks stood their ground: "When [the Turks] realized that the attack was made by the devilish Tepes and that he himself led it, the soldiers remained still, allowing him to get closer to the Turkish army. When he was right in the middle of the army, the soldiers shouted, 'Allah be blessed!' and slaughtered them so badly that more than half of the infidels were killed."

Greek chronicler Laonic Chalkondyles may have written the most balanced view of the attack: "Using torchlight, [Dracula] proceeded with his army in closed ranks and in good order they headed directly for the Emperor's tents. Missing their target, they fell upon the tents of the vizier Machmut and Vizier Issac; and here there was a great battle and they killed the camels, donkeys and other pack animals. Fighting in closed ranks, they had no losses worth mentioning, but if one of them went astray he was immediately killed by the Turks."

The fighting continued until daybreak, but Dracula eventually fled the scene. He had done considerable damage, but he had failed to get to his primary target, Mehmed. Furious at the indecisive outcome, Dracula rewarded men who had been wounded in the front of their bodies, but told any who were wounded in the back, "You are not a man but a woman," and then had them impaled.

Dracula's bold but ultimately fruitless night attack was the turning point of the campaign. Weary of a bloody, ruinous war in which the prospects of victory seemed hopeless, most of his boyars were defecting to Radu, now backed by the sultan as successor to the Wallachian throne.

Mehmed proceeded to Tirgoviste, flanked by Radu and his army, at dawn's first light. As they approached the city, smoke filled the air—a byproduct of Dracula's scorched earth policy. Unmanned cannons stood in dormant impotence. Mehmed expected Dracula to defend his capital, but there was no food, water, cattle or men. The place was uninhabited, save for the inhuman spectacle that greeted them. In a mile-long ditch surrounding the city, the remains of Turkish prisoners, including Hamza Pasha, were rotting away on stakes. The troops found themselves in a veritable forest of the impaled.

"And there were large stakes on which they could see the impaled bodies," wrote Chalkondyles, "about twenty thousand of them. . . . The Emperor himself, in wonder, kept saying that he could not conquer the country of a man who could do such terrible and unnatural things. . . ."

That night, the Turks dug a deep trench around their camp in anticipation of Tepes' return. In the morning, when Dracula failed to show up, Mehmed, disheartened and dealing with an outbreak of plague that was decimating his troops, signaled a retirement eastward. Perhaps, for the first time, Mehmed felt the terror he had struck in other men's hearts when he impaled hapless victims after conquering Constantinople in 1453.

Meanwhile, Dracula's army was coming apart at the seams. Wallachian boyar Gales (Galesh) jumped ship. Dracula's heart had hardened toward Gales ever since he failed to mobilize his men during the night attack. Then, later in June 1462, Dracula's cousin, Stephen the Great, backed by the Ottoman fleet, attacked the fortress at Chilia, probably to ensure his borders. For eight days the two forces brutalized the castle with cannon fire, but incredibly, the small Wallachian and Hungarian garrison held off the double assault.

Some historians seriously doubt that there was ever a Moldavian-Turkish alliance, but it seems that Wallachian, Moldavian, Hungarian and Ottoman armies did clash at Chilia, though Dracula himself never reached the fortress. The siege of Chilia was unsuccessful (Stephen claimed it after a second attempt in 1465), but the mood in Wallachia had shifted. With his armies depleted (the losses in one battle totaled 2,000 as Wallachian heads danced at the ends of Turkish swords), Dracula managed to win one final victory at Buzau, about 40 miles southeast of the site of his night raid. It had little effect. He had already lost Bucharest, Braila and Tirgoviste. For Dracula, the cost in human life was immeasurable, and the sultan simply had more lives to spend for his cause.

In the fall of 1462, Dracula retreated southeast along the Arges River toward Poienari. Led by Radu, his pursuers set up camp on the opposite side of the Arges. Eventually, the Turkish infantry slinked across the river to administer a massive dose of gunpowder and cannon balls to Dracula's Poienari castle. Still, its sturdy walls did not crumble and the Turks paused to reorganize and storm it the next day. According to a popular Romanian legend, when Dracula's Transylvanian wife was given a written warning of the castle's impending doom, she cried, "I would rather have my body rot and be eaten by the fish of the Arges than be led into captivity by the Turks," then flung herself into the river below.

Dracula did not stay to see his castle wasted, and instead fled in darkness while his cannons fired on the Turks as a diversionary tactic. Some reports say he left behind a son who would later be raised by a Wallachian peasant. With a small band of men, Dracula reached the Transylvanian mountains and, having sent notice to Matyás Corvinus of his situation, hoped the Hungarian king would send relief. None came. Corvinus was still in Buda, anxiously awaiting the campaign's outcome. Desperately in need of money and men, Dracula traveled to Brasov, thinking he would get an audience with the king. Instead, he was detained and, in November 1462, arrested by Corvinus. There has been much speculation as to why Corvinus imprisoned Dracula, including his having made a secret treaty with Mehmed II, though there is no evidence of that. What is known is that Corvinus used forged letters to accuse and convict Dracula of siding with the Turks against Hungary.

Romanian folklore often blames the boyars for Dracula's downfall. But the fact is that he ran out of resources, men and support. Radu was already on the throne by July 1462, and many of the boyars who ruled under Dracula were expelled once Radu became prince.

Dracula was taken to Buda and spent nearly 12 years in the castle of Visegrad. Ironically, with Radu on the throne, Sultan Mehmed agreed to let Wallachia maintain its autonomy. One has to wonder what effect Dracula really had on the Ottoman Empire. Did his terror tactics make the Turks think twice about making it a pashalik (a Turkish province with an appointed ruler)? Kurt W. Treptow, in his book, *Vlad III Dracula: The Life and Times of the Historical Dracula,* pointed to an Ottoman chronicle as proof that the sultan had no intention of making it such, and invaded Wallachia simply to seat Radu: "The conquering Sultan gave the throne of that country to the brother of that wicked man, named Radu voievod [sic], who had been accepted by the Porte a long time before. . . ."

Some Romanian historians still maintain that the sultan's unwillingness to turn Wallachia into a Turkish province proved Dracula to be the ultimate victor in his 1462 campaign. Still, that view has been fiercely disputed and has all but left a historical hole in the last days of Dracula's second campaign.

Corvinus held Dracula in captivity until 1474, when he was released under the condition that he convert from Orthodox to Catholic Christianity. By November 1476, Dracula had regained the throne with the help of Hungary and Moldavia. Stephen finally made good on his promise and left behind troops to protect Dracula from internal squabbles. Later that same year, however, Dracula died in battle near Bucharest.

There is also much speculation about how the impaler prince died. Austrian chronicler Jacob Unrest wrote that Dracula fought the Turks unmercifully, only to be killed by assassins. Dracula, having dressed as a Turk, may have been done in by his own men. Either way, his head was chopped off, put in preservative honey and sent to the sultan, where it sat on the main parapet of his palace. Vlad III Dracula's third and final reign had lasted only two months.

# Article 35

# Women in War

**In the roughly organized armies of 16th century Europe, there was literally a woman with every man. They were partners in pillage.**

JOHN A. LYNN

"When you recruit a regiment of German soldiers today, you do not only acquire 3,000 soldiers; along with these you will certainly find 4,000 women and children." So observed Johann Jacob von Wallhausen in his 1615 treatise on war, Kriegskunst zu Fuss. During the 16th and 17th centuries, great crowds of camp women were not unusual; they were the rule. Not mere camp followers, women were an essential element of military forces in the field, providing many services to the troops. In fact, the presence of these women helps explain the very existence of early modern European armies and the conduct of war.

The tasks performed by camp women did include prostitution, but also traditional women's work like laundry, meal preparation and petty commerce, and even heavy camp labor—contemporary woodcuts often illustrate a soldier paired with a woman, who is usually bent under a heavier load than that borne by her male companion. The most important contribution of women in this era, however, was the seizing and managing of pillage. Without pillage, armies could not exist.

During the 16th and 17th centuries, European rulers, including Philip II of Spain and Louis XIII of France, commonly fielded armies they could not afford to pay or supply. Troops from the Spanish army of Flanders, for instance, charged in 1594 that they had not been paid for 100 months. Even when men did receive their pay, it was often insufficient to sustain them. A 1574 document complained that whereas a frugal soldier would need 10 pattards per day just for food, he received only four. Although soldiers were supposed to be fighting to earn money, one observer of the Thirty Years' War (1618–48) wrote, "If you will consider how their wages are paid, I suppose, you will rather think them Voluntaries, at least very generous, for doing the greatest part of their service for nothing." Some commanders even saw an advantage to paying troops irregularly. "To keep the troops together, it is a good thing to owe them something," observed the great Spanish general Ambrosio Spinola. His harsh logic held that troops would be less likely to desert if they expected to receive back pay in the future. However, while underpaying troops might keep an army together, it practically guaranteed a breakdown in discipline, as troops turned to plunder as a form of compensation.

Troops with empty pockets and empty stomachs took matters into their own hands. Some responded by mutiny; the Spanish army of Flanders, commanded by such great generals as the dukes of Alva and Parma, suffered more than 45 mutinies between 1572 and 1607, including the horrendous 1576 Sack of Antwerp.

Most troops sought sustenance and compensation on campaign by pillaging the civilian communities that lay in their paths. "It is deplorable that our soldiers dedicate themselves to pillage rather than to honourable feats," wrote Pierre de Brantôme of his experience during the French Religious Wars (1662–74). "But it is all due to their not being paid." Princes might issue high-sounding declarations condemning troops for abusing civilian populations, but the bitter reality was that if those same rulers actually eliminated such excesses, they would have had to disband their armies as unaffordable.

The practice of allowing soldiers to pillage permeated the era. It was accepted as a distasteful but practical necessity. "One finds enough soldiers when one gives them the freedom to live off the land, and allowing them to pillage supports them without pay," concluded the annual register of current affairs, the Mercure François, in 1622. French monarch Louis XIV (r. 1643–1715) offered the same observation in his memoirs for the year 1666: "Of late, some commanders are found who have made great armies subsist for a long time without giving them any pay other than the license of pillaging everywhere."

Pillage and its associated savagery—beatings, torture, rape and murder—certainly warranted condemnation, even when inflicted on civilians loyal to the enemy, However, raiders made little distinction between friend and foe, even victimizing the loyal subjects of the government served by the soldiers. One observer described shameful conduct by the Florentine Black Bands as they marched through friendly territory in 1527: "[They are] worse than Turks. In the Valdarno, they have sacked three Florentine villages, raped women and perpetrated other very cruel things." Troops fielded by the Bourbon kings of

France notoriously ravaged the French countryside during the first half of the 17th century.

Because pillage was officially outlawed—if actually tolerated—the take from plunder was not tallied in royal accounts, even though it constituted a high proportion of military personnel expenses. Consequently, the true size of the pillage economy will always remain more or less unknown. This is further compounded by the fact that pillage supported not only soldiers, but also the vast array of civilians who accompanied them in the field, including camp women, who mastered the brutal business of plundering.

A military force in the field during the early modern period did not resemble an army as we know it today. Soldiers constituted only part of a campaign community, in which they lived symbiotically with male and female noncombatants. Officers and soldiers employed servant boys. Teamsters hauled wagons and cannon using draught animals supplied by private contractors. Entrepreneurs supplied bread to armies, sending their own staffs, including bakers, into the field. A large collection of other tradesmen—blacksmiths, wheelwrights, carpenters—served the community. Merchants and sutlers sold essentials and amenities to the troops.

Comprising such a varied multitude, a campaign community rivaled in complexity and size all but the largest towns of the day. A force of 25,000 soldiers with its accompanying supporters represented a larger population than that of contemporary Bordeaux, Strasbourg, or Turin. It is no exaggeration to describe military camps as cities on the march.

The campaign communities, moreover, formed a world apart, living according to their own rules, which were often quite hostile to civilian society—and vice versa. A mercenary principle drove enlistment; most common soldiers joined the ranks because they had few other options and hoped to fare better on campaign. A German woodcut dating from the 1530s makes this point with a poem attached to an illustration of a would-be Landsknecht, the much-feared, heavily armed Germanic mercenary of the 16th century: A tailor complains, "I must sit long hours for little pay with which I can hardly survive," so he decides to try his luck in "the open field to the sound of pipes and drums." The Englishman Sydnam Poyntz confessed a similar reason for enlisting in the 1620s: "My necessitie forced mee, my Money being growne short, to take the manes of a private soldier." Women opted for camp life with much the same rationale.

This need to survive and a desire to prosper ensured that men and the women who joined them on campaigns would prey upon the unfortunate civilian communities that lay in their paths. Troops quartered in civilian homes abused their hosts; pillagers stole, raped and murdered. The result of such violence was a pervasive animosity toward armies that, in turn, inspired the campaign community to reject the civilian world, its mundane life and its standards of propriety.

Although common soldiers came from the peasantry and urban working classes themselves, they announced their separation from such origins by sporting distinctive and often outlandish apparel. Most extreme was the bizarre multicolored and slashed garb of Landsknechts, though soldiers of other nations adopted their own extreme fashions. An early 17th century description of Spanish infantry claimed, "It is the finery, the plumes and the bright colors which give spirit and strength to a soldier so that he can with furious resolution overcome any difficulty or accomplish any valorous exploit." These sons of the laboring classes transformed themselves from subservient sparrows to aggressive peacocks.

Campaign communities lived by codes that were libertine and brutal. Soldiers of the early modern era were known for drinking, gambling, wenching and fighting. The novelist Johann Jacob Christoffel von Grimmelshausen, who had fought in the Thirty Years' War, summed up the soldiers' lifestyle with its violence, suffering and poverty:

Their whole existence consisted of eating and drinking, going hungry and thirsty, whoring and sodomizing, gaming and dicing, guzzling and gorging, murdering and being murdered, killing and being killed, torturing and being tortured, terrifying and being terrified . . . pillaging and being pillaged.

Within this hard and hostile community, women performed a broad range of tasks. The most obvious, but by no means the most characteristic, employment was prostitution. The term "camp follower" is often regarded as synonymous with prostitute, and there is no question that prostitutes plied their trade with the troops. Many military authorities favored having them in camp for reasons of public order and efficiency. Public order argued that soldiers who relied on camp prostitutes for sex would be less likely to trouble respectable women; according to Mathieu de la Simonne, writing in the 1620s, "It is good for the local inhabitants, it is said, because their wives, daughters and sisters will be more in security." Efficiency justified bringing along a limited number of prostitutes to satisfy the men's urges instead of dragging along a far greater number of wives who would encumber armies.

Over time, however, tolerance of camp prostitution declined. Rising rates of venereal disease led commanders to see prostitutes as dangers to health, and the strict moral codes brought about by the Reformation and Counter-Reformation advocated marriage and condemned prostitution outright. Frederick William, the great elector of Brandenburg, banned prostitutes from his army by an article of war in September 1656, as did Louis XIV from French forces in the 1680s.

The great majority of camp women belonged to two other categories: wives and so-called "whores"—the unmarried female partners of soldiers. These women were not prostitutes, as each accompanied a single man, yet contemporary accounts often refer to them as "whores," and the officer in charge of keeping order among camp women on the march was known in German as a Hurenweibel, or whoremaster. The nature of the relationship between a soldier and his whore is suggested by the German practice of "May marriages," agreements to stay together for the campaign season, which traditionally began in May. Dionysius Klein, writing at the end of the 16th century, described such liaisons and their rationales:

German soldiers, no sooner an expedition arrives, saddle themselves with frivolous and loose women with whom they contract "May marriages," whom they drag here and there just as millers do their sacks. The soldiers enhance the situation by pretending that in war they cannot get along without women; they are needed to take care of clothes, equipment and valuables; and in cases of illness, injury or any other personal harm, the women are needed to nurse and take care of them.

Wives and whores applied themselves to traditional and necessary women's work. Laundering, for one, was almost exclusively a feminine chore that soldiers regarded as unmanly. In *The Life of Courage: The Notorious Thief, Whore and Vagabond,* Grimmelshausen has his female antiheroine, Courage, declare, "I refused to let [my husband] stay in the castle without me for fear he would be eaten up by lice, as there were no women to keep the men clean." Basic needlework also fell to women, who repaired clothes, stitched shirts and sewed linens. Nursing, too, was considered a particularly feminine talent. When Robert Venables, one of Cromwell's favored generals during the English Civil Wars, was censured for including his wife and allowing some soldiers to bring their wives on his disastrous expedition to the West Indies in 1654–55, he replied that experience in the Irish wars had demonstrated "the necessity of having that sex with an army to attend upon and help the sick and wounded, which men are unfit for." Cooking, although not narrowly defined as a woman's task, also fell to camp women.

Such gender-defined work was so valuable to an army's health and well-being that a certain number of useful women remained with regiments in the field even after most wives and whores were driven from camps in the late 17th century. From then until the French Revolution, a contingent of 15 to 20 women usually marched in the train of a French regiment, while the British brought along about six wives per 100 soldiers until the late 18th century.

Camp women also scrambled to earn whatever they could through petty commerce. Some became suffers (vivandières in French), peddling food, liquor, tobacco and sundries to officers and men. And camp women could be extremely creative in garnering money by more extraordinary schemes. During the occupation of Freiburg by the Swedes in the 1630s, one citizen complained of "the soldiers' abominable wives," who trespassed in local gardens, cut produce as soon as it appeared, and had the gall to sell what they did not consume in the Freiburg market.

Men with female partners enjoyed an advantage. Sir James Turner, in his Pallas Armata (1683), argued that during the 1624–25 Spanish siege of Breda, in the Netherlands, "The married Soldiers fared better, look'd more vigorously, and were able to do more duty than the Batchellors; and all the spite was done the poor women was to be called their husbands' mules by those who would have been glad to have had such mules themselves."

Turner's use of the term "mules" points to the heavy labor these formidable women performed. An anonymous handwritten German manuscript of 1612 detailed the load carried by women on the march:

Seldom is one found who does not carry at least 50 or 60 pounds. [The] soldier … loads straw and wood on her, to say nothing of the fact that many of them carry one, two or three children on their back. Normally, however, aside from the clothing they are wearing, they carry for the man one pair of breeches, one pair of stockings, one pair of shoes. And for themselves the same number of shoes and stockings, one jacket, two Hemmeter [shifts], one pan, one pot, one or two spoons, one sheet, one overcoat, one tent and three poles. They receive no wood for cooking in their billets, and so they pick it up on the way. And to add to their fatigue, they normally lead a small dog on a rope or even carry him in bad weather.

The presence of so many women in the train of the army constituted a sizable labor pool that field commanders were quick to exploit. They even participated, according to Wallhausen, in the hard physical labor of siege work: "The whores and the boys [of the camp] also helped in binding fascines, filling ditches, digging pits and mounting cannon in difficult places."

The most important contribution made by camp women lay beyond their traditional women's work, petty commercial ventures and taxing manual labor. First and foremost, they took part in pillaging, without which early modern forces could not have maintained themselves on campaign. Grimmelshausen's antiheroine Courage boasted, "No one could match me at foraging." Peter Hagendorf, author of the only extant diary by a common soldier in the Thirty Years' War, reported how wives, his own included, pillaged the fallen city of Magdeburg in 1631 even after the fires that would destroy the city had broken out:

A cry then came from throughout the city as houses all fell on each other. Many soldiers and their wives who were searching to steal something died. God indeed protected [my wife]. After an hour and a half, she came out of the city accompanied by an old holy woman, who helped her carry bedding. She also brought me a large tankard with four liters wine. In addition, she found two silver belts and clothes, which I was able to cash in for 12 thaler in Halerstadt.

But women did more than steal; there is good reason to believe they guarded the booty and held the money gained by selling it. In woodcuts showing Landsknechts and their women, the men carry the weapons, ready for battle, while women are often shown with fat purses. Free from the immediate risks of fighting in the front rank, they held the money for their fighting men. The preceding description of May marriages confirms that women carried their men's clothing and other personal items, including their "valuables." A poem accompanying a 16th century woodcut claims that among a whore's duties was guarding the plunder:

Do well with me, my pretty lass
And stay with me in the Landsknechts
You'll wash my shirts
Carry my sacks and flasks
And if some booty should be mine
You shall keep it safe and fine
So when we put paid of this crew
We'll sell the booty when we are through.

Among artisan couples in the civilian community, women were similarly entrusted with holding goods and managing funds. Masters' wives regularly made sales and tended the till.

If the business maintained a market stall, this was the wife's preserve, for the husband was needed back at the shop. Pillage was a form of this early modern family economy.

Pillage was also the business of the army. Because the campaign community was based on mercenary principles, versus those of state service or patriotism, its members were easily seduced by greed. In his 1516 colloquy "Of a Soldier's Life," the great Dutch humanist Desiderius Erasmus confronted a soldier with the charge, "It was not the Love of your Country, but the Love of Booty that made you a Soldier," to which the soldier replied, "I confess so, and I believe very few go into the Army with any better Design." He also admits, "The Hope of Booty made me valiant." In fact, only a few common soldiers and their women profited, but it was just enough to tempt others in a kind of lottery psychology. When Erasmus inquires of his soldier, "Well, have you brought home a good Deal of Plunder then?" the soldier replies with a shrug, "Empty Pockets."

The unintended consequence of such unrealistic hopes of riches was the survival of military forces on campaign. Before European states developed the capacity to maintain their armies in the field, it was pillage that sustained them. The fact that women were key agents in securing and managing pillage explains the need for great numbers of them in the campaign community, as well as the radical reduction in their numbers after 1650.

Ultimately, pillaging and the abuses inescapably associated with it imposed limits on the reliability, efficiency and size of armies. To overcome these limits, European states developed the political power and administrative means to command revenues and tap credit sufficient to maintain their armies. Rulers curbed pillage by holding officers responsible for their soldiers' conduct and by imposing and enforcing stricter codes of discipline, but such efforts would have been fruitless were it not for major improvements in military administration and logistics, which in turn required advances in the state's ability to mobilize and disperse resources. These critical military and political changes affected different countries at different times, but in general the transformation occurred during the latter half of the 17th century. With distinct national twists, they were the work of Louis XIV in France, Frederick William the Great Elector (1640–1688) in Brandenburg-Prussia and Peter the Great (1682–1725) in Russia.

These monarchs' accomplishments demonstrate that war was the engine that drove state formation in Europe. Thus the history of camp women and their involvement in pillage merges with far greater issues—the rise of the modern army and the emergence of the modern state.

---

For further reading, **John A. Lynn** recommends: Battle Cries and *Lullabies: Women in War from Prehistory to the Present,* by Linda Grant De Pauw.

*Article 36*

# Will the Real Henry VIII Please Stand up?

**Henry VIII may be our most famous monarch, a man who still bestrides English history as mightily as he dominated his kingdom nearly 500 years ago—but how well do we really understand him? Eric Ives looks for the man behind the bluster.**

ERIC IVES

School children in Mussolini's Italy were given a cartoon history book. The page devoted to Henry VIII showed him in the Tower of London, leaning on the headsman's axe. In front was the block and a kneeling wife holding up an infant in supplication; behind, a queue of other wives waiting their turn. Henry taking a breather: the basket beside the block is already full of heads. Italy and much of Europe had long seen Henry that way. In Donizetti's opera *Anna Bolena* (1830), he is a Machiavellian who bates a trap for Anne by recalling her former suitor from abroad. He says to the Captain of his Guard,

> It is for you to ensure that the execution of my grand design does not miscarry. Keep their every step and every word under constant scrutiny.

English opinion could be equally damning. The young Jane Austen wrote:

> The crimes and cruelties of this prince were too numerous to be mentioned, and nothing can be said in his vindication but that his abolishing religions houses and leaving them to the various depredations of time has been of infinite use to the landscape of England.

Go even further back to student plays at the Jesuit seminary at St Omer in the early 1600s. One ended with Henry being dragged down to Hell, in close anticipation of Don Giovanni.

Talking pictures brought this monstrous Henry to life. The archetype is Charles Laughton's Oscar-winning king in The *Private Life of Henry VIII* (Alexander Korda 1933). This established the macho, totally self-regarding, totally self-absorbed Henry, and, incidentally the popular notion that the Tudors had no table manners. The message of the film is clear. Henry VIII's reign can be reduced to wife trouble. The opening announces that Katherine of Aragon will not appear because 'her story is of no particular interest—she was a respectable woman so Henry divorced her', and the film ends with the king saying of Katherine Parr—more a bossy nurse than subservient wife—'Six wives and the best of them is the worst'. Laughton is a lustful monarch, a cock among a bevy of sweet chicks, each with eyes on the royal bed; a man who sees women as objects. That, too, is the Henry of *Carry On Henry,* the most widely circulated of all later films about the King. Television's The *Six Wives of Henry VIII* (1970) served history better and Keith Michell's performance was more deeply drawn than Laughton's, but as the title made clear, the focus was once again on Henry the married man. In his *Six Wives: The Queens of Henry VIII* (2003) even David Starkey, who knows better, had to succumb to the expected.

The alternative Henry is the Henry of the Reformation. Indeed, the battle of Protestant versus Roman Catholic was for many years fought out over his character and motivation. Henry himself established the Protestant reading. The Great Bible, to which each of his subjects had access by law, has an engraved frontispiece of Henry enthroned, with God in the margin endorsing him with texts such as 'I have found a man after my own heart who shall fulfil all my will'. The opposing Catholic view was put by Henry's cousin Cardinal Reginald Pole. He wrote in 1536:

> At your age in life and with all your experience of the world, you were enslaved by your passion for a girl. But she would not give you your will unless you rejected your wife, whose place she longed to take.

Henry driven by lust was hard for Protestants to counter. Bishop Burnet fell back on an omnipotent God who uses frail humans to achieve his will. It was a good line, often repeated, but Catholics undoubtedly held the high moral ground. For good measure, they could also accuse Henry of greed in destroying the monasteries and so producing massive social distress.

That even persuaded the non-Catholic William Cobbett who declared:

> The reformation was engendered in beastly lust, brought forth in hypocrisy and perfidy, and cherished and fed by plunder, devastation, and by rivers of English and Irish blood.

Henry and sex, Henry and religion. The King's first major biographer, Herbert of Cherbury, argued that together these explained the posthumous collapse of Henry's reputation.

> It may truly be said, all his pomp died with him; his memory being now expos'd to . . . obloquy . . . either by discontented clergymen (for his relinquishing of papal authority, and overthrowing the monasteries) or offended women (for divers severe examples against their sex).

More nuanced and secular interpretations only begin to appear in the mid-nineteenth century. James Anthony Froude presented Henry as a statesman who had led England out of medieval bigotry to moderation, saved it from invasion and religious war, and the British constitution was in large measure built 'on foundations laid in his reign'. Henry's faults were great but forgivable in 'a sovereign who in trying times sustained nobly the honour of the English name and carried the commonwealth securely through the hardest crisis in its history'. A.F. Pollard dismissed Anne Boleyn in a sentence: 'her place in English history is due solely to the circumstance that she appealed to the less refined part of Henry's nature'. His monumental biography of the King claimed a deep symbiotic relationship between the monarch and the people of England and an astute, perhaps instinctive, identification with the contemporary zeitgeist. That in making omelettes Henry smashed a large number of valuable eggs was beside the point; the alternative was civil strife and bloodshed on a huge scale.

Since Pollard's death in 1948 historical knowledge has been revolutionized by research on a scale he could not have imagined. And not simply scale. From the late fifteenth century, source material for English history begins to expand in both quantity and subject matter. Froude and Pollard were pioneers in exploiting this but, understandably did not fully appreciate the radically new approach that was required. It was, for example, no longer satisfactory to infer motivation. Under Henry VII the purpose of a statute has to be assumed from its text; there is no certainty that it even represents the King's wishes. Under his son, not only can we now follow the drafting of the legislation but often much of the actual debate which lay behind it. And what is true of statutes is true generally. The statements 'Alfred the Great decided' and 'Henry VIII decided' are of quite different orders.

Compare Henry's last will with that of his grandfather Edward IV (d.1483). On his deathbed Edward, so the Croyland Chronicle says, made 'sagax dispositio'—'a wise settlement' for governing during his son's minority. Precisely what this sagacity amounted to we do not know; neither evidence nor the final will and codicils survive. For Henry VIII, we have will-related material and eyewitness accounts of what took place at the royal bedside. Research has demonstrated, for example, how wrong Cardinal Pole was when he wrote to Henry after Anne Boleyn's execution: 'God has got rid of the cause of all your mistakes. Cutting off her head has removed the chance for further offences and God has given you a good new wife'. What explains Henry's commitment to religious change is not lust but self-image. This was neatly summed up in the inscription beneath Holbein's great 1537 wall painting in Whitehall Palace, showing the King with his parents and his wife Jane Seymour. It compared the achievements of Henry VII who established civil peace, with Henry VIII who

> born to still greater things, turns unworthy men away from the altars and brings in men of integrity. The presumptuousness of popes has yielded to unerring virtue: with Henry VIII bearing the sceptre in his hand, religion has been restored, and with him on the throne the truths of God have begun to be held in due reverence.

The sum of this half-century of research has, ironically, been to recover Henry's personality and private life for the serious history of his reign. For example, we now know that late in the reign a 'dry stamp' of the King's signature was produced. This was politically risky; it might fall into the wrong hands, but how else to get over the problem that even minutiae required the King's signature. Otherwise, a chronically ill Henry would, in the last four weeks of his life, have been pestered to endorse over eighty papers including a letter of thanks for a gift of fruit trees, and a missive to a London widow recommending a suitable second husband.

So out with the cartoon Lawton and in with the monograph. For the hugely influential Geoffrey Elton, Henry was a negative, 'far from masterful, competent or in charge'. The result was a vacuum filled by others. Jack Scarisbrick saw Henry as more of a force but essentially selfish: 'Rarely, if ever, have the unawareness and irresponsibility of a king proved more costly to the material benefit of his people'. To L.B. Smith, Henry was the universal spider. David Starkey, has advanced the opposite view, 'Henry the vulnerable', with 'the essential features of his rule [being] determined by other intelligences and shaped for other purposes'. The conclusions differ, but for all of them the character of Henry is central. It is a view which would have been passionately endorsed by the King's contemporaries.

What, then, should readers of *History Today* make of Henry? There are two indisputables. First, Henry was personally dominant in both court and government. As James Gairdner put it,

> Strictly speaking Henry was not an unconstitutional sovereign; all his doings were clothed with legality. But the whole machinery of the state, both legislative and executive, moved simply in accordance with his pleasure.

But dominant need not mean domineering. In any power structure where gaining and keeping the confidence of the head person is crucial to success, individuals are found in 'sets' and 'subsets' acting for mutual support and advantage. They are often described as 'factions' but the political dimension of that term can mislead. 'Sets' are organic, formed through natural ties of family, friendship, locality, taste, common concern, ambition and self interest. They vary in how tight or loose they are and they can overlap. Such patterns of relationship are observable in the courts of Byzantium, or around Hitler and Stalin or, for that matter around the Vice-Chancellor of a modern university. Henry VIII's court was just like that.

The second certainty is that Henry the man and Henry the king cannot be separated. Henry was as convinced as Louis XIV that *'l'état c'est moi'*. True he did say, when about to marry Anne of Cleves: 'If it were not to satisfy the world and my realm, I would not do that I must this day for none earthly thing', but 'satisfy' meant no more than 'do what is expected'. He was not marrying for the sake of the realm but because he couldn't, with honour, get out of it. Henry's private character and private life and his public persona and political life interpenetrated. Pollard's generation and its successors covered many pages with evaluations of Henry's supposed foreign policy. Egoism, however, provides the simple explanation. Henry's constant objective was to be recognized as a monarch of European standing. An exception to this is the 1530s but then only because the object was to resolve his personal matrimonial problems and then to defend the outcome. Egoism is equally obvious in domestic matters. Henry responded to the Lincolnshire protesters in the Pilgrimage of Grace in 1536 with abuse:

> How presumptuous then are ye, the rude commons of one shire, and that one of the most brute and beastly of the whole realm, and of least experience, to find fault with your prince . . . whom ye are bound by all laws to obey and serve, with both your lives, lands and goods, and for no worldly cause to withstand.

His conviction that he possessed superior wisdom and absolute authority was total. It was unforgivable presumption to challenge him, an impertinence towards the Lord's anointed which was conclusive evidence of 'a cankered heart'.

Egoism was compounded by falsity and deceit. Henry was very much the *faux bonhomme;* after Thomas More had been seen walking with the royal arm round his shoulders, he warned that the King would behead him without a qualm if it 'could win him a castle in France'. Indeed Edmund de la Pole, Earl of Suffolk, was beheaded in 1513 precisely to free Henry to invade France. The Earl had been extradited on promise that his life would be spared, but since that guarantee had been given by his father, Henry himself felt absolved. He was nothing if not legalistic, provided it suited him.

Linked to this was an ability to deny reality, an obstinate conviction that facts were as he wanted to them to be. At the height of the Pilgrimage of Grace he wrote to the embattled Duke of Norfolk: 'it is much to our marvel to receive so many desperate letters from you'. If things were as bad as the Duke said, he was obviously falling down on the job, unless, that is, he was so concerned about problems that he was overlooking the good news which must be there. Henry was the world's best armchair strategist.

Opinionated self-righteousness made Henry both the most forgiving and the most unforgiving of men. An alleged offender who could reach the King, abjectly confesses himself guilty of whatever Henry suspected, true or not, and throw himself on royal mercy, could expect to be pardoned. In so doing he had confirmed Henry's perspicacity. On the other hand, if the King suspected 'dissembling', 'stiffness' or ingratitude he would be harsh in the extreme. Pole again:

> he has robbed every kind of man, made sport of the nobility, never loved the people, troubled the clergy, and torn like a wild beast the men who were the greatest honour to his kingdom.

Between 1509 and 1547, more English notables were executed than under any other monarch before or since.

All these traits fed a failing which the French ambassador Marillac identified in 1540: 'distrust and fear'. Henry was insecure. This is where the sets and subsets mattered. If the person at the top is open to influence they can exert pressure, and Henry was at times very susceptible. Wolsey fell, not because the King planned his downfall but because Henry was pressured. After the fall of his second great minister, Thomas Cromwell, Henry grumbled that his counsellors 'upon light pretexts, by false accusations, had made him put to death the most faithful servant he ever had'. Herbert of Cherbury concluded that: 'Impressions privately given to the king by any court-whisperer were hardly or never to be effaced'. On the other hand, the qualification 'susceptible at times' is important. Henry was not a puppet. His vulnerability does not contradict the proposition that he was truly dominant. His word was law and he was capable of initiative and decision. The point is that his innate suspiciousness meant that he could on occasion be persuaded. As the dying Wolsey famously said to Sir William Kingston, constable of the Tower, 'Be well advised and assured what matter ye put in [the King's] head, for ye shall never pull it out again'. Thomas More, too, said much the same.

In the search for the real Henry the hardest question is to explain why was he as he was. The evidence is almost all second-hand; Henry left no diary and only a handful of his more than a thousand letters are at all personal. Take upbringing. Modern psychology leaves no doubt about the formative influence of childhood, but there is little evidence for Henry the child and the adolescent. Was he repressed, as some ambassadors say? How was he affected by the early death of his elder brother? Was he influenced by his formidable grandmother, Lady Margaret Beaufort? In the Royal Collection is a terracotta bust believed to be of the young Henry. What is the relationship between that laughing happy child and the man he became? What did he really feel about marrying his sister-in-law Katherine and what weight should we place on the admission in a youthful letter to Erasmus that the news of her brother's death had reopened the wound 'of the death of his dearest mother' 'which time had brought to insensibility'?

Marillac, who fastened on Henry's obsessive suspiciousness, also reported that he was 'so covetous that all the riches in the world would not satisfy him'. Henry was avarice personified. This trait is evident in page after page of his inventories. That a king should regard a full treasury as desirable is understandable, but Henry was obsessed with ownership. When he died he had thousands of yards of cloth of gold in store, far more than could ever be needed. Why over a hundred pairs of embroidered sleeves? Why in the cash-strapped 1540s did his agents conspire to keep him from hearing about jewels on the market? And why, having inherited thirteen houses did he acquire and retain thirty or so more, many of which he never visited?

Henry would, no doubt, be gratified that his inner psychology is hard to understand: 'if my cap knew what I was thinking, I would burn it'. The only truly private letters which survive are those to Anne Boleyn. They reveal genuine passion and a true psychological dependency on her, something borne out by contemporary comments. But they cover only two years in a ten year relationship. As for its collapse, even if we assume that by 1536 Henry's feelings for Anne were dead and that she was an obstacle to his desires, what do we make of a man who as an act of grace summons the executioner from Calais to behead her in the French manner?

The difficulty in reaching the inner Henry explains the speculation and psycho history which appears all too often. However there are clues. One thing which obsessed him was status. This is not surprising; the whole of his upbringing and environment was designed to emphasise regal distance. Hence the egoism. He alone mattered. Henry, of course, did not see egoism as a fault but as a response to God. He was God's anointed in reality, not merely in coronation theory, and it would be a sin to tolerate any slur on that high calling. This conviction freed him to destroy anyone, however intimate. Status is the ultimate explanation of the break with Rome. Matrimonial difficulty opened Henry's eyes to the fact that human authority was frustrating what God had decreed. As the years passed, his version of Christianity became increasingly idiosyncratic but the changes he forced on the English Church are explicable only as an attempt to obey God. As the Whitehall inscription announced 'religion has been restored, and with him on the throne the truths of God have begun to be held in due reverence'.

Yet if possessing a God-given status, why the insecurity? One factor undoubtedly was having no male heir until he had reached middle age, and the birth of Edward only meant that the focus of anxiety shifted. But circumstances alone cannot account for the depth of Henry's vulnerability. Despite his bluff extrovert performance, he had a deep need to rely on other people. Given ideas, he could pursue them—the work he put in on the divorce shows that—but he rarely initiated. The radical solution to his matrimonial dilemma was sold to him in the teeth of traditionalists who advised otherwise. Moderate religious reform progressed in the 1530s because Anne Boleyn, Thomas Cranmer and Thomas Cromwell had command of the King's ear. He was at his least secure when his deepest convictions were engaged. The succession problem which followed the death of Edward VI and rumbled on for the rest of the century was because Henry was determined that the crown should go to his daughters Mary and Elizabeth, but equally determined to maintain that both were illegitimate.

Insecurity is probably the key factor in understanding Henry and sex. Once again historians differ. Did he, as one of his subjects claimed, 'want only an apple and a fair wench to dally with'? Was the assertion that he had never spared a man in his anger or a woman in his lust genuine or locker room bragging? The latter seems probable for Henry's extramarital activity is markedly restrained, in contrast to, say, Charles V, Francis I or more than one pope. Couple the good evidence that in the 1530s Henry suffered episodes of impotence with remarks he made which show that he identified virility with producing children, especially a son, and the obvious conclusion is that the sexual disfunction of his mature years was caused by anxiety. When this began it is hard to say. Katherine of Aragon's record of six conceptions in fifteen years is not good and all but one of them ended in miscarriage or neonatal death. It would have been only human to wonder what was wrong. In the 1520s Henry rationalized it as a consequence of his unwitting disobedience to God in marrying his brother's widow and a similar anxiety surfaced in the last months of his marriage to Anne Boleyn. Viagra, of course, had not been invented.

Asking the real Henry to stand up reveals to twenty-first century eyes a figure both monstrous and inadequate, but the perspective and values of Henry's contemporaries were markedly different. What first impressed them was his magnificence, the essential virtue expected of a king. They would have found nothing to query in a superfluity of embroidered sleeves. At the sight of Henry in full Garter robes, the Venetian diplomat, Pasquaglio, declared: 'he is handsomest potentate I ever set eyes on'. Henry was a big man with big ideas. His summit meeting with Francis I at the Field of Cloth of Gold was one of the marvels of Europe. It was regal glory in action. Henry was the greatest builder of all the English kings. Hampton Court alone was enlarged three times; Whitehall was essentially his creation, so was St James. With only limited modifications, his palaces lasted English monarchs for two hundred years. Their walls were bright with over three hundred tapestries. The gold, silver gilt and silver plate was prodigious; he possessed over a hundred ornate salts, while his gold and silver candlesticks alone together weighed a quarter of a ton. To the sixteenth-century mind, magnificence was, not egregious waste: it was of the essence of monarchy.

A similar contrast applies to Henry's foreign policy. We may dismiss it as egoistical posing, and his military successes as trivial and bought at wholly unreasonable expense. Some of his subjects felt the same, but by no means all. Henry VIII was the first king for more than a century to conquer territory in France. In the last four years of his reign the English laity contributed £750,000 towards war with no hint of rebellion. When Parliament voted the taxes for 1545 it declared that:

> We the people of this his realm have for the most part of us so lived under his Majesty's sure protection and do yet so live out of all fear and danger as if there were no war at all, even as the small fishes of the sea, in most stormy and tempestuous weather, do lie quietly under the rock or bank side, and are not moved with the surges of the water, nor stirred out of their quiet place, howsoever the wind bloweth.

The early Elizabethan Ballad of Flodden Field, begins its peroration with the lines:

> This noble King Henry won great
> victories in France
> Through the might that Christ Jesus
> did him send

lists the towns he conquered, and ends with the brag that he kept to Calais, 'plenished with Englishmen until the death that he did die'. For the bulk of the nation 'Henry had to do what a king had to do'.

It may, of course, seem that this was not true for Henry VIII's religious policies. Current revisionist historians have gone to great lengths to show that the traditional Church was deeply rooted in English society and that change was not wanted. But Henry met active opposition only in the North in 1536 and nobles who were deeply traditional in religion, were active in suppressing it. As for the more populous parts, they would threaten revolt over taxes but not over Henry's religious spoliation. Spectators might be shocked at the martyrdom of priests but not sufficiently moved to try to save the martyrs. When six years after Henry's death the country had the opportunity to reverse the ruin of the Church, it did not put its hands in its pocket. The late medieval Church was more vigorous than was once thought, but support for it was clearly too superficial to cause Henry concern.

The third quality that dazzled contemporaries was personality. In the desperate crisis of the summer of 1549, Henry's erstwhile secretary implored Protector Somerset to act on behalf of the young King Edward:

> Sir, for a king, do like a king. Go no further than to him who died last of noble memory, Henry VIII. Kept he not his subjects from highest to lowest in due obedience? And how? By the only maintenance of justice in due course.

Mary I faced with male counsellors ready to treat her orders as an invitation to debate, burst out on one occasion that 'she only wished her father might come to life for a month'. Early in James I's reign, the theatrical company 'Prince Henry's Men' had a huge success at the Fortune Theatre with a play with the significant title *When you see me you know me.* Indeed, so successful were they that His Majesty's Players, their rivals at the Globe, had to get Shakespeare and John Fletcher to write *Henry VIII.* Each play assumes that Henry's personal foibles and mannerisms would be immediately recognized by a London audience despite the years since the King's death. Henry was remembered as a proper king.

There is a chasm between the ways historians see Henry VIII and the way his subjects saw him. But it would be wrong to reject the latter because today we are so much better informed. Both characterizations have to be held in tension. Fallible though Henry was, modern criticism cannot destroy the reality that to his people he was a great king. A ballad written soon after his death summed him up in these words.

> For if wisdom or manhood by any
> means could
> Have saved a man's life to ensure for
> ever,
> The King Henry the 8th so noble and
> so bold
> Out of this wide world he would have
> passed never.

Not even Henry could manage that, but it is no little achievement that 450 years after his death it remains true that 'When you see me, you know me'.

## For Further Reading

Henry VIII in *The Oxford Dictionary of National Biography* (OUP, 2004 and on line); Robert Hutchinson, *The Last Days of Henry VIII* (Weidenfeld & Nicholson, 2005); Eric Ives, *The Life and Death of Anne Boleyn* (Blackwell, 2004); David Starkey, *Six Wives: the Queens of Henry VIII* (Chatto & Windus, 2003); Alison Weir, *Henry VIII, King and Court* (Jonathan Cape, 2001). See page 60 for related articles on this subject in the History Today archive and details of special offers at www.historytoday.com

**Eric Ives** is Emeritus Professor of History at the University of Birmingham.

# Test-Your-Knowledge Form

We encourage you to photocopy and use this page as a tool to assess how the articles in *Annual Editions* expand on the information in your textbook. By reflecting on the articles you will gain enhanced text information. You can also access this useful form on a product's book support Web site at *http://www.mhcls.com/online/*.

NAME: DATE:

---

TITLE AND NUMBER OF ARTICLE:

---

BRIEFLY STATE THE MAIN IDEA OF THIS ARTICLE:

---

LIST THREE IMPORTANT FACTS THAT THE AUTHOR USES TO SUPPORT THE MAIN IDEA:

---

WHAT INFORMATION OR IDEAS DISCUSSED IN THIS ARTICLE ARE ALSO DISCUSSED IN YOUR TEXTBOOK OR OTHER READINGS THAT YOU HAVE DONE? LIST THE TEXTBOOK CHAPTERS AND PAGE NUMBERS:

---

LIST ANY EXAMPLES OF BIAS OR FAULTY REASONING THAT YOU FOUND IN THE ARTICLE:

---

LIST ANY NEW TERMS/CONCEPTS THAT WERE DISCUSSED IN THE ARTICLE, AND WRITE A SHORT DEFINITION:

# We Want Your Advice

ANNUAL EDITIONS revisions depend on two major opinion sources: one is our Advisory Board, listed in the front of this volume, which works with us in scanning the thousands of articles published in the public press each year; the other is you—the person actually using the book. Please help us and the users of the next edition by completing the prepaid article rating form on this page and returning it to us. Thank you for your help!

## ANNUAL EDITIONS: Western Civilization, Volume 1, 15/e

### ARTICLE RATING FORM

Here is an opportunity for you to have direct input into the next revision of this volume.
We would like you to rate each of the articles listed below, using the following scale:

**1. Excellent: should definitely be retained**
**2. Above average: should probably be retained**
**3. Below average: should probably be deleted**
**4. Poor: should definitely be deleted**

Your ratings will play a vital part in the next revision.
Please mail this prepaid form to us as soon as possible.
Thanks for your help!

| RATING | ARTICLE |
|---|---|
| ________ | 1. Modern Archaeology |
| ________ | 2. The Queen Who Would Be King |
| ________ | 3. Journey to the Seven Wonders |
| ________ | 4. The Coming of the Sea Peoples |
| ________ | 5. Before Tea Leaves Divination in Ancient Babylonia |
| ________ | 6. Millennia of Murex |
| ________ | 7. Troy's Night of the Horse |
| ________ | 8. The First Olympics |
| ________ | 9. Can We Trust the Ancient Texts? |
| ________ | 10. Unlocking Mysteries of the Parthenon |
| ________ | 11. Outfoxed and Outfought |
| ________ | 12. Mighty Macedonian |
| ________ | 13. Etruscan Women |
| ________ | 14. Rome's Craftiest General |
| ________ | 15. The End of the Roman Empire |
| ________ | 16. The Volcano Explains Everything—Or Does It? |
| ________ | 17. Holy Family Values |
| ________ | 18. Adrianople |
| ________ | 19. The Survival of the Eastern Roman Empire |
| ________ | 20. Islam's First Terrorists |
| ________ | 21. Rediscovering Arabic Science |
| ________ | 22. A Turbulent Reputation |
| ________ | 23. What Did Medieval Schools Do For Us? |
| ________ | 24. Lackland |
| ________ | 25. The Fourth Crusade and the Sack of Constantinople |
| ________ | 26. East Meets West in Venice |
| ________ | 27. Genghis Khan |
| ________ | 28. How a Mysterious Disease Laid Low Europe's Masses |
| ________ | 29. The Guns of Constantinople |
| ________ | 30. Joan of Arc |
| ________ | 31. The Luther Legacy |
| ________ | 32. Explaining John Calvin |
| ________ | 33. The Third Way |
| ________ | 34. Vlad Dracula's War on the Turks |
| ________ | 35. Women in War |
| ________ | 36. Will the Real Henry VIII Please Stand up? |

NO POSTAGE NECESSARY IF MAILED IN THE UNITED STATES

**BUSINESS REPLY MAIL**
FIRST CLASS MAIL PERMIT NO. 551 DUBUQUE IA

POSTAGE WILL BE PAID BY ADDRESSEE

**McGraw-Hill Contemporary Learning Series**
501 BELL STREET
DUBUQUE, IA 52001

## ABOUT YOU

Name Date

Are you a teacher? ❒ A student? ❒
Your school's name

Department

Address City State Zip

School telephone #

## YOUR COMMENTS ARE IMPORTANT TO US!

Please fill in the following information:
For which course did you use this book?

Did you use a text with this ANNUAL EDITION? ❒ yes ❒ no
What was the title of the text?

What are your general reactions to the Annual Editions concept?

Have you read any pertinent articles recently that you think should be included in the next edition? Explain.

Are there any articles that you feel should be replaced in the next edition? Why?

Are there any World Wide Web sites that you feel should be included in the next edition? Please annotate.

May we contact you for editorial input? ❒ yes ❒ no
May we quote your comments? ❒ yes ❒ no